… Studies in Economic Transition

Series Editors
Jens Hölscher
The Business School
Bournemouth University
Bournemouth, Dorset, UK

Horst Tomann
Department of Economic Policy and Economic History
Freie Universitaet (FU) Berlin
Berlin, Germany

This series brings together theoretical and empirical studies on the transformation of economic systems and their economic development. The transition from planned to market economies is one of the main areas of applied theory because in this field the most dramatic examples of change and economic dynamics can be found. It is aimed to contribute to the understanding of specific major economic changes as well as to advance the theory of economic development. The implications of economic policy will be a major point of focus.

More information about this series at
http://www.palgrave.com/gp/series/14147

Michael Landesmann • István P. Székely
Editors

Does EU Membership Facilitate Convergence? The Experience of the EU's Eastern Enlargement - Volume I

Overall Trends and Country Experiences

palgrave
macmillan

Editors
Michael Landesmann
Vienna Institute for International
Economic Studies (WIIW)
Vienna, Austria

István P. Székely
DG ECFIN, European Commission
Brussels, Belgium

Corvinus University of Budapest
Budapest, Hungary

ISSN 2662-6675 ISSN 2662-6683 (electronic)
Studies in Economic Transition
ISBN 978-3-030-57685-1 ISBN 978-3-030-57686-8 (eBook)
https://doi.org/10.1007/978-3-030-57686-8

© The Editor(s) (if applicable) and The Author(s), under exclusive licence to Springer Nature Switzerland AG 2021
This work is subject to copyright. All rights are solely and exclusively licensed by the Publisher, whether the whole or part of the material is concerned, specifically the rights of translation, reprinting, reuse of illustrations, recitation, broadcasting, reproduction on microfilms or in any other physical way, and transmission or information storage and retrieval, electronic adaptation, computer software, or by similar or dissimilar methodology now known or hereafter developed.
The use of general descriptive names, registered names, trademarks, service marks, etc. in this publication does not imply, even in the absence of a specific statement, that such names are exempt from the relevant protective laws and regulations and therefore free for general use.
The publisher, the authors and the editors are safe to assume that the advice and information in this book are believed to be true and accurate at the date of publication. Neither the publisher nor the authors or the editors give a warranty, expressed or implied, with respect to the material contained herein or for any errors or omissions that may have been made. The publisher remains neutral with regard to jurisdictional claims in published maps and institutional affiliations.

This Palgrave Macmillan imprint is published by the registered company Springer Nature Switzerland AG.
The registered company address is: Gewerbestrasse 11, 6330 Cham, Switzerland

Praise for *Does EU Membership Facilitate Convergence? The Experience of the EU's Eastern Enlargement - Volume I*

"The volume is an excellent account of how the EU convergence machine worked for the CEEC. Questions arise: will it continue? why has it stalled with some "older" EU members?"

—Marek Belka, *member of the European Parliament, former Prime Minister and Finance Minister of Poland*

"To create greater convergence, we need more integration". This message, conveyed recently by a distinguished European statesman, perfectly reflects the key hypothesis this book discusses. By relevant and balanced synthesis of theory, empirical findings and country experiences, the book provides comprehensive and multi-dimensional insight into all important aspects of the linkages between integration and convergence, a rich material of a value-added to scholars, policymakers and corporate managers. Researchers will particularly value the model-based framework that builds on the various channels through which EU membership influences convergence. For policymakers such as myself, this book serves as a reminder of unique changes and reforms we witnessed and contributed to in the recent past but, more importantly, as an inspiration on how to face and address current challenges, from climate change, ageing to migration."

—Boris Vujčić, Governor, *Croatian National Bank*

"This two-volume study is a truly major contribution to our understanding of key issues related to the convergence of the New Member States of the European Union (EU11) to the frontier. The editors, Michael Landesmann and István P. Székely, and authors are among the most experienced analysts in this area and their contributions constitute a veritable tour de force. The focus on economic, institutional and social aspects of convergence, together with their interaction, is very appropriate and provides a rich set of insights into the past evolution and likely future trends. The two volumes are important by providing an in-depth analysis of the convergence of EU11, but their relevance is much broader, including the importance of what I would call the terminal conditions – the possibility of entering the EU – a factor with great effects that cannot be analyzed in the context of other emerging market economies. The authors identify the weakness of institutions as a major potential limitation on the speed of EU 11 convergence in the future. The EU 11 countries have performed remarkably well and I am hopeful, together with the authors of these two volumes, that these countries will tackle successfully their present and future challenges. The two volumes are a must read for everyone interested in EU11 and emerging market economies in general."

—Jan Svejnar, *James T. Shotwell Professor of Global Political Economy and Founding Director of the Center on Global Economic Governance at Columbia University's School of International and Public Affairs*

"This two volume collection is a treasure chest of timely information on the accession to the Economic Union (EU) of former Warsaw-Pact nations. Volume I presents overall analysis of convergence and extensive background information on the new members. Volume II contains careful analyses of four major linkages among new and old EU members, namely trade, finance, migration, and institutional reform, with a focus on the impacts of interdependencies across countries and their role in convergence. The authors of the individual chapters are well-known scholars in transition economics and in-country specialists in the topics. Experts in the field, the editors have compiled scholarship that is invaluable to anyone, researcher and student alike, who is interested in the future prospects for the newly constituted EU. This two-volume book is a must for academic libraries and the bookshelves of researchers. Students will find much useful information to supplement course materials."

—John Bonin, *Chester D. Hubbard Professor of Economics and Social Science at Wesleyan University*

"Economic convergence in Central and Eastern Europe is an absolutely central question for public policy in national but also EU context. This volume provides sound analysis about the long-term trends, especially for the period following the first EU enlargement in 2004. Readers must be pleased to see that the attention of the editors and authors expanded beyond macroeconomics, finance and trade to sensitive issues like migration, corruption and climate as well."

—László Andor, *Former European Commissioner*

"What was the impact of the Eastern Enlargement of the European Union regarding the convergence of new and existing members? This is a splendid collection of essays that cover an rich body of national experiences and offer detailed analysis about the main channels through which accession affected convergence. It is required reading for scholars and policy-makers interested in globalization, integration, and transition."

—Nauro F. Campos, *Professor of Economics, University College London, and Director, UCL Centre for Comparative Economics*

"From this an informative and interesting volume, readers may learn more than they may have wanted to learn, about the process of convergence of the 11 "transition economies" that became EU members in past years. The main message in the book, perhaps a not surprising one, is that, joining the EU gave the EU11 access to a large market and to a lot of foreign investment. These contributed to their economic "growth". Unfortunately, as the first development economists learned 70 years ago, and as many modern economists forgot, economic growth is not the same thing as developments. Development depends on the existence of institutions that distribute widely the benefits of economic growth. The creation of these institutions is more difficult than the generation of growth because it depends on established local cultural traits. In the EU11 countries, institutional or social development has lagged behind their growth. This is likely to create potential future problems."

—Vito Tanzi, *former Director of the Fiscal Affairs Department of the IMF*

Contents

1 **Introduction: The Story and the Lessons**   1
Michael Landesmann and István P. Székely

Part I   Framework for Analysis and Overall Trends   25

2 **Convergence of the EU Member States in Central-Eastern and South Eastern Europe (EU11): A Framework for Convergence Inside a Close Regional Cooperation**   27
István P. Székely and Robert Kuenzel

3 **Towards a New Growth Model in CESEE: Three Challenges Ahead**   91
Luca Gattini, Áron Gereben, Miroslav Kollár, Debora Revoltella, and Patricia Wruuck

4 **Regional Dynamics in EU11**   123
Dino Pinelli and Gábor Márk Pellényi

Part II Country Experiences of EU Members   149

5 How the European Union Made Poland European Again   151
   Marcin Piatkowski

6 Transformation of the Trade and Financing Model
   of the Hungarian Economy After EU Accession   173
   Anna Boldizsár, Zsuzsa Nagy-Kékesi, and Erzsébet-Judit Rariga

7 Macroeconomic Trends in the Baltic States
   Before and After Accession to the EU   211
   Martti Randveer and Karsten Staehr

8 Bulgaria and Romania: The Latecomers to the
   Eastern Enlargement   239
   Rumen Dobrinsky

Part III Convergence to Frontier as a Future
          Member of the European Union   283

9 Convergence of Non-EU Countries in the
   CESEE Region   285
   Richard Grieveson and Mario Holzner

Index   323

Notes on Contributors

Anna Boldizsár is an economist at the Magyar Nemzeti Bank, the central bank of Hungary. Her work mainly focuses on macrofinancing and external vulnerability, especially balance of payments and IIP dynamics. Her current projects examine how the external vulnerability of Hungary has changed since the 2008 crisis and the transformation that has taken place in the financing structure of the economy over the past decade.

Rumen Dobrinsky is Senior Research Associate at the Vienna Institute for International Economic Studies (WIIW) and former Chief of Economic Cooperation and Integration Division, United Nations Economic Commission for Europe. He has published extensively on the process of economic transformation in Central and Eastern Europe and the related policy reforms. His publications also cover the topics of economic integration in Europe, knowledge-based development, innovation and competitiveness policies.

Luca Gattini is currently Senior Economist in the Economics Department – Country and Financial Sector Analysis Division of the European Investment Bank. He is lead economist for the Eastern Neighbourhood and Central Asia region. He coordinates the efforts and publication on the CESEE Bank Lending Survey and manages the activities related to the EIB Group macro scenario analysis and stress testing. He worked for the European Central Bank, the European Financial Stability Facility and Prometeia.

Áron Gereben works as Deputy Adviser – Senior Economist at the European Investment Bank's Economics Department. His current work focuses on the economic growth and investment dynamics in Central and Eastern Europe, the links between finance and innovation, and the impact assessment of public support to access to finance. He has a background in central banking and held various management and analytical positions in the National Bank of Hungary and in the Reserve Bank of New Zealand. He graduated from the Budapest (Corvinus) University of Economic Sciences.

Richard Grieveson is Deputy Director at WIIW, coordinator of the WIIW country analysis team and country expert for Serbia and Turkey. His main area of research is CESEE country analysis and economic forecasting, with a particular focus on the Western Balkans. He holds a graduate diploma in economics from the University of London, Birkbeck, a Master in Advanced International Studies degree from the University of Vienna and a BA in history from the University of Cambridge.

Mario Holzner is Executive Director at WIIW. He is also coordinating economic policy development and communication with a focus on European economic policy. He has recently worked on issues of infrastructure investment in greater Europe, proposing a European Silk Road. He is also a lecturer in applied econometrics at the University of Vienna, Department of Economics. He obtained his PhD in economics at the Vienna University of Economics and Business in 2005.

Miroslav Kollár is a partner of 4 Gimel Investments SICAV. Prior to that, he was an economist at the European Investment Bank, an executive board member of the International Monetary Fund, and an advisor to the Bank Board at the Czech National Bank. He holds a PhD in economics from University of Economics in Prague, and he is a CFA Charterholder. He graduated from Staffordshire University in the UK and University of Antwerp in Belgium.

Robert Kuenzel is Assistant to the Deputy Director General in DG Economic and Financial Affairs, European Commission. He entered the UK Government Economic Service in 2003, before joining the Commission in 2007. He has since held various positions, including as Co-editor of the Quarterly Report on the Euro Area and Team Leader for Slovakia and the Czech Republic. In 2014–15 he was

Director for Euro Area Economic Research at Daiwa Capital Markets Europe, a London-based investment bank.

Michael Landesmann is Senior Research Associate, former Scientific Director (1996–2016), of the Vienna Institute for International Economic Studies (WIIW), and Professor of Economics at the Johannes Kepler University, Austria. He has a DPhil degree from Oxford University and taught and researched at Cambridge University's Department of Applied Economics and Jesus College, Cambridge. He held many visiting professorships including the Pierre Keller and Schumpeter professorships at Harvard University.

Zsuzsa Nagy-Kékesi is a senior economist at the Magyar Nemzeti Bank, the central bank of Hungary. She analyses the savings dynamics of Hungarian households and is an expert in the field of balance of payments processes and the central bank's balance sheet, as well as the profit and loss account. She is a student of the Doctoral School of Business and Management of the Corvinus University of Budapest and a lecturer at the Department of Finance.

Gábor Márk Pellényi is an economist at the European Commission, Directorate-General Economic and Financial Affairs. He previously worked at Magyar Nemzeti Bank and OTP Research. His research areas include macroeconomic forecasting and issues related to economic development in Central Eastern Europe. He gained his PhD at Budapest Corvinus University.

Marcin Piatkowski is an Associate Professor of Economics at Kozminski University in Warsaw and a senior economist at the World Bank. Previously, he was a visiting scholar at Harvard University's Center for European Studies, Chief Economist and Managing Director of PKO BP, the largest bank in Poland, economist in the European Department of the IMF and Advisor to IMF's Executive Director. He also served as Advisor to Poland's Deputy Premier and Minister of Finance. His personal website is at www.marcinpiatkowski.com.

Dino Pinelli is Deputy Head of Unit at the European Commission, Directorate-General Economic and Financial Affairs. He previously worked for Fondazione Eni Enrico Mattei and Cambridge Econometrics carrying out research on regional growth and convergence, migration and cultural diversity. He holds a PhD in economics from the University of Bologna.

Martti Randveer is Head of the Economics and Research Department of Eesti Pank, the central bank of Estonia. He holds master's and PhD degrees from Tallinn University of Technology. His research interests include issues in monetary economics, public economics, comparative economics and international finance.

Erzsébet-Judit Rariga is an economist at the Magyar Nemzeti Bank, the central bank of Hungary. Her work mainly focuses on firm behaviour, corporate finance and international trade. Her current projects examine firms' long-term borrowing decisions and network effects in firms' bank choice.

Debora Revoltella is Director of the EIB's Economics Department. The department comprises 30 economists and provides economic analysis and studies to support the bank in defining its policies and strategies. She holds a PhD in economics. She is member of the Steering Committees of the Vienna Initiative and the CompNet, and a member of the Boards of the Joint Vienna Institute, the SUERF and the Euro 50 Group.

Karsten Staehr is a professor of macroeconomics at the Department of Economics and Finance at Tallinn University of Technology, Estonia, and a part-time research supervisor at Eesti Pank. He holds a master's degree from the Massachusetts Institute of Technology and master's and PhD degrees from the University of Copenhagen. He carries out research and policy analysis within monetary economics, international finance, public economics, European integration and comparative economics.

István P. Székely is a Principal Advisor in the Directorate-General for Economic and Financial Affairs at the European Commission and Honorary Professor of Corvinus University in Budapest. He has a PhD in economics from the University of Cambridge. Before joining the European Commission in 2007, he worked at the International Monetary Fund and in the National Bank of Hungary as a General Manager and Adviser to the Governor. His research focuses on financial market and macroeconomic policy issues and on Central and Eastern European economies.

Patricia Wruuck is an economist in the Economics Department of the European Investment Bank where she is responsible for research on skills. She contributes to EIB publications such as the EIB Investment Report and EIB Working Papers. Her research interests are in European policy, political economy, trade and human capital development. Previously, she worked at Deutsche Bank Research and Google. She holds a master's degree from Freie Universität Berlin and a doctoral degree from Mannheim University.

LIST OF FIGURES

Fig. 1.1   Distance to the EU frontier at different parts of the income distribution in EU11 in 2005 and 2018. (Source: Eurostat, EU-SILC and ECHP surveys. Note: Columns show the ratios between equivalised per capita total disposable income of households (in PPS) in a given segment of the income distribution in EU11 and in the most developed EU countries (the group used in Chap. 2, including Austria, Denmark, Netherlands and Sweden). Values are the averages for the groups as a whole of cut off values for the income distribution segments shown (lowest 5% and 10%, the fifth decile and the top 10% and 5%))   14

Fig. 1.2   Distance to the EU frontier at different parts of the income distribution in the Czech Republic and Bulgaria in 2005 and 2018. (Source: Eurostat. Note: For a description of the variables shown in these figures, see the note to Fig. 1.1)   15

Fig. 1.3   Income convergence among EU11 countries, 2005–2018. (Source: Eurostat, EU-SILC and ECHP surveys. Note: Income refers to per capita equivalised total disposable income of households in purchasing power standard. Red dots are observations for the cut-off income for the lowest 5% of the income distribution in the EU 11 country concerned, grey dots are for the cut-off income for the 5th decile, while the green dots are for 95%. Values are expressed as percent of the corresponding value for EU frontier countries (Austria, Denmark, Netherlands, Sweden). On the horizontal axe, the

	initial position in 2005 is shown, while on the vertical axe, the change between 2005 and 2018. For the 5th decile and 95%, the trends suggest that the lower the initial income relative to the frontier the faster the convergence, while for the lowest 5%, there is no such trend) (Color figure online)	16
Fig. 2.1	Economic and social convergence in the world. Note: *EU Frontier* includes Austria, Denmark, Netherlands and Sweden; *EU11* includes Bulgaria, Croatia, Czech Republic, Estonia, Hungary, Latvia, Lithuania, Poland, Romania, Slovakia and Slovenia. *EU Candidates* include Albania, North Macedonia, Montenegro and Serbia; *Latam* includes Argentina, Chile, Costa Rica, and Uruguay; *North Africa* includes Algeria, Jordan, Morocco and Tunisia; SEA includes Indonesia, Korea, Malaysia and Philippines. Simple, unweighted averages of country observations. (Sources: For per capita GDP World Bank, for Human Development Index, UNDP)	37
Fig. 2.2	Economic and social convergence in EU11 countries. Note: *B3* includes Estonia, Latvia and Lithuania; *EU11 High-income* includes Czechia and Slovenia; *EU11 Low-income* includes Bulgaria and Romania. For the definition of the other groups, see the Note to Fig. 2.1. (Sources: For per capita GDP World Bank, for Human Development Index, UNDP)	39
Fig. 2.3	Economic and social convergence in EU11 and EU S4. Note: EU S4 includes Greece, Italy, Portugal and Spain. For the definition of the other groups, see the Note to Fig. 2.1. (Sources: For per capita GDP World Bank, for Human Development Index, UNDP)	40
Fig. 2.4	The Gini coefficient for income distribution, 2005–2015. Note: For the definition of country groups, see the Notes to Figs. 2.1 and 2.3. (Source: World Bank, World Development Indicators)	41
Fig. 2.5	The Gini coefficient for income distribution in EU countries in 2005 and 2018. (Source: Eurostat)	42
Fig. 2.6	Human Development Index (HDI) and Inequality-Adjusted HDI (AI-HDI), 2017. (Source: UNDP)	43
Fig. 2.7	Historical Human Development Index (HIHD) 1870–2015. Note: Frontier includes Austria, Denmark, Netherlands and Sweden; Southern Europe includes Greece, Italy, Portugal and Spain. For a description of the HIHD indicator see Prados de la Escosura (2019). (Source: http://espacioinvestiga.org/inicio-hihd/ Downloaded on July 2, 2019)	44

Fig. 2.8	Export openness, 2000–2017. Note: For the definition of country groups, see the Note to Fig. 2.1. (Source: World Bank)	45
Fig. 2.9	Change in export openness, 2000–2017. Note: For the definition of country groups, see the Note to Fig. 2.1. Columns are the countries in the world that are covered by the database. (Source: World Bank)	46
Fig. 2.10	Stocks of Inward and outward FDI. Note: For the definition of country groups, see the Note to Fig. 2.1. (Source: UNCTAD)	48
Fig. 2.11	Current account balance and banking credit to the private sector, 2000–2018. Note: For the definition of country groups, see the Note to Fig. 2.1. (Source: World Bank)	52
Fig. 2.12	Share of foreign-owned banks in the balance sheet total of the banking sector, 2008. Note: For the definition of country groups, see the Note to Fig. 2.1. (Source: Claessens and Van Horen 2014)	54
Fig. 2.13	Share of foreign-owned banks in the balance sheet total of the banking sector, 2008. Note: For the definition of country groups, see the Note to Fig. 2.1. (Source: Claessens and Van Horen 2014)	55
Fig. 2.14	Current account balance and banking credit to the private sector in the Czech Republic and Slovenia, 1990–2018. Note: For the definition of country groups, see the Note to Fig. 2.1. (Source: World Bank)	56
Fig. 2.15	Ratio between people living in EU15 countries and total population in EU11 countries. (Source: Eurostat)	61
Fig. 2.16	Income and outward migration in EU11 in 2004 and 2017. Note: Scatter diagram, with GDP per capita (PPP constant 2011 international $, log scale) on the horizontal axis and the ratio of the nationals living abroad to resident population of the country concerned (in percent) on the vertical axis. Countries are ordered according to their per capita income in the year concerned (2004 and 2017) and every point represents a pair of observations for an EU11 country (per capita GDP and emigration stock). Global curves are based on Clemens 2014, approximate curves to indicate global trends. (Sources: World Bank for per capita GDP and OECD International Migration Database for migration)	62
Fig. 2.17	Population trends, 2000–2017. (Source: Eurostat)	63
Fig. 2.18	Share of non-nationals in resident population, 2018. Note: Ordered according to total excluding non-nationals from countries with which the country concerned was formerly in one state. For the Czech Republic the latter category includes	

xx   LIST OF FIGURES

	Slovakia, and for Slovakia, the Czech republic. For the Baltic countries, this includes Russia, Ukraine and recognised non-citizens. For Malta and Cyprus, no breakdown is available between EU 11 and EU15, the light blue column shows the sum of these two categories. (Source: Eurostat)	65
Fig. 2.19	FDI and migration in EU11, 2000–2017. Note: Change in the stock of EU11 citizens living in another EU country (ΔMIGR) on the vertical axis, change in the inward stock of FDI, three-year moving average delayed by one year (ΔFDI) for the stock. Observations are for individual EU11 countries and years. The two points in red are for Bulgaria and Romania for 2008, the year after accession into the EU. (Source: Eurostat for migration, UNCTAD for FDI)	66
Fig. 2.20	FDI and migration in Czech Republic and Slovenia, and Bulgaria and Romania. Note: Stock of EU11 citizens living in another EU country (Emigration) and stock of FDI, three-year moving average delayed by one year. (Sources: Eurostat for migration, UNCTAD for FDI)	66
Fig. 2.21	Trends in Governance Indicators. (**a**) Voice and Accountability; (**b**) Political Stability; (**c**) Government Effectiveness; (**d**) Regulatory quality; (**e**) Rule of Law; (**f**) Control of Corruption. Note: For the definition of country groups, see the Note to Fig. 2.1. Unweighted group averages. Values for 1997, 1999 and 2001 are interpolated. (Source: Worldwide Governance Indicators, 2018 Update (World Bank 2019))	68
Fig. 2.22	Trends in Governance Indicators and income convergence. Note: For the definition of country groups, see the Note to Fig. 2.1. Institutional quality (right axis) is the distance to the EU Frontier, based on an average of the WGI indices, and it is the average for the three preceding years. Per capita GDP in PPP relative to EU Frontier (left axis). (Source: World Bank for per capita GDP; World Bank (2019) for Worldwide Governance Indicators, 2018 Update)	71
Fig. 2.23	Public debt relative to GDP. Note: For the definition of country groups, see the Note to Fig. 2.1. The panel on the left shows central government debt relative to GDP as internationally no consistent data are available for general government debt. The panel on the right shows general government gross debt (as defined in the Excessive Deficit Procedure of the EU). (Source: Central government debt, IMF; general government gross debt, Eurostat)	73

Fig. 2.24	Potential output growth in the EU in 2001–2018. Note: EU15 small open includes Austria, Belgium, Denmark, Finland Netherlands, and Sweden. EU11 is as defined in the Note to Fig. 2.1. (Source: Buti and Székely 2019)	76
Fig. 2.25	Regional differences in inward FDI, convergence trends and institutional quality in EU11 countries. (**a**) FDI; (**b**) Convergence; (**c**) Institutional Quality. Note: For the chart in the middle Level of per capita GDP in 2000, and growth in 2000–2014, regions are classified as: Red = regions with GDP per capital level and growth above national average Yellow = regions with GDP per capital level above the national average and growth below Green = regions with GDP per capita level below the national average and growth above Blue = regions with GDP per capital level and growth below the national average. (Sources: Buti and Székely (2019), Pinelli and Pellényi (2021). https://ec.europa.eu/regional_policy)	78
Fig. 2.26	Human Development Index for the country groups used in the analysis in 2017. Note: Columns represent countries, which were ordered according to their HDI index in 2017. *EU Frontier* includes Austria, Denmark, Netherlands and Sweden; *EU S4 includes Greece, Italy, Portugal and Spain*. *EU11* includes Bulgaria, Croatia, Czech Republic, Estonia, Hungary, Latvia, Lithuania, Poland, Romania, Slovakia and Slovenia. *EU Candidates* include Albania, North Macedonia, Montenegro and Serbia; *Latam* includes Argentina, Chile, Costa Rica, and Uruguay; *North Africa* includes Algeria, Jordan, Morocco and Tunisia; SEA includes Indonesia, Korea, Malaysia and Philippines. (Source: UNDP)	86
Fig. 3.1	Factor decomposition of potential GDP growth in a Cobb-Douglas accounting framework (in percentage points). (Source: European Commission. Used with permission from EIB)	96
Fig. 3.2	Correlation between GDP per capita and share (%) of intangible investment in total corporate investment, 2017. (Source: EIB Investment Survey, Eurostat. Used with permission from EIB)	100
Fig. 3.3	EIBIS digitalisation index, 2019. (Source: European Investment Bank, 2019. Used with permission from EIB. Note: Digital intensity is based on a score assigning value 1 if a firm has implemented in part of its business at least one of 4 digital technologies specific to the sector, and value 2 if the firm's entire business is organised around at least one of	

	the 4 technologies. The results are then summed up, creating a score ranging from 0 to 8, with 8 assigned to the firms that have organised their business around all 4 digital technologies. Digital infrastructure is based on a question whether access to digital infrastructure is an obstacle to investment or not. Investments in software and data and in organisation and business process improvements are measured as a percentage of total investment in the previous fiscal year. Strategic monitoring system is based on a question asking whether the firm uses a formal strategic business monitoring system or not. The five components of the EIBIS digitalisation index are aggregated at the country level and given the following weights: 0.4 to digital intensity, 0.3 to digital infrastructure and 0.1 to the other 3 components)	101
Fig. 3.4	Smart regions (EU rankings and within CESEE rankings, NUTS 3 regions). (Source: Kollár et al. (2018). Used with permission from EIB)	102
Fig. 3.5	Gross domestic expenditure on R&D, by country, 2008 and 2016. (Source: Eurostat. Used with permission from EIB)	103
Fig. 3.6	CESEE – Active innovators by firm size, 2019. (Source: EIB Investment Survey, 2019. Used with permission from EIB. Note: Active innovators refer to those that spend actively on R&D and fall into the categories of leading)	104
Fig. 3.7	CESEE – Active innovators by sector, 2019. (Source: EIB Investment Survey, 2019. Used with permission from EIB. Note: Active innovators refer to those that spend actively on R&D and fall into the categories of leading)	104
Fig. 3.8	Beveridge curve in CESEE. (Source: Eurostat. Used with permission from EIB. Note: The Beveridge curve shows the coexistence between vacancies and unemployment for CESEE countries from 2009-end of 2018 using four quarter averages.)	106
Fig. 3.9	Limited availability of skills in CESEE and the EU. (Source: EIB Investment Survey, 2016–2018. Used with permission from EIB. Note: Percentage of firms reporting the limited availability of skills as an obstacles to investment. Dark colours indicate the share of firms reporting the limited availability of skills as a major obstacle and light colours as a minor obstacle respectively.)	107
Fig. 3.10	Share of firms reporting mathematics, sciences and technical skills hardest to find. (Source: EIB Investment Survey 2018, special module on digitalisation and skills. Used with permission from EIB)	108

LIST OF FIGURES   xxiii

Fig. 3.11   Participation in lifelong learning, last 12 months. (Source: Eurostat. Used with permission from EIB)   110
Fig. 3.12   Strategies to cope with skill gaps in current workforce (% of all enterprises. Source: EIB Investment Survey special module (2018). Used with permission from EIB)   111
Fig. 3.13   Usual reaction to future skill needs. (% of all enterprises. Source: CVTS (2015). Used with permission from EIB)   112
Fig. 3.14   External positions of BIS reporting banks vis-à-vis CESEE countries – index 100=2007Q1. (Source: Authors calculation based on BIS data. Used with permission from EIB. Note: Index 100=2007Q1 based on billions of US$, exchange-rate adjusted, vis-à-vis all sectors; grey bars correspond to the global financial crisis and the Eurozone sovereign debt crisis)   113
Fig. 3.15   Banking group's total exposure to CESEE (net percentages). Source: Authors' calculation based on EIB – CESEE Bank Lending Survey. Used with permission from EIB. Note: Cross-border operations involving CESEE countries – Net percentages: positive (negative) figures refer to increasing (decreasing) exposure. Question from the survey:: Group's exposure to CESEE: Concerning cross-border operations to CESEE countries, your group did/intends to increase/decrease/maintain the exposure compared to the previous six months   114
Fig. 3.16   International banking groups' exposure to CESEE by type (net percentages). (Source: Authors' calculation based on EIB – CESEE Bank Lending Survey. Used with permission from EIB. Note: Cross-border operations involving CESEE countries – Net percentages: positive (negative) figures refer to increasing (decreasing) exposure in the specific category. "Other" refers to an average of direct cross border lending to domestic clients and funding to banks not part of the group. Question from the survey:: Group's exposure to CESEE: Concerning cross-border operations to CESEE countries, your group did/intends to increase /decrease/maintain the intra-group/capital/other) exposure compared to the previous six months)   115
Fig. 3.17   Share of foreign ownership in the banking system (per cent). Source: Raiffeisenbank International. Used with permission from EIB. Note: data refer to 2017 and represent foreign owned assets over total assets   116
Fig. 3.18   NPL ratio in CESEE. Source: Authors' calculation based on wiiw (Vienna Institute for International Economic Studies)

	database and national central banks' data. Used with permission from EIB. Note: Regional average computed using EUR based GDP weights (average 2012–2018) and it is based on Albania, Bosnia and Herzegovina, Bulgaria, Croatia, Czech Republic, Hungary, Poland, Romania, Serbia, Slovakia and Slovenia	117
Fig. 3.19	Foreign currency loans to non-financial private sector in CESEE (% of total and y/y growth). Source: Authors' calculation based on WIIW and National Central Banks. Used with permission from EIB. Note: Regional average for shares and growth rates computed using EUR based GDP weights (average 2012–2018) and it is based on Albania, Bosnia and Herzegovina, Bulgaria, Croatia, Czech Republic, Hungary, Poland, Romania, Serbia, Slovakia and Slovenia	118
Fig. 4.1	Average and regional dispersion of GDP per capita in the EU11. (Source: Own calculations on data from the Annual European Regional Database, European Commission)	127
Fig. 4.2	Regional dispersion of GDP per capita within and between EU11 countries. (Source: Own calculations on data from the Annual European Regional Database, European Commission)	128
Fig. 4.3	Regional dispersion of GDP per capita in the EU11: within and between groups based on different levels of urbanisation. (Source: Own calculations on data from the Annual European Regional Database, European Commission)	129
Fig. 4.4	Distribution of regional GDP per capita in the EU 11, 2000 and 2015. (Source: Own calculations on data from the Annual European Regional Database, European Commission)	130
Fig. 4.5	Distribution of regional GDP per capita in the EU11, by level of urbanisation. (Source: Own calculations on data from the Annual European Regional Database, European Commission)	131
Fig. 4.6	Employment-population ratio in the EU11 and old EU member states. (Source: Own calculations on data from the Annual European Regional Database, European Commission)	132
Fig. 4.7	Dispersion of the employment-population ratio, within and between EU 11 countries. (Note: Romania is excluded due to data issues. Source(s): Own calculations on data from the Annual European Regional Database, European Commission)	133
Fig. 4.8	Dispersion of the employment-population ratio in the EU 11, within and between groups based on different levels of urbanisation. (Note: Romania is excluded due to potential data issues. Source: Own calculations on data from the Annual European Regional Database, European Commission)	134

Fig. 4.9	Net migration and GDP per capita in the EU 11 regions. (Source: Own calculations on data from the Annual European Regional Database, European Commission)	135
Fig. 4.10	Growth and levels of GDP per capita in EU11 regions. (Note: With reference to the year 2000 for the level of GDP per capita and to the period 2000–2014 for its growth, regions are classified as: Type 1 = regions with GDP per capital level and growth above national average; Type 2 = regions with GDP per capital level above the national average and growth below; Type 3 = regions with GDP per capita level below the national average and growth above; Type 4 = regions with GDP per capita level and growth below the national average. Source: Own calculations on data from the Annual European Regional Database, European Commission)	138
Fig. 4.11	Spatial dependency among EU11 regions – Moran's scatterplot. (Source: Own calculations on data from the Annual European Regional Database, European Commission)	141
Fig. 4.12	Spatial clusters – localised Moran's I. (Source: Own calculations on data from the Annual European Regional Database, European Commission)	141
Fig. 5.1	GDP growth per capita, 1990–2018, 1989 = 100. (Source: author's own based on the Conference Board Total Economy Database)	153
Fig. 5.2	Top 10 upper-middle/high-income large economies in GDP per capita growth rate, 1993–2018. (Source: author's own based on the Conference Board Total Economy Database)	153
Fig. 5.3	Share of total population (in deciles), whose income since 1989 has increased faster than the G-7 average, 1989–2016. (Source: author's own based on data from EBRD 2016)	155
Fig. 5.4	Indicators of institutional quality for Poland and upper-middle-income countries, 2004 and 2018. (Note: Upper-middle-income countries as defined by the World Bank. Source: http://info.worldbank.org/governance/wgi/#reports)	159
Fig. 5.5	Changes in GDP per capita for Poland, Mexico, Malaysia, South Korea and South Africa, 1990–2018, PPP, in constant 2011 international $. (Source: author's own based on the World Bank World Development Indicators database)	162
Fig. 5.6	Changes in poverty headcount for Poland, Mexico, Malaysia, South Africa and South Korea, 1992–2016, poverty gap at $5.50 a day (2011 PPP) (%). (Note: Poland and South Africa: 1992 = 1993; Malaysia: 1996 = 1997; Malaysia: 2000 assumed to equal 4; South Africa: 2004 = 2005, Malaysia: 2016 = 2015	

	and South Africa: 2016 = 2014, South Korea: 2006 = 2004, 2016 = 2012. Sorted by the lowest poverty rate in 2016. Source: author's own based on the World Bank World Development Indicators database)	164
Fig. 5.7	Changes in Gini coefficient for Poland, Mexico, Malaysia, South Korea and South Africa, 1992–2016. (Note: Poland and South Africa: 1992 = 1993; Malaysia: 2005:2004; 2010 = 2011, 2016 = 2015; South Africa: 2016 = 2014, South Korea, 2005 = 2006, 2016 = 2012. Sorted by the lowest Gini coefficient. Source: author's own based on the World Bank World Development Indicators database)	165
Fig. 5.8	Tertiary school enrollment in Poland and selected global peers, % gross, 1970–2017. (Source: World Bank's World Development Database)	167
Fig. 5.9	Length of highways and expressways in Poland, 2000–2019. (Source: https://en.wikipedia.org/wiki/Highways_in_ Poland#/media/File:PL-Motorways-en.svg)	168
Fig. 5.10	Hourly compensation costs in manufacturing, as a percent of costs in the United States (US = 100), 2016. (Source: author's own based on The Conference Board)	168
Fig. 5.11	Exports of goods and services as % of GDP in Poland, Germany and selected global peers, 1990–2018. (Source: World Bank's World Development Database)	169
Fig. 6.1	Developments in trade openness in Hungary. (Source: Eurostat 2019, UN Comtrade, Fred. Note: Exports and imports as a share of GDP. New member states are countries joining in 2004 or later)	175
Fig. 6.2	Top export partners of Hungary. (Source: UN Comtrade)	176
Fig. 6.3	Top import partners of Hungary. (Source: UN Comtrade)	177
Fig. 6.4	Composition of Hungarian exports and imports. (Source: Eurostat 2019)	178
Fig. 6.5	Hungary's investment-to-GDP ratio, financing and real growth (as a percentage of GDP). (Source: Pellényi et al. 2016)	180
Fig. 6.6	Changes in households' net savings (as a percentage of GDP). (Source: MNB, own compilation)	181
Fig. 6.7	Main financing factors of external net borrowing (as a percentage of GDP). (Source: MNB, own compilation)	182
Fig. 6.8	Changes in the yields on Hungarian government securities. (Source: Bloomberg, own compilation)	182
Fig. 6.9	Changes in the average credit rating of countries acceding to the EU prior 2004. (Note: The respective credit rating of the countries is calculated as the average of the ratings provided by	

	Fitch, Moody's and S&P. The credit rating shown for the two groups is calculated as the average credit rating of the countries belonging to the given group. Source: tradingeconomics.com, own calculations)	183
Fig. 6.10	External debt, swap holdings and retail FX loan portfolio of the banking sector (as a percentage of GDP. (Source: MNB, own compilation)	187
Fig. 6.11	Structure of public debt (as a percentage of GDP). (Source: ÁKK, MNB, own compilation)	188
Fig. 6.12	Net lending of the sectors (as a percentage of GDP). (Source: MNB, own compilation)	191
Fig. 6.13	Financing of external net borrowing (in EUR billions). (Source: Pellényi et al. 2016)	191
Fig. 6.14	Measures affecting the change in the financing structure. (Source: own compilation)	193
Fig. 6.15	Net savings of the household sector (as a percentage of GDP). (Source: MNB, own compilation. Note: * The values reflect underlying trends and are adjusted for the effect of pension savings, the early repayment scheme, real yield payments, the indemnification of the depositors of liquidated savings cooperatives and the HUF conversion and settlement. Two points show the original data without the corrections)	195
Fig. 6.16	Cumulative change in households' main financial assets. (Source: MNB, own compilation)	196
Fig. 6.17	Breakdown of the net issuance of the public sector. (Sources: ÁKK, MNB, own compilation)	197
Fig. 6.18	Ownership share of debt securities issued by the central government. (Source: MNB, securities statistics)	198
Fig. 6.19	Distribution of loan purposes in the individual phases of the FGS. (Source: MNB 2017)	200
Fig. 6.20	Absorption of EU funds and the investment rate. (Source: MNB)	202
Fig. 6.21	Breakdown of funds of EU programme periods by development objective. (Source: Boldizsár et al. 2016)	203
Fig. 6.22	Changes in net external debt by sector (as a percentage of GDP). (Source: MNB, own compilation)	205
Fig. 6.23	Correlation between economic development and NIIP position (2018). (Source: Eurostat (2019), own compilation)	206
Fig. 6.24	Real GDP per capita calculated from the PPP-based indicator in 2017, EU28 = 100. (Source: Eurostat 2019, own calculation)	207
Fig. 7.1	GDP growth, per cent per year, 1995–2018. (Source: Eurostat (code: *nama_10_gdp*), Ameco (code: *OVGD*) for 1995)	217

Fig. 7.2	Current account balance, per cent of GDP, 1995–2018. (Source: WEO (label: Current account balance))	218
Fig. 7.3	Unemployment rate, 15–74 years, per cent of labour force, quarterly data 2000:1–2018:4. (Note: The quarterly unemployment rate is from labour force surveys. Source: Eurostat (code: une_rt_q))	220
Fig. 7.4	Net emigration, per cent of population, 1995–2018. (Source: Eurostat (code: $demo\_gind$))	221
Fig. 7.5	Budget balance, per cent of GDP, 2000–2018. (Source: Ameco (code: $UBLG$))	226
Fig. 7.6	GDP per capita PPP, per cent of EU15, 1995–2018. (Source: Ameco (code: $HVGDPR$))	228
Fig. 7.7	Population at the beginning of the year, millions, 1995–2018. (Source: Ameco (code: $NPTN$))	230
Fig. 7.8	Old-age dependency ratio, per cent, 1995–2018. (Note: The old-age dependency ratio is computed as the population aged 65 or older in per cent of the population aged 15–64 at the beginning of the year. Source: Eurostat (code: $demo\_pjanind$))	230
Fig. 8.1	FDI inflows and GDP growth in Bulgaria and Romania, 2000–2018. (Source: wiiw macroeconomic database)	244
Fig. 8.2	Stock of inward FDI in Bulgaria and Romania, % of GDP. (Source: wiiw macroeconomic database)	245
Fig. 8.3	Breakdown of the inward FDI stock in Bulgaria and Romania by NACE sectors, 2017, %. (Source: wiiw macroeconomic database)	247
Fig. 8.4	Breakdown of exports from Bulgaria and Romania by SITC categories, 2002 and 2018, % of total. (Source: Eurostat)	250
Fig. 8.5	Exports of machinery and transport equipment (SITC 6) from Bulgaria and Romania, 2000–2018, % of total exports. (Source: Eurostat)	251
Fig. 8.6	Real effective exchange rate and current account balance by sectors in Bulgaria and Romania, 2000–2018. (Source: Eurostat, wiiw macroeconomic database, author's calculations)	254
Fig. 8.7	Public and gross external debt in Bulgaria and Romania, 2000–2018, % of GDP. (Source: wiiw macroeconomic database)	255
Fig. 8.8	Population, employment, activity rate and unemployment rate in Bulgaria and Romania, 1991–2018. (Source: wiiw macroeconomic database)	256
Fig. 8.9	Labour productivity and real wage dynamics in Bulgaria and Romania, 2000–2017, annual % change, 3-year moving averages. (Source: wiiw macroeconomic database)	257

LIST OF FIGURES   xxix

Fig. 8.10   Net financial position of the new EU member states, 2004–2017, % of GNI. (Source: Eurostat)   264
Fig. 8.11   Public capital expenditure (left scale) and gross fixed capital formation (right scale) in Bulgaria and Romania, 2000–2018, % of GDP. (Source: wiiw macroeconomic database, author's calculations)   265
Fig. 8.12   Real GDP per capita at PPS in the NMS-10 relative to the EU-15, 2000–2018, %. (Source: Eurostat)   269
Fig. 8.13   Speed of catching up and structural effects. (Source: author's calculations based on Eurostat and wiiw macroeconomic database)   271
Fig. 8.14   Gini coefficient of equivalised disposable income in selected EU member states, 2000–2017, %. (Source: Eurostat)   275
Fig. 8.15   Young people neither in employment nor in education and training in Bulgaria and Romania, 2000–2018, %. (Source: Eurostat)   277
Fig. 9.1   Exports of goods and services, % of GDP, 1995. (Note: Horizontal line indicates the global average. Source: World Bank)   289
Fig. 9.2   Real GDP, % per year, 3-year moving average. (Note: simple averages for each region. Data for the early years are missing for some countries. Source: wiiw)   291
Fig. 9.3   GDP per capita, PPS, Germany = 100, simple averages for each sub-region. (Note: *Does not include Estonia for 1990; **Insufficient data available for 1990. Source: wiiw)   294
Fig. 9.4   Share of merchandise exports going to EU15, %, 2018 or latest data. (Note: Horizontal lines represent simple averages for each sub-region. Source: wiiw)   297
Fig. 9.5   Inward FDI stock, % of total in CESEE countries, selected industries, 2017 or latest data. (Source: wiiw FDI database. Simple averages for each country group)   299
Fig. 9.6   Average EBRD transition indicators score, change 1989–2014. (Note: Simple average of change in six scores: large-scale privatisation, small-scale privatisation, governance and enterprise restructuring, price liberalisation, trade and forex system, competition policy. Orange line = sub-regional simple average. Source: EBRD)   301
Fig. 9.7   PISA scores, 2015. (Source: OECD)   304
Fig. 9.8   Average World Bank Worldwide Governance Indicators scores, simple averages for each country group in selected years, 2.5 = best, −2.5 = worst. (Note: Scores represent simple averages of change in five categories: control of corruption, government

	effectiveness, rule of law, regulatory quality, voice and accountability. Source: World Bank Worldwide Governance Indicators. Some 1996 data unavailable for Kosovo and Montenegro)	305
Fig. 9.9	Average World Bank Worldwide Governance Indicators scores; Change versus Germany, 1996–2017. (Note: Scores represent simple averages of change in five categories: control of corruption, government effectiveness, rule of law, regulatory quality, voice and accountability. Source: World Bank Worldwide Governance Indicators. Some 1996 data unavailable for Kosovo and Montenegro)	307
Fig. 9.10	V-Dem Democracy Index for CESEE countries, 1 = best, 0 =worst. (Note: Simple averages for each country group. Source: V-Dem)	308
Fig. 9.11	World Bank's Logistics Performance Index (LPI), 2018. (Source: World Bank)	310
Fig. 9.12	Estimated infrastructure investment needs for the period 2018–2022, in % of GDP, by investment type. (Note: Catch-up infrastructure investment needs refer to the cost of catching up with the levels expected on the basis of the experiences of more advanced comparator economies. Supporting future growth infrastructure investment needs refer to the cost of improving infrastructure to support future growth in GDP and population. Source: EBRD Transition Report 2017–18)	310
Fig. 9.13	Chinn-Ito Financial Openness Index. (Note: The index is normalised with the highest degree of financial openness captured by the value of one and the lowest by the value of zero. The CIS+UA average is constructed from data for BY, MD, KZ, RU, UA; the WB average from data for AL, BA, MK. Source: Chinn and Ito (2006), 2016 update, own calculations)	312

List of Tables

Table 4.1	Summary statistics	137
Table 5.1	Countries that have become high-income since 1960	166
Table 6.1	Transformation of Hungary's financing model	208
Table 8.1	GDP growth in the NMS-10, national accounts data	268
Table 8.2	Implied rates of GDP growth in the NMS-10 (GDP at PPS of 2018, Eurostat)	272

CHAPTER 1

Introduction: The Story and the Lessons

Michael Landesmann and István P. Székely

Starting on 1st of May 2004, 11 countries in Central-Eastern and South Eastern Europe and in the Baltics (EU11) joined the European Union in three consecutive waves.[1] Half a generation later, and a full generation after the start of transition in the region, we thought it would be opportune to

---

The views expressed are solely those of the authors and do not necessarily represent the official views of the European Commission.

[1] We will refer to the region as CESE and the 11 countries as EU11 and to the process as the eastern enlargement of the EU throughout the two volumes.

M. Landesmann
Vienna Institute for International Economic Studies (WIIW), Vienna, Austria
e-mail: landesmann@wiiw.ac.at

I. P. Székely (✉)
DG ECFIN, European Commission, Brussels, Belgium

Corvinus University of Budapest, Budapest, Hungary
e-mail: istvan-pal.szekely@ec.europa.eu

© The Author(s), under exclusive license to Springer Nature Switzerland AG 2021
M. Landesmann, I. P. Székely (eds.), *Does EU Membership Facilitate Convergence? The Experience of the EU's Eastern Enlargement - Volume I*, Studies in Economic Transition,
https://doi.org/10.1007/978-3-030-57686-8_1

look into the convergence experience of these countries. The two volumes of this book offer a collection of contributions on this matter.

This volume, Volume I, sets out the framework for analysis and focuses on the country experiences, that is, it looks at the various issues involved and the way they emerged and interacted with each other in these countries.

Volume II, looks into the channels of interaction between the EU and EU11 countries. That is, the contributions in this volume focus on the different channels relevant for convergence processes for all the countries or a subset of them.

A unique characteristic of the convergence process in this part of Europe relative to other European countries and to middle-income countries in other parts of the world is EU membership. Thus, the focus is on this and the authors ask the following basic research questions: What impact did the EU have on the convergence process in EU11? What difference did it make, relative to other converging economies, that these countries were part of a closely knit supranational organization?

1.1 Framework for Analysis

Chapter 2 sets out a framework to analyse convergence in a country, or a group of countries, which belongs to the EU. Convergence in this framework means that the outcome in a given area approaches the level we can observe in the most developed countries. Outcome in this context can refer to production, income, health and educational outcomes, quality of institutions, as measured by objective outcome indictors, or judged by people living and working in these countries. While economic, institutional and social models can be different in different countries, people generally thrive for a better life and better opportunities in life. So convergence to the most developed countries in this sense is what everybody wants, whatever economic, institutional or social model a country adopts.

Economic convergence is a global process. People in countries all over the world that are not at the global frontier of economic and social development have the desire to get closer to the frontier, ideally to reach it and then push it out further. Put simply, they want to have the same quality of life, the same chances in life for themselves and for their children, as people in the countries at the frontier have. Thus, we will look at economic and social convergence as a process to approach the global frontier of economic and social development, and not as the convergence of these countries among themselves, or to simply to an EU average.

Using the EU average as a reference point would raise several problems. With the exceptions of the most developed EU countries, quite a few of the countries that formed the EU before the eastern enlargement themselves were at a distance from the frontier. Thus, some of the member countries themselves were "converging" economies, albeit not always at a speed that would have satisfied their citizens' desire. Moreover, since then, and in some cases starting even before the eastern enlargement, some of the "old" member states of the EU have been diverging from the frontier. The eastern enlargement of the EU interacted with this process in important ways, albeit globalization and the financial and later the European crises in 2008–2013 were probably much stronger forces in this regard.

While our focus is on the global frontier of economic and social development, the fact that EU11 countries are in Europe and are part of the EU is highly relevant. To address this issue, the analysis in Chap. 2 uses a group of EU countries that are at or very close to the global frontier of economic and social development—and have been there for long, in some cases since the middle ages—as a reference group.

This framework that guides our analysis looks at convergence as a multi-dimensional process, which has economic, social and institutional dimensions. Economic convergence increases the "means", the productive capacity of a society. This is the basis to achieve social convergence, which constitutes the "ends". Institutional convergence improves the quality of institutions, the "ways" of achieving economic convergence and turning it into social convergence. The interactions among these aspects are strong. Good institutions are conducive to fast economic convergence. Conversely, lack of sufficient institutional convergence is likely to slow, or even reverse economic convergence at some point. Equally, deficiencies in social convergence can lead to political reactions hindering progress (and possibly leading to reversals) in economic and institutional convergence.

The relationship among these dimensions is of course very complex, and the delay with which it works in either direction is not easy to establish. In fact, it is very likely that both, the strength of the impact and its timing may change over time and/or may be state dependent. There can be times when markets are forgiving, and lack of institutional convergence has no traceable short- or even medium-term impact on the speed of economic convergence. But there can be punishing times when the negative impact comes fast and strong. Conversely, there can be times when institutional improvements do not lead to an acceleration of economic convergence, and there can be, and our analysis clearly shows there were, times when doing the right reforms at the right time was richly rewarded. We do not yet know how exactly this relationship works. Nonetheless, the broad lesson is clear, economic and institutional convergence should go hand in hand.

Equally, there might be complex relationships and lags in the way that social convergence is linked to economic convergence. Beyond that, there can also be trade-offs between achieving social vs. economic convergence (if the latter is simply measured in average GDP per capita) as the fruits of economic convergence might be differently distributed across people and regions of a country. Furthermore, mixed market economies offer a range of "socio-economic models" with regard to achieving social convergence consistent with economic convergence (such models differ in the ways social security systems are set-up, public goods provision, redistributive measures, regional policies, etc.) Different socio-economic models go along with differentiated institutional set-ups and these in turn depend on economic and social-behavioural development levels.

Thus institutional development is essential for enhancing the capacity of a country to transform economic convergence into social convergence. While economic convergence provides the basis (means) for social convergence, the correspondence is not automatic. The pace of social convergence may well trail economic convergence if institutions are not appropriately developed, that are specifically aimed towards social convergence and are effective in targeting it. The lack of sufficient social convergence, in turn, can lead to institutional reversals, and through this, can eventually undermine economic convergence.

Regarding economic, institutional and social convergence, it is important to emphasize that we do not suggest there is a unique economic, institutional or social model that these countries, or any other country, should converge to. There are certain areas of the economy, domestic institutions and of social issues in the member states in which EU law directly governs things. However, by design, these laws and rules leave ample room for different models in different countries, reflecting the preferences and choices of people in member states.

In a way, the convergence process is also a competition of different economic, social and institutional systems, and not only in EU11. In healthy societies, such as those in the EU, this is a positive force. Countries watch each other and try to learn from the more successful ones, as companies do in markets. There are several mechanisms present in the EU that promote constructive peer review and peer learning among member states.

On the other hand, economic transition was fundamentally triggered by the fact that the soviet-type central planning system lost the competition with modern social-market economies. These countries did not have healthy societies during this period, and thus could not deliver to their citizens a sufficient degree of economic, social and institutional convergence. No political or military force was strong enough to avoid the inevitable consequences of such outcome.

The framework which guides the two volumes identifies the channels through which EU membership influences economic, institutional and social convergence. The trade, investment, finance, mobility and institutional channels. The first four of these channels are related to the four freedoms in the EU, albeit structured somewhat differently, the free movement of goods, services, capital and people. The institutional channel captures the way the EU shapes national institutions, as defined by Douglas North (1990), that is, laws, rules, norms and institutions. The channels also interact, strengthen or weaken each other. These interactions are very important as they can change the nature of the process over time, and can make it state dependent.

The EU is not the only supranational institution that affects the development of EU11, and that of their peer groups of converging middle-income countries in other parts of the World. There are several international organizations that facilitate the channels this framework identifies, such as for example the WTO which was created to facilitate and regulate the trade channel at the global level. There are other regional organizations that promote regional integration in other parts of the world, such as ASEAN. However, the EU represents a much deeper integration of its member states (see Lawrence 1996; Sapir 2011). Thus, its impact is more direct and much stronger than that of other such organizations.

Measuring the different dimensions of convergence is a very difficult undertaking, and there is no perfect way of doing this. Neither the data nor the methodologies that are available would ever allow researchers to do a perfect job in this regard. Nevertheless, in these two volumes, academic researchers from all over Europe, researchers and economists working in global, European and national public institutions make a joint effort to answer the basic issues we raised above.

1.2 The Convergence Story of EU11: A Major Success with Emerging Policy Issues

EU11 countries were part of a Soviet-dominated and largely isolated economic area of centrally planned economies until the late 1980s-early 1990s.[2] Thus, they all went through an economic transition to turn their economies into modern market economies. This transition not only led to major changes in relative prices, but it also wiped out a large part of their productive capital stock. Moreover, as Chap. 2 points out, during central planning, their human capital stock relative to the rest of Europe had also deteriorated, and—of course—there was the major challenge to change fundamental institutions compatible with the move towards a market economy. Thus, it was natural for them to look to Europe for help to make up for the lost decades. By 1996, they had all applied for EU membership, except Croatia which was just emerging from a devastating war at that time.

The eastern (as previously the southern) enlargement of the EU was a political project, and people's desire in EU11 countries to join the EU was also driven by their "want" to belong to "Europe". Europe defined broadly and vaguely, including all dimensions, political, institutional, social, cultural and economic ones. Nonetheless, on both sides, there was a clear economic rational as well, based on expectations about costs and benefits. On both sides, politicians and people wanted to achieve rapid economic convergence.

The historical experience of the EU with economic convergence of low-income EU members is mixed. Italy, the (then) low-income founding member of the EU had an unprecedentedly rapid and in fact full (albeit not lasting) convergence within the EU until the early 1990s. By that time, it had reached the income level of the most developed EU countries (starting at about 60% of their level in 1957). Since then, however, it has continuously diverged from the frontier of economic development. By now, it has erased about half of the convergence gain it had made as an EU

---

[2] Slovenia and Croatia were parts of the former Yugoslavia. Politically and in its everyday life, Yugoslavia was much less isolated than the rest of the region and Soviet domination was much less direct. The form of collective ownership of productive assets in Yugoslavia was also somewhat different from that in other countries in the region and its economy was less isolated. Nevertheless, the fundamental characteristics of its economic system were very similar to those of the other countries in the region, regarding relative prices, distortions in resource allocation and incentive structures that strongly influenced—although in somewhat different ways—corporate behaviour, employment and productivity.

member by the early 1990s. Ireland entered the EU in 1973 at a relative income level slightly below that of Italy back in 1957. The first 15 years of Ireland's EU membership was characterized by slow convergence, but starting in the late 1980s-early 1990s, Ireland converged rapidly and reached the EU frontier by the turn of the century. Since then, despite a sizable temporary drop during the crisis in 2008–2010, it has remained among the most developed EU countries, making it the most successful convergence episode in the history of the EU. Greece joined in 1981 at an income level slightly above the relative level of Italy back in 1957, but it never really converged as an EU member, except for a short period of unsustainable (debt-driven) increase in its income level after euro introduction. Portugal and Spain joined in 1986, Spain roughly at Italy's relative income level back in 1957, Portugal at much lower relative income level. Both got stuck by the early nineties, at the same time as Italy, and just 5 years after joining the EU. They started to diverge after the introduction of the euro.

In light of this historical experience, but also globally, as the chapters in Volume I show, the economic convergence of EU11 as a whole has been highly successful so far. Despite the biggest economic crisis in the history of the EU, triggered by a major global financial crisis, EU11 has been consistently the fastest converging group of middle-income countries in the world since the turn of the century. Rapid economic convergence started some four years before the first wave of EU accession in 2004. This suggests that the accession process was well managed, in the sense that it created strong incentives for reforms and it anchored the expectations regarding future membership. In fact, on almost all fronts, these were the most successful years of the entire period. What is not so encouraging though is that institutional convergence has largely stopped in EU11 since EU accession, and social convergence has paused since the crisis (we return to this issue later in this Introduction).

In the accession process, there was a great emphasis on institutional convergence. It was convergence in the sense of adopting the EU institutions (the *acquis*), and convergence in the sense of ensuring that also the quality of institutions, as operating in reality, approaches that of the most developed countries. The process was carefully monitored, politically and technically in the official accession process, but also by the EBRD in a very structured and analytically sound way (transition index; EBRD 1989–2014), and by the economics profession.

However, by that time, the deterioration of institutional quality in the Southern European EU member states was at full speed, underlying their economic divergence. This is not to say that—given the tight monitoring of developments during the accession process—the EU11 countries were treated unfairly. After all, the reforms they undertook during this period was the best investment they have ever made, and produced huge returns. But it seems they needed this external push to progress with reforms, and once the pressure was taken away, reforms slowed and institutional convergence stopped, as it did in Southern Europe earlier.

Hopefully, EU11 countries will learn the lesson, and will not allow institutional divergence to kick in. We say hopefully they will not, but the fact is that in some countries, this process has already started (Székely and Ward Warmedinger 2018). So far, it has not slowed economic convergence in the countries concerned. The growth push the EU gives through increased trade and FDI, combined with overall solid macroeconomic policies and reforms in certain areas, is still sufficient for these countries to maintain their economic convergence, more or less at a similar average speed across the EU11, which is still among the highest in the world.

But this does not negate the lesson. On the contrary, as incomes of EU11 countries approaches a certain level, institutional quality becomes a critical factor. Thus, unless institutional convergence is restarted before the countries concerned reach that point, their convergence is bound to be brought to a halt, or even reversed. Chapter 3 (Volume I) offers a detailed discussion of the underlying process that makes the quality of institutions critical at a certain point in economic convergence. When "low-hanging fruits" of convergence have been reaped and innovation becomes the key driver of growth, human capital accumulation and allocative efficiency, both regarding physical and human capital, become critical factors (Acemoglu et al. 2006). Economic literature suggests that there is a close relationship between these factors and the quality of private and public institutions. Chapter 3 argues that EU11 countries, most certainly the most developed ones, are getting close to the point where they should adopt a new growth model based on innovation.

1.3 The Working and Interactions of Channels

Regarding the role of the channels discussed above, the overall analysis in Chap. 2 suggests that the trade and investment channels worked well and provided a strong growth impetus to EU11.[3] Regarding foreign trade, within this rather short period, EU11 countries became the most open economies in the world. This was a unique development in the world, very few other countries outside Europe followed a similar trend, and trade openness in the world economy as a whole did not change much during this period. Without a *single market* for trade, EU countries would have much lower income levels (see Chap. 2 in Volume II). In fact, the gain the single market offers is bigger for EU11 than the rest of the EU, because these countries on average are more open than the rest of the EU.

As to the private part of the investment channel, the stock of inward FDI relative to GDP in EU11 rapidly reached the levels observed in countries at the frontier of economic development. While FDI became a main driving force in many successful middle-income countries, too, this development in EU11 was closely linked to EU membership. A large part of inward FDI came from other EU countries, and a significant portion was related to global/regional value chains set up by EU companies in industries that went through such developments globally, such as car production.

There is a strong interaction between the trade and investment channels. Close trade integration, the single market of the EU, induces major FDI flows. This, in turn, creates further trade flows. Institutional convergence further amplifies this positive interaction by creating a legally safe environment for FDI.

Regarding the public part of the investment channel, EU funds have made a major contribution to accelerating growth in EU11 countries, and during the crisis stabilized their external and fiscal balances. While a large contribution of FDI to growth is a global phenomenon, such a strong role of the public part of the investment channel is a unique characteristic of the convergence process of EU11.[4] Official financing for other middle-

---

[3] Volume II contains contributions on the working of these channels. The introduction to that volume provides a more detailed overview of the main findings and discusses their relevance to the nature of the convergence process in EU11.

[4] More recently, China's Belt and Road strategy also targets large infrastructural investment projects. However, these projects are financed by loans, financing is linked to the projects and promotes Chinese companies, and the total size is much smaller than EU funding of investment.

income countries, particularly the grant component of it, is much less and of narrower focus, and it is phased out at a much lower income level.

The role of the finance channel in the convergence process was mixed. The eastern enlargement took place during a period of rapid increase in cross-border financial flows in the world and in the EU. A large part of the globally significant surplus savings of some of the EU countries found its way into the rest of the EU, in Southern European countries mostly into the financial system, and more or less equally distributed between FDI and financial flows in EU11. As a result, credit to the private sector relative to the GDP reached historical heights in both groups. However, the crisis that started in 2008–09 quickly reversed this trend, in fact fully erased the former gain of a credit-led expansion in Southern Europe. However, in EU11, a significant part of the increase in the degree of financial intermediation has been preserved and despite the ups-and-downs, this brought them in line with the levels observed in other middle-income countries. Given their very low starting point in this area, a legacy of their central planning past, this is a major development. The expansion of corporate lending was largely healthy in EU11 (in contrast to some of the lending to households), and thus was preserved even after the crisis. Misallocation among sectors, most importantly an inordinate growth in lending to the real estate and construction sectors, and to households in form of mortgage loans, was a general phenomenon in both groups, and globally. Hence the strong re-adjustment in both sets of economies.

The migration channel also shaped the convergence process in EU11 in important ways. Cross-border migration increased significantly after EU accession, albeit from rather low levels in international comparison and to greatly varying extents in individual EU11 countries. While evidence in the literature suggests that the overall welfare impact of increased mobility in EU11 was positive for the EU as a whole, the gains were distributed unequally. The mobility impacts on the EU11 countries were considerably higher in relative (and absolute) terms than for the other EU countries, but with mixed short- and longer-term results. Thus the "migration rent" is distributed between the migrants themselves and the countries of destination, and in the countries origin there can be positive short-term (reduced unemployment rates, remittances) but also substantial negative longer-term term impacts (such as on the age structure, labour force and skill shortages). Further there are differential impacts on low-skill and high-skill people in EU11 and in the rest of the EU (often in opposite directions).

The impact on the sections of the low-skill labour force in the receiving countries which might have suffered a rather small (but significant) loss, deserves special attention. In light of Brexit, this is an important lesson, which suggests that it is crucial to understand how these channels work and interact, and to complement their working with public policies that mitigate negative side effects. The gains are plenty to pay for this, albeit they may not emerge in the same fiscal constituency where the need arises, so internal and cross-border fiscal transfers might be needed. Such transfers are never easy to implement politically.

The analysis also shows strong interaction between the investment (FDI) and migration channels. An increase in FDI tended to go together with a moderation in net outward migration, and vice versa. As FDI was highly concentrated in certain geographical areas of EU11 countries, mostly in capitals and in regions close to those companies in EU15, mostly in Germany, which created global value chains. FDI also induced internal migration inside EU11 countries, mostly of young low-/medium-skill people.

Overall, the institutional channel has not worked well in the EU (Chap. 2). The rapid economic convergence was not matched by a comparable institutional convergence in EU11. In fact, most of the institutional convergence took place before EU accession. It also became apparent that formal adoption of an advanced legal and regulatory framework (such as the *Acquis*) does not guarantee its transmission into the working of actual institutions and behaviour. This might be particularly the case when such adoption takes place very rapidly in order to fulfil conditions imposed from outside. Slow institutional convergence is also likely to be a factor that explains why rapid economic convergence was not turned into a commensurate social convergence (see also Chap. 9 in Volume II).

Corruption is a particularly important mechanism that can undermine improvements in institutional quality, which in turn weakens the trade, investment and financial channels, and thus slows economic convergence. Moreover, it also reduces the capacity of a country to turn economic convergence into social convergence.

1.4 Emerging Asymmetries and Imbalances of Economic and Social Convergence

Asymmetric FDI flows resulting in a rapid increase in the stock of inward FDI relative to GDP while outward FDI remains scarce, together with other characteristics of EU11 economies—such as vulnerability on the external accounts leading, at times, to high external borrowing, low and unequally distributed household savings—make these economies structurally volatile (Southern EU economies suffered from similar situations).

Imbalances in cross-border migration, a large increase in net outward migration, combined with negative demographic trends that were present in the region well before the eastern enlargement (in many cases, well before economic transition), resulted in an unprecedented decline in population in EU11, including in some of the most successful countries (such as the Baltic countries, see Chap. 7). This is yet another unique characteristic of the convergence process of EU11. Mobility in an integrated economic area is overall a helpful process, and is seen as a positive factor for an integrated monetary zone (either a full monetary union or for a set of countries that with largely pegged exchange rates vis-à-vis each other). However, the segmented nature of fiscal systems affects the sustainability of social security systems, and particularly the large share of national public pension and health care systems can turn this into a negative development. Furthermore, the characteristics of migration flows involving particularly the young and often also those with important qualifications has implications for long-term growth (Chap. 8).

Emerging regional inequalities in EU11 (Chap. 4) are closely related to the existence of strong investment (FDI) and migration channels, and their interaction with an uneven institutional quality of subnational government. Successful regions, those that have better subnational governments and thus tend to attract more FDI, pulled ahead and lost their previously existing positive impact on surrounding areas. Less successful areas, on the other hand, were increasingly left behind and pulled back each other stronger than before.

This happened in a period in which FDI subsided because of the crisis and the disbursement of EU funds picked up as EU11 countries were approaching the end of the programming period. So the pressure on the system from market forces somewhat subsided while the resources specifically targeted to deal with such regional inequalities increased. However, this was only sufficient to reduce the increase in regional inequality.

Moving forward, as FDI can be expected to pick up and transfers from EU funds will most likely somewhat decline, it is essential that these funds are used more efficiently. Regionally unbalanced growth can feed into the political process, creating a hotbed for reform reversals and further weakening the institutional channel.

1.5 Social Coherence: Different Convergence Journeys for Different Groups in Society?

We define convergence as getting closer to the frontier. However, to begin with, at any point in time, distance to frontier can be very different for different groups of people in society. And so can be the speed with which a certain group in a country approaches the frontier. So how did the journey to the frontier looked like for different income groups in EU11?

As Fig. 1.1 shows, different income groups, those at the lower end of the income distribution (5 and 10 percentiles), those in the middle (50 percentile), and those at the top (90 and 95 percentiles) travelled broadly at the same speed, reducing the distance to their peers in the EU frontier countries (people at the same percentile) by more or less the same percentage points.

However, this overall trend masked rather different development paths across countries. EU11 countries positioned themselves very differently regarding the degree of income inequality within the EU upon accession. The (then) high-income new member states (Slovenia and the Czech Republic) were close to the countries with the most equal income distribution (Scandinavian countries), while most of the (then) low-income new member states (Baltic countries and Romania) were at the other end of the distribution, among countries with the most unequal income distribution (Sothern European countries and the UK).[5] As the analysis also shows, the convergence process following EU accession made these differences among EU11 countries more pronounced, with the high-income EU11 countries, Slovenia, Slovakia and the Czech Republic, becoming the EU countries with the most equal income distribution, while Bulgaria moving from the middle to become the EU country with the highest degree of income inequality. As Fig. 1.2 shows, this meant very different journeys for their poor and rich people. Overall, Bulgaria converged faster than the Czech Republic, in line with the standard theory of convergence,

[5] As measured by the Gini coefficient, see Fig. 2.5 in Chap. 2.

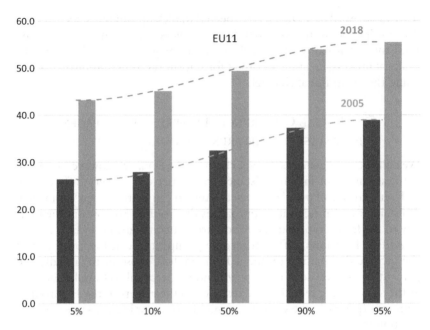

Fig. 1.1 Distance to the EU frontier at different parts of the income distribution in EU11 in 2005 and 2018. (Source: Eurostat, EU-SILC and ECHP surveys. Note: Columns show the ratios between equivalised per capita total disposable income of households (in PPS) in a given segment of the income distribution in EU11 and in the most developed EU countries (the group used in Chap. 2, including Austria, Denmark, Netherlands and Sweden). Values are the averages for the groups as a whole of cut off values for the income distribution segments shown (lowest 5% and 10%, the fifth decile and the top 10% and 5%))

as it started from a significantly lower income level. However, poor people in Bulgaria gained much less than their peers in the Czech Republic, and the opposite was true for people at the higher end of the income distribution in the two countries.

On the one hand, EU11 countries not only converged fast to the frontier, faster than any other group of medium-income economies in the world, but they also converged among themselves. However, this overall trend masks very different developments for different income groups. As Fig. 1.3 shows, there was no convergence among EU11 countries at the lower end of the income distribution, while a relatively strong

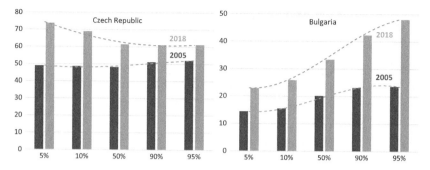

Fig. 1.2 Distance to the EU frontier at different parts of the income distribution in the Czech Republic and Bulgaria in 2005 and 2018. (Source: Eurostat. Note: For a description of the variables shown in these figures, see the note to Fig. 1.1)

convergence took place among income groups in the middle and at the top of the income distribution. The analyses in the two volumes point to several mechanism that might have led to this outcome: high concentration of FDI (Chap. 2 in Volume II); cross-border and internal migration, the latter also interacting with FDI and uneven quality of subnational governments. Furthermore, turning economic convergence into social convergence depends upon the evolution of a policy-making framework that is targeting the congruence between these two convergence domains and, furthermore, institutions that are effective and of good quality to achieve this. A weak institutional channel would therefore hinder the capacity of EU11 countries to turn economic convergence into social convergence, as would an inefficient use of EU funds (Chap. 3 in Volume II).

Another important issue is the generational aspect of convergence. There is no contribution in these two volumes that would cover this issue in its entirety, albeit in many countries in EU11 being a pensioner confines people to the lower part of the income distribution. Thus, the brief analysis above relates to their convergence experience. Chapter 11 (Volume II) does however provide a rather comprehensive analysis of a very important issue of the generational aspect in a society, pension reforms. While the design of the pension (and social support) system is a major issue in any modern society with broad pension coverage, and the demographic transition that (high- and middle-income) countries in the world are going through is perhaps the strongest force shaping pension reforms, the experience of EU11 countries is of particular importance.

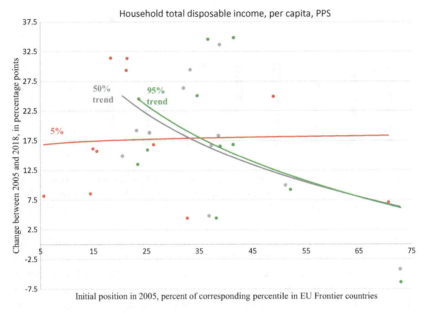

Fig. 1.3 Income convergence among EU11 countries, 2005–2018. (Source: Eurostat, EU-SILC and ECHP surveys. Note: Income refers to per capita equivalised total disposable income of households in purchasing power standard. Red dots are observations for the cut-off income for the lowest 5% of the income distribution in the EU 11 country concerned, grey dots are for the cut-off income for the 5th decile, while the green dots are for 95%. Values are expressed as percent of the corresponding value for EU frontier countries (Austria, Denmark, Netherlands, Sweden). On the horizontal axe, the initial position in 2005 is shown, while on the vertical axe, the change between 2005 and 2018. For the 5th decile and 95%, the trends suggest that the lower the initial income relative to the frontier the faster the convergence, while for the lowest 5%, there is no such trend) (Color figure online)

As part of their shared legacy, EU11 countries embarked on transition with poorly designed and highly non-transparent fiscal systems, particularly regarding pension and health care systems. Moreover, the first phase of transition, the (in most cases) large initial decline in economic activity and massive layoffs put strong pressure on both systems, particularly on the pension system. For many, retirement was offered as an escape route to avoid long-term unemployment. Thus, sustainability became an issue early on, also because of the obscurity of financing and the arbitrariness and over-generous nature of the rules for benefits (relative to revenues). Moreover, as mentioned above, a rapid population decline has been a unique characteristic of the convergence process in EU11. EU accession greatly accelerated outward migration from EU11 to EU15 countries, with few exceptions, reflecting the income gaps within the EU. The interaction of migration and demographic processes produced a decline in population in EU11 (and accelerated a strong change in the age distribution) that is unprecedented in peacetime and put further strong pressure on pension systems in the region.

The transition process also had a major impact on the approach to pension reforms in EU11 countries as well as on the development of other pillars that are of great importance for social convergence (such as the health and educational systems). A general enthusiasm about reforms and market-based solutions in the public sphere, combined with (or perhaps even induced by) a push by international organizations led to rather radical pension reforms in EU11 (and in some other medium-income countries in the world). Most of this happened well before EU accession became a major force shaping institutional reforms, and by the time EU11 countries joined the EU, this was a rather unique characteristic of these countries, very few EU15 countries had similar pension systems. These reforms were neither induced by EU membership, nor did EU legislation cover this area. Nevertheless, through the fiscal rules of the EU, there was a strong interaction between these reforms and the institutional setup of the EU, particularly when the crisis put strong pressure on the fiscal system in EU11. Chapter 11 (Volume II) offers an excellent analysis of the policy responses in EU11 and the subsequent reforms of the previous pension reforms.

The outcome of this process will greatly shape the life-time experience of different generations in EU11 with economic and social convergence, possibly making their convergence journeys as active and retired people rather different. This in turn, may affect the political economy of convergence in important ways.

1.6 Convergence and Climate Change

Climate change is among the biggest challenges humankind faces at this stage. 93% of European Union citizens see climate change as a serious problem. The EU has been at the forefront of the fight against climate change. As one of its actions, the newly elected European Parliament declared a climate and environment emergency in November 2019, and the newly elected European Commission proposed a European Green Deal in December (European Commission 2019).

As a legacy of their shared Soviet-type centrally planned past, EU11 countries started economic transition with highly energy- and carbon-intensive economies. As the analysis in Volume II (Chap. 10) shows, since then, they embarked on a unique path of rapid decarbonization of their economies. No other group of medium-income countries have managed to follow such a path so far. EU membership played an important role in bringing about these positive developments, directly and indirectly. It helped EU11 countries to quickly catch up with high-income countries regarding the CO2 intensity of their economies.

1.7 Lessons for Other Countries

While the main focus is on EU11, our approach is directly applicable to other countries that in the past joined the EU as upper-middle income countries. Chapter 2 uses the Southern European member states (EU S4) as a reference group and concludes that most of the key findings of the analysis for EU11 also hold for this group. Chapter 8 analyses the convergence process in European countries outside the EU. Some of them are EU candidate or potential candidate countries, with a perspective of future EU membership, albeit with uncertain timing or, in the case of Turkey, with very high uncertainty surrounding eventual membership. Others, such as Belarus, Moldova, Ukraine, Russia and Kazakhstan (which is outside Europe) at this stage have no perspective of future EU membership, or not even the desire for it. Nevertheless, they are in the proximity of the EU, and thus, their convergence process is strongly influenced by the EU.

1.8 Looking Forward: Will Rapid Economic Convergence in EU11 Continue?

While most of the analyses focus on the historical experience of EU11, the main messages of these two volumes concern the future of the region. The weakness of the institutional channel is clearly a major potential limitation on the speed of convergence in the future. While this is an important finding for EU11, it fits with the main findings of the traditional convergence/development literature. Social cohesion and climate change are however newly emerging areas of development that can put severe limitations on the pace of convergence in the future, hence the separate discussion on these aspects in this Introduction. Weakening social cohesion not only reduces the growth potential of a country by limiting human capital accumulation and labour force participation, it can also lead to weakening institutions and to reform reversals. This is the political economy of convergence, which is as important as the economics of the process. Moreover, a deteriorating environment, and particularly aggravating climate change will no doubt also limit the development of high-income countries at or close to the frontier and the convergence of others to the frontier. Any hindrances to the development of the global frontier also makes convergence a much more vulnerable process, increasing inter alia the likelihood of geo-political tensions.

As the experience of Sothern European EU members shows, and as the vast literature on the middle-income trap points out, getting closer to the frontier changes the nature of the economic convergence process. The relative importance of different factors changes rapidly. While this is well described in the literature in general and historically, there is yet little research available on the impact of the current wave of rapid and disruptive technological change and on the reforms that are necessary to break through the middle-income threshold inside the EU. Chapter 3 fills some of this gap by drilling into the key factors that will determine future convergence in EU11, allocative efficiency and innovation. The legacy of massive migration flows from some of the EU11 countries over the past 2 decades (analysed in Chap. 8 in Volume II) will also have non-negligible implications on age structure, the labour force and hence on innovation and the adaptability of institutions to deal with future challenges.

1.9 The Corona Crisis and the Future of Convergence in the European Union

Since the submission of the manuscript to the publisher a rather dramatic break in global developments has taken place: the outbreak of a severe health crisis in the form of the Covid-19 virus epidemic. For months, Europe became the epicentre of a worldwide health crisis, having the highest infection and deaths rates in the world.

Most EU11 countries did relatively well during the epidemic maintain relatively low infection and death rates. Studies show that this was due to early and rigorous lockdown policies. However, the early economic impact with sharply declining production and GDP levels was rather similar to that experienced in most Western European countries. The most vulnerable countries were those that depended most on trade, in particular those that hosted cross-border production networks, and those that depended strongly on tourism (see Grieveson 2020).

What is the likely impact in the future? In the immediate future, these countries face similar problems as other European countries. Public spending will be crucial to compensate for the hesitant resumption of consumption and private investment after a relaxation of the lock-down. Public debt will increase sharply as GDP declines and fiscal stimulus kicks in. While this is likely to be a general trend in Europe, there are important specific factors that will shape macroeconomic developments in the region.

Like other severely affected countries, EU11 countries will receive massive financial support from the EU. At the time of writing, the next financial framework (MFF) for the years 2021–27 is still being negotiated. Nevertheless, it is likely that due to the corona-crisis, the EU budget will be significantly strengthened, through the Next Generation EU facility, and front-loaded and targeted towards countering the effects of the crisis, while maintaining longer-term priorities by investing in a green, digital and resilient Europe. Moreover, CEE countries will be able to benefit from the various new schemes that the EU has been setting up as a collective response to the economic crisis, such as SURE, a new instrument for temporary Support to mitigate Unemployment Risks in an Emergency, or the Pan-European Guarantee Fund set up by the EIB to support SMEs. Financial support from the EU will take away some of the pressure on their national budgets and will allow them to spread their additional borrowing over a long period.

In the countries where public debt was relatively high prior to the pandemic, such as Croatia, Hungary and Slovenia, "fiscal space" available to governments to give a stimulus to the economy from their own budgets is somewhat smaller than in other EU11 countries. Thus, their structural deficit is likely to deteriorate less and/or for shorter period. Consequently, the increase in the public debt ratio is not likely to be sizable in these countries either, albeit their policy responses may be somewhat hindered by this limitation. Therefore, albeit for different reasons, debt sustainability is unlikely to be a major issue in the region. The first post-pandemic economic forecast of the European Commission confirms these trends.

Developments regarding international trade and external finance in the region will also be somewhat different from general trends in Europe and globally. The dependence of EU11 countries on foreign capital fell quite dramatically because of the improvements in their current accounts position following the financial crisis. Hence, they are less affected by short-term capital outflows than emerging economies globally.

However, the situation in this regard is different in the South East European (SEE) countries (particularly in the West Balkan) which had sizable trade deficits prior to the pandemic, in large part covered by remittances. As people from these countries who work abroad are going to face very harsh labour market situations, and as many of them have already returned home, remittance flows are likely to subside for an extended period. Foreign direct investment will also ebb for a while, as international companies will be hesitant to expand (or even maintain) their operations abroad.

On the other hand, EU11, and perhaps even more so SEE countries that attracted FDI later, are likely to benefit from the newly emerging trend of "regionalist" production networks. If this trend gets stronger, those in closer geographic and legal/institutional proximity to highly developed countries will gain from the retrenchment of global production networks.

Apart from these factors directly linked to the impact of the Coronavirus crisis, the longer-term development of EU11 and associated Eastern European economies will continue to be shaped by the general factors that are extensively analysed in these two volumes. Amongst these, we would single out demographic trends, differences in institutional and political-economic developments in the region and the evolution of the European Union as a whole. Moreover, global developments will also influence the region, such as the increasing US-China rivalry, challenges to the international trading system, the climate crisis, and migration challenges.

1.10 Structure of Volumes

The two volumes of this book are both stand-alone collections of novel contributions to the literature on the convergence process in Europe. They can be fully enjoyed separately.

In Volume I, after spelling out the overall framework adopted in the two volumes and describing and analysing the main trends for the EU11 as a whole by Székely and Kuenzel (2021) in Chap. 2, Gattini et al. (2021), Chap. 3 looks into the future challenges that the EU11 will face to maintain rapid economic convergence. In Chap. 4, Pinelli and Pellényi (2021) analyse regional dynamics in the EU11, an area where the different channels strongly interact, with a potential to lead to a regionally unbalanced convergence process.

This is followed by a set of country studies looking into the convergence process in individual countries or group of countries: in Poland by Piatkowski (2021) in Chap. 5, in Hungary by Boldizsár et al. (2021) in Chap. 6, in the Baltic countries by Randveer and Staehr (2021) in Chap. 7, and in Bulgaria and Romania in Dobrinsky (2021) in Chap. 8. Holzner and Grieveson (2021) in Chap. 9 complement this part with a joint analysis of European countries that are not members of the EU.

Volume II contains the contributions that discuss in detail the various aspects of the working of the individual channels outlined in this Introduction.

1.11 Thanks

We would like to thank the institutions and people who helped and supported these two volumes and the underlying collaborative project on the 15th anniversary of the eastern enlargement of the EU. DG ECFIN of the European Commission launched a Theme for Team project on this topic, which initiated the work underlying the contributions of authors from DG ECFIN, Chaps. 2 and 4 in Volume I and Chaps. 2, 3, 5, 10 and 11 in Volume II. Moreover, as part of the T4T project, DG ECFIN financed contract studies that formed the basis for Chap. 9 in Volume I and Chaps. 4, 9 and 12 in Volume II. We are grateful to Marc Puig and Melanie Ward Warmedinger for their contribution to organizing this project, and to Peter Koh for copy editing several chapters.

As part of the project, DG ECFIN, EPSC and WIIW jointly organized a two-day international conference in Vienna and Bratislava on 8–9 April 2019, which focused on the policy issues involved. The materials of this conference can be found at https://ec.europa.eu/info/conference-15th-anniversary-2004-eu-enlargement-looking-back-looking-forward_en. DG ECFIN provided finance, and the participants of the T4T in DG ECFIN contributed in a major way to the organization of the international conference. We are particularly thankful to Marc Puig for helping to organize this conference. We are also grateful to EPSC, particularly Lucio Vinhas de Souza, the head of EPSC's economics team, Vladimir C. Isaila and Matthias Busse for their major contribution to putting together the program of this conference and to organizing this conference. We are also thankful to WIIW, particularly to Elisabeth Hagen, for the great help with the organization of this conference and for the active participation of WIIW staff in the conference. We are also grateful for the contribution of WIIW staff to these two volumes, Chap. 9 in Volume I and Chap. 8 in Volume II.

Related to this conference, WIIW published the *Faces of Convergence*, an open access e-book that carries the personal testimonies of many of the authors of this volume, as well as many other people who made major contribution to the transition process in their own countries and/or across the region. This book can be freely downloaded at https://wiiw.ac.at/faces-of-convergence-p-4908.html We are grateful to Mario Holzner for his support for this publication. We are also grateful to Gábor Székely for designing and producing the electronic version of this publication, and to Peter Koh, Ayesha Landesmann and Melanie Ward Warmedinger for their help with editing.

Finally, we are particularly grateful to Marco Buti and Maarten Verwey from the European Commission for their strong support to the entire project.

References

Acemoglu, D., Aghion, P., & Zilibotti, F. (2006). Distance to Frontier, Selection, and Economic Growth. *Journal of the European Economic Association, 1*, 37–74.

Boldizsár, A., Nagy-Kékesi, Z. S., & Rriga, E. J. (2021). Transformation of the Trade and Financing Model of the Hungarian Economy After EU Accession. In Landesmann and Székely (2021).

Dobrinsky, R. (2021). Bulgaria and Romania: The Latecomers to the Eastern Enlargement. In Landesmann and Székely (2021).

EBRD. (1989–2014). *Transition Reports* (Consecutive Issues). London: European Bank for Reconstruction and Development.

European Commission. (2019). *The European Green Deal. Communication from the Commission to the European Parliament, the European Council, the Council, the European Economic and Social Committee and the Committee of the Regions; COM(2019) 64*. Brussels: European Commission.

Gattini, L., Gereben, Á., Kollár, M., Revoltella, D., & Wruuck, P. (2021). Towards a New Growth Model in CESEE: Three Challenges Ahead. In Landesmann and Székely (2021)

Grieveson, R. (2020). Regional Overview. In *Looking for Shelter from the Storm: Economic Forecasts for Eastern Europe 2020–21*. WIIW Monthly Report 5/2020. Vienna: The Vienna Institute for International Economic Studies.

Holzner, M., & Grieveson, R. (2021). Convergence of Non-EU Countries in the CESEE Region. In Landesmann and Székely (2021).

Landesmann, M., & Székely, I. P. (Eds.). (2021). Does EU Membership Facilitate Convergence? The Experience of the EU's Eastern Enlargement. Palgrave Macmillan.

Lawrence, R. Z. (1996). *Regionalism, Multilateralism and Deeper Integration*. Washington, DC: Brookings Institution Press.

North, D. C. (1990). *Institutions, Institutional Change, and Economic Performance*. New York: Cambridge University Press.

Piatkowski, M. (2021). How the European Union Made Poland European Again. In Landesmann and Székely (2021).

Pinelli, D., & Pellényi, G. (2021). Regional Dynamics in EU11. In Landesmann and Székely (2021).

Randveer, M., & Staehr, K. (2021). Macroeconomic Trends in the Baltic States Before and After Accession to the EU. In Landesmann and Székely (2021).

Sapir, A. (2011). European Integration at the Crossroads: A Review Essay on the 50th Anniversary of Bela Balassa's Theory of Economic Integration. *Journal of Economic Literature, 49*(4), 1200–1229.

Székely, I. P. (Ed.). (2019). *Faces of Convergence*. Vienna: WIIW. Open-access e-book.

Székely, I. P., & Kuenzel, R. (2021). Convergence of the EU Member States in Central-Eastern and South Eastern Europe: A Framework for Convergence Inside a Close Regional Cooperation. In Landesmann and Székely (2021).

Székely, I. P., & Ward Warmedinger, M. (2018). *Reform Reversal in Former Transition Economies (FTEs) of the European Union: Areas, Circumstances and Motivations* (IZA Policy Paper No. 142).

PART I

Framework for Analysis and Overall Trends

CHAPTER 2

Convergence of the EU Member States in Central-Eastern and South Eastern Europe (EU11): A Framework for Convergence Inside a Close Regional Cooperation

István P. Székely and Robert Kuenzel

2.1 Introduction

Countries in Central-Eastern and South Eastern Europe and in the Baltics decided to join the Western alliance system soon after the start of transition in the late 1980s. The desire to belong to the West was a major factor politically anchoring these countries and making the necessary reforms

---

The views expressed are solely those of the authors and do not necessarily represent the official views of the European Commission.

I. P. Székely (✉)
DG ECFIN, European Commission, Brussels, Belgium

Corvinus University of Budapest, Budapest, Hungary
e-mail: istvan-pal.szekely@ec.europa.eu

© The Author(s), under exclusive license to Springer Nature Switzerland AG 2021
M. Landesmann, I. P. Székely (eds.), *Does EU Membership Facilitate Convergence? The Experience of the EU's Eastern Enlargement - Volume I*, Studies in Economic Transition,
https://doi.org/10.1007/978-3-030-57686-8_2

more palatable. Later in the process, the desire to join the EU became the main force, the most important external anchor to foster development.

The strong desire in the region to join the EU was based on an expectation about the benefits of EU membership. As many expressed it clearly (see, e.g. Vértes 2019), the expectation was that by joining the EU, these countries would get on a convergence path that leads to a quality of life and opportunities that, in their perception, people in the (then) EU countries had. Starting in May 2004, in three waves (in 2004, 2007 and 2013), 11 of these countries joined the EU (in what follows, we will refer to them as EU11) and subsequently they benefitted from their membership.

There were several ex-ante assessments of the likely impact of EU enlargement on EU11 and on the rest of the EU starting as early as in the mid-1990 (Baldwin 1995; Baldwin et al. 1997), and there are several recent assessments of the actual impact (Keereman and Székely 2010; Caliendo et al. 2017; Campos et al. 2019). These assessments focused on economic convergence and on the free movement of production factors, the four freedoms.

The framework we offer makes several extensions to the traditional ones. It focuses on the interaction between EU membership and convergence, and it defines convergence as approaching the global frontier of economic, institutional and social development. It looks at the EU as a set of rules and institutions, which not only create the environment for free trade of goods and services and for free movement of capital, people and enterprises, but also impact and anchor the development of institutions in the member states. We argue that as EU11 countries get closer to the global frontier, the quality of their institutions becomes more important, in fact, at some point critical. Moreover, it not only affects the speed of economic convergence, but it also influences the capacity of a country to turn economic convergence into social convergence.

In what follows, we do not aim to quantify the impact of EU accession using a formal model. Several chapters in this volume present analyses that attempt to quantify the impact of EU accession through particular channels using formal models. As these chapters show, even in a relatively narrow area, such as trade (Chap. 1 in Volume II) or EU transfers (Chaps. 3 and 4 in Volume II), it is a difficult task to identify the counterfactual scenario. Producing a plausible counterfactual scenario to describe the

---

R. Kuenzel
DG ECFIN, European Commission, Brussels, Belgium
e-mail: Robert.KUENZEL@ec.europa.eu

(hypothetical) outcome of no EU accession of EU11 would be a very challenging task. To build a model that captures the quality of institutions, which is of central importance in our framework, and thus could describe the institutional channel through which the EU and its member states interact with each other would add to the challenge. Instead, we use a set of control groups, relatively homogeneous groups of countries in different parts of the world to which we compare our group of interest (EU11). This does not provide any quantitative estimate, but can perhaps offer an indication of the impact EU membership had on the development of these countries.

The rest of the chapter is structured as follow. First, in Sect. 2.2, we will develop a conceptual framework to discuss the interaction between EU membership and convergence in EU11, breaking down the matter into well-contoured aspects, or channels as we call them, such as trade, investment, finance, migration and institutions and laws. In Sect. 2.3, we will investigate whether convergence accelerated in EU11 since EU accession, relative to the period before and relative to similar (middle-income) countries in other parts of the world. In the subsequent sections (Sects. 2.4, 2.5, 2.6, 2.7, and 2.8) we present some basic evidence on the working of the channels we identified. The subsequent chapters in Volume II elaborate further on the working of these channels. In Sect. 2.9, we look into some of the issues the integration of EU11 countries into the EU raised. In Sect. 2.10, we discuss those institutional changes in the EU that took place as a reaction to the crisis and are relevant to the issues we raise in our analysis. Finally, we draw some conclusions in Sect. 2.11.

2.2 A Framework for Analysis

Our focus is on the role of EU in economic convergence of EU11 countries. However, to understand this role, we apply a broader framework that includes economic ("means"), institutional ("ways") and social development ("ends"), because these three main dimensions of development strongly interact with each other. Analysing the role of EU in such broader framework is also important because the main aims of EU include all three dimensions.[1] In our analysis, we will also look into the distributional

---

[1] Article 3 of the Treaty on European Union (2012) sets out the aims of the European Union, which explicitly includes the promotion of the well-being of its people, the four freedoms discussed earlier in the Introduction, highly competitive social market economy, social progress, and economic, social and territorial cohesion. As we focus on outcome, we will aim to translate these general goals into measurable indicators in our framework.

aspects of the convergence process in all three dimensions, and into the impact of EU membership in this regard.[2]

We will define economic, institutional and social convergence (or divergence) as a trend of declining (increasing) distance between the country (or group of countries) concerned and the global frontier of economic ("means"), institutional ("ways") and social ("ends") development. In all three dimensions, we will focus on outcome, instead of any particular form or structure (of economy, society or institutions). Thus, in or framework, convergence is defined and measured (admittedly in imperfect ways) as the difference in performance in these three dimensions, and not as convergence of economic, institutional or societal structures.

We will analyse the interaction between the EU as a legal-institutional structure, a set of laws, institutions and institutional culture[3] and economic convergence of EU11 in a framework, which breaks down this interaction into channels. These channels capture the key mechanisms through which the impact of EU membership works.

From the viewpoint of our analysis, one of the most important functions of the EU is to provide a legal and institutional framework that allows people and companies in the EU to fully exercise their four basic freedoms, the free movement of goods, services, capital and people. Four of the channels we will analyse, trade (of goods and services), cross-border investment (FDI and EU funds that support private and public investment), finance (cross-border financial flows and foreign-owned financial firms which is FDI in the financial sector), and mobility (cross-border movement of people) are directly related to these basic freedoms. We break up the cross-border movement of private capital into two channels, FDI (which is part of the investment channel) and cross-border financial investment (which is part of the finance channel) because they are of fundamentally different natures and have different dynamics. What we investigate in our analysis is the outcome, the impact of EU membership on trade openness, FDI, cross-border financial flows and financial deepening, and cross-border migration, and through these channels, on

---

[2] Article 3 explicitly mentions this aspect as well when it says: "It shall promote economic, social and territorial cohesion, and solidarity among Member States."

[3] In short, institutions as defined by North (1991): "Institutions are the humanly devised constraints that structure political, economic and social interactions. They consist of both informal constraints (sanctions, taboos, customs, traditions, and codes of conducts) and formal rules (constitutions, laws, property rights)."

economic and social convergence of EU11 to the frontier of economic and social development.

The direct impact of EU membership in the areas discussed above (trade, investment, finance, migration) is on the laws and institutions that govern these activities, as many of these aspects are either directly governed by European Law, or strongly influenced by them, and by practices in other member states. The scope and intensity of such interactions is perhaps a unique characteristic of the convergence process in EU11, compared with the convergence process of other middle-income countries in the world.

To capture this impact, we also define the institutional channel of interaction between the EU and its member states. What we will investigate here is the impact of EU membership on the quality of economic governance in EU11 relative to other groups of countries that are not part of such a closely knit supranational organisation. That is, we will investigate the outcome, the way institutions actually work and the way people in these countries perceive their own economic institutions, as measured by Worldwide Governance Indicators of the World Bank.

Albeit EU membership has a very strong impact on the economic and social development of these countries, it was not the only force at work. Global integration has also played an important role through all these channels. There are several international organisations that promote better legal and institutional frameworks at the global level to facilitate cross-border trade and investment, financial integration and labour mobility. Industries such as car manufacturing have seen the creation of global value chains (GVC), which have championed trends also inside the EU. Trade agreements, such as NAFTA, and investment support initiatives have facilitated this process, and have revealed the alternative model of a looser form of integration than the EU via partial agreements. A large part of FDI flows and financial market integration in the world have been created by globalisation through such arrangements.

Moreover, several of the global institutions also promote improvements in governance in the public and private spheres. The World Bank, the IMF and the OECD are among such institutions. By their very nature, these institutions influence and anchor economic, institutional and social development everywhere, in EU11 and in other middle-income countries that try to converge to the global frontier. The question we ask here is whether the EU had a stronger, more positive impact on the convergence of EU11 (and EU Candidate countries) in this regard, whether it could add to the impact of global institutions and global integration.

2.2.1 Interactions Among the Channels

The different channels interact with each other. These interactions can strengthen or weaken the working of the channels, that is, the total impact is not simply the sum of the impact through the individual channels in isolation. These interactions are richly discussed in the literature. Some of these interactions have been particularly strong in EU11 during the period under investigation here. As we will see below, a large part of the EU accession induced inward FDI was concentrated in the automotive industry and in the financial (mostly banking) sector (roughly one quarter of the total each, albeit unevenly distributed within EU11). The former was driven by the creation of GVCs and thus generated large gross trade flows in both directions. The sizable share of financial sector FDI translated into very high shares of foreign banks in the banking sectors of EU11. This in turn strongly influenced the working of the financial integration channel, and its interaction with the trade and investment channels (FDI).

For our analysis, the interactions among the four channels above and the institutional channel will be of particular importance. As widely demonstrated in the literature, well-designed and well-functioning (good-quality) domestic (public and private) institutions enhance the working of the trade, investment and financial integration channels, as they create a favourable environment for private enterprises, foreign and domestic, while poor-quality institutions can hinder the working of other channels (North 1990; Acemoglu et al. 2005; Tridico 2011). We shall discuss some of the most important interactions among these channels as we go along.

The working of these channels unleashes powerful market mechanism, which if left to their own, can distribute large gains and burdens in very uneven ways in society, according to income, social position or geographical location (prosperous vs backward regions, urban vs rural). The quality of domestic economic institutions and/or major unevenness in institutional quality across subnational institutions can amplify this problem.

Inequalities in economic development, in turn, have major implications on the speed and nature of social development. Economic institutions considered here are not designed to promote social development, or to prevent or mitigate inequalities. In fact, if they function well, they unleash strong market forces that can create challenges for social development.

These challenges are to be tackled by institutions that focus on promoting social development, such as social support, health care or educational systems. Likewise, these institutions focus on social development, and not on economic development. If they function well, they can indirectly help economic development, as they better and more equal social conditions, and help people to have long and healthy life and better education in an equitable manner. These are important factors that influence economic development.

It is the overall quality of domestic economic and social institutions that influence the capacity of a country to turn economic convergence into social convergence, and to do so in an equitable manner, which is the ultimate aim of EU member states individually, and collectively in the EU.

2.2.2 *The Impact of EU Through the Channels*

The impact EU membership has had through these channels could in turn manifest itself in specialisation patterns and more broadly in the change of economic structure, higher capital stock, faster innovation, better corporate governance, better government quality and faster human capital accumulation. Put more broadly, in the strengthening of "deep growth fundamentals", relative to other converging countries, and relative to countries at the frontier.

To disentangle the impact of EU membership, two strategies could be applied. First, a model-based prediction of developments without EU membership (a model generated counter factual) could be compared with actual developments. Second, developments in EU11 countries could be compared with those countries in Europe which are not EU members (yet) and with a broader set of control group (e.g. middle-income developing countries). Both approaches have major limitations. Models that we could possibly use to describe the (past) development of countries without EU membership are surrounded by major model uncertainties, and the assumptions we would have to make to define the counterfactual almost by design were too restrictive. Calibrating or estimating the parameters of these models would also be a challenging task. Most importantly perhaps, these models may not fully capture the role of institutions (rule of law, corruption, government efficiency, etc.) and the interaction of the different channels (trade, investment, financial integration, migration, institutions).

Comparing EU11 with non-EU countries in the region is also problematic, since the selection of EU members has not been random and unrelated to their convergence potential. Put differently, countries that have become EU members since 2004 are the ones that had proved themselves ready to join the EU and benefit from EU membership. The characteristics needed for this are in all likelihood the same as the ones necessary to converge fast.[4] Despite these difficulties, such an approach may help disentangle the impact of EU membership and that of global forces.

While EU membership was an important factor promoting development through various channels, it was not the only one. Convergence has also taken place at the global level and the speed of convergence has never been as fast globally as it is today. Convergence is towards the global frontier, so our analysis will not focus on convergence to the EU average (which itself includes these countries), but to the global frontier.

We identify the global frontier of economic, institutional and social development with four small open EU economies, Austria, Denmark, Netherlands and Sweden (we refer to this group as *EU Frontier*). These countries have real income levels among the highest in the world, and they are also among the most competitive countries with high-quality institutions. In almost all global rankings, they are in the top 10–20, and among the top EU countries. They have well-established democracies; thus policy choices fully reflect people's preferences. People from EU11 travel to these countries, work and live there, companies from these countries have important presence in EU11 economies. Ideas flow back and forth between these countries and EU11 countries, their national soccer teams play frequently. These are countries policy makers and ordinary people can relate to, and perhaps most importantly, they embody the hopes and expectations of people in EU11. Thus, they serve for them as natural, meaningful benchmarks. These countries are in Europe but they are undoubtedly also at the global frontier of economic and social development, and provide inspirations for people all over the world.[5]

---

[4] Moreover, several EU candidate countries in the Western Balkan experienced war (e.g., Serbia), stronger negative consequences of war elsewhere (e.g., North Macedonia, Albania) or changing composition and/or boundaries of states (e.g., Montenegro) in the past that may have long lasting impact on their economic and social development.

[5] Székely (2019) uses a broader set of small open economies to define the global frontier, including additional countries from other continents (such as Canada, New Zealand, Australia or Singapore). In almost all respect, these additional countries are very similar to the ones chosen here.

To gauge whether EU11 countries are converging faster because of EU membership than global trends alone would suggest, we use several benchmark groups from different regions of the world, such as Latin America, South-east Asia and Northern Africa. We selected from each region four countries with sizes and income levels that are close to EU11 countries. As EU11 countries are medium-income small open economies, we selected from each region countries that are the most similar in this regard. *Latam* includes Argentina, Chile, Costa Rica, and Uruguay; *North Africa* includes Algeria, Jordan, Morocco and Tunisia; *SEA* (South-East Asia) includes Indonesia, Korea, Malaysia and Philippines. While these choices are inevitably ad hoc, as the figures in subsequent sections show, they form meaningful groups for comparison. They are rather homogeneous along most dimensions investigated here, reflecting similarities in the nature of their convergence process. Many of these countries, particularly those in North Africa, have close relationship with the EU, including long-standing trade (association) agreements.[6] Most importantly, comparisons with such groups are easier for policy makers to interpret than those involving synthetic comparators, and thus are perhaps more inspiring.[7]

We also added a group of candidate countries from the Western Balkan, that is, countries that are on the path towards EU membership. The group includes Albania, Montenegro, North-Macedonia and Serbia, and we refer to them as *EU Candidates*. Finally, we also use Southern European EU countries (*EU S4*, which comprises Greece, Italy, Portugal and Spain) as a benchmark group, as these countries went through a similar convergence process in the past when they joined the EU, Italy as a founding member. They are also an important group because they, as group, have started to diverge from the frontier. As the sustainability of convergence is an important aspect of our analysis, the comparison with this group may help inform policy makers in EU11 countries about this crucial aspect.

We use the same groups as benchmarks throughout our analysis. Thus, the indicators for them in different areas of comparison represent coherent

---

[6] For more details on the trade agreements with the EU, see Sect. 2.4.

[7] The synthetic comparators calculated in Campos et al. (2019) include several countries in these groups. While such synthetic comparators are data driven and thus more objective, they also include countries with which a comparison of economic, institutional and social convergence in EU11 is somewhat difficult to interpret. For example, large resource-based economies, such as Russia. Moreover, using different synthetic comparators for rather similar countries may not appear intuitive for policy makers.

development strategies, policy choices that take into account the trade-offs and the economic, social and political constraints policy makers face in real life. The same argument applies to using the same group of countries to represent the frontier of economic and social development in different areas. For further information on these groups, see Annex A.

The metric along which convergence is measured is also an important choice. We will measure economic convergence by per capita GDP (in PPP). GDP is a relatively good proxy for the resources available to generate household income and government revenue. Albeit widely used, social development is not a well-defined concept. We will define it as the well-being of people, that is, their capability, their real opportunity to do and be what they have reason to value.[8] This also corresponds well with what people in EU11 expected from EU accession. They wanted to have a life similar to the one people in EU15 countries had. That is, expectations covered a much broader area than just income, it also included health care, education and work conditions. In our analysis, we use the UNDP Human Development Index (HDI) to measure social development. Equity is another important aspect of economic and social development. We will capture by the Gini coefficient for income distribution and by the Inequality-Adjusted HDI (IA-HDI).

The analysis we present here is in not an attempt to quantify the impact of EU membership on the economic, institutional and social development of these countries. The comparison with these groups, based on a limited set of indicators, is illustrative; it helps to make useful observations and to raise issues that might be relevant for future policy formulation.

2.3 Convergence: How Have EU11 Countries Fared in Global Comparison?

Figure 2.1 shows the per capita GDP in PPS and the HDI for EU11 countries as a group, and compares these with the respective values for other middle-income groups in the world to see whether EU membership helped accelerate convergence to the frontier.

Without trying to establish causality, we can make a few important points related to Fig. 2.1. In the 1990s, the first decade of economic

---

[8] Article 3 of the Treaty on European Union (2012) also explicitly mentions well-being as one of the main aims of the EU: "The Union's aim is to promote peace, its values and the well-being of its peoples."

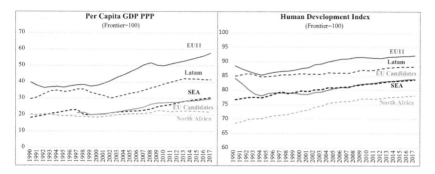

Fig. 2.1 Economic and social convergence in the world. Note: *EU Frontier* includes Austria, Denmark, Netherlands and Sweden; *EU11* includes Bulgaria, Croatia, Czech Republic, Estonia, Hungary, Latvia, Lithuania, Poland, Romania, Slovakia and Slovenia. *EU Candidates* include Albania, North Macedonia, Montenegro and Serbia; *Latam* includes Argentina, Chile, Costa Rica, and Uruguay; *North Africa* includes Algeria, Jordan, Morocco and Tunisia; SEA includes Indonesia, Korea, Malaysia and Philippines. Simple, unweighted averages of country observations. (Sources: For per capita GDP World Bank, for Human Development Index, UNDP)

transformation, similarly to the other benchmark groups, EU11 did not converge to the frontier. However, since the turn of the century, EU11 has been the fastest converging group of middle-income countries in this sample. The acceleration of convergence started in 2000, which coincides with the period in which EU membership became a plausible option and preparations for EU membership started in earnest. Since then, the relative position of this group improved significantly over all the groups used here as benchmark. The 2008–09 crisis led to a lull and slowed the pace of convergence in a seemingly lasting manner, but EU11 remains the fastest converging group, albeit not so much as before.[9]

---

[9] Campos et al. (2019) use a synthetic benchmark country approach and start to account for the positive impact of (future) EU enlargement in 1998. They estimate that in the first 10 years (1998–2008) on average (average over the period and the 8 EU11 countries that joined in 2004) EU accession increased per capita GDP by some 15% (relative to the predicted value for no EU membership). The average gain in the first 5 years is estimated at close to 10%, so the gain is estimated to have increased over time. These estimates are for a period that ends just before the crisis started. Thus, they are strongly influenced by the rapid growth in the Baltic countries. However, the estimates seem to be rather robust to the choice of the synthetic benchmark. These estimated gains are very much in line with what Fig. 2.1 sug-

Regarding social convergence, as measured by HDI, Fig. 2.1 suggests that rapid economic convergence of EU11 prior to the crisis also resulted in social convergence to the frontier, but this was not commensurate to the pace of economic convergence. Since the crisis, however, economic convergence does not seem to have led to social convergence, neither towards the frontier nor relative to other groups of countries. This suggests that EU11 countries have limited capacity to turn economic convergence into social convergence, and thus may need a rather fast economic convergence to achieve tangible social convergence. Moreover, this relationship may not be linear and may depend on other factors. There may also be a structural break in this relationship, a hypothesis that has been raised by some regarding social convergence within the EU (Eurofound 2018).[10] We shall return to this point after analysing the institutional channel and discussing some issues related to European integration and economic convergence.

Regarding convergence within the region, EU11 countries broadly moved together in this period (Fig. 2.2), but there are a few noteworthy changes in relative positions within the group. Baltic countries as a group converged much faster on both metrics, moving from the bottom of the group after the disruptive part of the transition from central planning (and the break-up of the USSR) ended, to above the group average by 2007. The crisis temporarily set back the group, as they were more vulnerable to the shock. However, they bounced back much faster than other EU11 countries and stabilised their relative position above the group average. By now, in terms of per capita GDP, Estonia and Lithuania have approached the two countries that traditionally led this group, the Czech Republic and Slovenia. Per capita GDP and HDI broadly show the same trends. Slovakia was also a country, which improved its relative position, albeit more in

gests for that period. Figure 2.2 shows why the estimated gain for the Baltic countries are so high, and seem to suggest that in a longer period including the crisis years, a considerable part of these extra gains might have been lost. Estimates for the individual countries vary greatly, but with the exception of Slovakia and Poland, are all double digit.

[10] Albeit using a different concept of convergence and analysing social convergence within the EU, based on a large set of multidimensional socio-economic indicators, Eurofound (2018) also identified a structural break in social convergence following the outbreak of the crisis. Our analysis focuses on the relationship between economic and social convergence to the frontier. What our finding adds to theirs is that following the crisis social convergence of EU11, to the frontier and relative to other groups of countries, seems to have paused while economic convergence continued albeit at a slower pace.

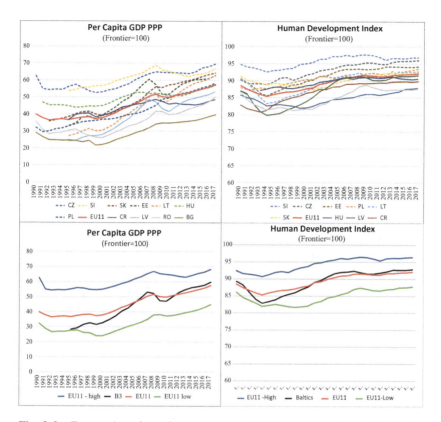

Fig. 2.2 Economic and social convergence in EU11 countries. Note: *B3* includes Estonia, Latvia and Lithuania; *EU11 High-income* includes Czechia and Slovenia; *EU11 Low-income* includes Bulgaria and Romania. For the definition of the other groups, see the Note to Fig. 2.1. (Sources: For per capita GDP World Bank, for Human Development Index, UNDP)

terms of economic than social convergence. On the other hand, Hungary experienced a major deterioration in its relative position until 2013, and stabilised it afterwards. Its human development has however continued to lag behind the overall trend for the group.

In general, income convergence to the frontier slowed and within the group stopped after the 2008–09 crisis. Convergence in human development has largely stopped after the crisis, a trend which perhaps explains the disappointment with the EU and European integration (Vértes 2019).

Southern European EU (EU S4) countries relative income position gradually declined during the period under investigation. The crisis in Europe accelerated somewhat this decline, and the relative income position of this group stabilised as the crisis ended (Fig. 2.3). As this case shows, EU membership does not guarantee continuous convergence.[11] In fact, it can entail divergence from the frontier if growth fundamentals are allowed to weaken in EU member states. Human development in EU S4 followed a different trend, it slightly improved relative to the frontier until the crisis, from an already very high level, and suffered only a temporary and small setback during the crisis.

Reflecting different trends, per capita income in EU11 has been approaching rapidly the level in EU S4 (Fig. 2.3). In fact, the two groups started to overlap. Regarding human development, the convergence between the two groups has been much less pronounced. In fact, it has almost stopped since the beginning of the crisis.

An important aspect of development is equity. Due to their shared central planning past, EU11 countries entered transition with rather egalitarian societies. They had significantly narrower income distribution than other countries at comparable level of economic and social development,

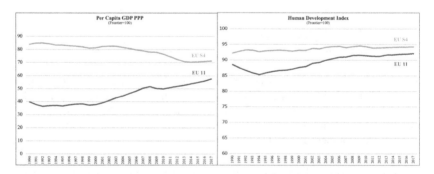

Fig. 2.3 Economic and social convergence in EU11 and EU S4. Note: EU S4 includes Greece, Italy, Portugal and Spain. For the definition of the other groups, see the Note to Fig. 2.1. (Sources: For per capita GDP World Bank, for Human Development Index, UNDP)

---

[11] Ridao-Cano and Bodewig (2018) calls the attention to this issue in a broader context and using a different concept of convergence, but pointing to same group of EU countries and regions in Southern Europe. On the regional aspect of EU11 convergence, see Sect. 2.9.

and an even more compressed wealth distribution. The first period of economic transformation, particularly privatisation and liberalisation of the economy, widened income distribution. Nonetheless, as Fig. 2.4 shows, at the time of EU accession, the income distribution in EU11 was still rather equitable by international comparison.[12] The Gini coefficient declined somewhat after EU accession. However, as countries in the other groups experienced a similar trend, the relative position of EU11 did not change in this regard.

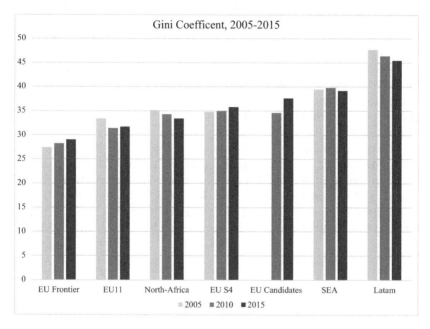

Fig. 2.4 The Gini coefficient for income distribution, 2005–2015. Note: For the definition of country groups, see the Notes to Figs. 2.1 and 2.3. (Source: World Bank, World Development Indicators)

---

[12] For several countries, the Gini coefficient was not calculated for the years shown in Fig. 2.4. Thus, we used the closest available estimate, or an average of those if they were available on both sides. For this reason, and because of frequent changes over time and differences across estimates in methodology, these numbers should be treated with great caution. They probably give a broad indication of major trends, but certainly not a precise measure of income inequality. For the same reason, any comparison over time and across countries needs to be taken with a pinch of salt.

Figure 2.5 shows the Gini coefficients for individual EU countries in 2005 (the year after the first wave of eastern enlargement) and in 2018 (the latest available year). The new member states had rather different positions within the EU in 2005 in this regard, spanning the distribution of Gini coefficients in the EU. Slovenia and the Czech Republic were close to the Scandinavian countries, while Poland, Romania and the Baltic countries populated the other end of the distribution. The overall picture changed little by 2018, albeit the countries at the two ends of the distribution changed somewhat. Slovakia caught up with Slovenia and the Czech Republic, and these countries replaced the Scandinavian countries at the lower end of the distribution. These countries were in the top 5 in the world by 2015 regarding income equity (based on World Bank estimates). At the other end of the distribution, Estonia moved to the centre, while Bulgaria moved from the centre to the far end of the distribution. As the chart for 2018 shows, the EU Candidate countries populate the higher half of the distribution, with Serbia and Montenegro close to the higher end.[13]

Equity is a crucial aspect of human development, too. To capture this, the UNDP started to calculate an inequality-adjusted HDI. While no time series are yet available, Fig. 2.6 shows a cross section of estimates for the country groups used in our analysis for 2017. Reflecting the relatively high degree of equitable development in EU11 and EU Candidate countries, relative to other middle-income countries but also relative to EU S4,

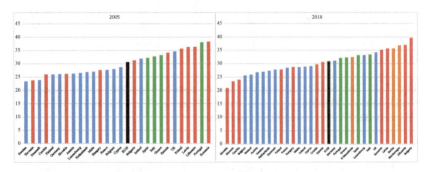

Fig. 2.5 The Gini coefficient for income distribution in EU countries in 2005 and 2018. (Source: Eurostat)

---

[13] Eurostat does not publish estimates for Albania, but based on World Bank estimates, the Gini coefficient for Albania is likely to be close to the EU average.

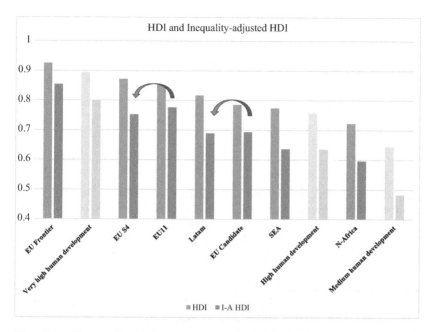

Fig. 2.6 Human Development Index (HDI) and Inequality-Adjusted HDI (AI-HDI), 2017. (Source: UNDP)

the positions of EU11 countries regarding human development is more favourable when measured by IA-HDI. EU11 countries move ahead of EU S4, and EU Candidate countries move ahead of Latam countries.

We do not have the estimates for IA-HDI for the entire period. Nonetheless, based on the estimates for Gini coefficient by the World Bank discussed earlier, the situation was probably the same at the time when the eastern enlargement of the EU started, and the trend in IA-HDI since then has probably been broadly similar to that in HDI.

Taking a longer-term perspective, EU11 countries had a long period of rapid convergence in income and human development in the past, under much less favourable conditions than the ones they enjoy today as EU members (Fig. 2.7). This period ended when the last reserves of extensive growth had been depleted under the Soviet-dominated central planning system by the late 1950s. Czechoslovakia by then was very close to the global frontier, in fact, it was already in that position before the Communist takeover in 1948. At that point, people in Czechoslovakia were better

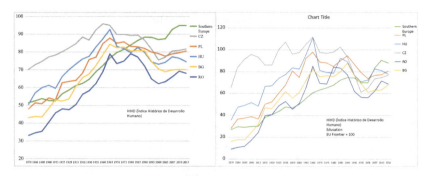

Fig. 2.7 Historical Human Development Index (HIHD) 1870–2015. Note: Frontier includes Austria, Denmark, Netherlands and Sweden; Southern Europe includes Greece, Italy, Portugal and Spain. For a description of the HIHD indicator see Prados de la Escosura (2019). (Source: http://espacioinvestiga.org/inicio-hihd/ Downloaded on July 2, 2019)

educated than people at that time were in the group we use as EU Frontier here (Austria, Denmark, Netherlands and Sweden). We can perhaps recall that in the late 1930s, there was a young assistant professor at the University in Prague called Albert Einstein. At that point, Czechoslovakia, Hungary and Poland were more developed than Southern European countries (EU S4) on average, and people in these countries were better educated than people in Southern Europe. Soviet-dominated central planning system had eroded this advantage, and the difficult transition to market economy further aggravated the trend of relative deterioration in this group.

2.4 Trade Channel

The core element of the EU is the single market. It ensures unfettered access to domestic markets within the EU for a dominant part of trade.[14] Common legal frameworks for competition and state-aid, and harmonisation of technical standards further facilitate trade within the EU. As the EU is the largest trading block in the world, access to the single market is one of the main advantages of EU membership for EU11 relative to other middle-income countries. The advantages include not only the absence of

---

[14] This section and Sect. 2.9 build on Buti and Székely (2019).

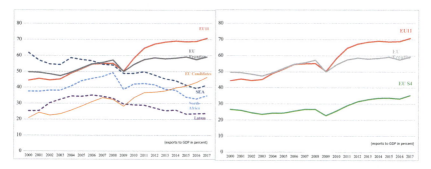

Fig. 2.8 Export openness, 2000–2017. Note: For the definition of country groups, see the Note to Fig. 2.1. (Source: World Bank)

tariffs and quotas, but also the ease with which trade can be conducted within the single market.

Many countries have different forms of trade arrangements with the EU, some in Europe are even members of the single market. Among the countries in the benchmark groups, Northern African countries have long-standing trade (association) arrangements with the EU, which remove or reduce customs tariffs in bilateral trade. The one with Tunisia entered into force in 1998, so it helped trade throughout the entire period under investigation here.[15] Regarding EU Candidate countries, the EU granted autonomous trade preferences to all the Western Balkans in 2000. These preferences, last renewed in 2015, allow nearly all exports to enter the EU without customs duties or limits on quantities.

As Fig. 2.8 shows, EU membership increased the trade openness of EU11 to an unprecedented extent. As a result, EU11 economies are now among the most open economies globally. The increase in their trade openness in this millennium is among the highest in the world (Fig. 2.9). Trade openness continuously increased in EU Frontier countries, and following the crisis in EU S4, as well. The rapid increase in trade openness in EU11 (and EU Candidate) countries is in sharp contrast with developments in the non-European groups of countries.

What we measure is actual trade, so it not only reflects favourable trade arrangements but also the private activities that better access to foreign

---

[15] For a complete list of trade arrangements that are in place with the EU, see https://ec.europa.eu/trade/policy/countries-and-regions/negotiations-and-agreements/#_in-place

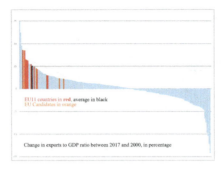

Fig. 2.9 Change in export openness, 2000–2017. Note: For the definition of country groups, see the Note to Fig. 2.1. Columns are the countries in the world that are covered by the database. (Source: World Bank)

markets induces. The latter, as we will see when we analyse the investment channel, also entails significant FDI flows. A large part of the increased export capacity in EU11 was created by FDI, heavily concentrated in industries with global value chains (Coeuré 2018).[16] Thus, trade creation led to a significant increase in intra-industry and intra-company trade in intermediate goods, both in exports and imports. Other factors also contributed to the increase in trade openness, such as the strong reform drive involved in their transition from central planning to market economy and in the preparations for EU entry (Székely and Ward Warmedinger 2018). Nevertheless, the impact of EU accession is very visible in these charts, and not only on EU11, but also on EU Candidate countries.

Roeger and in 't Veld (2021) (Chap. 2 in Volume II) assess the impact of access to the single market (in goods and services) on EU11 economies by using a structural macroeconomic model. In the counterfactual scenario, tariffs and non-tariff barriers to intra-EU trade are set at levels that would apply if trade reverted to WTO rules and Most Favoured Nation (MFN).[17] They simulate the combined impact of higher trade barriers and higher mark-ups, that is, it also captures the (negative) impact on competition. On average, under the counterfactual scenario, the level of GDP in

---

[16] Boldizsár et al. (2021) (the country study on Hungary in this volume) emphasizes the importance of this aspect for Hungary. The share of the automotive industry in total inward FDI in Hungary was above 30%.

[17] For non-tariff barriers (NTBs), estimates are based on those calculated for trade between the EU and the US. The analysis used a multi-country version of the QUEST model.

EU11 would decline by more than 13% in the long run, significantly more than in the EU or in the euro area (about 9%), reflecting the fact that EU11 economies are more open to trade than the EU (euro area) as a whole. The decline in consumption and investment would be close to 25%. These estimates are within the range of estimates other studies produced.

As we mentioned earlier, it is very difficult to quantify the benefits of EU membership using formal models, because of the difficulties involved in translating the broad question we ask into a concrete counterfactual scenario. As Roeger and in 't Veld (2021) emphasise, EU membership entail several other important advantages which are not removed in this counterfactual scenario, such free movement of capital, firms and people. On the other hand, the alternative to EU membership is not necessarily trade based on WTO rules and MFN. As the authors mention, non-EU countries also participate in the single market for goods and services, and candidate countries have access to EU markets under much better conditions than the ones used in this analysis for the counterfactual scenario. Moreover, as we mentioned earlier, several countries in the control groups have trade agreements with the EU.

To sum up, trade was probably the channel through which the impact of EU membership on economic convergence was the strongest. Campos et al. (2019) using a different approach come to the same conclusion. As we will argue below, the investment and finance channels magnified the impact through the trade channel. The econometric estimates probably also capture this interaction effect, hence the overwhelming share of the trade channel in the overall impact.

2.5 Investment Channel

The public component of the investment channel includes the common legal and institutional environment the EU creates for cross-border investment from within the EU and from outside, for the protection of investors, for contract enforcement and dispute resolution. This promotes private cross-border investment, including by commercially operated state-owned enterprises. Moreover, EU funds also generate sizable public and private investments in the recipient countries. EU11 has been the biggest beneficiary of EU funds that generate such investment.

The private component of the investment channel is FDI. The process of trade integration and the creation of GVCs also drove a significant

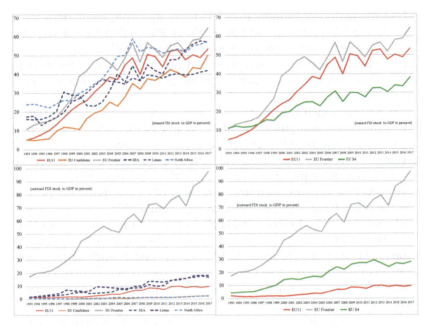

Fig. 2.10 Stocks of Inward and outward FDI. Note: For the definition of country groups, see the Note to Fig. 2.1. (Source: UNCTAD)

inflow of FDI into EU11 countries (Fig. 2.10). FDI brought in modern technology and led to capital deepening, as well as to a rapid modernisation of the product structure, having a positive impact on productivity of local suppliers (Harding and Smarzynska Javorcik 2011; Hagemejer and Muck 2019). As with trade, many of the underlying forces that promoted FDI were global, and geographical proximity also played an important role. Nonetheless, EU accession provided a fertile ground for these forces to work. It helped improve institutions and create a higher degree of legal certainty for investors (Buiter and Lubin 2019).

Moreover, as we showed in the previous section, EU11 countries benefited significantly from the reduction of trade barriers, which in turn made FDI into these countries more attractive for foreign investors. Merlevede and Purice (2019) estimate that supplying inputs to a multinational just across the border is productivity enhancing only when countries share an EU border. These spill-over effects become even stronger when borders become seamless, as it is the case in the Schengen Area. That is, the trade and investment channel mutually strengthened each other.

As a result, inward FDI (excluding special purpose entities, SPEs) relative to GDP in EU11 countries has caught up with global trends. The trend was also upward for EU S4 countries, but less so than for EU11, especially during the crisis.

Developments regarding outward FDI have been different (Fig. 2.10). The increase in the stock of outward FDI relative to GDP in EU11 was modest prior to the crisis, significantly less than in the EU Frontier countries, and less than in several other groups of middle-income countries.

Durán and Szabo (2021) (Chap. 3 in Volume II) confirm the strong impact of FDI on trade and economic development in EU11, which started to kick in when accession to the EU became a plausible future path for these countries. In fact, high inward FDI made EU11 on average more integrated into the single market than EU15. The share of FDI from other EU (mostly EU15) countries in total FDI is very high in EU11 (typically above 80%, in Slovakia above 90%), much higher than in EU15. Inward FDI is heavily concentrated in car manufacturing (some 7% of total stock) and financial services (mostly banking) (some 25%). FDI is also highly concentrated geographically. Capitals and regions close to manufacturing firms that created GVCs (mostly in Germany) seem to have benefitted most from FDI.

As a model-based analysis by Varga and in 't Veld (2021) (Chap. 5 in Volume II) shows, EU funds play an important role in fostering the convergence of EU member states. According to their calculations, by 2030, EU Cohesion fund spending may increase the level of GDP in EU11 by close to 8% (relative to a counterfactual scenario with no EU support), ranging from about 3% in Slovenia to above 10% in Latvia. Moreover, as Czelleng and Vértes (2021) (Chap. 4 in Volume II) emphasise, EU transfer played a major role in stabilising EU11 economies during the crisis, as they helped increase budget revenues through increasing corporate and household incomes, and helped increase central bank reserves.

As we pointed out earlier, and the authors themselves emphasise, these are estimates of the potential gains from the public and private investments into physical and human capital induced by the spending from EU funds (the public component of the investment channel). In interaction with the other channels, including the institutional channel, the actual impact can be higher or lower than these estimates, overall for the regions as a whole, and in different EU11 countries.

These funds are targeted on poorer regions, so they not only support growth and development at the aggregate level, but they also aim to help reduce income dispersion among regions. In Sect. 2.9 below, we shall look into this aspect.

2.6 Finance Channel

The finance channel is an important and potentially helpful channel in every middle-income converging economy (Aghion et al. 2005). Albeit cross-border lending is increasing in importance, most of the financial capital finds its way into a middle-income economy through the domestic financial system, in Europe predominantly the banking system of the country. The allocative efficiency of the banking system is thus an essential prerequisite for sustained convergence. This is important not only because of the efficient use of imported financial capital, but also because it helps use well the part of domestic savings that is intermediated through the financial system. Besides allocative efficiency, prudent management of the inherent risks involved in financial intermediation is also essential. Whether these preconditions will be satisfied in an emerging economy depends on the quality of relevant public and private institutions.

On the public side, the quality of financial regulation and the quality of the central bank and financial supervision are critical factors, and they are to a large extent determined by the overall quality of institutions in the country concerned. Hence the important interaction with the institutional channel (Fernández and Tamayo 2017). There are global institutions, such as the IMF, the World Bank, BIS, OECD, that are mandated to promote high-quality financial regulation and to help central banks and financial regulatory agencies to improve their institutional quality. These institutions have supported also EU11 countries from the very beginning of economic transition.

On the private side, the quality of the private (and publicly owned) enterprises in the financial sector (lending side) and in the corporate sector (borrowing side) is a critical prerequisite of efficient and safe financial intermediation.

EU membership plays an important role in determining how the finance channel works in EU11, in fact an increasingly important role as the EU is building the Banking Union and the Capital Market Union. The benefits of EU membership entail the free flow of financial capital across borders; a legal and institutional environment that fosters safe and efficient intermediation of foreign capital through the financial system, and helps domestic financial intermediation as well; and a stable and well-developed overall legal and institutional environment.

EU11 countries entered the EU during times when cross-border capital flows, mostly through the financial system increased significantly in the EU. However, soon after the eastern enlargement of the EU started in 2004 a crisis broke out and capital flows within the EU reversed sharply. The deep-seated problems with financial intermediation in Europe surfaced. Hence, the crisis episode dominates the experiences of EU11 regarding the impact of the EU as an institution on their overall convergence process through the finance channel.

Prior to the crisis, a significant part of the large savings pool in the EU found its way into EU11 and EU S4 countries (Fig. 2.11). As we have shown in Sect. 2.5, EU11 absorbed a large part of this inflow through FDI. Nevertheless, a significant portion entered through the banking sector. As a result, bank credit to the private sector increased rapidly, much faster than in other groups.

Figure 2.11 also shows that the reversal of capital flows following the outbreak of the crisis was a unique European development (EU11, EU S4 and EU Candidate). No other group of countries considered here experienced such major reversal of capital flows in this period.

The reversal of cross-border financial flows led to a reversal in the trend for private credit. Similarly to capital inflows, this was a development rather unique to middle-income economies in Europe (EU11 and EU Candidate). Figure 2.11 shows that similar development took place in EU S4 countries. As FDI was a less important in these countries than in EU11, a larger part of the cross-border capital flows entered through their banking systems. Hence, the increase and the subsequent decline in bank credit was more pronounced.

The banking system was apparently not prepared for managing such massive capital inflows, neither in EU11, nor in EU Candidate and EU S4 countries.[18] Cross-border financial flows of this magnitude were not sustainable and were eventually reversed. The reversal took place earlier and

---

[18] In an early assessment of the challenges of EU accession, Feldman and Watson (2002) emphasize the importance of sustainability of capital flows and the critical role of the quality of the financial system. They also point to the importance of the quality of macroeconomic policies, monetary and fiscal, and that of the institutions that are conducive to prudent macroeconomic policies.

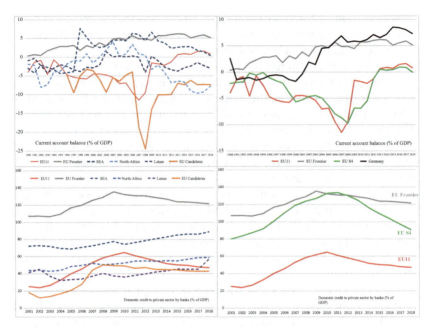

Fig. 2.11 Current account balance and banking credit to the private sector, 2000–2018. Note: For the definition of country groups, see the Note to Fig. 2.1. (Source: World Bank)

faster in EU11 and EU Candidate countries than in EU S4, but more of the increase in financial deepening has been preserved in the former groups.[19]

Coricelli and Frigerio (2021) (Chap. 7 in Volume II of this book), using firm-level micro data, present an econometric analysis on the relationship between credit growth and efficiency in resource allocation in

---

[19] To help these countries to adjust with less economic and social cost to the reversal of financial capital flows and to limit the reversal to the unavoidable minimum, the Vienna Initiative brought together policy makers, central bankers, supervisors and bankers from the CESEE region and from EU15. It was a joint initiative of the EBRD, the IMF and the European Commission and it promoted concerted policy actions and business strategies to help the countries and banks concerned to manage this difficult process and to safeguard financial stability. This was a good example of the EU working with other regional and global anchoring institutions in a particular area. For more information on the Vienna Initiative, see http://vienna-initiative.com/

Europe. They find no evidence of intra-sector misallocation as a consequence of rapid credit expansion in the pre-crisis period in EU11. Indeed, during the credit boom, misallocation decreased in EU11, while it increased in the older EU members.[20] This evidence suggests that part of the credit boom in Emerging Europe coincided with an equilibrium phenomenon of financial deepening. The difference in the quality of financial intermediation may be one of the factors that explains why more of the financial deepening that had taken place prior to the crisis could be preserved in EU11 rather than in EU S4 countries.

While this is an important and encouraging result regarding EU11, as the authors themselves point out, there might have been misallocation across sectors. Indeed, the most important form of misallocation in the region (and in EU S4) was among sectors, the massive over financing of the real estate sector, including residential real estate (e.g. in Spain and Baltic countries). Hence the reversal of a large part of the rapid increase in financial deepening in EU11 as well. But what was soundly intermediated survived and the overall trend throughout this entire period is an upward one in EU11, bringing them up to the level of most other groups of middle-income converging economies (Fig. 2.11).

A particular aspect of the banking sector in a middle-income converging economy is the role of foreign(-owned) banks. Following the liberalisation of capital flows in the early 1990s, the role and share of foreign banks increased significantly in most parts of the world (Claessens and Van Horen 2014). By 2008, just before the global crisis, it has reached significant levels in all of our control groups (Fig. 2.12). The typical pattern is that the majority of owners of foreign banks in a country are from the region where the country is. Distance, including cultural and institutional, matters. In fact, foreign banks with owners from countries that are geographically, but also culturally and institutionally closer function better and contribute more to the financial deepening and development of the host country. However, as Claessens and Van Horen (2014) convincingly show, the characteristics of the host country also matter. In countries with good business environment and strong institutions, foreign banks help

---

[20] Calligaris et al. (2016) analysed allocative efficiency in the Italian enterprise sector and found that the extent of misallocation had substantially increased since 1995, and that this increase could account for a large fraction of the Italian productivity slowdown since then. While they use a broader concept of allocative efficiency and look into the overall efficiency of resource allocation in the enterprise sector, their finding points to the same direction.

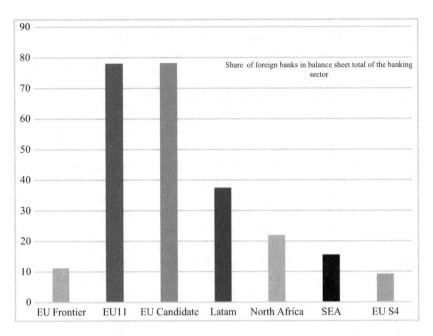

Fig. 2.12 Share of foreign-owned banks in the balance sheet total of the banking sector, 2008. Note: For the definition of country groups, see the Note to Fig. 2.1. (Source: Claessens and Van Horen 2014)

financial deepening and financial development, and through this accelerate economic convergence.

These global trends also worked in EU11 (and EU Candidate) countries. From early on after economic transition started, foreign banks played a central role in the banking sector in most EU11 countries. The share of foreign banks in EU11 (and EU Candidate) countries is very high by international comparison, albeit Slovenia until very recently has been a notable exception (Figs. 2.12 and 2.13).[21] Foreign banks in EU11 tend to be parts of European banking groups with headquarters in EU15. The only mentionable exception is the OTP group in Hungary, which has a sizable regional network.

---

[21] Following a banking crisis and a subsequent recapitalization of a large part of the banking system by the state in 2013, all the recapitalized banks have been privatized or wound up.

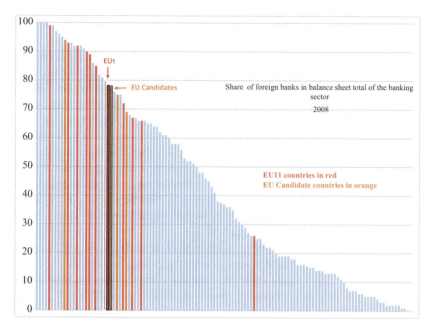

Fig. 2.13 Share of foreign-owned banks in the balance sheet total of the banking sector, 2008. Note: For the definition of country groups, see the Note to Fig. 2.1. (Source: Claessens and Van Horen 2014)

Most of the financial capital channelled to EU11 originates from Europe, albeit following the crisis and the subsequent rapid adjustment, very little additional capital has been channelled to EU11 countries through the banking sector. But it is not only foreign banks that channel foreign capital into EU11 countries. A high share of foreign banks in a country did not necessarily mean more excessive capital inflow prior to the crisis. Moreover, foreign banks played an unquestionably important role in modernising the banking sector in EU11 (Voljč 2019).

Nevertheless, to a considerable extent foreign banks were responsible for excessive capital inflow prior to the crisis, for the misallocation of imported capital and for failing to ensure prudent financial intermediation. However, foreign banks paid for their own mistakes. Their parents provided the funds to clean up their portfolios and to recapitalise them, even when their owners were from a country that itself went through a major crisis (such as Greece or Portugal). In Slovenia, where banks were domestically (mostly publicly) owned, it was the taxpayer who shouldered most of the costs of the banking crisis.

The experience of EU11 regarding foreign banks and their contribution to the financial development and economic convergence of the host countries confirms the main findings of Claessens and Van Horen (2014). The quality of institutions in the host country determined the role of foreign banks. What we can add to their findings is the importance of prudent macroeconomic policies and high-quality home and host supervision. Financial regulation and supervision in EU11 also had its own share of responsibility in creating an environment in which cross-border capital movements and domestic financial intermediation became excessive and unsustainable. So did their counterparts in the home (mostly EU) countries of foreign banks. It is the quality of institutions on both sides, in the home and host countries, that matters.

A brief comparison of developments in the Czech Republic and Slovenia regarding capital inflow and bank credit to the private sector demonstrates our point and sheds some light on how the different aspects interacted. These two countries are historically the most developed in EU11 (Fig. 2.2). As Fig. 2.14 shows, both could largely avoid the excesses of capital inflows prior to the crisis. Overall, both countries had rather sound macroeconomic policies.

However, they chose rather different models regarding FDI and the banking system. The Czech Republic had one of the highest inflows of FDI while Slovenia one of the lowest. The banking sector of the Czech

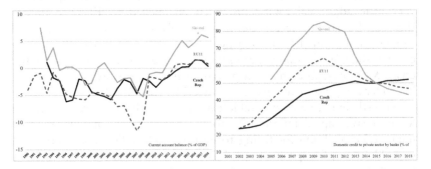

Fig. 2.14 Current account balance and banking credit to the private sector in the Czech Republic and Slovenia, 1990–2018. Note: For the definition of country groups, see the Note to Fig. 2.1. (Source: World Bank)

Republic was mostly foreign owned, while in Slovenia banks were mostly domestically, in large part publicly owned during this episode.[22] So if foreign banks had been responsible for excessive credit in the region, we would expect to see a bigger upswing in the Czech Republic than in Slovenia. But just the opposite was true (Fig. 2.14). There was some acceleration also in the Czech Republic, but much less pronounced and apparently sustainable.

In Slovenia, a relatively short period of increased capital inflow, which in total size was not significantly different from what happened in the Czech Republic during the same period, created a large and unsustainable increase in domestic credit to the private sector. The subsequent collapse of a large part of the banking system was a clear indication of massive misallocation of financial resources. As there were no foreign owners to pick up the cost of the banking failures, a large part of the loss was borne by the tax payer.

Székely and Ward Warmedinger (2018) sheds some light on the behavioural reversals in central banking and banking supervision that resulted in the failure of the banking system to efficiently and safely intermediate the capital inflow in Slovenia. As FDI was rather limited, the large inflow fell entirely on the banking system, and apparently, neither the banks, nor the financial authorities had sufficiently strong institutions to manage this inflow safely and efficiently.

Developments in the Czech Republic suggest that the opposite was true there. The pressure on the banking system was smaller as a large part of the inflow was through FDI. Nevertheless, like in Europe (and globally), bank credit accelerated. However, the banking system, mostly foreign-owned banks, and the financial authorities managed the inflow rather well. Good-quality public and private institutions in the financial system helped the country to remain resilient.

Many tend to attribute higher macroeconomic volatility in euro area countries during the crisis to the euro. Slovenia was the first EU11 country to enter the euro area in 2007 (the ERM2 in 2004), while the Czech Republic is still outside. But if this was a major factor here, it should have worked through the current account. However, as Fig. 2.14 shows, this is exactly the part where the two countries show similarities.

Lending behaviour of foreign banks, more broadly, their business model changed fundamentally after the crisis, and so did the lending

---

[22] Since then, following the crisis, recapitalized banks have been privatized or wound down.

behaviour and business model of domestic banks.[23] Following the crisis, foreign banks in EU11 (and in EU Candidate) countries returned to the traditional business model. Claessens and Van Horen (2014) identified: high capital adequacy, strong liquidity and reliance on own sources, mostly own deposits. This regime change also reflects the positive impact of major EU initiatives to strengthen financial supervisory and macro prudential institutions, most importantly the launching of the Banking Union (the creation of the joint euro area banking supervision, SSM). We will discuss these reforms in Sect. 2.10.

In some countries, such as Hungary and Poland, the share of foreign banks is declining, a process which is also driven by government policies. With EU11 countries rapidly converging, there is a room for domestic banks to increase their share in the banking system. In fact, it would be natural for large and strong banks (financial groups) in the region to start turning themselves into regional or European groups. The important issue is not whether a bank (financial group) is domestic or foreign owned. What matters is the quality of private organisations (banks and financial and non-financial firms), and private (corporate culture) and public (central banks, financial supervisors) institutions in EU11. As Székely and Ward Warmedinger (2018) argue, it is the motivation and mechanisms which drive this new development that will determine whether this new trend will be conducive to continued fast convergence or not.

Regarding the interaction among channels, De Bonis et al. (2015) investigated the relationship between bank-firm relationship and outward FDI. They find a significant impact of the nature of bank-firm relationship on the likelihood of outward FDI by a firm in their sample for Italian firms. The more established the relationship, the higher the likelihood of FDI. If the bank involved is an international bank, the impact is stronger. If such relationship existed for a broader set of countries, the large share of European banking groups in EU11 should have helped promote outward FDI by EU11 firms. However, as the analysis in Sect. 2.5 shows, this is was not the case. A positive impact in this regard would probably also require a more established (longer) relationship between (foreign-owned) banks and firms in EU11.

---

[23] An empirical analysis by Temesváry and Banai (2017) covering also post-crisis years (2002–2013) provides empirical evidence for a fundamental change in foreign banks' lending behaviour. They also find that the Vienna Initiative helped to smooth adjustment in bank lending in the region.

To summarise our findings, the eastern enlargement of the EU took place during a period in which cross-border capital flows within the EU intensified. The large pool of excess savings in the surplus countries found its way into EU11 and Southern EU countries. The crisis brought to the surface deeply seated problems in the European banking sector leading to a rapid reversal of these flows. The crisis hit EU11 countries hard and the degree of financial intermediation started to recede. However, the healthy part of financial intermediation was preserved. Thus, despite a crisis and a hump in the degree of financial deepening, EU11 countries caught up with other groups of middle-income economies regarding financial deepening.

As a response to the crisis, the EU strengthened its institutions in a major way relatively quickly.[24] The creation of the ESM, setting up of the Macroeconomic Imbalances Procedures, the launching of the Banking Union,[25] which involved the creation of a common rule book for the EU and a joint banking supervision (SSM) and joint resolution mechanism (SRM) in the Euro Area, and the launching of Capital Market Union are among the most important measures.

Looking forward, the creation of the Banking Union (SSM) addresses the issues surrounding banking supervision in EU11 countries that are in the euro area. The institutional channel in this area produced a joint EA institution. This is a unique feature of the EU relative to any other supranational organisation in which middle-income converging economies participate. Nevertheless, the way this new set up will work in the future will continue to depend on the quality of other domestic public and private institutions in EA member states as well.

For non-EA EU11 countries, the impact of newly created European institutions is also strong but not as strong as for EA members. As Székely and Ward Warmedinger (2018) describe in detail, there were major episodes of reform reversals in this area, perhaps the most dangerous ones. With no intention to join the EA and with a reversed trend in the role of foreign banks, this will be an issue to watch out for in some non-EA EU11 countries.

The quality of public and private institutions that are important for financial intermediation will remain critical to ensure that EU11 countries

---

[24] A Roadmap towards a Banking Union was issued in September 2012 (European Commission 2012).

[25] For detailed information on the Banking Union, see European Commission (2019a).

can import financial capital, and together with their own domestic financial savings, can intermediate it in an efficient and safe manner. The ultimate lesson from the experience of Europe during the crisis episode is that, in the longer run, only good-quality financial intermediation is sustainable and conducive to fast convergence.

2.7 Migration Channel

One of the four basic freedoms in the EU is the free movement of people, to live and work in another EU country. While this right induces relatively large migration flows within the EU, this is not the only source of cross-border migration in the EU. A significant part of inward migration in EU countries has been from non-EU European countries. This was true also for EU11 prior to their accession. Nevertheless, the legally guaranteed right to work anywhere in the EU (after a transitory period which for most EU11 is over by now) triggered massive outward migration from the EU11 to EU15 countries. By 2017, some 8% of the EU11 population was reported as living in an EU15 country, up from about 1½% before the first wave of EU eastern enlargement (Fig. 2.15). These large migration flows have been unevenly distributed both among sending and receiving countries. The ratios of migrants from EU11 to EU15 countries to domestic population vary greatly among EU11 countries, ranging from above 15% in Romania to below 1½% in the Czech Republic. The differences are equally large among the receiving EU15 countries regarding the share of migrants from EU11 to their population, with Ireland, Austria, Luxembourg, UK and Germany receiving significantly more than proportional (four to two times).[26]

As Fig. 2.15 shows, the gradual phasing out of restrictions on free movement of labour following EU accession accelerated the process, and

---

[26] In the southern EU enlargement waves of 1981 and 1986, upon entry, the share of Spanish nationals living in the (then) EU was, 1.5% of resident population of Spain, similar to the average level in EU11. The same ratio for Greece was 3.7% in 1985, the first year for which observation is available, and for Portugal, it was 8.8%. But unlike in EU11, following EU accession these shares changed little until the recent crisis, when they started to increase, albeit much less than in most EU11 countries. Similarly to EU11, the distribution among receiving countries was highly uneven, close to 80% of Spanish nationals stayed in France and Germany, the same share of Greeks in Germany, and slightly higher share of Portuguese in France (all data are from the OECD International Migration Database). The population of these countries didn't decline following EU accession, as it did in EU11 (Figure 2.17).

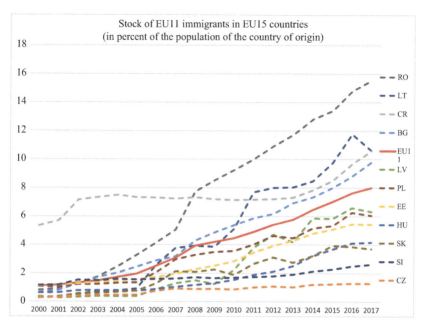

Fig. 2.15 Ratio between people living in EU15 countries and total population in EU11 countries. (Source: Eurostat)

made the difference among EU11 countries in this regard more pronounced. According to the literature on economic migration, the strongest factor driving outward migration is income differential. Clemens (2014) documents an inverted-U relationship between emigrant stocks and real income per capita throughout the late twentieth century, with outward migration peaking at around 10 thousand dollars (PPP 2005). He also finds that the inverted-U became more pronounced as years passed, that is, the stock of emigrants (as percent of resident population of the sending country) at a given income level is growing over time. EU11 countries were all above the (real) per capita GDP level where the distribution is peaking already in 2004, so they would be all situated on the declining side of the inverted-U curve. Fig. 2.16 shows the cross-section curves for EU11 countries for 2004 and 2017.[27] In 2004, with the exception of Croatia, all EU11 had very low shares, way below what the global trends

---

[27] For an explanation of the chart, see the Notes to the chart.

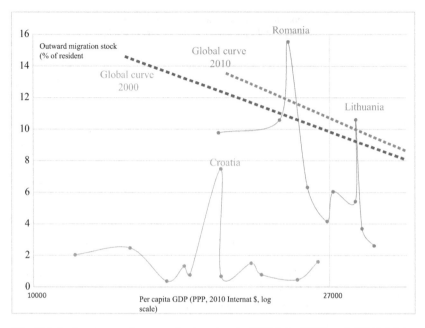

Fig. 2.16 Income and outward migration in EU11 in 2004 and 2017. Note: Scatter diagram, with GDP per capita (PPP constant 2011 international $, log scale) on the horizontal axis and the ratio of the nationals living abroad to resident population of the country concerned (in percent) on the vertical axis. Countries are ordered according to their per capita income in the year concerned (2004 and 2017) and every point represents a pair of observations for an EU11 country (per capita GDP and emigration stock). Global curves are based on Clemens 2014, approximate curves to indicate global trends. (Sources: World Bank for per capita GDP and OECD International Migration Database for migration)

would suggest and the shape for the curve (almost flat) is rather different from that of the global curve (Clemens 2014).[28] By 2017, the curve moves up and gets closer and more similar to the global curve. With few exceptions, the higher the income, the lower the stock of outward migration. But the curve for EU11 is still below the global curve and its slope (the

---

[28] The relatively high stock for Croatia, which is still below the global trend, is related to the Yugoslav war.

rate of decline as income rises) is much steeper, with Romania and perhaps Lithuania (slightly) being above the global curve for 2010.[29]

A unique characteristic of EU11 among middle-income countries is that their population is rapidly declining. By 2017, net migration to EU15 countries accounted for about 2/3 of the difference between population trends in the EU as a whole and that in EU11 (Fig. 2.17). As Fig. 2.15 shows, the number of people from EU15 countries living in EU11 relative to the local population is rather small, less than one percent in all EU11 countries, and so is the stock of immigrants from other EU11 countries and from non-EU countries, except the Russian and Ukrainian citizens and recognised non-citizens living in Baltic countries.

Regarding the interaction between migration and other channels, As Schmieg (2019) points out, increased migration is almost always associated with increased trade. This certainly holds for this period in the EU, trade openness increased in the EU despite a stagnating level worldwide.

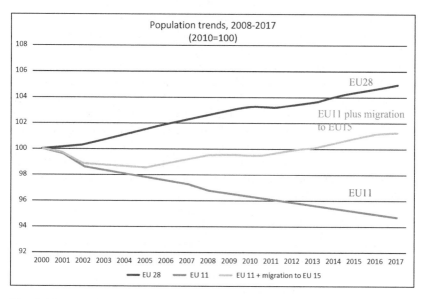

Fig. 2.17 Population trends, 2000–2017. (Source: Eurostat)

---

[29] The latest estimate in Clemens (2014) is for 2010. The global curve moved up continuously every decade since 1960, so the global curve for 2017 would in all likelihood be above the one for 2010.

It is not clear what part of this is attributable to migration as there have been other major forces at work that are known to generate trade, such as FDI.

The other important interaction is between FDI and cross-border migration, albeit empirical evidence is inconclusive on the nature of this link (Schmieg 2019). The scatter diagram for EU11 in Fig. 2.19 shows that large increases in the stock of EU11 migrants in EU15 were associated with small increases or declines in the FDI stock relative to GDP, while large increases in the latter were associated with small increases or declines in the former. That is, it seems, there is substitution between FDI and outward migration. Figure 2.20 shows this relationship for Bulgaria and Romania, the two lowest income EU 11, and for Slovenia and the Czech Republic, the two highest income EU11 countries. For both pairs, higher FDI is associated with smaller outward migration.

Using a quantitative multi-country dynamic general equilibrium model with trade in goods and labour mobility across countries, Caliendo et al. (2017) estimate the welfare (consumption equivalent) effect of labour mobility of the 2004 EU enlargement. They take into account the way free movement of labour was phased in, which explains some of the variation among receiving countries shown in Fig. 2.18. They estimate that the average welfare effect for the EU as a whole, average over all EU countries and all skill classes, was some 0.6%. The main beneficiaries were low-skilled workers in Poland and Hungary (those who stayed and those who moved), while low-skilled workers in the UK suffered a small loss in their welfare.

Generally, according to their model-based estimates, countries that joined the EU gained some four times more than the rest of the EU, and high skill workers gained less than low skill ones in the new member states, while the opposite was true in the rest of the EU.

Looking forward, the facts that the current levels of the stock of outward migration are still below the global curve, particularly for higher income EU11, that the global curve seems to continue to move upwards (Clemens 2014) and that the stock of FDI is levelling off (Fig. 2.10) point to further increase in outward migration. However, rapidly declining population and labour force, and the consequent historically lowest levels of unemployment will work in the opposite direction. In fact, in some areas such as tourism and construction there is anecdotal evidence suggesting a direct wage arbitrage emerging between EU15 and EU11 economies.

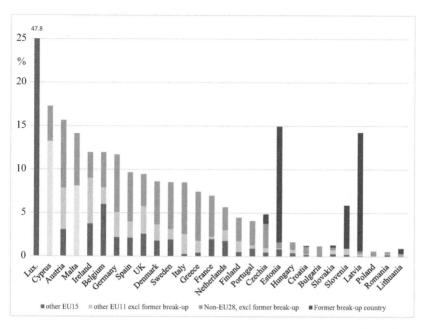

Fig. 2.18 Share of non-nationals in resident population, 2018. Note: Ordered according to total excluding non-nationals from countries with which the country concerned was formerly in one state. For the Czech Republic the latter category includes Slovakia, and for Slovakia, the Czech republic. For the Baltic countries, this includes Russia, Ukraine and recognised non-citizens. For Malta and Cyprus, no breakdown is available between EU 11 and EU15, the light blue column shows the sum of these two categories. (Source: Eurostat)

Besides wage, there are other push/pull factors at work, such as the quality of health care and education and the quality of institutions, particularly corruption. While individual decisions may be perfectly rational and very much in line with the way people in other high middle-income countries make such decisions, there may be a need for public policy intervention. The fiscal implications of migration, particularly on the pension system, and the implications on social developments, but also on innovation or firm creation, may create strong negative externalities, and path dependency may make these negative effects long lasting.

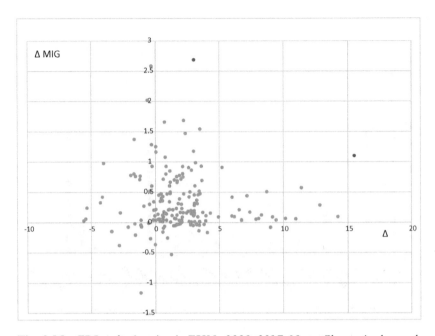

Fig. 2.19 FDI and migration in EU11, 2000–2017. Note: Change in the stock of EU11 citizens living in another EU country (ΔMIGR) on the vertical axis, change in the inward stock of FDI, three-year moving average delayed by one year (ΔFDI) for the stock. Observations are for individual EU11 countries and years. The two points in red are for Bulgaria and Romania for 2008, the year after accession into the EU. (Source: Eurostat for migration, UNCTAD for FDI)

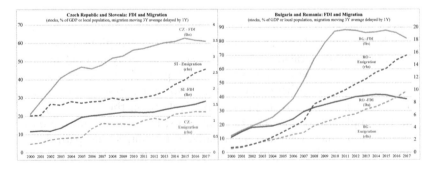

Fig. 2.20 FDI and migration in Czech Republic and Slovenia, and Bulgaria and Romania. Note: Stock of EU11 citizens living in another EU country (Emigration) and stock of FDI, three-year moving average delayed by one year. (Sources: Eurostat for migration, UNCTAD for FDI)

2.8 Institutional Channel

A unique characteristic of the convergence process in EU11, compared to other middle-income countries, is the strong impact of EU membership on institutions. The adoption of the *acquis communitaire* shaped in a major way the legal system and the institutional setup in these countries. They adopted at a massive scale laws and institutions originating from much more developed countries (Baldwin 1995, Baldwin et al. 1997).

There was a similar process in the private sector with an increasing presence of EU (and other foreign) firms in EU11. Similarly to the economic effects discussed earlier in the chapter, many of the changes took place before accession. The impact on public and private institutions did not stop upon accession, as public and private institutions have been evolving in the EU since then.

While the formal, legal adoption of legislation, rules and institutions has been important, what matters for convergence is the actual functioning of these institutions. In fact, what matters is the functioning of the whole system of laws and institutions, which entails the part that is driven by domestic legislation, and the interaction between the two parts. As recent research for EU11 countries showed (Székely and Ward Warmedinger 2018), the actual working of institutions can be very different from the one envisaged in the legislation and can change over time, sometimes in ways not very visible, at least for a while, to the public.

The development of domestic legislation, institutions and policies in the EU is also influenced by peer learning and pressure. The different Council formations and Committees supporting these meetings of national policy makers, and the country specific recommendations issued in the European Semester process are examples of channels through which this works. Recommendations for reforms and policy coordination are not unique to the EU, several international organisations, such as the IMF, World Bank or OECD, perform similar functions. But the scope and intensity of this activity of the EU again sets apart EU11 countries from other groups of middle-income countries regarding the functioning of the institutional channel.

Using the World Bank (2019) Worldwide Governance Indicators, we can check whether, as measured by these indicators, EU membership improved institutions in EU11 and EU Candidate countries, in absolute and relative terms, relative to countries on the frontier of development and relative to other middle-income converging economies in the world (Fig. 2.21).

Fig. 2.21 Trends in Governance Indicators. (**a**) Voice and Accountability; (**b**) Political Stability; (**c**) Government Effectiveness; (**d**) Regulatory quality; (**e**) Rule of Law; (**f**) Control of Corruption. Note: For the definition of country groups, see the Note to Fig. 2.1. Unweighted group averages. Values for 1997, 1999 and 2001 are interpolated. (Source: Worldwide Governance Indicators, 2018 Update (World Bank 2019))

2 CONVERGENCE OF THE EU MEMBER STATES IN CENTRAL-EASTERN...

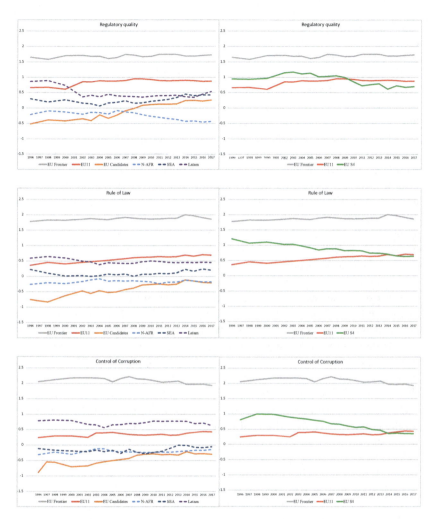

Fig. 2.21 (continued)

As these charts show, EU accession led to improvements in the quality of governance in EU11 countries on all fronts, bringing them somewhat closer to the countries in the EU that are at the global frontier in terms of economic and social development. After accession, however, improvements slowed, or even stopped. This confirms the finding in the literature, that the EU was more successful in promoting reforms before accession than afterwards (Schönfelder and Wagner 2015, Székely and Ward Warmedinger 2018).[30]

Before the outbreak of the crisis in 2008–2009, a strong positive pre-accession impact was also observable for the EU candidate countries. In fact, more so than for the EU11 countries prior to their accession. The impact was so strong that the relative position of these countries, relative to other groups of middle-income countries, changed significantly. This suggests that the EU's positive pre-accession effect can be stronger for countries that are further away from the frontier.

The improvement in institutional quality in these countries was an important factor explaining their relatively good performance regarding economic convergence that we found in our earlier analysis. A less encouraging development is that since the outbreak of the crisis, on most fronts, improvement slowed or stopped. That is, a positive pre-accession impact is not guaranteed either. If EU membership is not viewed as a plausible option in the foreseeable future, the anchoring role of the EU may weaken.

Prior to EU accession, EU11 countries were ahead of the other groups of middle-income countries considered here. Since then, however, their position relative to these groups has changed little. Overall, the institutional channel in the EU has been weak. It did not induce EU11 countries to improve their global position regarding institutional quality. As Fig. 2.22 shows, institutional quality in EU11 improved nonetheless and this certainly helped convergence, and to some extent explain the improvement in the relative position of EU11 within the EU. But the fast economic convergence that the trade and investment channels generated has not been fully matched by improvements in institutions. As we will argue below, this imbalance in development contributed to the emergence of vulnerabilities and other imbalances that can endanger the sustainability of fast convergence. It has also weakened the capacity of EU11 countries to turn fast economic convergence into commensurate social convergence.

As Fig. 2.3 above shows, EU11 is rapidly reaching the income level of EU S4, partly as a result of their rapid convergence but also because of the

---

[30] Schönfelder and Wagner (2015), based on an econometric analysis of these indicators, go a step further and conclude that EU membership after accession has no impact on institutional quality, as measured by WDI. Based on an econometric model to explain the development of the EBRD transition indicators, Staehr (2011) finds that already the start of the EU membership negotiations had a negative effect on reforms.

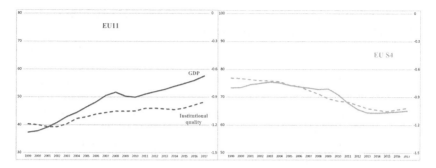

Fig. 2.22 Trends in Governance Indicators and income convergence. Note: For the definition of country groups, see the Note to Fig. 2.1. Institutional quality (right axis) is the distance to the EU Frontier, based on an average of the WGI indices, and it is the average for the three preceding years. Per capita GDP in PPP relative to EU Frontier (left axis). (Source: World Bank for per capita GDP; World Bank (2019) for Worldwide Governance Indicators, 2018 Update)

divergence of the latter group. Fig. 2.22 shows that the deterioration in the relative income position of EU S4 countries was preceded by a deterioration in the relative quality of governance.[31] The continuous decline in the area of corruption control is a particularly important development in this regard (Fig. 2.21).[32]

Importantly for EU 11 countries, these developments also suggest that EU membership in itself is no guarantee for good governance. In fact, it can entail a deterioration in the quality of governance, in absolute terms and relative to other countries. Such reversal in the trend of institutional quality can in turn reverse economic convergence and lead to economic divergence.

By now on almost all fronts, EU11, as measured by the WGI indicators, have better quality of governance than EU S4. This suggests that the

---

[31] A comparison of the numbers for 2010 and 2017 of the European Quality of Government Index also shows a rapid deterioration in institutional quality in EU S4 relative to EU11, and relative to the EU Frontier.

[32] The analysis in Tóth and Hajdu (2021) (Chap. 12 in Volume II) provides micro-level empirical evidence for the weakening of corruption control in public procurement in EU S4 countries. Schönfelder and Wagner (2015) present econometric evidence to suggest more broadly that euro introduction led to a deterioration in the WDI for control of corruption, possibly capturing the developments in these countries.

relative trend between these two groups of countries regarding their per capita GDP (Fig. 2.3) is likely to continue.

An important aspect of the institutional channel is the impact of EU membership on the quality of institutions of macroeconomic policymaking. Central bank independence is in the very core of EU legislation, perhaps the most guarded element of it. In fact, central bank independence as a key building block of a modern market economy was introduced early in in the transition process (Siklos 1994). Nevertheless, as described in detail in Székely and Ward Warmedinger (2018), there have been several attempts to change national legislation in a way that would have violated EU law. Given the strong legal power of European institutions, these attempts never succeed. However, behavioural reversals happened, there were episodes in which the actual functioning of central banks, mostly in the area of banking supervision changed in a way that created major problems in the functioning of the banking sector.

Fiscal institutions and rules is another important area in which the institutional channel in the EU can help member states to improve their institutions. As Jankovics et al. (2021) (Chap. 11 in Volume II) describes in details, EU membership brought about major improvements in fiscal institutions in EU11 countries. However, unlike in other areas, the acceleration of institutional convergence took place recently, chiefly as a result of the EU economic governance legislation of 2011–2013. Reforms concerned all pillars of national fiscal frameworks, including numerical rules, medium-term budgetary frameworks and independent fiscal institutions.

High-quality fiscal institutions not only help ensure that macroeconomic policies are conducive to growth, but they also help transform economic convergence into social convergence. Both impacts work through the quality and predictability of public finances. Predictability is important because it promotes forward-looking behaviour of the private sector, and through this investment. Quality concerns the composition and effectiveness of public sector revenues and expenditures. Regarding income distribution, tax and benefit systems play a central role, while for equity in social development, health and education systems are the most important. To ensure access to affordable and good-quality education and health care for all requires reliable and timely information on outcomes, high level of transparency, good policy design, and strong and evenly distributed implementation capacities. While these are important aspects of institutional development, they are not covered here, as we focus on economic institutions.

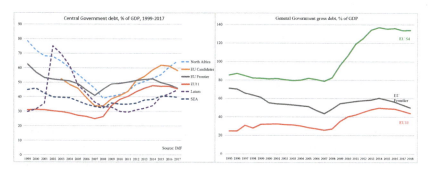

Fig. 2.23 Public debt relative to GDP. Note: For the definition of country groups, see the Note to Fig. 2.1. The panel on the left shows central government debt relative to GDP as internationally no consistent data are available for general government debt. The panel on the right shows general government gross debt (as defined in the Excessive Deficit Procedure of the EU). (Source: Central government debt, IMF; general government gross debt, Eurostat)

Overall, fiscal policy in EU11 as a group has been disciplined and public debt has been kept at safe levels (Fig. 2.23). Nevertheless, there have been major episodes of reversals in this area too (Székely and Ward Warmedinger 2018). In the absence of market discipline, and in countries where the institutional channel was weak, fiscal policies deteriorated. They became strongly pro-cyclical further adding to the vulnerability of these economies to economic shocks (see Sect. 2.9 below). The less impressive convergence in human development indicators also suggests that the quality of public finance may not have improved as much as necessary to transform economic convergence into social convergence while keeping public debt at safe levels.

The trade-off between the level of public debt and social convergence at a given level of institutional (and public finance) quality is also apparent from the chart on the right-hand side in Fig. 2.23. Taken together with Fig. 2.3, this chart shows that the consequence of maintaining the relative level of human development while the relative income position deteriorated led to a rapid increase in public debt in EU S4 during the crisis. Moreover, during the recovery since 2013, public debt remained at this elevated level. EU11 countries seem to have followed a different strategy, the restart of convergence led to a gradual decline in public debt while the restart of social convergence was postponed. The best way to remove this apparent trade-off is to improve the quality of public finances, and more broadly institutional quality.

The pension system is a central element of a country's fiscal system. EU legislation has very little direct formal impact on the design of the pensions system of a country. Nevertheless, as described in details in Chłoń-Domińczak (2021) (Chap. 12 of Volume II) EU membership has had an important impact on the development of pension systems in EU11 countries. In fact, developments in this area demonstrate well how the interaction of the different channels described in this chapter earlier can shape developments in an area where EU membership has very little direct, formal impact. The combined effect of (a) rapid aging together with increased migration; (b) fiscal rules in the EU that initially may not have fully taken into account the specific characteristics of the early radical pension reforms in EU11 countries; (c) the imbalances in integration (see Sect. 2.9 below) that made EU11 economies more vulnerable to shocks than the rest of the EU; (d) the crisis that hit budgets in EU11 countries much harder than in the rest of the EU because of their vulnerabilities; and (e) weak institutions lead to pauses, or in some cases even reversals in pension reforms.

While there is no consensus on the optimal design of pensions systems, and the pension reforms that were introduced earlier in the transition process suffered from several design problems and poor implementation (Székely and Ward Warmedinger 2018), the lack of institutional stability in such a central area may hinder economic and social convergence in the future.

EU funds play an important role in fostering the convergence of EU member states. As the analyses of Czelleng and Vértes (2021) and Varga, and in 't Veld (2021) (Chaps. 4 and 5 in Volume II) show, the net receipt from EU funds were very large in EU11 and they had sizable positive impact on the level of economic activity (GDP). As Czelleng and Vértes (2021) emphasise though, their analysis does not capture the impact of corruption on this relationship. The chart on control of corruption in Fig. 2.21 shows only a modest improvement for EU11, particularly after EU accession when most of the EU funds were released.

Tóth and Hajdu (2021) (Chap. 9 of Volume II) offers a quantitative micro-level analysis to measure corruption risk in public procurement, a channel through which a large part of EU funds is eventually released into the economy. The results of this analysis show very diverse developments in EU11 countries, which seem to correlate closely with the relative economic and social performance of the individual countries shown in

Fig. 2.2. Countries that managed to improve the control of corruption in public procurement are the countries that managed to improve their relative positions both economically and socially. In all likelihood, this not a causal relationship, but perhaps an important indication of a common underlying factor, the quality of institutions, that produced improvement in both indicators.

Besides corruption, the effectiveness of government is also likely to be an important factor which determines the impact of EU funds on the economic and social development of a member state. This also a factor that the models used in Chaps. 3 and 4 in Volume II do not capture. The observation we make based on this is that institutional quality is a channel that is likely to interact with all the other channels discussed earlier and this interaction may become more important as countries get closer to the frontier.

2.9 The Dangers of Convergence: Imbalances and Policy Reversals

EU membership has accelerated economic convergence by facilitating rapid trade integration and inward FDI. EU11 economies are now among the most open economies in the world. Moreover, inward FDI reached levels observed in the highly developed small EU15 countries, cross-border labour mobility increased significantly, foreign ownership in the banking sector reached very high levels, and overall, institutions improved albeit slowly. In short, EU membership has led to a deep economic integration of EU11 countries into the EU and improved their growth potential.

However, these positive results came at a cost. Rapid trade integration made these countries highly open and thus vulnerable to external shocks, much more than before and much more than the rest of the EU. While trade integration has been rather symmetric, trade flows increased in both directions and trade between EU15 and EU11 is broadly balanced, major imbalances emerged on other fronts. FDI flows have been particularly unbalanced. As we have shown in Sect. 2.5, inward FDI stock in EU11 relative to GDP reached levels very similar to those in highly developed EU15 countries. However, outward FDI has not followed the same trend, it has remained rather low even compared with other middle-income economies (Fig. 2.10). Similarly, outward migration has been significant, but inward migration from EU15, or form non-EU countries, has remained insignificant. EU15 banking groups own a large part of the banking sector in EU11 but very few banking groups from EU11 have managed to develop even a regional network.

As Buti and Székely (2019) argue, model simulations show that large differences between inward and outward FDI, combined with relatively low levels of domestic savings and a large share of households with little savings to absorb temporary income loss, may make EU11 more vulnerable to shocks than the rest of the EU. The impact of a shock is bigger and more lasting than in an economy with less imbalances of this kind. Thus, potential output may become more volatile as well. That is, EU11 economies may become structurally more volatile. As Fig. 2.24 shows, this has indeed be the situation.

If fiscal policy is pro-cyclical and fails to rebuild fiscal buffers during good times, as it happened recently in some EU11 countries, the

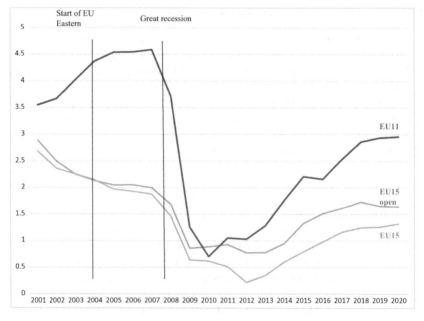

Fig. 2.24 Potential output growth in the EU in 2001–2018. Note: EU15 small open includes Austria, Belgium, Denmark, Finland Netherlands, and Sweden. EU11 is as defined in the Note to Fig. 2.1. (Source: Buti and Székely 2019)

inevitable pro-cyclical fiscal tightening during the shock further adds to the volatility of actual and potential output.

An increased structural volatility of the economy may be an inherent characteristic of the early phase of the convergence process. But if so, macroeconomic policies and institutions should do their utmost to mitigate the impact of this characteristic on the economy and society. This requires particular attention to the quality of macroeconomic policies, including macro prudential policies, and to the quality of the institutional framework that is in place to ensure prudent macroeconomic policies and financial stability.

Pinelli and Pellényi (2021) (Chap. 4 in Volume I) show that, as EU11 countries converged towards the frontier, income dispersion among EU countries, and among countries within EU11 declined (there was sigma convergence). Nevertheless, income dispersion within EU11 countries, i.e. among their (NUTS3) regions, increased (no sigma convergence). They also find evidence of stronger localised agglomeration effects, which underpin strengthening urban/rural divides. This is consistent with Buti and Székely (2019), which highlights that increasing FDI has further accelerated the already strong agglomeration effects of trade integration and increased the demand for, and the wage premium on higher skills. FDI is indeed highly concentrated in main urban areas particularly in capitals and in areas that host the main west European manufacturing firms participating in GVCs (Durán and Szabo (2021) and Fig. 2.25).[33]

Pinelli and Pellényi 2021 also show that the most prosperous regions in EU11 have pulled ahead fast and de-linked from their neighbouring regions as economic convergence progressed. Connecting this analysis to the one on FDI suggests that these are likely to be the same regions that benefitted most from FDI (Fig. 2.25) and from internal (skilled) labour migration. That is, FDI driven by trade integration, that is, the trade and investment channels created prosperous regions. But with no sign of positive spill-over to the less fortunate parts of these countries.

On the other hand, some connected areas of poor and slow growing regions, sometimes spreading over national borders, remain. Unlike with

---

[33] As Table 5 in Annex C in Durán and Szabo (2021) show, in EU11, the share of FDI in regional GDP in the regions that benefit the most from FDI in a country (with the exception of Hungary this is the region where the capital is) is 3½ to 17 times higher than the same share in the regions that benefits least. The highest (double-digit) ratios are in Poland and Romania, the lowest ones in Slovenia and Bulgaria.

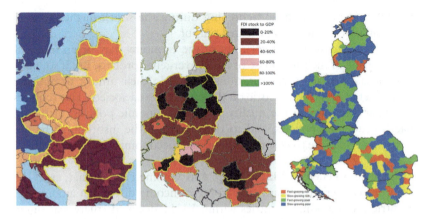

Fig. 2.25 Regional differences in inward FDI, convergence trends and institutional quality in EU11 countries. (**a**) FDI; (**b**) Convergence; (**c**) Institutional Quality. Note: For the chart in the middle Level of per capita GDP in 2000, and growth in 2000–2014, regions are classified as: Red = regions with GDP per capital level and growth above national average Yellow = regions with GDP per capital level above the national average and growth below Green = regions with GDP per capita level below the national average and growth above Blue = regions with GDP per capita level and growth below the national average. (Sources: Buti and Székely (2019), Pinelli and Pellényi (2021). https://ec.europa.eu/regional_policy)

prosperous regions, there are signs of negative spill-over among these regions. That is, the same process, the working of the trade and investment channels can also create pockets of persistent backwardness with negative regional spill-over. This is another form of imbalance that characterises the otherwise rather successful convergence process in EU11.[34]

Andor (2019) calls the attention to the fiscal and social implications of asymmetries in migration described above. In the absence of an efficient state with high-quality public expenditure and social support system, this may destabilise societies and domestic politics. As we mentioned above, Caliendo et al. (2017) present model-based estimations that suggest a

---

[34] Ridao-Cano and Bodewig (2018) calls the attention to this issue for the EU as a whole, particularly concerning Southern Europe. Pilati (2019) argues that the "fourth industrial revolution" will further exacerbate already strong agglomeration effects in Europe, and argues for a geographically fair EU industrial strategy, and for policies that can break agglomeration bubbles. As the former analysis shows, for this policies to work, regional institutions need to be strengthened first.

sizable overall welfare gain from (dominantly low skill) labour migration in the EU following the eastern enlargement. They show that this gain is unevenly distributed among countries and skill classes, with low skill labour in EU11 gaining the most (those who migrated and also those who stayed at home, and the most in Poland and Hungary) and low skill labour in the rest of the EU less (in the UK even suffering a small loss). However, as the analysis by Pinelli and Pellényi (2021) suggests, this sizable overall welfare gain from migration in EU11 may have been distributed rather unevenly within the countries. The prosperous regions, which emerged in EU11 because of unevenly distributed FDI and strong unidirectional internal migration among regions, might have received most of the welfare gain from outward migration. This is because these are the regions where there were vibrant local labour markets in which low skill workers who had stayed (had not migrated to EU15) could realise higher wages (higher than what they would have been without increased migration in the EU).

That is, even though there might have been sizable overall welfare gains to EU11 countries from large net outward migration, an emerging regional divide might have turned this positive development into a new challenge for policymakers in EU11. This is not an argument against FDI and outward or internal migration. Rather, it is an important lesson that the market forces that global and European integration unleashes, combined with weak national and local institutions in member states, can create major economic and social challenges, even if the overall effect on a country is positive.

The EU provides large financial support from its Cohesion funds to EU member states to promote regional cohesion. As in 't Veld and Varga (2021) and Czelleng and Vértes (2021) (Chaps. 4 and 5 in Volume II) show, potentially, these funds have large positive impact on economic growth in EU11, both in the short to medium and in the long run. Moreover, these funds are by design targeted on the less fortunate regions and on projects that are known to enhance their growth potential, such as infrastructure. Nevertheless, they produce actual gains only if the money is allocated well across projects and if the projects are implemented well.[35]

---

[35] Tóth and Hajdu (2021) describe a very important aspect of allocation of EU funds, control of corruption risk in public procurement.

This depends on the quality of national and regional institutions, and the working of the institutional channel in the EU.[36]

The dispersion in per capita income among regions within EU11 countries increased until 2010 and has flattened out since then (Pinelli and Pellényi 2021). In the period after 2010 the disbursement of regional funds picked up strongly while FDI subsided. This would suggest that significantly more targeted help from the EU, despite less pressure on the system from FDI, could arrest but not reverse the increasing dispersion. Moving forward, FDI is likely to increase while EU funds to be somewhat reduced. Hence, national and subnational institutions need to improve to avoid a further increase in the already sizable regional and urban-rural divide.[37] Moreover, the institutional channel in the EU should also work better to help this process.

The idea that EU accession is a way to lock in democratic and pro-market reforms in EU11 (through the institutional channel) has been around from the beginning of transition (Baldwin 1995). The emergence of reform reversals in the region (Székely and Ward-Warmedinger 2018) however suggests that this lock in is not automatic. As Fig. 2.24 shows, the growth potential of EU11 at the aggregate level has been largely restored. Nevertheless, the economic and social vulnerabilities discussed above may have increased. Low skill workers in Hungary and Poland might have benefitted the most from the working of the migration channel in the EU. Moreover, EU funds provided major financial support targeted on the poorest regions in EU11. Nevertheless, major reform reversals in these countries might have been supported the most by low skill workers in the poorest regions.

More broadly, the full impact of EU enlargement on certain parts of society may be very different from what an aggregate analysis would suggest. This in turn may change the political economy of European integration. To avoid this, it is important to understand the underlying forces and to identify public policies and institutional reforms at the EU and national

---

[36] The econometric analysis in Rodríguez-Pose and Ganau (2019) shows that the quality of regional institutions improve productivity both directly and indirectly through increasing the return to physical and human capital and local innovative capacity.

[37] This applies not only to the average quality of regional institutions, but also to the dispersion in quality among regions within a country. As the European Quality of Government Index shows, the dispersion in institutional quality among regions is much higher in EU11 then in EU15 countries, except EU S4. For the latter, this is an important factor that contributed to the decline in relative income in the past decades.

levels that can mitigate such imbalances and vulnerabilities. Such reforms would also concern areas that are not analysed here, most importantly social policies and institutions.

2.10 The EU's Response to the Crisis: Strengthening EU Institutions

Economic and social convergence is one important aspect of EU membership for these countries, but it does not take place in isolation. EU integration has its own course of development and dynamics. Not surprisingly, many of the issues we identified here have been identified in other areas of the functioning of the EU, particularly during the crisis as it brought to the surface many of the problems of European integration and the functioning of the EU.

The Five Presidents Report (Juncker 2015) put a greater focus on employment and social performance in the future design of EMU and the European Semester process was enhanced to monitor social developments. In 2017, the European Pillar of Social Rights was issued.[38]

The deep-seated problems of financial integration and intermediation in the EU came to the surface early on in the crisis. There were major banking crises in Europe and many of the countries concerned required massive financial and institutional assistance to cope with the situation. The reaction on the part of the EU was decisive, leading to the launching of the Banking Union and the Capital Market Union.

These reforms address many of the problems that caused excessive cross-border financial flows and domestic credit to the private sector in EU11. Nevertheless, our analysis suggests that it will remain important to improve national institutions and to strengthen the institutional channel. Moreover, these reforms will be less effective in EU11 countries that are not euro area members or not opted into close cooperation with the SSM. Improving the quality of domestic institutions and strengthening the institutional channel will thus remain critical for these countries.

---

[38] The European Pillar of Social Rights expresses principles and rights essential for fair and well-functioning labour markets and welfare systems in twenty-first century Europe. It reaffirms some of the rights already present in the Union acquis. It adds new principles that address the challenges arising from societal, technological and economic developments. For more information, see European Commission (2019b).

The crisis also revealed problems with economic policy coordination and with macroeconomic policies that create imbalances and vulnerabilities. To address these problems, fiscal policy coordination was strengthened (Jankovics et al. 2021), the Macroeconomic Imbalances Procedures and the European Semester process was introduced, also to promote reforms.

These measures were taken to ensure a better functioning of the EMU, and more broadly that of the EU. However, as always, good institutions have beneficial impact also in other areas, in this case they help the convergence process in EU11. Nevertheless, our analysis suggests that the institutional channel in the EU needs to be further strengthened.

2.11 Conclusions

This chapter offered a framework to analyse the impact of EU membership on economic ("means"), institutional ("ways") and social ("ends") convergence of EU11 countries to frontier. Using this framework, we find that EU membership shaped the convergence process in important ways. As a group, EU11 countries have been among the fastest converging countries in the world in terms of per capita GDP since the turn of the century, when EU accession became a realistic future path for them. The main drivers were trade and FDI. EU membership brought about a rapid increase in trade openness, transforming EU11 countries into the most open economies in the world. The remarkable fact about this development is that trade openness in the world as a whole levelled off during this period, in some parts of the world even started to decline. The investment channel, through a massive inflow of FDI, greatly supported rapid trade integration. These two channels strongly interacted and supported each other.

The finance channel injected major volatility into the economic convergence process. Prior to the crisis, it poured large amount of foreign, mostly European savings into the financial system of EU11, dominated by banking systems with a high share of foreign banks. As a result, financial deepening increased rapidly. However, this was unsustainable, as the financial system poorly allocated a large part of the funds. The crisis put a sudden end to the process. Cross-border financial flows reversed and the financial system rapidly delivered. However, as lending to the corporate sector was overall efficient, a significant part of financial deepening has been preserved. Thus, the rather large gap between EU11 and other middle-income countries in this area prior to EU accession has been closed by now.

Through the trade, investment and finance channels, EU membership unleashed strong market forces. They boosted economic convergence in the region despite a major crisis.[39] However, the unleashed market forces also caused negative side effects because of weak institutions. Economic research shows that increased trade openness and a massive presence of capital and firms from countries with high quality of (public and private) institutions go hand-in-hand with better institutions in the host countries. The EU as an institution legally requires (the acquis) and through several channels (such as the European Semester) promotes better institutions. Thus, it is striking to find only a moderate convergence to the frontier in terms of institutional quality in the region, most of it before accession. As the experience of Southern European EU countries (EU S4) indicate, if the quality of institutions deteriorates, countries may start to diverge from the frontier. In such a situation, the potentially large advantages of EU membership regarding economic convergence may turn into disadvantages.

Fast economic convergence of EU11 has also brought about major imbalances and vulnerabilities. While the level of inward FDI in EU11 is among the highest in the world, and very similar to what we see in the most developed EU countries, the level of outward FDI is rather low by international comparison, and it has remained broadly flat since 2012 for the group as a whole. Very few local firms in EU11 invest abroad, create GVC or aspire to be multinational firms. This, together with other characteristics of their economies, seem to explain why EU11 countries turned out to be structurally so volatile during the crisis.

Another important imbalance emerged in migration patterns. Some 8% of EU11 citizens live now in other EU countries, mostly in EU15, while the share of EU15 citizens among residents in EU11 is below one percent, and the share of non-EU citizens is among the smallest in the EU. The total population of EU11 declined significantly, to a considerable extent due to the large net outward migration. With fiscal systems remaining national, this may have a major impact on budgets and pension systems in the future.

---

[39] Campos et al. (2019) estimate the contributions of the different factors to the gain from EU accession, including in the sample countries that joined the EU in the previous waves of enlargement. They confirm that the biggest gain is from trade openness followed by financial integration and the introduction of the euro, for a period that ends in 2008. As our analysis in Sect. 2.6 suggests, these estimates may overstate the impact of the finance channel as the period ends just before the crisis.

Regarding increased labour mobility in EU11, model-based calculations suggest sizable overall welfare gains for the EU as a whole. However, these gains were distributed unevenly among countries and among people with different skills, reflecting the uneven distribution of migration flows. Low skill people in EU11 are estimated to have gained the most, while low skill people in other parts of the EU the least. As the analysis of regional development patterns show, the interaction of the mobility channel with the investment channel (FDI) and the institutional channel (weak- and uneven-quality national and subnational institutions) and with internal migration may have made the distributional effects of labour migration more uneven. Most of the welfare gains in EU11 might have benefitted prosperous regions, while leaving other regions with the negative impacts of the strong agglomeration effects market forces create.

Massive EU funds could arrest a rapid opening of regional income inequalities but could not reverse them yet. The analysis could not find positive spill-over from prosperous regions but could find evidence supporting negative regional spill-over from poor regions. Moving forward, EU funds will be smaller and FDI is likely to be higher. Hence, available resource to mitigate the negative distributional effects of market forces need to be used more efficiently in the future. This requires improvement in national and subnational institutions in EU11 countries.

Rapid economic convergence has not translated into a commensurate social convergence, neither relative to the frontier nor relative to other middle-income economies. In fact, based on HDI, social convergence seems to have paused in EU11 since the start of the crisis in 2008. Slow social convergence and imbalances in economic convergence may in turn jeopardise the sustainability of the rapid economic convergence the region has achieved so far. These developments have already created a fertile ground for reform reversals in many areas and countries, in some cases of more systematic nature.

In light of this, it is important to find ways to reduce the emerging imbalances of economic convergence. Not by trying to limit the four freedoms, either legally or in practice. The challenge for governments in the region and for the EU is to identify and implement public policies that help EU11 firms to become European or global firms, policies that help circular migration, promote domestic savings and can create new agglomeration dynamics that can counterbalance the ones that globalisation creates.

Looking forward, unless institutions improve faster, the convergence of EU11 countries to the global frontier of economic and social development may slow in the future. As these countries get closer to the frontier, innovation and allocative efficiency becomes increasingly important development factors (Acemoglu et al. 2006; Gattini et al. 2021). The quality of public and private institutions has a major impact on these factors. Therefore, to avoid a slowdown in convergence, EU11 countries should focus on improving institutional quality and the institutional channel in the EU should be improved. The latter would also help the overall functioning of the EU.

ANNEX 1: THE SELECTION OF THE COUNTRY GROUPS USED IN THE ANALYSIS

In order to benchmark the developments in EU11 countries, the group that is in the focus of our analysis, we selected from each region four countries that were the most similar in size, trade openness, and overall economic and social development to the countries in the EU11 group. We did not select very large economies, such as China and India, or mostly resource-based economies. Figure 2.26 below shows the position of the countries in the different benchmark groups used in our analysis.

As Fig. 2.26 shows, with the exception of the group of South-East Asian countries (SEA), these groups are rather homogenous. The wider range of development in SEA is due to South Korea, which by 2017 reached the income level of Italy. At the beginning of the period, however, this was not yet the case. In 2004, South Korea's per capita GDP (in PPP) was at the level of the per capita GDP of the Czech Republic, somewhat below that of Slovenia, and way below that of Italy (or Spain). Broadly, the same is true for South Korea's relative position regarding its human development (HDI), albeit in this regard South Korea was ahead of the Czech Republic and much closer to Italy or Spain in 2004. Thus, by including Korea in the SEA group, we incorporate one of the most successful convergence episodes, which is highly relevant for EU11 countries. During the period under investigation here, South Korea reached the income level of highly developed countries starting from the level of the most developed EU11 countries. But this success was not repeated by the other countries in this group; thus by 2017, the range of per capita incomes in SEA became rather wide.

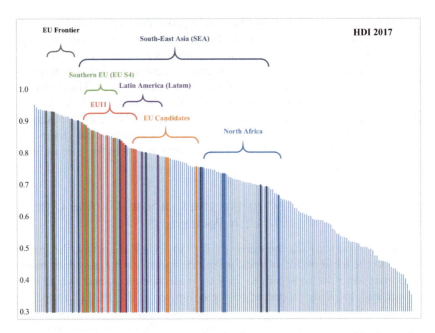

Fig. 2.26 Human Development Index for the country groups used in the analysis in 2017. Note: Columns represent countries, which were ordered according to their HDI index in 2017. *EU Frontier* includes Austria, Denmark, Netherlands and Sweden; *EU S4 includes Greece, Italy, Portugal and Spain*. EU11 includes Bulgaria, Croatia, Czech Republic, Estonia, Hungary, Latvia, Lithuania, Poland, Romania, Slovakia and Slovenia. *EU Candidates* include Albania, North Macedonia, Montenegro and Serbia; *Latam* includes Argentina, Chile, Costa Rica, and Uruguay; *North Africa* includes Algeria, Jordan, Morocco and Tunisia; SEA includes Indonesia, Korea, Malaysia and Philippines. (Source: UNDP)

As explained in Sect. 2, we identify the global frontier of economic and social development with four small open EU economies, Austria, Denmark, Netherlands and Sweden. As with the other groups, we selected only small open economies, and thus left out Germany and France. As Fig. 2.26 shows, these countries are among the economically, socially and institutionally most developed countries in the world. Regarding other small open EU economies in this group, we left out Finland because of two major idiosyncratic shocks to its economy during the period under investigation, and Ireland because of high volatility in its statistics. While

Belgium is also a high-income and very open economy, it is less closely linked to EU11 than those included in this group, and its institutional development is rather uneven.

REFERENCES

Acemoglu, D., Aghion, P., & Zilibotti, F. (2006). Distance to Frontier, Selection, and Economic Growth. *Journal of the European Economic Association*, 4(1), 37–74.

Acemoglu, D., Johnson, S., & Robinson, J. A. (2005). Institutions as a Fundamental Cause of Growth. In P. Aghion & S. N. Durlauf (Eds.), *Handbook of Economic Growth* (Vol. 1a, pp. 386–454). New York: North-Holland.

Aghion, P., Howitt, P., & Mayer-Foulkes, D. (2005). The Effect of Financial Development on Convergence: Theory and Evidence. *Quarterly Journal of Economics*, 120, 173–222.

Andor, L. (2019). EU Enlargement: The Social Dimension Human Capital and East-West Imbalances. In I. P. Székely (Ed.), *Faces of Convergence* (pp. 9–15). WIIW Vienna.

Baldwin, R. (1995). The Eastern Enlargement of the European Union. *European Economic Review*, 39, 474–481.

Baldwin, R., Francois, J., & Portes, R. (1997). The Costs and Benefits of Eastern Enlargement: The Impact on the EU and Central Europe. *Economic Policy*, 12, 125–176.

Boldizsár, A., Nagy-Kékesi, Zs., Rriga, E. J. (2021). *Transformation of the Trade and Financing Model of the Hungarian Economy After EU Accession.* In: Landesmann and Székely (2021).

Buiter, W., & Lubin, D. (2019). Did EU Membership Bring Economic Benefits for CESEE Member States? In I. P. Székely (Ed.), *Faces of Convergence* (pp. 33–37). WIIW Vienna.

Buti, M., & Székely, I. P. (2019). *Trade Shocks, Growth and Resilience: Eastern Europe's Adjustment Tale*, VoxEu.org.

Caliendo, L., Opromolla, L. D., Parro, F., & Sforza, A. (2017). *Goods and Factor Market Integration: A Quantitative Assessment of the EU Enlargement* (CEP Discussion Paper No 1494).

Calligaris, S. Del Gatto, M., Hassan, F., Ottaviano, G. I. P., & Schivardi, F. (2016). *Italy's Productivity Conundrum a Study on Resource Misallocation in italy* (European Economy Discussion Paper 030). European Commission, DG ECFIN.

Campos, N. F., Coricelli, F., & Moretti, L. (2019). Institutional Integration and Economic Growth in Europe. *Journal of Monetary Economics*, Elsevier, 103(C), 88–104.

Chłoń-Domińczak, A. (2021). *Towards Sustainable and Adequate Pension Systems: Old-Age Pension Reforms After Economic Transition and EU Accession in Central-Eastern and South-Eastern Europe*. In: Landesmann and Székely (2021).
Claessens, S., & Van Horen, N. (2014). Foreign Banks: Trends and Impact. *Journal of Money, Credit and Banking*, Supplement to Vol. 46(1), 295–326.
Clemens, M. A., 2014. *Does Development Reduce Migration?* (IZA Discussion Paper 8592). Bonn: Center for Global Development, Institute for the Study of Labor (IZA).
Coeuré, B. (2018). *The Role of the European Union in Fostering Convergence*. Speech Delivered at the Conference on European Economic Integration (CEEI), Vienna.
Coricelli, F., & Frigerio, M. (2021). *15 Years from the Eastern Enlargement: Financial Integration and Economic Convergence in Europe*. In: Landesmann and Székely (2021).
Czelleng, A., & Vértes, A. (2021). *The Impact of EU Cohesion Funds on Macroeconomic Development in the Visegrad Countries After the 2008–2009 Financial Crisis*. In: Landesmann and Székely (2021).
De Bonis, R., Ferri, G., & Rotondi, Z. (2015). Do Firm–Bank Relationships Affect Firms' Internationalization? *InternationalEconomics, 142*(2015), 60–80.
Durán, J., & Szabo, S. (2021). *FDI as Vector of Convergence in the CESEE Countries*. In: Landesmann and Székely (2021).
Eurofound. (2018). *Upward Convergence in the EU: Concepts, Measurements and Indicators*. Luxembourg: Publications Office of the European Union.
European Commission. (2012). *A Roadmap Towards a Banking Union, Communication from the Commission to the European Parliament and the Council*, COM(2012) 510 final.
European Commission. (2019a). *What Is the Banking Union?* https://ec.europa.eu/info/business-economy-euro/banking-and-finance/banking-union/what-banking-union_en
European Commission. (2019b). *European Pillar of Social Rights*. https://ec.europa.eu/commission/priorities/deeper-and-fairer-economic-and-monetary-union/european-pillar-social-rights_en
Feldman, R. A., & Watson, C. M. (2002). *Into the EU: Policy Frameworks in Central Europe*, International Monetary Fund.
Fernández, A., & Tamayo, C. E. (2017). From Institutions to Financial Development and Growth: What are the Links? *Journal of Economic Surveys, 31*(1), 17–57.
Gattini, L., Gereben, Á., Kollár, M., Revoltella, D., & Wruuck, P. (2021). *Towards a New Growth Model in CESEE: Three Challenges Ahead*. In: Landesmann and Székely (2021).
Hagemejer, J., & Muck, J. (2019). Export-Led Growth and Its Determinants Evidence from CEEC countries. *The World Economy*, forthcoming.

Harding, T., & Smarzynska Javorcik, B. (2011). *FDI and Export Upgrading* (University of Oxford, Department of Economics Discussion Paper Series, Number 526).

Jankovics, L., Ormaetxea Igarzabal, L., & Ciobanu, S. (2021). *The Impact of the EU on National Fiscal Governance Systems*. In: Landesmann and Székely (2021).

Juncker, Jean-Claude. (2015). *Completing Europe's Economic and Monetary Union*. Report by Jean-Claude Juncker in Close Cooperation with Donald Tusk, Jeroen Dijsselbloem, Mario Draghi and Martin Schulz. Brussels.

Keereman, F., & Székely, I. P. (Eds.). (2010). *Five Years of an Enlarged EU – A Positive Sum Game* (p. 256). Berlin/Heidelberg: Springer-Verlag.

Landesmann, M., & Székely, I. P. (Eds.). (2021). *Does EU Membership Facilitate Convergence? The Experience of the EU's Eastern Enlargement*. Volumes I and II. Palgrave Macmillan, London, UK.

Merlevede, B., & Purice, V. (2019). *Border Regimes and Indirect Productivity Effects from Foreign Direct Investment* (Working Paper 965). Department of Economics, Ghent University, Belgium.

North, D. C. (1990). *Institutions, Institutional Change, and Economic Performance*. New York: Cambridge University Press.

North, D. C. (1991). Institutions. *Journal of Economic Perspectives*, 5(1), 97–112.

Pilati, M. (2019). *A Geographically Fair EU Industrial Strategy*. EPC Policy Brief, EPC, Brussels.

Pinelli, D., & Pellényi, G. (2021). *Regional Dynamics in EU11*. In: Landesmann and Székely (2021).

Prados de la Escosura, L. (2019). *Human Development in the Age of Globalisation* (CEPR Discussion paper Series, DP 13744).

Ridao-Cano, C., & Bodewig, C. (2018). *Growing United: Upgrading Europe's Convergence Machine*. (Vol. 2, English). Washington, DC: World Bank Group.

Rodríguez-Pose, A., & Ganau, R. (2019). *Institutions and the Productivity Challenge for European Regions* (Discussion Paper 116, European Commission, DG ECFIN).

Roeger, W., & in 't Veld, J. (2021). *The Economic Impact Of Single Market Membership on the EU Enlargement Countries*. In: Landesmann and Székely (2021).

Schönfelder, N., & Wagner, H. (2015). *The Impact of European Integration on Institutional Development* (MPRA Paper No. 63392) posted 2. April 2015 01:17 UTC. Online at http://mpra.ub.uni-muenchen.de/63392/

Schmieg, E. (2019). *Connections Between Trade Policy and Migration. A Sphere of Action for the EU* (SWP Research Paper 15). German Institute for International and Security Affairs, Berlin.

Siklos, P. (1994). *Central Bank Independence in the Transitional Economics: A Preliminary Investigation of Hungary, Poland, the Czech and Slovak Republics*.

In J. P. Bonin & I. P. Székely (Eds.), *The Development and Reform of Financial Systems in Central and Eastern Europe.* Edward Elgar, Cheltenham, UK.

Staehr, K. (2011). Democratic and Market-Economic Reforms in the Post-Communist Countries. The Impact of Enlargement of the European Union. *Eastern European Economics, 49*(5), 3–28.

Székely, I. P. (2019). *Convergence to the Global Frontier in South East Asia and CESEE: The Role of External and Internal Anchors and Their Interactions* (Paper Presented at the Asia Economic Community Forum 2019). Incheon, Korea.

Székely. I. P., & Ward Warmedinger, M. (2018). *Reform Reversal in Former Transition Economies (FTEs) of the European Union: Areas, Circumstances and Motivations* (IZA Policy Paper No. 142).

Temesváry, J., & Banai, A. (2017). The Drivers of Foreign Bank Lending in Central and Eastern Europe: The Roles of Parent, Subsidiary and Host Market Traits. *Journal of International Money and Finance, 79*(2017), 157–173.

Tóth, I. J. & Hajdu, M. (2021). *Corruption, Institutions and Convergence.* In: Landesmann and Székely (2021).

Treaty on European Union. (2012). Consolidated Version of the Treaty on European Union. *Official Journal of the European Union*, English Version, C 326/13.

Tridico, P. (2011). *Institutions, Human Development and Economic Growth in Transition Economies.* Basingstoke: Palgrave Macmillan.

Varga, J., & in 't Veld, J. (2021). *The Impact of the EU Cohesion Policy Spending: A Model-Based Assessment.* In: Landesmann and Székely (2021).

Vértes, A. (2019). Unfulfilled Dreams In Székely, I. P. (ed.) *Faces of Convergence* (pp. 151–155). WIIW Vienna.

Voljč, M. (2019). Financial Integration in Central and Southeastern Europe – The "Soft Power" of EU Membership. In Székely, I. P. (ed.) *Faces of Convergence* (pp. 160–164). WIIW Vienna.

World Bank (2019). *The Worldwide Governance Indicators,* 2018 Update. www.govindicators.org downloaded on June 20, 2019.

CHAPTER 3

Towards a New Growth Model in CESEE: Three Challenges Ahead

Luca Gattini, Áron Gereben, Miroslav Kollár, Debora Revoltella, and Patricia Wruuck

3.1 INTRODUCTION

Until the onset of the financial crisis in 2008, economies of Central, Eastern and South Eastern Europe (CESEE) established a record of significant growth and economic progress.[1] The process leading to the EU

The views expressed in this document are those of the authors and do not necessarily reflect the position of the EIB or its shareholders.

[1] For the purpose of this study, we define Central, Eastern and South Eastern Europe (CESEE) as the former Eastern bloc countries that were part of the 2004 wave of EU enlargement (the Czech Republic, Estonia, Hungary, Latvia, Lithuania, Poland, Slovakia and Slovenia), together with those of the 2007 wave (Bulgaria and Romania), and Croatia that

L. Gattini • Á. Gereben (✉) • M. Kollár • D. Revoltella • P. Wruuck
Economics Department, European Investment Bank (EIB), Luxembourg, Luxembourg
e-mail: l.gattini@eib.org; a.gereben@eib.org; d.revoltella@eib.org; p.wruuck@eib.org

© The Author(s), under exclusive license to Springer Nature Switzerland AG 2021
M. Landesmann, I. P. Székely (eds.), *Does EU Membership Facilitate Convergence? The Experience of the EU's Eastern Enlargement - Volume I*, Studies in Economic Transition,
https://doi.org/10.1007/978-3-030-57686-8_3

accession, and the accession itself, have unleashed the inherent potential of these economies. Previously state-owned industries were privatised, important reforms were implemented, which laid the foundations of market economy. This in turn attracted capital and foreign direct investment that drove productivity improvements and GDP growth. In many instances, however, unsustainable levels of consumption and borrowing propelled to some extent the pre-crisis growth, thus exacerbating the recession following the 2008 crisis. While the regions' economies recovered successfully from the downturn, there are strong arguments supporting that to continue the process of economic convergence, CESEE countries need to revisit their economic models.

We first briefly elaborate on the drivers of post-accession convergence of CESEE member states, highlighting the role of low labour costs, the role of exports, the capital inflows intermediated through foreign direct investments and banking sector, and their role in creating external vulnerabilities. Next, we present how the conditions underlying this model have changed following the financial crisis and its aftermath, and how these changes have been rendering this model less and less capable to be the engine of economic convergence. To avoid being confined in the middle income trap, the countries of CESEE need a new, innovation and knowledge-based growth model, which can fuel productivity growth in the long run.

The obstacles of implementing such a model are emerging in three important areas. The first critical area is the innovation itself, where – despite ongoing efforts and policy initiatives – the region is still lagging well behind the EU. The second of these areas is the labour market. The availability of skilled labour at relatively low costs has been one of the factors raising the region's attractiveness as a destination for foreign direct investment. However, CESEE countries are increasingly experiencing labour shortages on a broad scale and wage dynamics often outpace productivity increases. This risks to lower attractiveness to investors and to impose constraints for domestic firms as they have difficulties finding skilled personnel. Third, we look at the area of financial intermediation, where cross-border inflows have dwindled and had to be replaced by domestic savings, while at the same time the financing of young and innovative companies would require a shift away from the traditional,

joined the EU in 2013. The only exception is aggregate data from the EIB CESEE Bank Lending Survey, which uses a somewhat different definition (see EIB 2018a).

bank-dominated intermediation towards (venture) capital markets. Finally, we highlight some of those policy areas where action is needed to relaunch further catching-up with a new engine of growth.

As countries move upwards on the development ladder, the role of innovation and skilled labour increases in generating productivity improvements and economic growth. Economies of CESEE show a fair amount of heterogeneity when it comes to the distance from the global productivity frontier. Innovation capacity and skills are more likely to be the bottlenecks of growth in the more developed areas of the region, such as the Baltics, the Czech Republic or Slovenia. Romania and Bulgaria may still have sufficient room to base growth and convergence on technology imports, so the fact that they lag behind the rest of the region in terms of indicators of the knowledge-based economy is not yet a key constraint of development. That said, it usually takes decades to build well-functioning innovation ecosystems, our analysis applies to all parts of the region when considering a medium – to long-term view.

3.2 The Pre-crisis Growth Model

Economic growth in CESEE before the crisis was driven chiefly by export, propelled by low wages, capital inflows and technology import. Integration through trade well preceded the actual EU accession. Geographical proximity, reforms and competitiveness helped to integrate quickly into the EU supply chains (particularly into the one of the German automotive manufacturing sector), granting indirect access to global markets. This ushered in an era of export-driven growth, particularly of machinery and transport equipment manufacturing. Over time, the CESEE countries have moved up somewhat the production value chain, with more and more complex technological processes being disseminated to the local subsidiaries of the multinational companies.[2]

The labour market situation – the combination of low wages and a skilled labour force –, catalysed by the EU membership, contributed significantly to the export-led growth model. The transition from central planning to market-based economies was initially accompanied with a severe increase in unemployment and inactivity. Deregulation and privatisation resulted in large job shedding. Yet, it facilitated the development of

---

[2] The development and convergence of the region is documented in detail, among others by Roaf et al. (2014).

the previously practically non-existent private sector through improved conditions for job matching during the times of radical enterprise restructuring. Job shredding also helped putting a check on real wages dynamics, making the relatively skilled labour force of the region highly competitive relative to Western Europe.

At the same time, EU membership brought down the legal barriers and other cross-border frictions, giving CESEE a strong advantage over other geographical regions with similar characteristics. Moreover, the availability of specific skillsets in the region (including command of Western European foreign languages) and geographic proximity made CESEE countries a particularly attractive destination for nearshoring.

Private investment – to a large extent in the form of foreign direct investment – flourished in most CESEE countries, supporting also productivity growth. Investment was largely fuelled by economic and political transition, privatisation, the prospect of EU accession, and financial deepening. Large-scale private greenfield investments helped build up and modernise the capital stock in the CESEE countries, and facilitated rapid export growth. While foreign direct investment had a beneficial impact on capital deepening, even more importantly it also enabled the implementation of new technology and know-how, thereby supporting the rapid increase of total factor productivity (Damijan et al. 2013).

As the convergence process continued, an increasing part of capital inflows were intermediated by the banking sector. The majority of the financial sector became owned by large international banking groups. To take advantage of lending and profit opportunities in these new markets, intra-group funding was channelled to the CESEE subsidiaries, pushing loan-to-deposit ratios well above 100% by the late 2000s. In the years preceding the crisis, capital inflows intermediated by the banking sector have been increasingly used to finance private consumption, property development and housing loans, rather than productivity-enhancing investments.

The pre-crisis growth model came hand-in-hand with high level of external imbalances in some countries of the region. The flipside of large-scale capital inflows was the increase in external deficits and international indebtedness.[3] Initially the capital inflows took the form of foreign direct

---

[3] Current account deficits to GDP ratios reached double-digit GDP levels in Bulgaria, the Baltic States and Romania in the years before the crisis, and elevated to high single digit levels in other countries of the CESEE region, with the exception of the Czech Republic.

investment (FDI). These inflows typically financed productive assets, and reflected long-term commitments from the investors' side. However, in the years before the crisis, growth was largely driven by external borrowing for consumption and construction, and became increasingly unsustainable.

3.3 NEED FOR A WIND OF CHANGE?

With the onset of the crisis, the region experienced a protracted reversal of the strong capital inflows leading to a recession in most CESEE countries. The lack of new funding triggered declines in credit and domestic demand. The output slowdown in the euro area, and deleveraging by Western European parent banks exacerbated and prolonged the sudden stop, and weighed heavily on macroeconomic and financial developments.

Cyclical fluctuations aside, the conditions on which the pre-crisis growth model was based have also changed after the global financial crisis that started in 2008. While some of these changes – such as the slowdown of capital inflows – were direct consequences of the crisis itself, some other ones – for instance demographic changes and migration – are of a structural nature. Emigration from CESEE countries has been a structural trend affecting economies in the region with persistent and large-scale outflows during the last 25 years and accelerating with EU accession.[4]

While the CESEE countries recovered from the downturn by 2014, and are showing a robust cyclical upswing since, their potential growth slowed down significantly during the crisis. Furthermore, the slowdown of potential growth was not particular to a single factor of production. While the decline of total factor productivity (TFP) was the largest, other factors – capital and labour also contribute negatively to the post-2009 decline in potential growth (Fig. 3.1). While the latest estimates of potential growth are now approaching the pre-crisis levels (see Székely and Buti 2019), the upside is much more limited by factor constraints than 15 years ago.

When it comes to the post-crisis level of investment, it appears to be below the level necessary for economic convergence towards the core of the EU.[5] Investment in CESEE has been below the levels experienced in

---
[4] See Atoyan et al. (2016).
[5] Bubbico et al. (2017) covers in detail the post-crisis development of investment in CESEE, and provide estimates of an investment gap.

Fig. 3.1 Factor decomposition of potential GDP growth in a Cobb-Douglas accounting framework (in percentage points). (Source: European Commission. Used with permission from EIB)

countries that successfully graduated from middle income to high income status in the past. Furthermore, for most CESEE economies the current investment levels are not even sufficient to maintain the size of the capital stock relative to GDP under reasonable growth assumptions. As to public investment, European structural and investment funds (ESIF) have played a crucial role in maintaining a healthy level of public investment during the post-crisis downturn in capital availability. Private investment, particularly by the corporate sector, however, declined sharply after the crisis along with foreign private capital inflows, and still has not fully recovered.

Low private investment is partially related to the slowdown of capital inflows. With the advent of the financial crisis, capital flows to the region, both gross and net, collapsed and have remained at a low level. The largest decline came from inward FDI, which was reduced to a third by the 2012–2014 period relative to 2005–2007 (EIB 2016). This decline contributed significantly to the decline of corporate investment, not only through its direct effect but also through an indirect impact: FDI has a catalytic effect on domestic investment that has been reduced with this decline. Large foreign banks changed their strategies for the region, too. They reduced cross-border loans and intra-firm financing of their subsidiaries, switching to a domestically financed banking model for the region. While international banks remained committed to keep their subsidiaries well-capitalised, they started to repatriate profits and in some cases sold their participations to national or international investors. Portfolio investment in the region halved.

Labour markets in CESEE countries are increasingly tight, to the extent that labour shortage became a drag on investment and competitiveness. The post-crisis rise in unemployment reversed, and countries of the region are now close to full employment. Reasons behind the skill shortages are both cyclical and structural.[6] Structurally, emigration and aging have exacerbated shortages. The fast and strong rebound after the crisis increased demand. At the same time, sectoral shifts within CESEE economies – higher job creation in high technology intensive activities and job losses in some traditional activities such as agriculture, mining etc. – can add to shortages as required skillsets are less readily available. Altogether, the abundant, competitive, skilled labour force that fuelled growth from the mid-1990s until the late 2000s in not manifest anymore, and firms have difficulties finding skilled staff.[7]

With the moderation of inwards FDI, the pace of technological change has also slowed down, reflected in lower total factor productivity growth. Lower TFP growth is partially due to the fact that it has become more difficult to find those "low-hanging fruits", where the replacement of old, outdated technology to modern production facilities led to large-one off productivity improvements. The extra productivity gains for any additional FDI are lower now than it used to be around the time of the enlargement. Besides that, exogenous factors, such as the crisis and the related shift in risk perceptions, also contributed to the slowdown of FDI and lower TFP growth as a result. In any case, so far technology importation has not been substituted with home-grown innovation.

The slowdown of potential growth casts the shadow of the middle-income trap over the countries of the region. Despite the cyclical upturn, growth is still lagging behind the levels seen in those countries that successfully graduated from middle income to high income. Furthermore,

---

[6] See EIB (2018b) for further discussion.

[7] That said, unused or underused reserves of labour still exist in most CESEE countries. However, policy actions would be necessary to access these reserves. For instance, unemployment and inactivity is still high in many rural regions, but the large mismatch in skills often prevent the affected population from engaging in the labour market. Previously relocated low-value added FDI, such as white products assembly, could give way to higher value added facilities by leaving and freeing up labour. Furthermore, the public sector employs a significant part of the highly skilled labour force, therefore improving the efficiency of the state could also help alleviating labour shortage in the private sector.

many of the other conditions of a successful continuation of the convergence towards the most developed economies of Europe – for instance, high levels of private investment – are not present either.[8]

In the light of these developments, a prospective "new growth model" is emerging as a candidate to be the driving force of the region's economic convergence for the coming years. Such a model has been put forward by various policy analyses and recommendations in the past years.[9] Although the recommendations differ in the details, some common elements are recurrent. These include, among others, the followings:

- Stronger role for home-grown innovation to increase productivity. While building on the already existing strong manufacturing base, it is time for CESEE economies to begin to move upwards on the value chain. While there is still scope to move upstream in the "functional specialization" in manufacturing (see Stöllinger 2019), the momentum of economic growth can only be maintained with a stronger role of innovation, switching from manufacturing/industrial production towards the – increasingly tradable – services.
- Preservation and development of the productive labour force. A skills-based growth model can only be successful when supported by policies that enable reversing the brain drain, and help to preserve and develop a skilled labour force. Also, policies should address the low participation of certain parts of the population at the labour market. These could include dedicated programmes for the inactive population in underdeveloped rural regions, or programmes aiming at increasing the currently often low female participation in the labour force.

---

[8] The problem of reaching and maintaining a level of economic development that corresponds to high income is not unique to CESEE. Spence (2008) present a broad set of empirically established conditions that can be considered as prerequisites of successfully graduating from the middle-income trap. They derive these from the experience of 13 countries, mostly from the Far East. He highlights the role of high investment levels, in particular to infrastructure, human capital development, early childhood and higher education and healthcare, among others. The EU membership have been helping the countries of CESEE towards meeting these conditions, both directly through providing access to various forms of investment support (ESIF, EIB, EFSI), and indirectly through the four freedoms provided by the single market.

[9] See for example Piatkowski (2014), Bubbico et al. (2017), and EBRD (2017).

- A system of financial intermediation that supports domestic savings. While the region will continue to be a strong potential target for capital inflows, domestic savings should play an increasing role, by providing a stable, local-currency funding source that supports investment.

In the following we will look more deeply at these three areas – innovation, labour market, and financing. We will elaborate more on the challenges the countries of the CESEE region will face in these fields, and suggest policies that may bring them closer to the successful implementation of the "new growth model".

3.4 The Innovation Challenge

Declining technology import has not been successfully substituted with home-grown innovation, and as a consequence, productivity growth has declined together with FDI inflows. Figure 3.2 illustrates the strong association between investment in knowledge and innovation – in the form of intangible assets, such as research, development, software, data, training or business process improvements – and the level of economic development. It also reveals that CESEE economies as a group are lagging behind the rest of the EU.[10]

At the moment, most countries in the CESEE region are regarded as modest or moderate innovators. The European Innovation Scoreboard (EIS) is an annual ranking summarising innovation performance across EU Member States.[11] All of the CESEE countries fall under the categories of "Moderate innovators" (Czech Republic, Estonia, Lithuania, Slovakia, Hungary, Latvia, Poland, Croatia), or "Modest innovators" (Bulgaria and Romania) – except Slovenia, which is the only country in CESEE that qualifies as a "Strong innovator".

Nevertheless, substantial heterogeneity exists in the evolution of innovation performance across CESEE countries. Some countries – such as Lithuania, Slovakia and Latvia – have increased their innovation capacities, while in others – including Slovenia, Poland, Croatia and Bulgaria – innovation performance has stagnated.

---

[10] The crucial role of innovation in the future convergence of CESEE countries is discussed in detail by Correia et al. (2018).
[11] http://ec.europa.eu/growth/industry/innovation/facts-figures/scoreboards_en

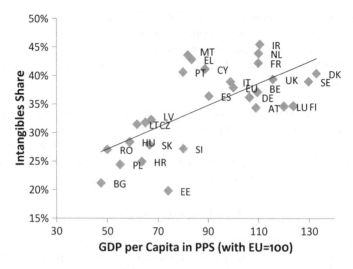

Fig. 3.2 Correlation between GDP per capita and share (%) of intangible investment in total corporate investment, 2017. (Source: EIB Investment Survey, Eurostat. Used with permission from EIB)

The level of digital readiness – a key enabler of innovation in the twenty-first century – varies across CESEE, but with only few countries performing above the EU average. Digital technologies are increasingly becoming innovation drivers. The impacts and dynamics of innovation are changing with the rise and convergence of digital technologies with the physical world: understanding the level of technological readiness is thus a prerequisite to understanding the innovation capacity of an economy. Despite cross-country disparities, the CESEE region has made some progress towards increasing digital capacity and performance. Most CESEE countries still lag behind in their digital competitiveness – with some exceptions. Measured by the EIBIS Digitalisation Index, most CESEE countries are well below the EU average and are far behind the United States (Fig. 3.3). The exceptions are the Czech Republic and Estonia, and to some extent also Croatia and Slovakia, where the Digital Environment Index is above the EU average and above other CESEE countries.[12]

At the regional level, the innovation gap is also significant. Based on the Smart Regions Index (Kollár et al. 2018), the CESEE regions and cities lag behind their EU peers (see Fig. 3.4). In the CESEE, the regions

---

[12] Eurostat, and European Investment Bank.

3 TOWARDS A NEW GROWTH MODEL IN CESEE: THREE CHALLENGES AHEAD   101

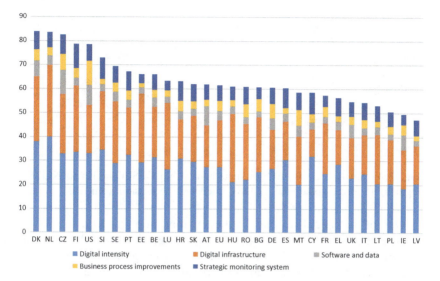

Fig. 3.3 EIBIS digitalisation index, 2019. (Source: European Investment Bank, 2019. Used with permission from EIB. Note: Digital intensity is based on a score assigning value 1 if a firm has implemented in part of its business at least one of 4 digital technologies specific to the sector, and value 2 if the firm's entire business is organised around at least one of the 4 technologies. The results are then summed up, creating a score ranging from 0 to 8, with 8 assigned to the firms that have organised their business around all 4 digital technologies. Digital infrastructure is based on a question whether access to digital infrastructure is an obstacle to investment or not. Investments in software and data and in organisation and business process improvements are measured as a percentage of total investment in the previous fiscal year. Strategic monitoring system is based on a question asking whether the firm uses a formal strategic business monitoring system or not. The five components of the EIBIS digitalisation index are aggregated at the country level and given the following weights: 0.4 to digital intensity, 0.3 to digital infrastructure and 0.1 to the other 3 components)

registering the highest "smartness" scores are located in Slovenia, the Czech Republic and Estonia. In most CESEE economies, the capital regions register the highest score, and a large divide exists between them and the rest of the country. Aggregating the common strengths and weaknesses of the CESEE region, the smartness gap between the CESEE countries and the rest of the EU shows that CESEE regions and cities lag the rest of the EU in all areas (Fig. 3.4).

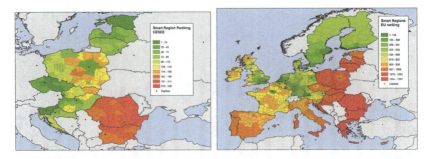

Fig. 3.4 Smart regions (EU rankings and within CESEE rankings, NUTS 3 regions). (Source: Kollár et al. (2018). Used with permission from EIB)

One of the crucial reasons for the low innovation performance in the CESEE region is low investment in intangible assets, such as R&D. As the rest of the EU, CESEE countries are not making sufficient strides to improve their R&D investment and continue to lag significantly behind. R&D intensity in the CESEE region remains significantly below the EU average, with the exception of Slovenia (Fig. 3.5). However, with the exception of Romania, Latvia and Croatia, all the other CESEE countries show some signs of progress in increasing their R&D intensities, particularly after 2007.

There is still substantial room for improvement in the CESEE region when it comes to transforming innovation investment into scientific and technological outputs. In many cases, reforms of their science and innovation system are needed to improve the performance of the scientific and innovation systems.

Private R&D investment plays a lesser role in CESEE than on average in the rest of the EU. Furthermore, foreign financing and public R&D play a much stronger role, notably in certain countries where they account for the vast majority of R&D investment. Compared to the EU average, the CESEE region relies more heavily on government financing and financing from abroad. This reflects, on the one hand, the importance of intra-group financing of R&D due to a large presence of multinationals based in the region, and, on the other hand, the importance of European funding (e.g. the European Structural and Investment Funds) in the financing of much of domestic R&D investment.

When it comes to translating research into business opportunities, CESEE firms are lagging behind the EU average in terms of innovation activity. Correia et al. (2018) show, using data from the EIB Investment

3 TOWARDS A NEW GROWTH MODEL IN CESEE: THREE CHALLENGES AHEAD   103

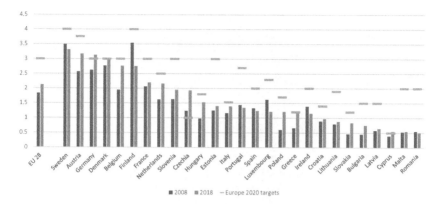

Fig. 3.5 Gross domestic expenditure on R&D, by country, 2008 and 2016. (Source: Eurostat. Used with permission from EIB)

Survey, that the share of firms with active R&D expenditures in all CESEE countries rank below the EU average. About 77% of CESEE firms either do not innovate, or are only adopting innovation from elsewhere, with no active R&D expenditures – compared to an EU average of 72%. Given the slowdown of the pace of convergence and productivity growth after the crisis, sustaining high levels of economic growth going forward will require a shift in the growth model in the region to a model that will need to be increasingly based on innovation and innovation diffusion. This innovation imperative will be crucial if rising prosperity is to be sustained and a fall into the middle income trap is to be avoided. The situation across the region is diverse as many countries find themselves at different stages of development. However, most countries in the region seem to face a development ceiling that can only be broken through innovation driven productivity growth.

Innovation activity in the CESEE countries is driven by manufacturing firms, large companies, but young firms are also in the forefront. Looking at firms with active R&D spending (i.e. leading, incremental and developing innovators), about 64% of active innovators are large firms, almost 18% are medium-size firms and less than 14% are among small firms (Fig. 3.6). About 65% of active innovators are manufacturers, 20% are in the infrastructure sectors and 11% in services (Fig. 3.7).

Firms' readiness to innovate is closely linked to the availability of staff with the right skill sets. Besides uncertainty about the future, an overwhelming majority of CESEE firms asked in the EIB Investment Survey

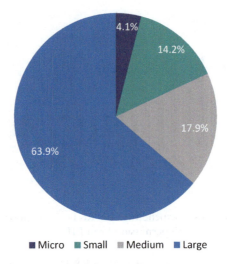

Fig. 3.6 CESEE – Active innovators by firm size, 2019. (Source: EIB Investment Survey, 2019. Used with permission from EIB. Note: Active innovators refer to those that spend actively on R&D and fall into the categories of leading)

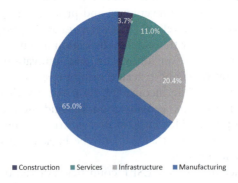

Fig. 3.7 CESEE – Active innovators by sector, 2019. (Source: EIB Investment Survey, 2019. Used with permission from EIB. Note: Active innovators refer to those that spend actively on R&D and fall into the categories of leading)

report availability of skilled staff as the key impediment for investment. Labour market regulations and business regulations are also obstacles that are mentioned by a vast majority of firms. The lack of skilled staff is even more burdensome for more innovative firms. The EIB investment survey reveals that 90% of innovating firms in the CESEE countries are constrained in their investment decisions by the lack of staff with the right skills. This can negatively affect the potential of CESEE firms when it comes to boosting their innovation activity. We elaborate on the factors behind labour and skill shortages in the next section.

3.5 The Labour Market Challenge

Hitherto a large untapped potential, the labour force has become a key constraint to investment and growth. Labour markets in CESEE have increasingly tightened. This is reflected in low unemployment, high job vacancy rates and pronounced wage increases well above the EU average. Recent wage increases reflect to some extent a catch-up after a phase of stagnation following the crisis.[13] However, demographics and migration have contributed to the dynamics.[14] Wage increases have outpaced productivity growth in a number of countries, potentially adding to challenges in competitiveness (EIB 2018b). While labour shortages in CESEE have increasingly broadened, emigration of highly skilled labour, a longstanding feature, can be a bottleneck to move up the value chain. To that extent, we find that innovative firms in the region report skill gaps more often.[15] (See the comments on the role of increasing wages in freeing up labour for higher value added production).

Firms face increasing difficulties in finding personnel. Labour shortages in the region are broad-based across different skill levels. Wage increases are similar or even higher in some low-skilled occupations.[16] Aggregate vacancies are higher and unemployment lower than before the crisis. Vacancy rates are high in some high-skilled categories but also in certain low-skilled ones. Compared to the rest of the EU, more CESEE firms post open positions at all skill levels but positions are sometimes hard to fill. This is particularly the case for higher-level occupations, for which 16% of firms report having long-term vacancies (more than six months to fill positions), i.e. above the EU average (14%).

---

[13] Ibid.
[14] For instance Astrov et al. (2018) find stronger wage dynamics for countries like Romania and Bulgaria that have been strongly affected by emigration.
[15] See EIB (2018b).
[16] Wage increases in the lower skilled occupations may reflect combinations of labour being scarce and country-specific policy measures such as minimum wage increases.

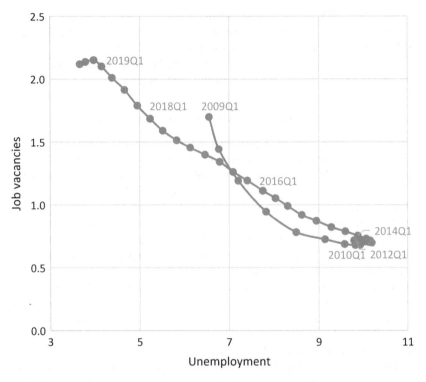

Fig. 3.8 Beveridge curve in CESEE. (Source: Eurostat. Used with permission from EIB. Note: The Beveridge curve shows the coexistence between vacancies and unemployment for CESEE countries from 2009-end of 2018 using four quarter averages.)

Lack of staff with the right skills poses key investment impediment. Beyond short-term effects of skill shortages, e.g. in terms of limiting production in firms and putting pressure on wages, they can also add to difficulties to adopt new technologies and dampen investment, thereby impacting on longer-term growth prospects.[17] The share of firms reporting the limited availability of skills as an investment impediment has been highest in CESEE compared to other EU regions for the last three years and corporate concerns have intensified with more firms reporting the issue as major (Fig. 3.9).

[17] See for instance Nickel and Nicolitsas (2000) for the effect of skill shortages on firms' investment in R&D.

3 TOWARDS A NEW GROWTH MODEL IN CESEE: THREE CHALLENGES AHEAD

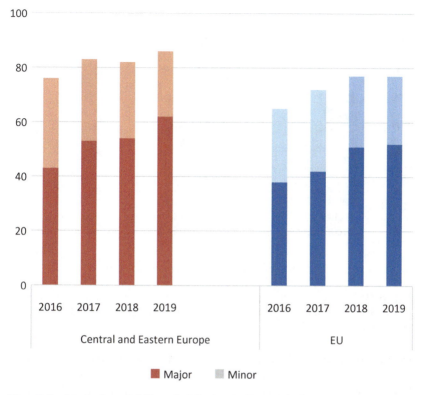

Fig. 3.9 Limited availability of skills in CESEE and the EU. (Source: EIB Investment Survey, 2016–2018. Used with permission from EIB. Note: Percentage of firms reporting the limited availability of skills as an obstacles to investment. Dark colours indicate the share of firms reporting the limited availability of skills as a major obstacle and light colours as a minor obstacle respectively.)

Reasons behind the skill shortages in CESEE are both cyclical and structural. Growth in 2017–18 has been strong, supported by robust domestic demand, favourable external conditions and EU funds inflows. The robust recovery rapidly increased labour demand. At the same time, structural factors have worked to constrain labour supply.

Emigration and population aging strongly affect the region and put pressure on labour supply. CESEE countries have experienced large-scale population outflows. During the last 25 years, almost 20 million people, i.e. about 5.5% of the population, left the region, many of them young and

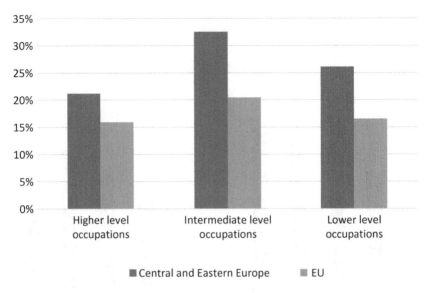

Fig. 3.10 Share of firms reporting mathematics, sciences and technical skills hardest to find. (Source: EIB Investment Survey 2018, special module on digitalisation and skills. Used with permission from EIB)

highly skilled (Batsaikhan et al. 2018; Atoyan et al. 2016). Pressure from brain drain is associated with more firms reporting skill shortages controlling for cyclical factors such as the labour market situation (EIB 2018b). CESEE countries have fertility rates below the EU average. This has led to a decline in overall population, an increase in the old-age dependency ratio and contributed to pressure on labour supply. Furthermore, this tends to be aggravated by poor health outcomes and lower labour force participation in some countries, particularly among women.[18]

Skillsets need to support transition to new growth model. When it comes to recruiting, firms in the region tend to miss job specific skills the most. While this is in line with EU peers (EIB 2018b) notably more firms in the CESEE region report mathematical, science and technical skills as hard to find, (Fig. 3.10), potentially impeding the transition to a more innovation-led growth model. This may point to needs for better

---

[18] Some countries in the region have both low female employment rates (60% or below) and a large wage gap between male and female employees (European Commission 2016).

alignment of education and training systems to market needs. At the same time, a lack of quality job opportunities in the region can be a push factor for emigration, particularly for the young and those with transferrable skillsets that are also in high demand elsewhere.

Education and training systems in the region face multiple challenges. Education systems in CESEE are heterogeneous in terms of funding as well as performance.[19] However, a common challenge for the region is preserving incentives for (sufficient) investment in education against the background of persistent emigration (Brutscher et al. 2019). Also, certain countries such as Estonia, Slovenia and the Czech Republic are close or above the EU average when it comes to lifelong learning, most countries in the region show below average participation (see Fig. 3.11). Possibilities to acquire new skills throughout careers, however, will be increasingly important for workers in the region given changing skill needs due to digitalisation but also pressure from automation, with CESEE countries facing concentrated sectoral exposures (potential car industry restructuring) and relatively high shares of jobs at risk of automation in European comparison (Nedelkoska and Quintini 2018; Pouliakas and Sekmokas 2018).

Attracting, keeping and developing a well-qualified work force is necessary to transition towards more innovation-led growth. About 20% of firms in the region report underinvestment in training. While this is similar to EU peers, firms' investment in training per employee and relative to wages is lower in CESEE. A high share of small firms, differences in management practices as well as retention problems may be factors behind lower investment in employees. Firms in the region tend to be more inclined to resort to automation, step up hiring efforts or improve remuneration and benefits to mitigate skill gaps (Fig. 3.12). Also, in most countries of the region few firms provided training with a view to future skill needs (see Fig. 3.13). Exceptions are Slovenia, the Czech Republic and Slovakia.

Demography and technological change make it eminent for the region to address skill gaps. Countries in the cohesion group are going to face greater pressure from both demography and potential automation than other EU regions. While the latter can also help to overcome labour shortages, it requires investment in the respective technologies, which might be

[19] While Bulgaria and Romania record the lowest levels of spending on education as a share of GDP in European comparison, education investment in the rest of the group except the Czech Republic is above the EU average in 2017.

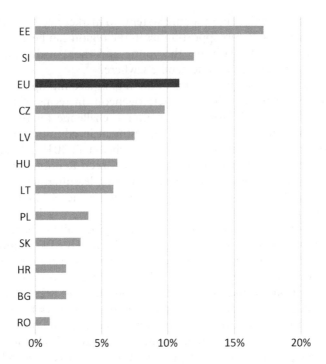

Fig. 3.11 Participation in lifelong learning, last 12 months. (Source: Eurostat. Used with permission from EIB)

challenging in particular for small firms due to a mix of financing and skill constraints. At the same time, where deployment of new technologies lead to worker displacement in the absence of policy measures that would facilitate transitioning to new jobs and acquire respective skills, the social costs can be high.

The labour market challenge in CESEE needs a comprehensive response. Skills are at the heart of a new growth model with greater emphasis on innovation. Nurturing skills in the region requires comprehensive strategies including steps to foster quality and inclusiveness in primary and secondary education, transversal skills in tertiary education and enhancing possibilities for upskilling and reskilling during working lives. Using active labour market policies can help ease labour market shortages by improving matching between jobs and workers, bringing parts of the inactive population in the labour market and providing pathways to better

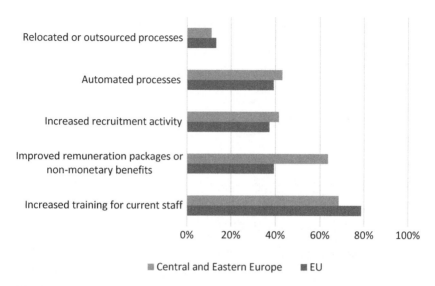

Fig. 3.12 Strategies to cope with skill gaps in current workforce (% of all enterprises. Source: EIB Investment Survey special module (2018). Used with permission from EIB)

jobs. Investment in quality early childhood education and care infrastructure can facilitate (re)entering the labour market for women, support future skill development and more inclusive growth in the long-run. Moreover, investment in social infrastructure, i.e. including education, childcare but also health, can help to mitigate pressure from brain drain, making it more attractive for workers to work and live in the region. Finally, strengthening government effectiveness, institutional quality and the business environment plays a key part to nurture a skilled workforce in the region, establish successful hubs and creative clusters and move into activities that are more knowledge intensive.

3.6 The Financing Challenge

With the advent of the financial crisis, capital flows to the region, both gross and net, collapsed and have remained at a lower level ever since. The largest decline came from inward foreign direct investment (FDI), which was reduced to a third (EIB 2016). This decline dealt a hard blow to corporate investment in CESEE, not only through its direct effect but also

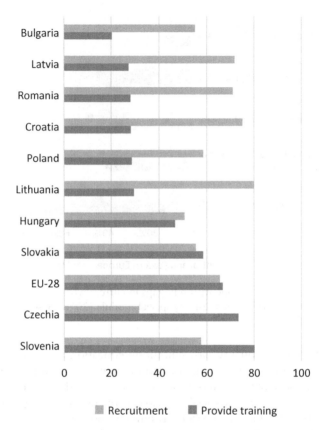

Fig. 3.13 Usual reaction to future skill needs. (% of all enterprises. Source: CVTS (2015). Used with permission from EIB)

through an indirect impact: FDI has a certain catalytic effect on domestic investment that has been reduced with this decline.

When looking at cross-border banking exposures vis-à-vis CESEE, there has also been at a steady decline since 2009.[20] The external position of BIS-reporting banks is down at levels comparable to early 2007 (Fig. 3.14). Self-reported exposures in the EIB-CESEE Bank Lending Survey is consistent with the BIS data. International banks reported on

---

[20] This section builds heavily on the analysis of Gattini et al. (2019), who cover extensively the post-crisis development of cross-border banking in CESEE.

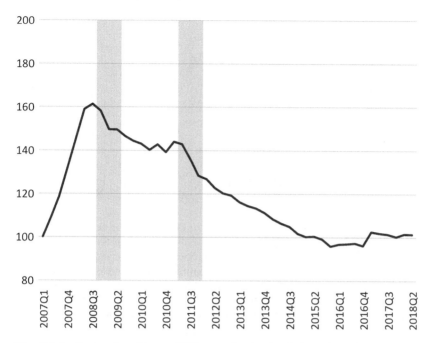

Fig. 3.14 External positions of BIS reporting banks vis-à-vis CESEE countries – index 100=2007Q1. (Source: Authors calculation based on BIS data. Used with permission from EIB. Note: Index 100=2007Q1 based on billions of US$, exchange-rate adjusted, vis-à-vis all sectors; grey bars correspond to the global financial crisis and the Eurozone sovereign debt crisis)

average to decrease their exposure to the CESEE region in the past years, including over the second half of 2018 (Fig. 3.15).

The reduction in bank exposures is specific to debt funding: ownership of the banking system remained predominantly cross-border. While a large part of banking groups operating in the CESEE region have been reducing their regional exposure over the past six years, most of the enduring negative contributions to the CESEE exposures stemmed from reduced intra-group *funding* to subsidiaries (Fig. 3.16). At the same time, most parent banks reported consistently that they have maintained their capital exposure to their subsidiaries. Data from the BLS confirms that on average, international banks contributed positively to their capital position in the CESEE – in stark contrast to the dynamics of intra-group funding.

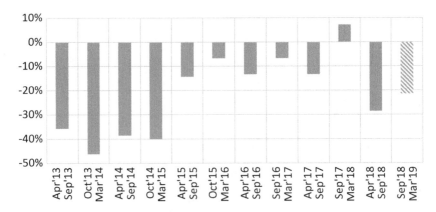

Fig. 3.15 Banking group's total exposure to CESEE (net percentages). Source: Authors' calculation based on EIB – CESEE Bank Lending Survey. Used with permission from EIB. Note: Cross-border operations involving CESEE countries – Net percentages: positive (negative) figures refer to increasing (decreasing) exposure. Question from the survey:: Group's exposure to CESEE: Concerning cross-border operations to CESEE countries, your group did/intends to increase/decrease/maintain the exposure compared to the previous six months

The stability of equity-type banking flows is also reflected in the stable share of foreign bank ownership in the region, which remains exceptionally high by global standards (Fig. 3.17). While there have been some exits in the region, and minor declines in the share of foreign ownership in certain countries, the overall picture have not changed: international banks continue to play a pivotal, determining role in the financial landscape of CESEE.

As a reaction to the crisis experience, self-sustainability became a fundamental drive in global banks' strategic decisions. Cross-border lending flows intermediated by the banking system may have indeed contributed to some extent to pre-crisis imbalances, and as a consequence, to the amplitude of the boom – bust cycles in credit and growth. International banks operating in CESEE have adapted to this lesson by calling for their subsidiaries to implement a more self-sustained financing model, with lending financed mostly via domestic funding – e.g. deposits.

This strategy can be observed in the development of loan-to-deposit ratios (LTDs), which went through a significant rebalancing over the last years. The average regional loan to deposit ratio was relatively high

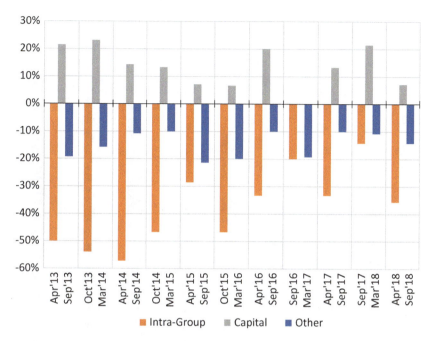

Fig. 3.16 International banking groups' exposure to CESEE by type (net percentages). (Source: Authors' calculation based on EIB – CESEE Bank Lending Survey. Used with permission from EIB. Note: Cross-border operations involving CESEE countries – Net percentages: positive (negative) figures refer to increasing (decreasing) exposure in the specific category. "Other" refers to an average of direct cross border lending to domestic clients and funding to banks not part of the group. Question from the survey:: Group's exposure to CESEE: Concerning cross-border operations to CESEE countries, your group did/intends to increase /decrease/maintain the intra-group/capital/other) exposure compared to the previous six months)

between 2007 and 2014, averaging above 110%, albeit improving over time. In 2016 the average LTD was already close to 100%. The loans-to-deposits ratio has improved further between 2017 and 2018; ultimately stabilising around 100%.

It appears that the more cautious strategy of the banks have contributed to the improvement of credit portfolios' quality. Originally, the crisis led to a marked deterioration in the ratio of non-performing loans (NPLs). The year 2015 was a turning point, and NPLs at an aggregate level have

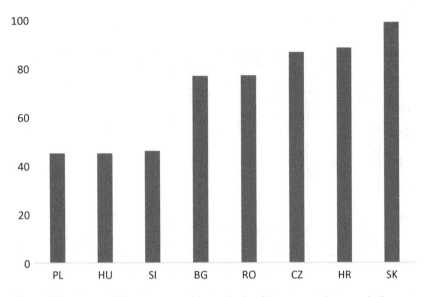

Fig. 3.17 Share of foreign ownership in the banking system (per cent). Source: Raiffeisenbank International. Used with permission from EIB. Note: data refer to 2017 and represent foreign owned assets over total assets

been improving ever since (Fig. 3.18). By mid-2018, the regional aggregate NPL ratios have normalised substantially and reached levels that are broadly in line with the pre-crisis ones. The commercial banks' efforts to eliminate the NPL legacy of the crisis was supported by a substantial set of reforms by domestic regulators. Safer bank lending practices are also reflected in the declining role of loans denominated foreign currency (Fig. 3.19).

Reliance on domestic funding allows for less, but possibly safer credit in the region. Total credit growth in the region has been positive again since 2016. This credit growth is driven primarily by demand, with the supply-side developments lagging behind. This cautious approach of banks has been reflected in the fact that so far credit growth went in parallel with the decline in the share of non-performing loans. Dependence on domestic deposits for lending may also limit the pro-cyclicality of credit dynamics,

3 TOWARDS A NEW GROWTH MODEL IN CESEE: THREE CHALLENGES AHEAD

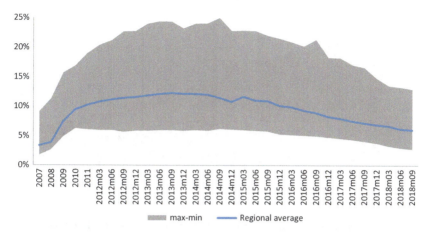

Fig. 3.18 NPL ratio in CESEE. Source: Authors' calculation based on wiiw (Vienna Institute for International Economic Studies) database and national central banks' data. Used with permission from EIB. Note: Regional average computed using EUR based GDP weights (average 2012–2018) and it is based on Albania, Bosnia and Herzegovina, Bulgaria, Croatia, Czech Republic, Hungary, Poland, Romania, Serbia, Slovakia and Slovenia

and could help avoiding overheating, bubbles, and could tie credit flows more in line with potential growth. The presence of additional safeguards and a more cautious approach are also reflected in the very limited role of foreign-currency lending in the recent credit growth.

Is there a role for more cross-border banking in CESEE? Stronger cross-border capital flows, in principle, could foster more rapid convergence of the CESEE economies, and would also strengthen international risk sharing. However, the crisis showed that cross-border capital flows can have detrimental impacts, especially if the institutional framework is not prepared.

If countries of CESEE have the ambition to reap the benefits of even higher level of cross-border capital flows, the pre-conditions and safeguards need to be laid down. This is particularly true when it comes to the regulation of the financial sector: large international capital flows should come hand-in-hand with a high level of international coordination of banking regulation, supervision and resolution policies.

Beyond bank credit, venture and growth capital is an essential financing source for young and innovative companies with high growth potential.

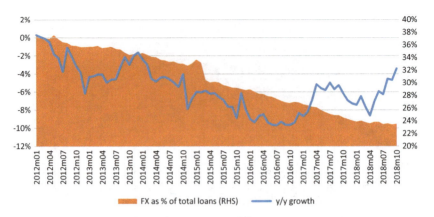

Fig. 3.19 Foreign currency loans to non-financial private sector in CESEE (% of total and y/y growth). Source: Authors' calculation based on WIIW and National Central Banks. Used with permission from EIB. Note: Regional average for shares and growth rates computed using EUR based GDP weights (average 2012–2018) and it is based on Albania, Bosnia and Herzegovina, Bulgaria, Croatia, Czech Republic, Hungary, Poland, Romania, Serbia, Slovakia and Slovenia

Bank (debt) finance is conventionally provided to companies which can demonstrate a consistent financial track record and put up sufficient collateral, and hence not suitable for younger, high growth firms, which lack both track-record and physical assets.[21] These financing forms, notably provided in the form of external equity, are not to be seen as a substitute for traditional, mainly bank-centred, SME financing instruments. Rather, they serve a specific and restricted group of SMEs and mid-caps (including start-ups), which, nevertheless, significantly contribute to the innovativeness, productivity and development of the overall economy.

As the financing of CESEE firms remains largely bank-centric, venture and growth capital markets still lag behind the EU average. Funding for venture and growth capital is coming mainly from outside CESEE, and from public sources. Venture capital volumes in the CESEE have been stagnating in the last few years. Venture capital accounts only for 6% of total private equity volume, with 70% of the recipients being start-ups.

---

[21] Correia et al. (2018) show using data from the EIB Investment Survey that while leading innovators in CESEE rely more on external funding than other firms, they are also more likely to be financially constrained than other companies.

The ICT sector accounts for almost half of the venture capital volume in the CESEE. Nevertheless, the VC market situation in the CESEE region is improving. The recent investment and divestment activity confirms the positive trends of the previous years, despite the significant influence of a limited number of large transactions.

In the CESEE countries, the VC market is characterised by the prevalence of public resources. IFIs and government agencies represent a key component of the VC market. A key feature of the VC market in the CESEE countries is the relatively easy access to seed-stage funds that are mainly backed by EU programs and the European Structural and Investment Funds (ESIF), e.g. under the JEREMIE initiative.

Despite the availability of public financing schemes, CESEE remains underfinanced and far from achieving its full market potential. The VC ecosystem is not yet complete, in particular with regard to later stage VC. While VC funds operating in a broader set of CESEE countries can provide larger investment sizes, VC investors with regional focus often share an investment round by means of co-investment amongst them. According to the EIF VC Survey (EIF 2018), fundraising is the top challenge for VCs in the CESEE region, followed by the number of high-quality entrepreneurs and the exit environment. Successful companies often (have to) move away from the region, partly because of the lack of growth capital funds and a low appetite for the region by non-CESEE and "pan-European" funds.

Improved cooperation between public and private sector is crucial to effectively respond to evolving market demands for financing innovation. For instance, public support available at the pre-seed, seed and early revenue stage, but support could more strongly address later stage VC and growth stage financing.

3.7 Conclusions

The CESEE countries established a record of significant growth and economic progress since their EU accession, and experienced a strong cyclical upswing in the recent years. Foundations of market economy attracted capital and foreign direct investment, which fuelled productivity and GDP growth. While excess consumption and borrowing from the mid-2000s exacerbated the recession following the 2008 crisis in some countries of the region, the CESEE has recovered successfully from the downturn, showing high GDP growth in the last few years.

However, CESEE countries need to revisit their economic models to continue the process of economic convergence. The conditions on which the pre-crisis growth model was based have changed after 2008. Capital flows reversed, technology imports through FDI have slowed down, and profound structural changes reshaped the labour market. In the light of these developments, a prospective "new growth model" is emerging as a candidate to be the driving force of the region's economic convergence for the coming years, based on home-grown innovation, knowledge and skills-based growth, and stronger reliance on domestic savings when it comes to financing the economy.

While domestic research and development is crucial for long-term convergence, the countries of CESEE have still a long way to go to base their productivity growth on home-grown innovation. In most indicators of research, development innovation, CESEE economies as a group are lagging behind the rest of the EU. Currently, innovation is happening mostly in large, foreign owned manufacturing firms. To translate research into tangible innovation, a broader set of private firms need to invest into intangible assets, particularly into R&D.

The labour market is a major bottleneck for long-term growth, and this is a challenge that needs a comprehensive response. Active labour market policies can help ease labour market shortages by improving job matching and bringing parts of the inactive population in the labour market. Investment in quality early childhood education and care infrastructure can facilitate (re)entering the labour market for women and support inclusive growth in the long-run. Moreover, investment in social infrastructure – including also healthcare – can help to mitigate pressure from brain drain. It is crucial to emphasise that strengthening government effectiveness, institutional quality and the business environment also plays a key part to nurture a skilled workforce in the region and to move into activities that are more knowledge intensive.

The post-crisis financing environment provides less, but safer credit through the banking system, yet sources of financing innovation should be established and developed. Capital flows to the region collapsed after 2008 and have remained at a lower level ever since. Reliance on domestic funding allows for less, but safer credit in the region. While credit growth in the region has been positive again since 2016, it appears to subdued. If countries of CESEE have the ambition to reap the benefits of higher cross-border capital flows, the pre-conditions and safeguards need to be laid down in the form of much stronger international coordination banking regulation, supervision and resolution policies. At the same time, strong support to venture and growth capital development is essential to provide financing to young and innovative companies with high growth potential.

REFERENCES

Astrov, V., Holzner, M., Leitner, S., Mara, I., Podkaminer, L., & Rezai, A. (2018, July). *Die Lohnentwicklung in den mittel – und osteuropäischen Mitgliedsländern der EU.* WIIW Research Report in German Language No. 12.
Atoyan, R., Christiansen, L., Dizioli, A., Ebeke, C., Ilahi, N., Ilyina, A., Mehrez, G., Qu, H., Raei, F., Rhee, A., & Zakharova, D. (2016). *Emigration and Its Economic Impact on Eastern Europe.* IMF Discussion Note. Washington, DC: International Monetary Fund.
Batsaikhan, U., Darvas, Z., & Raposo, I. (2018). *People on the Move: Migration and Mobility in the European Union.* Brussels: Bruegel.
Brutscher, P. B., Revoltella, D., & Wruuck, P. (2019, April 5). An EU Tax Credit to Preserve Incentives for Investment in Human Capital in the Context of Intra-EU Migration. *VoxEU.*
Bubbico, R. L., Gattini, L., Gereben, Á., Kolev, A., Kollar, M., & Slacik, T. (2017). *Wind of Change: Investment in Central, Eastern and South Eastern Europe.* EIB Regional Studies.
Correia, A., Bilbao-Osorio, B., Kollár, M., Gereben, Á., & Weiss, C. (2018, December). *Innovation Investment in Central, Eastern and South-Eastern Europe: Building Future Prosperity and Setting the Ground for Sustainable Upward Convergence.* EIB Regional Study.
Damijan, J., Rojec, M., Majcen, B., & Knell, M. (2013). Impact of Firm Heterogeneity on Direct and Spillover Effects of FDI: Micro-Evidence from Ten Transition Countries. *Journal of Comparative Economics, 41*(3), 895–922.
EBRD. (2017). *Transition Report 2017–18: Sustaining Growth.* London: European Bank for Reconstruction and Development.
EIB. (2016). *Investment and Investment Finance in Europe.* Luxembourg: European Investment Bank.
EIB. (2018a). *CESEE Bank Lending Survey H2-2018.* Luxembourg: European Investment Bank.
EIB. (2018b). *EIB Investment Report 2018/2019: Retooling Europe's Economy.* Luxembourg: European Investment Bank.
EIF. (2018). *EIF VC Survey 2018: Fund Managers' Market Sentiment and Views on Public Intervention* (EIF R&MA Working Paper 2018/48). Luxembourg: European Investment Fund.

European Commission. (2016). *Employment and Social Development in Europe 2016: Annual Review 2016* (Chapter 1). Luxembourg: Publications Office of the European Union.

Gattini, L., Gereben, Á., & Revoltella, D. (2019). Cross-Border Banking in CESEE – Through the Lens of the EIB Bank Lending Survey. In *Ten years of the Vienna Initiative 2009-2019*. Luxembourg: European Investment Bank.

Kollár, M., Bubbico, R. L., Arsalides, N. (2018). *Smart Cities, Smart Investment in Central, Eastern and South-Eastern Europe* (EIB Thematic Study). Luxembourg: European Investment Bank.

Nedelkoska, L., & Quintini, G. (2018). *Automation, Skills Use and Training* (OECD Social, Employment and Migration Working Paper No. 202). Paris: OECD Publishing.

Nickell, S., & Nicolitsas, D. (2000). Human Capital, Investment and Innovation: What Are the Connections? In R. Barrell, G. Mason, & M. O'Mahoney (Eds.), *Productivity, Innovation and Economic Performance, National Institute of Economic and Social Research Economic and Social Studies* (Vol. 40, pp. 268–280). Cambridge: Cambridge University Press.

Piatkowski, M. (2014). *"The Warsaw Consensus" – The New European Growth Model* (TIGER Working Paper Series 131).

Pouliakas, K., & Sekmokas, M. (2018). Automation, Skills Demand and Adult Learning. In *Investing in Europe's Future: The Role of Education and Skills*. Luxembourg: European Investment Bank.

Roaf, J., Atoyan, R., Joshi, B., Krogulski, K., & IMF Staff Team. (2014). *25 Years of Transition: Post-Communist Europe and the IMF*. Washington, DC: International Monetary Fund.

Spence, M. (2008). *The Growth Report: Strategies for Sustained Growth and Inclusive Development*. Washington, DC: World Bank.

Stöllinger, R. (2019). *Functional Specialisation in Global Value Chains and the Middle-Income Trap*. WIIW Research Reports 441, The Vienna Institute for International Economic Studies, WIIW.

Székely, I., & Buti, M. (2019, June 28). Trade Shocks, Growth, and Resilience: Eastern Europe's Adjustment Tale. *VoxEU, CEPR*.

CHAPTER 4

Regional Dynamics in EU11

Dino Pinelli and Gábor Márk Pellényi

4.1 INTRODUCTION

This chapter analyses the dynamics of regional disparities in the member states that joined the European Union in or after 2004, excluding Cyprus and Malta (EU11). Regional disparities are a crucial perspective of the assessment of real convergence. Through proximity, social and economic inequalities are magnified. Mobile, skilled people move to high-wage areas, further reinforcing the region's growth potential. Low-skilled people are less equipped to move and may remain locked in low-income areas, which further reduces their opportunities over their life-time. Recent

---

The views expressed are solely those of the authors and do not necessarily represent the official views of the European Commission. We would like to thank István P. Székely, Michael Landesmann, Gianmarco I.P. Ottaviano, Septimiu Szabo, Andrea Mairate and Angel Catalina Rubianes for their very helpful comments. Any errors or omissions are ours alone.

D. Pinelli (✉) • G. M. Pellényi
DG ECFIN, European Commission, Brussels, Belgium
e-mail: Dino.PINELLI@ec.europa.eu; Gabor-Mark.PELLENYI@ec.europa.eu

© The Author(s), under exclusive license to Springer Nature Switzerland AG 2021
M. Landesmann, I. P. Székely (eds.), *Does EU Membership Facilitate Convergence? The Experience of the EU's Eastern Enlargement - Volume I*, Studies in Economic Transition,
https://doi.org/10.1007/978-3-030-57686-8_4

research also shows how the spatial organisation of inequalities is relevant for people's perspectives and voting behaviour (Dijkstra et al. 2020).

The Treaty of the European Union itself stipulates upfront (Art. 3) that the Union should "promote economic, social and territorial cohesion". In particular, it "shall aim at reducing disparities between the level of development of the various regions and the backwardness of the least favoured regions" (Art. 174). Territorial cohesion is thus at the heart of the European project. Around one-third of the EU budget is devoted to this objective.

Economic theory is not conclusive on the impact of economic integration on regional disparities. Neo-classical growth models would predict convergence in income per capita. Capital and labour would move to low and high-wage locations, respectively, bringing about income equalisation across regions over time. On the other hand, endogenous growth models and new economic geography theory emphasise how increasing returns and benefits from the proximity of firms and people may sustain agglomeration. These forces are likely to act at different spatial levels. The processes of learning and knowledge transmission through informal interaction are very localised and thus likely to underpin the agglomeration of knowledge-intensive activities in urban areas. Conversely, the positive externalities deriving from the proximity of labour, customers and suppliers may act on a larger geographical scale.

Empirically, most studies found that convergence in income per capita across regions was prevailing until at least the 1980s, both within western Europe and the US. Thereafter, the process has stalled or even reverted, with a combination of globalisation and technological change underpinning this "great divergence" within countries (Moretti 2012), benefiting mostly urban agglomerations (Desmet et al. 2018). This seems to occur within a broader "great convergence" process taking place across countries, with some less developed countries catching up to more developed ones (Baldwin 2016). In Europe, Eurofound (2018) documents a process of divergence in income per capita across the EU regions over the period 1995–2015. The 7th Report on Economic, Social and Territorial cohesion by the European Commission (2017) shows, however, a broad process of convergence in income per capita and employment across EU regions over 2000–2008, which was interrupted by the crisis, and then recovered somewhat in the latest years. Taking a long-term perspective, Rosés and Wolf (2018) highlights that the traditional core-periphery pattern is opening to a more complex articulation characterised by an increasing role of within-country differences, cross-border regional clusters and "islands of prosperity" surrounded often by less developed areas.[1]

With regard to EU11 only, European Commission (2017) documents an overall process of regional convergence in income per capita over the period 2000–2008. This seems to have continued in 2008–2015, although with some weak spots. While cross-country disparities seem to be declining (Forgó and Jevčák 2015), many studies find evidence that they have been increasing within countries (Kotosz and Lengyel 2017; Bourdin 2019). The distance from the former Iron Curtain (Bourdin 2015, 2019) and the degree of urbanisation appear to have played a role. In particular, large urban areas and, notably capital cities, drove growth before the crisis. Capital cities however suffered most during the crisis while rural and urban areas close to cities showed more resilience (European Commission 2017; Dijkstra et al. 2015; Bourdin 2019). To a large extent, such internal regional divides had started to grow already in the transition phase (Ezcurra et al. 2007; Cuaresma et al. 2014; Artelaris et al. 2010). Bourdin (2019) finds that inter-territorial dependency, i.e., the extent to which development in one region affects the surrounding regions, has declined over 2000–2014 but remains robust.

This chapter complements the previous literature by integrating different methodologies and indicators to distil the key stylised facts that characterise regional dynamics in the EU11 before and after accession. The analysis shows that while differences between countries have been shrinking, regional disparities within countries have been increasing. In particular, there is evidence of a strong and growing divide between urban and rural areas, at least until the crisis. A similar picture emerges if one looks at the employment rate instead of income per capita. Consistently, population dynamics also point to increasing within-country agglomeration, with the areas that had lower income per capita in 2000 (prevailingly rural) experiencing very sizeable population outflows over the subsequent 15 years. While a region's prosperity depends on and affects that of neighbour regions, this spatial dependency has been declining over time, with

---

[1] This review is not exhaustive. Among many contributions, an important recent review of theoretical and empirical research is in Breinlich, Ottaviano and Temple (2014). Less recent, but more comprehensive, reviews of empirical research are in Magrini (2004), and, focused on Europe, Monfort (2008). Recent contributions include Ottaviano (2019), Alfaro, Chen and Fadinger (2019), Demertzis, Sapir and Wolff (2019). The definition of convergence, empirical methodology and findings vary across papers. Only the trends that are broadly consistent across papers, sometimes with many exceptions, are reported above.

geographical clusters of prosperous (poor) regions breaking up into more a granular spatial organisation.

In what follows, Section 4.2 analyses regional disparities in terms of GDP per capita. Sections 4.3 and 4.4 analyse respectively regional dynamics in labour market outcomes and demography. Section 4.5 provides a first summary of results. Section 4.6 brings geography into the picture and analyses patterns of spatial dependency. Throughout, regions are defined at NUTS 3 level, corresponding to megye in Hungary, podregiony in Poland, provinces in Italy or counties in the UK. This level of disaggregation is finer than in most of the other studies reported above. This allows distinguishing urban from rural areas within the larger NUTS 2 region comprising them. For instance, the NUTS 2 region Central Hungary includes the capital, Budapest, and the surrounding, less urbanised area, Pest county.[2] The data cover 2000–2015 (or 2016, when available). They are from the Annual European Regional Database (ARDECO), maintained by the European Commission.[3]

4.2 Convergence and Divergence in Income Per Capita

A crucial question in the assessment of regional convergence is whether disparities in the purchasing power of people living in different regions are diminishing or increasing. This is the primary focus of this first part. To this purpose, the regional GDP per capita is used to approximate purchasing power, the most widely used approach in literature.[4] Convergence is defined as reduction in disparities. In the economic literature, this is usually referred to as σ-convergence.[5] To measure regional disparities, the

---

[2] As a caveat, similar to all administrative units, even NUTS 3 regions may have arbitrary boundaries that do not correspond to actual geographical areas of economic activity.

[3] The database is available at: https://ec.europa.eu/knowledge4policy/territorial/ardeco-database_en. Data were downloaded in July 2019.

[4] In order to approximate better the average citizen's purchasing power across locations, GDP is usually corrected for differences in prices. Price indexes are however available only at national level. Since prices tend to be higher in higher income areas, it is likely that our measure of GDP per capita overestimates differences in real purchasing power at regional level.

[5] An alternative definition of convergence is β-convergence. There is β-convergence when the regions that were initially poorer are growing faster. It has been shown that σ-convergence is a sufficient condition for β-convergence. For a comprehensive review of the definitions and measurements of regional convergence, see Eurofound (2018).

Theil index is used, which is a standard measure of income inequality in the economic literature. Compared to other measures of inequality, the main advantage of this index is that it is decomposable by subgroup (Monfort 2008). In order to focus on regional disparities, rather on overall inequality, regions are not weighted by their population (Breinlich et al. 2014). Figure 4.1 shows that the rapid and continuous convergence of the EU11 average GDP per capita to the EU average (from just above 30% in 1995 to almost 70% in 2015) was accompanied by a broad process of declining internal regional disparities within the region as a whole, starting some years before accession and continuing thereafter. To a different degree, around 90% of the NUTS 3 regions in the EU11 managed to converge to the EU average. Although there is some sign of increasing dispersion since 2011, this could seem a success story at first sight.

It is possible to decompose the Theil index to its between-countries and within-countries components. Figure 4.2 shows that the declining

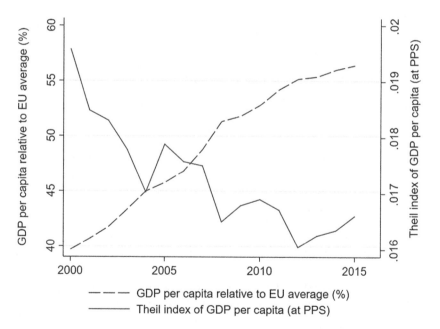

Fig. 4.1 Average and regional dispersion of GDP per capita in the EU11. (Source: Own calculations on data from the Annual European Regional Database, European Commission)

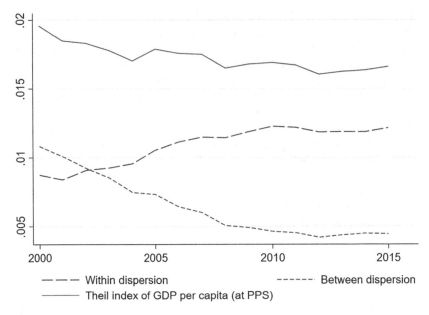

Fig. 4.2 Regional dispersion of GDP per capita within and between EU11 countries. (Source: Own calculations on data from the Annual European Regional Database, European Commission)

overall dispersion was driven by the decreasing differences between the EU11 countries, while disparities within countries have been increasing after 2000. A possible explanation is that while investment was indeed flowing from richer countries to EU11 searching for higher returns and lower wages (as neoclassical growth models would predict), it went into selected areas to benefit from localised agglomeration, increasing spatial disparities within countries (see Section 4.7).

Figure 4.3 shows the decomposition of the dispersion index when regions of the EU11 countries are classified depending on their level of urbanisation.[6] A nice symmetry can be noticed with Fig. 4.2. Here, disparities are increasing between groups, which are however becoming more equal internally. Investment seems to have gone into more densely

---

[6] Regions are categorised in four groups: in addition to urban, intermediate and rural (according to European Commission 2017, p. 21) regions, the NUTS 3 regions including the capital cities are treated separately from urban regions.

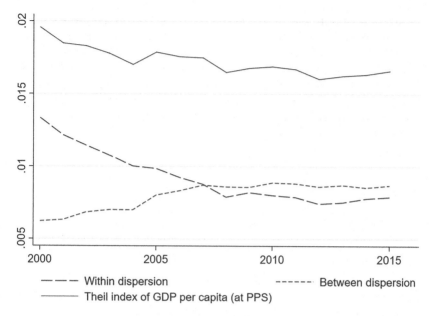

Fig. 4.3 Regional dispersion of GDP per capita in the EU11: within and between groups based on different levels of urbanisation. (Source: Own calculations on data from the Annual European Regional Database, European Commission)

populated areas in low wage countries, thereby forcing income per capita equalisation across similar areas in different countries. Since around 2010, disparities have stopped falling, both between countries and within groups of regions with similar levels of urbanisation. This is consistent with the finding of Dijkstra, Garcilazo, and McCann (2015) that, since the great financial crisis, capital cities strongly underperformed other metropolitan regions and rural areas close to cities outperformed other rural areas.

Indicators such as the Theil index offer very informative summaries of the underlying income distribution. However, they may also hide relevant information. For instance, a certain value of the dispersion index could be associated with regions clustering either around one or more values. In the second case, one could say that regions are forming different development "clubs" or that there is some form of "polarisation", whereby regions cluster together with either very rich or very poor regions. Some studies found that European regions showed a bimodal distribution of income per capita, at least until the 1990s (Eckey and Türck 2007). Figure 4.4 shows that this bimodality of the distribution was still evident in EU11 regions in 2000 but has disappeared over time.[7] This is even more evident when regions are categorised by their degree of urbanisation. In 2015, bimodality remains only for rural regions, with a very numerous group of very poor rural regions (Fig. 4.5). The figure for 2015 also shows a thick right tail of very rich urban regions, which are typically the capital cities (see also Kotosz and Lengyel 2017).[8]

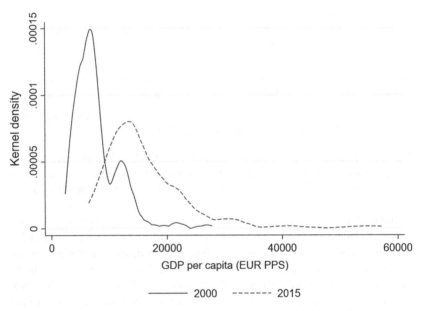

Fig. 4.4 Distribution of regional GDP per capita in the EU 11, 2000 and 2015. (Source: Own calculations on data from the Annual European Regional Database, European Commission)

[7] This seems a long-term trend. Ezcurra, Pascual and Rapún (2007) found multimodality in the regional distribution of income per capita in 1900, which substantially weakened by 2001.

[8] GDP per capita in capitals could be inflated by the concentration of company headquarters in these cities. This concentration allocates a disproportionate share of gross operating surplus to capitals, even though these firms may operate in several regions.

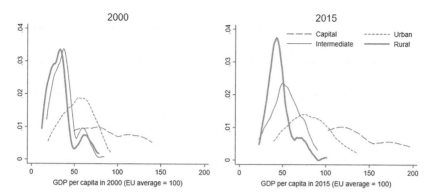

Fig. 4.5 Distribution of regional GDP per capita in the EU11, by level of urbanisation. (Source: Own calculations on data from the Annual European Regional Database, European Commission)

4.3 Convergence and Divergence in the Labour Market

This section complements the analysis of living standards by looking at convergence/divergence patterns in labour market outcomes. These are important from two viewpoints. Directly, unemployment and non-employment rates[9] per se (i.e., given the same income level), have been found to matter for a wide range of indicators of well-being, including crime, mortality, body weight, smoking initiation, as well reported happiness at individual and community level (Council of Economic Advisers 2016; Austin et al. 2018). Indirectly, the capacity of the labour market to allocate efficiently the labour force within and across regions is an important determinant of regional income per capita dynamics. Therefore, differences in labour market outcomes may contribute to explaining regional income disparities. For instance, Austin, Glaeser and Summers (2018) emphasise that enduring cross-regional differences in the non-employment rate underpin the deterioration of income per capita convergence process in the US.

---

[9] The unemployment rate is the number of persons not working but actively searching for employment, as a percentage of the labour force (unemployed plus those in paid or self-employment). The non-employment rate is the number of those not working (irrespective of whether they are searching for work) as a percentage of the working-age population.

Figure 4.6 shows that the average employment rate in the EU11 fell after the economic transition but has been converging to the EU average after accession. This convergence was interrupted during the crisis but it has recovered more recently. The overall dispersion of the employment rate remains quite stable after 2004, with declining between-countries dispersion broadly counterbalanced by increasing within-countries dispersion (Fig. 4.7). Looking into the urban-rural divide, dispersion has increased between groups while decreasing within, at least until the crisis (Fig. 4.8).

The convergence/divergence patterns for the employment rate are very much consistent with those found for GDP per capita in Section 4.2. The decline in cross-country disparities is however smaller, resulting in more persistent disparities overall than it was the case for GDP per capita. Given that local incomes per capita are positively correlated with employment rates, it could be deduced that labour demand factors are likely to play a bigger role than labour supply factors in explaining employment trends (Austin et al. 2018). Indeed, if labour supply factors were the main driver, the correlation would more likely be negative, because excess labour supply would lead to lower wages and thus lower income per capita.

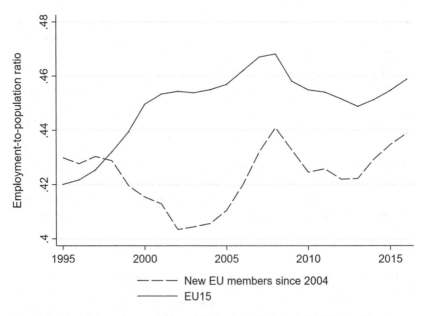

Fig. 4.6 Employment-population ratio in the EU11 and old EU member states. (Source: Own calculations on data from the Annual European Regional Database, European Commission)

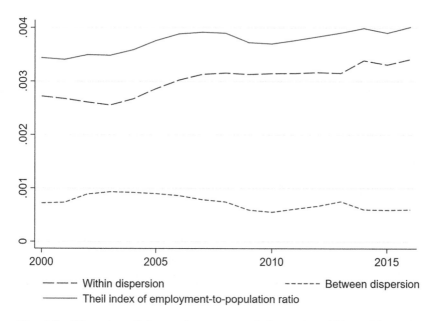

Fig. 4.7 Dispersion of the employment-population ratio, within and between EU 11 countries. (Note: Romania is excluded due to data issues. Source(s): Own calculations on data from the Annual European Regional Database, European Commission)

4.4 Agglomeration and Population Dynamics

If labour is mobile, which is likely to be the case across regions, regional advantages are reflected in population and local price dynamics rather than in income per capita, as labour moves to higher wage locations forcing real income equalisation across regions, ceteris paribus. Disparities in GDP per capita may therefore underestimate the real extent of regional divides. It is therefore important to investigate population dynamics to complement the income per capita analysis.[10]

---

[10] To see why, consider two opposing cases. First, assume that labour is fully mobile and individuals' utility is determined only by their real income (purchasing power). One would expect people to move to higher productivity places where they reap higher nominal incomes. This migration would continue until the prices of localised goods (e.g., land, property, local services) change sufficiently to equalise real income across locations. Second, assume instead that localities have the same productivity level but different non-monetary amenities. Then,

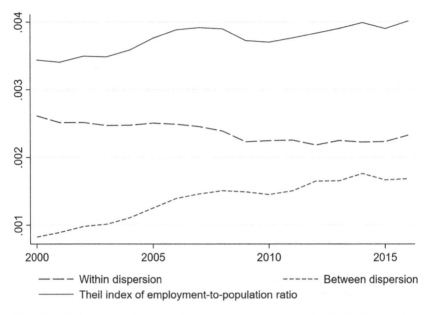

Fig. 4.8 Dispersion of the employment-population ratio in the EU 11, within and between groups based on different levels of urbanisation. (Note: Romania is excluded due to potential data issues. Source: Own calculations on data from the Annual European Regional Database, European Commission)

Figure 4.9 shows that the relation between income per capita in 2000 and net migration over the period 2000–2015. On average, EU11 regions have experienced negative net migration, with important differences, however. In particular, urban regions, typically rich, have been net beneficiaries of migration, while rural regions, typically poorer, have experienced important outflows (even 10–20% of 2000 population, see also Desmet

people may accept lower income in exchange for better amenities (e.g. better climate or nicer landscapes). The joint behaviour of local prices and local population dynamics can differentiate between these two cases. If higher income per capita is accompanied by higher population growth, productivity differences would be the main driver of local differences in income per capita. If higher income per capita is instead accompanied by lower population growth, local non-monetary amenities would be the main driver. In this chapter, we find that local population dynamics and incomes are positively correlated, which would suggest that they primarily reflect productivity differences. For a more complete explanation of these mechanisms, see for instance, Breinlich, Ottaviano and Temple (2014).

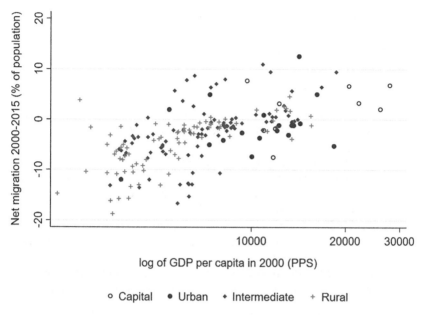

Fig. 4.9 Net migration and GDP per capita in the EU 11 regions. (Source: Own calculations on data from the Annual European Regional Database, European Commission)

et al. 2018). A very large number of intermediate regions, and in particular those with lower income per capita, have also seen large population declines. Initial income per capita and population density are not the only determinants of migration rates. The between-country component explains 45% of the variance in migration rates among regions of the EU11. Housing market characteristics at the national level could be relevant factors. The depth of the rental market and the extent of planning restrictions may affect migration decisions, particularly towards fast-growing urban areas (Moretti 2011; Austin et al. 2018).

The locational Gini coefficient (Krugman 1991) can be used to calculate the extent to which a certain quantity is agglomerated regionally (the index is equal to 1 when the quantity is agglomerated in one region and 0 when it is equally distributed across regions). Consistently with the above, the locational Gini coefficient for population has increased over the period, from 0.31 in 2000 to 0.34 in 2015. The locational Gini coefficient for

GDP is higher (0.49 in 2000 and rising to 0.52 by 2015), showing that GDP is more agglomerated than population (consistently with the fact that richer regions tend to be more densely populated).

4.5 Some Regional Groupings

Table 4.1 summarises the previous findings. Following European Commission (2017) and Iammarino, Rodríguez-Pose and Storper (2019), regions are grouped by their income per capita in 2015. On average, the richer are the regions, the higher their population density, net migration, and employment-to-population ratio (in level and change). Concerning GDP per capita, however, the top and bottom category show higher growth than the intermediate ones. This is consistent with European Commission (2017). The relatively high growth of GDP per capita in the poorest regions can however be explained by a denominator effect, given the sizeable population decline. Furthermore, income per capita growth in the numerous medium-income regions is slightly higher than in high-income regions, which could explain the declining Theil index overall.

4.6 Bringing in Geography

The preceding sections analysed regional disparities without taking into account geography. This Section takes a step further and tries to uncover any spatial relations underpinning regional disparities. Figure 4.10 maps EU11 regions according to whether their level and growth of GDP per capita are above or below the national average.[11] Type 1 regions are richer and growing faster than the national average. They are increasingly standing out, moving farther ahead of the rest. Type 4 regions are poorer and growing slower than the national average: they are left behind. A lot of Type 1 and 4 regions would imply therefore that disparities are increasing. On the contrary, a lot of Type 3 (poor regions growing faster than average) and Type 2 (rich region growing slower than average) regions would imply increasing convergence. On Fig. 4.10, two-thirds of regions are either Type 1 or 4, which is consistent with our previous finding of

---

[11] The position of regions (poor/rich and fast/slow growing) is always relative to their national average. This implies that a Type 1 region in Country A may grow slower than a Type 4 region in Country B, if Country B national average growth is sufficiently higher than Country A national average growth.

Table 4.1 Summary statistics

	Average growth of GDP per capita, 2000–2015 (%)	Population density (person per sq. km)	Average population change, 2000–2015 (%)	Net migration rate, 2000–2015 (%)	Average employment-to-population ratio (%)	Average change in employment-to-population ratio (p.p.)	Number of regions
Capitals	5.5	2004	0.1	2.1	62.3	0.6	11
Other very high income	5.4	1046	0.1	0.4	48.7	0.4	11
High income	4.6	241	0.0	1.9	44.9	0.1	33
Medium income	4.8	95	-0.3	-2.4	38.5	0.1	113
Low income	4.8	60	-1.1	-6.5	39.7	0.0	70

Note: The classification of regions is based on regional GDP per capita in 2015, relative to the EU11 average. Very high income: GDP per capita above 150% of average for EU11; this group includes all 11 capitals, and 11 other regions. High income: between 120% and 150% of group average (33 regions). Medium income: between 75% and 120% of group average (113 regions). Low income: below 75% of group average (70 regions)

Source: Own calculations on data from the Annual European Regional Database, European Commission

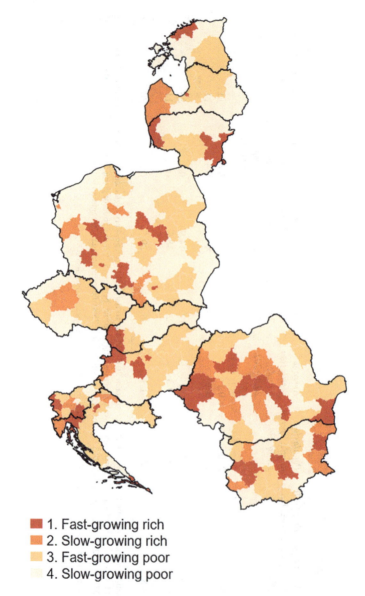

Fig. 4.10 Growth and levels of GDP per capita in EU11 regions. (Note: With reference to the year 2000 for the level of GDP per capita and to the period 2000–2014 for its growth, regions are classified as: Type 1 = regions with GDP per capital level and growth above national average; Type 2 = regions with GDP per capital level above the national average and growth below; Type 3 = regions with GDP per capita level below the national average and growth above; Type 4 = regions with GDP per capita level and growth below the national average. Source: Own calculations on data from the Annual European Regional Database, European Commission)

increasing internal divergence. There is no clear geographical pattern, which is our interest in in this section. Nevertheless, one can see that most capital cities are Type 1 and generally, but not always, surrounded by Type 1 or Type 3 regions, which could imply that growth is spilling over from the core urban areas to the surroundings. Furthermore, regions on the former Iron Curtain (i.e., at the borders with Austria and Italy) tend to be richer and/or growing faster. This is not true for the regions bordering with eastern Germany. There are also many slow-growing and poor regions along the external border of the EU, suggesting that it may be an obstacle for their economic development.

Moran's I is an index that provides a formal statistical testing of spatial correlations. A high value of Moran's I indicates strong similarity among neighbouring regions, e.g. that the GDP per capita (growth) of one region is significantly correlated with the GDP per capita (growth) in surrounding regions. This would correspond to clusters of geographically close rich (fast-growing) or poor (slow-growing), economies.

The Moran scatterplot maps regional GDP against the weighted average GDP of neighbouring regions (with weights inversely related to geographical distance).[12] If there is spatial dependency, the dots are scattered around an upward-sloping line (rich regions are surrounded by other rich regions). The 45° diagonal indicates perfect correlation (the region's GDP per capita is equal to the weighted average of GDP per capita in neighbour regions). The slope of the fitted line is the estimate of the Moran's I. The charts show that there is significant spatial dependency, as indicated by the positive slope of the interpolating line, which declined from 2000 to 2015.[13]

The vertical and horizontal lines are drawn at the respective averages. They divide the regions into four groups:

---

[12] Neighbouring regions more than 200 kilometres away are not considered for this analysis, their weights are set to zero. This implies that spillovers are considered negligible beyond this threshold. As a robustness check, various thresholds were tried between 100 and 500 kilometres, but the results did not change materially. The calculations also take into account the GDP per capita in bordering regions in Western Europe.

[13] In 2000, the slope coefficient I = 0.505 with a standard deviation of 0.033 (z = 15.441, significant at all levels). By 2015, the slope had halved (0.238) while remaining statistically significant (standard deviation of 0.033, z = 7.394, significant at all levels).

- HH (high-income regions, with high-income neighbours). These are the areas characterised by positive agglomeration: rich regions tend to be close and benefit each other.
- LL (low-income regions, with by low-income neighbours). These could be called depression zones, with poor regions surrounded by other poor regions.
- HL (high-income regions, with low-income neighbours). These could be called "islands of prosperity", where rich regions are not benefiting their surroundings.
- LH (low-income regions, with high-income neighbours), these are deprived regions among richer neighbours.

The main difference between the two charts is in the number of outliers on the right. While regions close to the average level of development are surrounded by similarly rich regions in both charts, by 2015 the richest regions have moved further away and are like islands, their neighbours are nowhere near as rich as them. This implies that the spatial spillovers from the most developed regions could be weak. This group of rich regions seems to be the main driver of the declining spatial dependency detected above.

The localised Moran's I indicates whether a region's GDP per capita is correlated with surrounding regions' GDP per capita. Figure 4.12 shows the maps of localised Moran's I for 2000 and 2015. Regions are classified in three categories: the various shadings indicate either that the region's high (low) GDP per capita is significantly correlated with the high (low) GDP per capita of surrounding regions (this correspond to the HH (LL) regions in Fig. 4.11 with statistically significant spatial dependency), or that a rich region is surrounded by relatively poor regions (HL regions in Fig. 4.11).[14] The white indicates that the region's GDP per capita is independent of the income of its neighbours. The maps for 2000 and 2015 are very different and confirm that the spatial correlation has substantially declined over the last 15 years, as shown in Fig. 4.11. While in 2000 poor/rich regions were robustly clustered, such clusters have broken up and poor/rich regions are now more randomly distributed.[15] In 2000,

---

[14] The calculations take into account the GDP per capita in bordering regions in Western Europe.

[15] Rosés and Wolf (2018) also find evidence of weakening spatial dependency in the EU as a whole over the long term (1900–2010).

4 REGIONAL DYNAMICS IN EU11   141

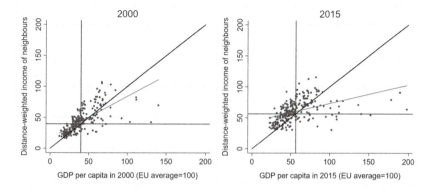

Fig. 4.11 Spatial dependency among EU11 regions – Moran's scatterplot. (Source: Own calculations on data from the Annual European Regional Database, European Commission)

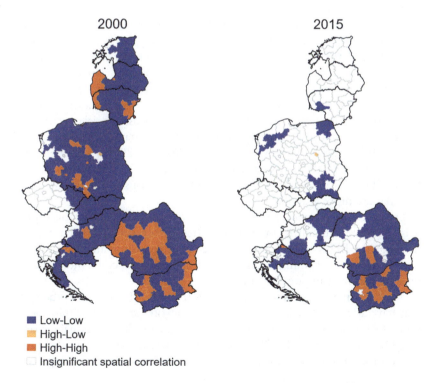

Fig. 4.12 Spatial clusters – localised Moran's I. (Source: Own calculations on data from the Annual European Regional Database, European Commission)

only the regions close to the former Iron Curtain were characterised by this finely grained articulation, possibly anticipating the dynamics that then spread out. There remain some clusters of poorer regions in Romania and Bulgaria, which are on average less developed that the rest of the EU11. There are clusters also in parts of Poland and Slovakia, Hungary and Croatia. These clusters appear to cross national borders, which may call for strengthening interregional cooperation.

4.7 Conclusions

Our findings are broadly in line with theoretical expectations and previous empirical findings, as discussed in Section 4.1. The decreasing return mechanisms emphasised by neo-classical growth theories could explain the convergence in income per capita across countries. At the same time, the benefits that firms and workers enjoy from locating closer to each other create powerful agglomeration effects that may underpin the increasing disparities within countries.

The spatial scale of agglomeration depends on the reach of agglomeration effects. In recent decades, technological progress and globalisation have reduced the costs of transporting goods and increased the relative importance of people and knowledge in the economy. This could have enhanced the importance of easy very short distance personal interactions relative to that of easy good transportation over longer distance (Glaeser 2011, 2013; Combes et al. 2011). This would boost the relative importance of e.g., conurbation, whose high density facilitates the transmission of knowledge and the matching of people (Brülhart 2009). These mechanisms may explain why spatial dependency across NUTS 3 regions has been reduced, with previous blocks of similar regions breaking into clusters that are more granular in space.

Developing a proper counterfactual was beyond the scope of this paper, it is therefore difficult to say whether these processes have been engendered by the EU accession. The consistency with existing literature, covering a broader set of countries and the transition period, could indicate that broader mechanisms are at work.

There are nevertheless several channels through which EU membership may have affected these processes. The EU devotes around one third of its budget to regional funds explicitly put in place to address regional disparities. Over the period 2014–2020, around half of these funds are attributed to EU11 countries. A vast literature has attempted to assess the impact of

EU funds on regional growth and convergence. The available evidence supports the conclusions that on average EU funds had a positive impact on the economic growth of less developed regions, thereby contributing to overall convergence. At the same time, it also points out that the impact of the funds is heterogeneous across regions. In particular, the impact of funds seems bigger in regions with better institutions, lower local corruption, higher human capital and closer to urban agglomeration, which would tend to reinforce existing disparities within countries (Becker et al. 2012, 2013, 2018; Bourdin 2019; Gorzelak 2017; Gagliardi and Percoco 2017).

A second channel concerns foreign direct investment (FDI). Chapter 3 in Volume II shows that (the perspective of) EU accession fostered FDI greatly. As a share of GDP, the FDI stock increased very rapidly from 4% of GDP in 1992 to almost 53% in 2017. This represented a powerful growth driver in these countries, facilitating their catching up to the rest of the EU. At the same time, FDI located primarily in or close to urban agglomerations, where they could benefit from the concentration of human capital and infrastructures and related agglomeration economies. The largest stocks are indeed in the regions including the capital cities. The local availability of skills and knowledge did not only attract FDI to those regions, it also facilitated technology transfers and technology absorption by local domestic firms, which further reinforced their positive impact on these locations (Tondl and Vuksic 2007; Bourdin 2015). FDI continued to flow but at a much lower rate after 2007, reaching 53% of GDP in 2017. This could help explain why the increase in rural/urban disparities flattened somehow after the crisis, in line with the findings of Dijkstra, Garcilazo and McCann (2015).

Agglomerations create winners and losers. People living in the core areas enjoy higher incomes and better living conditions compared to those living in the periphery. In practice, the young and high-skilled people are more mobile and can move to core areas, leaving behind the older and the lower skilled.

From a policy perspective, an important question is whether agglomeration delivers economic benefit at the aggregate level or not.[16] Ottaviano and Thisse (2002) show that agglomerations underpinned by the normal

---

[16] See Baldwin et al. (2003) for a detailed analysis of the welfare implications of New Economic Geography models. Ottaviano and Pinelli (2005) provides a summary of the relevant literature.

customer-client market interactions happening at intermediate spatial distance (one can think of regions within countries) do not deliver aggregate benefits for the overall economy. In this case, policies aimed at lowering territorial disparities would also deliver higher aggregate benefits. In all other cases, however, there would be a trade-off: pursuing a more equitable territorial development would have some price tag at the aggregate level. This happens when agglomeration occurs at very local (urban) or very high (national) level, or when it is underpinned by non-market interactions such as informal transmission of knowledge.[17]

The research and policy debate has frequently been articulated in terms of place-based vs. people-based policies, i.e. whether there is a case for differentiating policies according to location or to be place-blind and address specific problems (for instance, poverty) in the same way across the entire territory. When agglomeration does not deliver aggregate benefits, there is a clear case for place-based policies, such as financial support to poorer regions to reduce regional disparities. The case for place-based policies is less clear-cut when agglomeration does deliver aggregate benefits. For instance, if innovation benefits from localised knowledge transmissions, policies that hamper agglomeration, such as limits to internal migration or subsidies to keep people in the rural areas, could damage innovation and growth at the aggregate level (Moretti 2011; World Bank 2009).

Even in the latter case, the space for regional policies remains nevertheless large in practice. Policy-makers have limited information about the size and spatial reach of agglomeration effects, and one-size-fits-all policies are unlikely to work in practice because local situations are very different (Austin et al. 2018; Barca et al. 2012). Furthermore, the proximity of disadvantaged people in poorer areas may create spatial traps, which require specific policies to address. Well-designed regional policy measures could aim at removing local barriers to growth and unlock the full potential of local resources, including labour, without imposing any restriction on mobility. Adequately tailored to the specific characteristics of each region, they could address institutional inefficiencies, improve and adapt skills to the need of a changing economy, enact active labour market

[17] This is because these models include a non-linear relation between trade costs and agglomeration effects. Agglomeration effects are minimised when transport costs are either very high (firms have to locate close to their customers) or very low (firms' location becomes irrelevant). For intermediate costs, agglomeration effects are stronger – in this case, market outcomes tend to be inefficient. Combes et al. (2011) find evidence of such bell-shaped curve with regard to French regions over the period 1860–2000.

policies to facilitate job matching and reduce inactivity, provide the digital and physical infrastructure to increase interconnectedness and market access, address local hindrances to endogenous investment and entrepreneurship. Iammarino, Rodríguez-Pose and Storper (2019, p. 289) speak of "place-sensitive" policies aimed at "distributed development" that "should be both sensitive to the need for agglomeration and the need for it to occur in as many places as possible".[18] Rodríguez-Pose and Ketterer (2020) also stress the importance of government quality for sustained regional development.

A key issue is demographic decline (see also Chapter 8 in Volume II). This chapter has documented that many regions in EU11 are experiencing significant out-migration and population decline. In many economic models, migration is a re-equilibrating factor, which helps redistribute the benefits of agglomeration. However, declining population entails multiple negative effects locally: underutilised capital stock, deteriorating social relations, declining local public services and tax bases. This often empirically results in low trust and high crime levels.[19] These negative effects of outmigration are not taken into account by individual migration decisions, which therefore reinforces the case for region-specific policy interventions.

REFERENCES

Alfaro, L., Chen, M. X., & Fadinger, H. (2019). *Spatial Agglomeration and Superstar Firms: Firm-Level Patterns from Europe and US*. Working Paper 20-015, Harvard Business School.

Artelaris, P., Kallioras, D., & Petrakos, G. (2010). Regional Inequalities and Convergence Clubs in the European Union New Member States. *Eastern Journal of European Studies*, 1(1), 113–133.

Austin, B. A., Glaeser, E. L., & Summers, L. H. (2018). Jobs for the Heartland: Place-Based Policies in 21st-Century America. *Brookings Papers on Economic Activity*, 49(1), 151–255.

Baldwin, R. (2016). *The Great Convergence: Information Technology and the New Globalisation*. Cambridge: Harvard University Press.

---

[18] Breinlich, Ottaviano and Temple (2014), Austin, Glaeser and Summers (2018), Moretti (2012), Glaeser (2013) also provide comprehensive overviews of regional policies and regional growth drivers.

[19] Breinlich, Ottaviano and Temple (2014) provide a good overview of the topic and analyse the related important analytical gaps.

Baldwin, R., Forslid, R., Martin, P., Ottaviano, G. I. P., & Robert-Nicoud, F. (2003). *Economic Geography and Public Policy*. Princeton: Princeton University Press.

Barca, F., McCann, P., & Rodríguez-Pose, A. (2012). The Case for Regional Development Intervention: Place-Based Versus Place-Neutral Approaches. *Journal of Regional Science, 52*(1), 134–152.

Becker, S. O., Egger, P. H., & von Ehrlich, M. (2012). Too Much of a Good Thing? On the Growth Effect of the EU's Regional Policy. *European Economic Review, 56*(4), 648–668.

Becker, S. O., Egger, P. H., & von Ehrlich, M. (2013). Absorptive Capacity and the Growth and Investment Effects of Regional Transfers: A Regression Discontinuity Design with Heterogeneous Treatment Effects. *American Economic Journal: Economic Policy, 5*(4), 29–77.

Becker, S. O., Egger, P. H., & von Ehrlich, M. (2018). Effects of EU Regional Policy, 1989–2013. *Regional Science and Urban Economics, 69*, 143–152.

Bourdin, S. (2015). National and Regional Trajectories of Convergence and Economic Integration in Central and Eastern Europe. *Canadian Journal of Regional Science/Revue canadienne des sciences régionales, 38*(1/3), 55–63.

Bourdin, S. (2019). Does the Cohesion Policy Have the Same Influence on Growth Everywhere? A Geographically Weighted Regression Approach in Central and Eastern Europe. *Economic Geography, 95*(3), 256–287.

Breinlich, H., Ottaviano, G. I. P., & Temple, J. R. W. (2014). Regional Growth and Regional Decline. In P. Aghion & S. Durlauf (Eds.), *Handbook of Economic Growth* (Vol. 2B). Oxford: Elsevier.

Brülhart, M. (2009, January 7). Is the New Economic Geography Passé? *VoxEU*. https://voxeu.org/article/new-economic-geography-pass

Combes, P.-P., Lafourcade, M., Thisse, J.-F., & Toutain, J.-C. (2011). The Rise and Fall of Spatial Inequalities in France: A Long-Run Perspective. *Explorations in Economic History, 48*(2), 243–271.

Council of Economic Advisers. (2016). *The Long-Term Decline in Prime-Age Male Labour Force Participation*. Technical Report.

Cuaresma, J. C., Doppelhofer, G., & Feldkircher, M. (2014). The Determinants of Economic Growth in European Regions. *Regional Studies, 48*(1), 44–67.

Demertzis, M., Sapir, A., & Wolff, G. (2019). *Promoting Sustainable and Inclusive Growth and Convergence in the European Union*. Policy Contribution No. 7, Bruegel.

Desmet, K., Nagy, D., Nigmatulina, D., & Young, N. (2018). Chapter 4: Geographic Transition. In *Transition Report 2018–19*. London: EBRD.

Dijkstra, L., Garcilazo, E., & McCann, P. (2015). The Effect of the Global Financial Crisis on European Regions and Cities. *Journal of Economic Geography, 15*(5), 935–949.

Dijkstra, L., Poelman, H., & Rodríguez-Pose, A. (2020). The Geography of EU Discontent. *Regional Studies, 54*(6), 737–753.
Eckey, H.-F., & Türck, M. (2007). Convergence of EU-Regions. A Literature Report. *Investigaciones Regionales, 10*, 5–32.
Eurofound. (2018). *Upward Convergence in the EU: Concepts, Measurements and Indicators.* Luxembourg: Publication Office of the European Union.
European Commission. (2017). *Seventh Report on Economic, Social and Territorial Cohesion.* Luxembourg: Publication Office of the European Union.
Ezcurra, R., Pascual, P., & Rapún, M. (2007). The Dynamics of Regional Disparities in Central and Eastern Europe During Transition. *European Planning Studies, 15*(10), 1397–1421.
Forgó, B., & Jevčák, A. (2015). *Economic Convergence of Central and Eastern European EU Member States Over the Last Decade (2004–2014).* European Economy – Discussion Papers 001, Directorate General Economic and Financial Affairs, European Commission.
Gagliardi, L., & Percoco, M. (2017). The Impact of European Cohesion Policy in Urban and Rural Regions. *Regional Studies, 51*(6), 857–868.
Glaeser, E. L. (2011). *The Triumph of the City. How Our Greatest Invention Makes Us Richer, Smarter, Greener, Healthier and Happier.* Harmondsworth: Penguin.
Glaeser, E. L. (2013). A Review of Enrico Moretti's "The New Geography of Jobs". *Journal of Economic Literature, 51*(3), 825–837.
Gorzelak, G. (2017). Cohesion Policy and Regional Development. In J. Bachtler, P. Berkowitz, S. Hardy, & T. Muravska (Eds.), *EU Cohesion Policy. Reassessing Performance and Direction* (Regions and Cities). Oxon/New York: Regional Studies Association/Routledge-Taylor & Francis Group.
Iammarino, S., Rodríguez-Pose, A., & Storper, M. (2019). Regional Inequality in Europe: Evidence, Theory and Policy Implications. *Journal of Economic Geography, 19*(2), 273–298.
Kotosz, B., & Lengyel, I. (2017). *Regional Growth and Convergence of the NUTS 3 Regions of Eastern European Countries.* Draft manuscript, University of Szeged, presented at the 57th ERSA Congress: Social Progress for Resilient Regions, available at https://www.researchgate.net/profile/Balazs_Kotosz/publication/319768127_Regional_Growth_and_Convergence_of_the_NUTS_3_Regions_of_Eastern_European_Countries/links/59bbfa08458515e9cfc7bc97/Regional-Growth-and-Convergence-of-the-NUTS-3-Regions-of-Eastern-European-Countries.pdf.
Krugman, P. (1991). *Geography and Trade.* Cambridge, MA: The MIT Press.
Magrini, S. (2004). Regional (Di)Convergence. In V. Henderson & J. F. Thisse (Eds.), *Handbook of Regional and Urban Economics.* Amsterdam: Elsevier Science.
Monfort, P. (2008). *Convergence of EU Regions. Measures and Evolution.* Working Paper 1/2008, Directorate-General Regional Policy, European Commission.

Moretti, E. (2011). Local Labour Markets. In O. Ashenfelter & D. Card (Eds.), *Handbook of Labor Economics* (Vol. 4B). North Holland: Elsevier.

Moretti, E. (2012). *The New Geography of Jobs*. New York: Houghton Mifflin Harcourt Publishing.

Ottaviano, G. I. P. (2019). *Geografia economica dell'Europa sovranista*. Roma: Editori Laterza.

Ottaviano, G. I. P., & Pinelli, D. (2005). A 'New Economic Geography' Perspective on Globalization. *Italian Journal of Regional Science, 4*, 71–106.

Ottaviano, G. I. P., & Thisse, J.-F. (2002). Integration, Agglomeration and the Political Economics of Factor Mobility. *Journal of Public Economics, 83*(3), 429–456.

Rodríguez-Pose, A., & Ketterer, T. (2020). Institutional Change and the Development of Lagging Regions in Europe. *Regional Studies, 54*(7), 974–986. https://doi.org/10.1080/00343404.2019.1608356.

Rosés, J. R., & Wolf, N. (2018). *Regional Economic Development in Europe: 1900–2010: A Description of Patterns*. CEPR Discussion Paper 12749, Centre for Economic Policy Research.

Tondl, G., & Vuksic, G. (2007). Catching Up of Eastern European Regions: The Role of Foreign Investment, Human Capital and Geography. In R. Eisen, A. M. Díaz Cafferata, A. E. Neder, & M. L. Recalde (Eds.), *Trade, Integration and Institutional Reforms in Latin America and the EU*. Frankfurt: Lang.

World Bank. (2009). *World Development Report 2009: Reshaping Economic Geography*. Washington, DC: World Bank.

PART II

Country Experiences of EU Members

CHAPTER 5

How the European Union Made Poland European Again

Marcin Piatkowski

5.1 INTRODUCTION

Poland and the rest of Central and Eastern Europe have been economically underdeveloped, peripheral and lagging behind Western Europe for almost all of its history. During the last 400 years, Poland's GDP per capita PPP has hardly ever exceeded half of the average level of income in Western Europe (Bolt et al. 2018; Piatkowski 2018; Bukowski et al. 2018; Koryś 2018). In 1989, when Poland became the first country in the "Soviet Camp" to introduce democracy and open markets, the average Pole, adjusting for purchasing parity, earned less than a quarter of the

---

Senior Economist, the World Bank, and Associate Professor, Kozminski University in Warsaw. The views expressed are solely those of the author and do not represent the official views of the World Bank. The author is grateful to István P. Székely for his insightful comments on the draft version of the chapter.

M. Piatkowski (✉)
The World Bank, Washington, DC, USA

Kozminski University, Warsaw, Poland
e-mail: mpiatkowski@kozminski.edu.pl

© The Author(s), under exclusive license to Springer Nature Switzerland AG 2021
M. Landesmann, I. P. Székely (eds.), *Does EU Membership Facilitate Convergence? The Experience of the EU's Eastern Enlargement - Volume I*, Studies in Economic Transition,
https://doi.org/10.1007/978-3-030-57686-8_5

average German. The country was insolvent, uncompetitive, and unstable. Few predicted that Poland's transition would go well.

And yet 30 years later, Poland has become by far the most successful economy in Europe and one of the most successful middle-income and high-income economies in the world. Poland also became a champion of inclusive growth, where rising prosperity lifted all boats, and a well-being champion, where higher incomes translated into higher quality of life and a higher level of happiness.

What were the key drivers of this unexpected and unprecedented success? What was the role of the European Union in this process? What are the implications for the future?

This chapter is structured as follows: Sect. 5.1 provides details of Poland's economic performance since 1989. Section 5.2 looks at the proximate and ultimate drivers of Poland's success. Section 5.4 zooms in on the critical role of the European Union in Poland's success story. Section 5.4 zooms in on medium-term growth projections. Section 5.5 concludes.

5.2 Poland's Economic Success

Poland is Europe's growth champion. Since 1989, its GDP per capita has increased by almost 150 percent, more than any other post-transition economy, significantly more than France or Germany, and more than any other country in Europe (Fig. 5.1).[1]

In purchasing power parity terms, Poland's GDP per capita almost tripled in the same period, from $10,300 in 1990 to more than $28,600 in 2018 (in 2011 constant dollars). At the same time, Hungary's income, the early leader of transition, has not even doubled. France's GDP per capita has increased by barely a third.[2] Poland has also beaten Europe's record for the length of uninterrupted economic growth: in 2019, it completed its 28th year of growth, overshadowing the Netherlands' earlier 25-year record.

Poland was also the fastest-growing large economy in the world among upper-middle-income and high-income countries over the last 25 years, growing faster than the Asian Tigers and other top-performing economies (Fig. 5.2).

---

[1] Although, if the source statistics can be fully believed, Albania's GDP per capita during 1990–2018 increased by 149 percent, a shade higher than Poland's.

[2] Based on data from the World Bank's WDI database https://data.worldbank.org/indicator/ny.gdp.pcap.pp.kd, plus own projections for 2018.

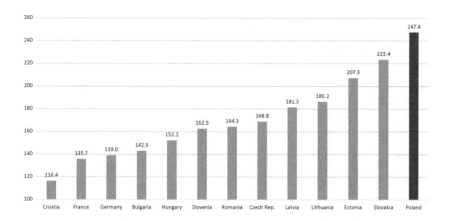

Fig. 5.1 GDP growth per capita, 1990–2018, 1989 = 100. (Source: author's own based on the Conference Board Total Economy Database)

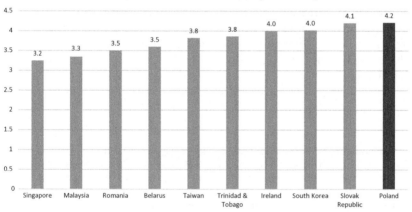

Fig. 5.2 Top 10 upper-middle/high-income large economies in GDP per capita growth rate, 1993–2018. (Source: author's own based on the Conference Board Total Economy Database)

As a result of this remarkable growth, the average level of income in Poland rose to over two-thirds of the average for Western Europe, the highest level in Poland's history and a testament to the arrival of Poland's new Golden Age (Piatkowski 2013, 2018).[3] In terms of actual individual consumption, which takes into account the availability of public services, Polish incomes now exceed 70 percent of the euro zone average, the highest level on record.[4]

Well-being and happiness have boomed too: according to the OECD's Better Life Index, well-being in Poland is as high as in South Korea even though the latter is about one-third richer.[5] More than 80 percent of Poles are also satisfied with their lives (Czapiński 2015), up from only around half at the beginning of transition.

This widespread increase in well-being and satisfaction had much to do with Poland's impressive record in inclusive growth: according to EBRD data, it was the only democratic post-socialist country in the region where incomes of even the poorest grew faster than the G-7 average (Fig. 5.3). Income inequalities also increased less than elsewhere: in 2019, Poland's Gini coefficient amounted to 29.2,[6] below the EU and the OECD average. That said, a different methodological approach based on the income shares in GDP of each population decile show a more nuanced picture of inequality.[7]

---

[3] Malinowski (2016) argues that Poland's GDP per capita in 1580 reached 85 percent of income in France. That said, given the much higher income and wealth inequality in premodern Poland, where the top 6–8 percent of the society—the ruling gentry and aristocracy—monopolized the economy, the median levels of income were lower than today. In addition, more than 80 percent of the society were serfs, whose status was in practice not that entirely different than that of slaves. They would be quite surprised to hear that they lived in a "golden age".

[4] From: https://ec.europa.eu/eurostat/statistics-explained/index.php?title=GDP_per_capita,_consumption_per_capita_and_price_level_indices. Accessed on April 10, 2019.

[5] From: http://www.oecdbetterlifeindex.org/

[6] From: http://appsso.eurostat.ec.europa.eu/nui/show.do?dataset=ilc_di12 and https://read.oecd-ilibrary.org/social-issues-migration-health/society-at-a-glance-2019_soc_glance-2019-en#page100

[7] A recent paper by Blanchet, Chancel and Gethin (2019) argues that Poland's inequality measured by income shares is the highest in Europe, with the top 10 percent of Poles taking over almost 40 percent of the national income versus less than 30 percent in the Czech Republic.

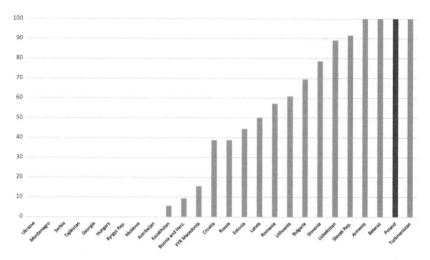

Fig. 5.3 Share of total population (in deciles), whose income since 1989 has increased faster than the G-7 average, 1989–2016. (Source: author's own based on data from EBRD 2016)

5.3 THE DRIVERS OF THE POLISH MIRACLE

How did Poland, a perennial economic underachiever, suddenly manage to become Europe's growth champion?

In my recent book (Piatkowski 2018), I argue that after 1989, Poland was successful because it adopted good economic policies. These policies included deep market reforms at the beginning of the transformation spearheaded by Leszek Balcerowicz, relatively fast institution building, including during the implementation of the "Strategy for Poland" (Kolodko 2000, 2011; Kolodko and Tomkiewicz 2019), and rapid improvement in both the quantity and quality of education. A successful restructuring of foreign debt—in the early 1990s governmental and private creditors cut Poland's debt by half—was also important. Lastly, a relatively well-managed privatization helped, even though it was driven more by luck than by design.[8]

---

[8] Owing to a strong resistance from a robust civil society, Poland's mass privatization was delayed until 1996, much later than among most other post-socialist countries. When it finally happened, strong institutions, independent media, and availability of market prices for

There were also other supportive factors for Poland's strong performance, such as a rebound from the economic stagnation of the 1980's (Vonyo 2017), which pushed Poland's economic growth further below potential than its peers. Large inflows of savings from abroad accumulated by Polish migrant workers also helped (Gomułka 2018), as did the legacy of pro-market reforms implemented in the late 1980's by the country's last communist governments (Bąk 2009) and its low starting point in 1989 in terms of income (in line with the conditional convergence theory).

Polish economic policy after 1989 could have been better—macroeconomic policies during 1990–1991 were overshot and the economy was unnecessarily cooled down in 2000–2001—but in general Poland's post-socialist transformation achieved much more than anyone could have expected. Even in an optimal scenario of almost perfect policies, Poland's GDP per capita in 2018 would have been only about 10 percent higher (Piatkowski 2018). In terms of economic growth, Poland achieved 9/10 of what was possible, more than two-thirds of growth potential argued by, for instance, Kolodko (2009).

If good economic policies drove good economic outcomes, then what drove the good economic policies?

Poland adopted good economic policies after 1989 for several fundamental reasons. First, Polish success was driven by the positive legacy of real socialism, which left behind an egalitarian, classless, inclusive and socially mobile society. The egalitarian distribution of economic resources helped ensure that in 1989, all social classes were interested in building institutions that would give equal opportunities to everyone and prevent a re-emergence of the pre-1939 extractive system, which had stymied Poland's development before.[9] The relatively high level of education, high level of gender equity and a strong civil society (which emerged in response to the state's oppression) also helped to give Polish society a fresh start, where—unlike in the past—(almost) anyone could flourish regardless of their socio-economic background. The fact that among the richest Polish businessmen listed on the Forbes Top 100 list today practically all of them are "self-made men" testifies to the open nature of the post-1989 society.

assets ensured that the privatization was much "cleaner" than elsewhere and did not lead to the emergence of oligarchs.

[9] In Piatkowski (2018), I focus on Poland's long-term development and propose a new model of institutional development based on the amended concept of "inclusive" and "extractive" institutions developed by Acemoglu, Johnson, and Robinson (2005) and Acemoglu and Robinson (2012).

Second, Poland has also developed a social consensus to "return to Europe" and absorb Western values and institutions. Such a strong consensus had never existed before, as for centuries Polish elites preferred to equivocate between the West and the East, very much like Ukraine and Russia today. It didn't end well for any of them.

Third, the country was ruled by a strong, professional and Westernized elite, which from the beginning knew that it wanted Poland to integrate with the developed part of Europe. Poland's economic elites were particularly strong, exemplified by the fact that, for instance, almost all the key policymakers in Poland studied or conducted economic research in the West before 1989.[10] In Bulgaria, by contrast, no minister of finance even spoke English before 2002.

Finally, Poland's success was underpinned by the rise of a nascent middle class and new business elite, which supported democracy and open markets. None of these classes existed earlier, as before 1939, there had been no middle class and the business elites largely comprised of non-ethnic Poles, whose political influence was limited.

5.4 The Fundamental Role of the European Union

There is one more fundamental driver of the Polish economic miracle: the European Union. Without it, Polish communists might not have relinquished power in 1989, early "shock" reforms might not have succeeded, institution building would largely have not happened, highways would not have been built and economic populism would have taken reign a long time ago. Any of these factors could have cut the Polish miracle short. Let me take each of these points in turn.

5.4.1 Political Economy Drivers

First, the prospect of joining the European Community, the predecessor of the EU, was one the drivers of the collapse of communism. In 1989, the Polish communists decided to share power with Solidarność because

---

[10] Leszek Balcerowicz, Grzegorz W. Kolodko, and Marek Belka, the three key economic policymakers of the last 30 years, were all Fulbright scholars in America in the 1970s and 1980s and have kept close touch with Western economics throughout their careers. Jacek Rostowski, Poland's finance minister during 2007–2014, was the most Western of all: he was born and spent most of his life in the UK, moving to Poland to assume the minister's position.

Western Europe and—to a lesser extent—the US played a critical role as implicit third-party enforcers of the "deal" between communists and Solidarność to create inclusive institutions and keep the country open and democratic. The lack of such a credible commitment mechanism is one of the key reasons why so many countries around the world are stuck with extractive, economically-harmful institutions: as I explain in Piatkowski (2018, p. 231), "in the absence of a third-party enforcer, the ruling elites cannot be sure that when they share or relinquish power, the new elites will keep their side of the bargain and will compensate the old elites for the lost rents. They also cannot be sure that new elites will keep the political and economic system open so that economic and political losses to the old elites will be limited. Thus, the old elites rarely let go.". It also mattered that the Polish communists themselves lost their communist religion a long time ago and—like their peers in Solidarność—they also craved Western European freedom and prosperity.

Second, Balcerowicz's "shock" reforms in 1990–1991 would have likely not succeeded had it not been for the existence of an implicit quid pro quo among the ruling elites and the society to allow the shock reforms to go through in exchange for the promise of future prosperity underpinned by moving towards the West. Without Western European openness to embrace Poland and early promises of Western politicians about future accession, the fundamental reforms might have met with much stronger social resistance and have never gotten off the ground.[11]

Third, the European Union was the key driver of institution building and structural reforms, during the EU accession process in the late 1990s and early 2000s and—to a lesser extent—after the EU accession in 2004. During the run-up to the accession, Poland "downloaded" more than 80,000 pages of *acquis communautaire*, including 50,000 new laws and regulations, that encapsulated the very institutions that took Western Europe hundreds of years to build and the same institutions that made Europe what it is today: the most prosperous, humane and happy continent on earth. Thanks to the accession process, Poland (and the rest of the CEE) built institutions that are much stronger, more robust and more effective than those of its upper-middle-income peers outside the EU

---

[11] In the early days of transition, the reforms were also anchored by the IMF and the World Bank financing support programs (Roaf et al. 2014), the US-led international effort to create a US$ 1 billion Stabilization Fund, and the need to follow the reforms underlying the agreed 50 percent debt restructurings with Paris Club and later London Club of creditors.

(Fig. 5.4). The newly built institutions were the critical driver of Poland's success (Piatkowski 2018). Institution building did not stop after the accession in 2004: EU's institutions, rules and regulations, including those on the size of the budget deficit, limits on state aid or the importance of the rule of law, restricted the scope for harmful economic policies. These rules made Polish politicians "behave" much better that they would have otherwise. Many emerging markets around the world lack such an "institutional straitjacket" (Piatkowski 2009), which leaves them at the mercy of economic populists, leads to repeated crises and thwarts their development.

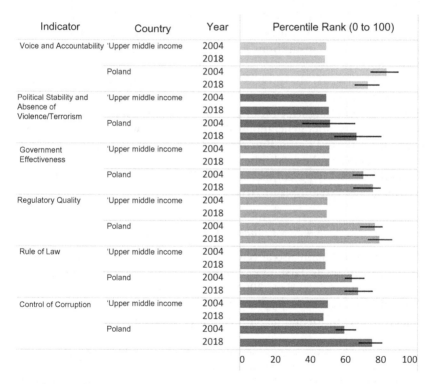

Fig. 5.4 Indicators of institutional quality for Poland and upper-middle-income countries, 2004 and 2018. (Note: Upper-middle-income countries as defined by the World Bank. Source: http://info.worldbank.org/governance/wgi/#reports)

Finally, accession to the EU also accelerated the otherwise slow process of cultural change. While everyone focuses on the incumbent government, which seems to embody values that are at variance with those in Western Europe, it is easy to forget that during the last parliamentary elections in October 2019 almost two-thirds of the society voted for pro-European parties and 88 percent of Poles, the fourth highest ratio in the EU, believe that Poland has benefited from the EU, double the proportion in Italy.[12]

It is also easy to forget that Poland's culture and values were never as Western and European as now: before 1939, the culture of Polish society, ruled by an autocratic elite that governed a largely poor, rural and even partly illiterate society, was incomparably less Western than today. It is only now that Poland's culture is (slowly) Westernizing.[13] The fact that such different values did not undermine the country's success is a testament to the key role of EU institutions and the attraction of the EU's fundamental values and norms.

Going forward, the process of cultural convergence will continue: Poland's younger generations are incomparably more Westernized, European, multilingual, educated, democratic, open-minded, tolerant and ethical than its older generations. Poland's culture will change with them. Time is on Poland's (and Europe's) side. In the meantime, however, the tensions between the newly absorbed Western institutions and the slower change in underlying cultural norms will continue (Székely and Ward-Warmedinger 2018; Roland 2014).

5.4.2 Economic Channels of Impact

The European Union also affected Poland's growth through other, more traditional channels. First, open borders to trade helped increase Poland's exports by three times since 2004 (and more than 25 times since 1989).[14] Second, open borders to capital allowed Poland to attract more than 200 billion dollars of foreign direct investment since 2004, which was critical

---

[12] http://www.europarl.europa.eu/news/en/press-room/20180522IPR04027/public-opinion-survey-finds-record-support-for-eu-despite-brexit-backdrop

[13] According to one perspective, Poland's culture is still in many ways closer to that of Latin America than to many other countries in Europe. See Inglehart–Welzel Cultural Map at http://www.worldvaluessurvey.org/WVSContents.jsp

[14] Based on data from https://data.worldbank.org/indicator/BX.GSR.TOTL.CD?locations=PL accessed on April 11, and Piatkowski (2018).

to enhance the country's competitiveness and support entrance into global value chains (World Bank 2017). Third, open borders for labor let more than two million Poles multiply their incomes when they moved to find jobs in the West, creating a classic win-win in the process, with little impact (at least so far) on the labor market and low "brain drain". Fourth, open borders also helped educate hundreds of thousands of young Poles in the West, a long-term investment into Poland's democracy and prosperity.

Finally, the more than 150 billion euros in net EU funds that Poland has received since its accession in 2004 have helped develop robust infrastructure, support investment in education and innovation, and strengthen institutions. Poland would have never been able to afford these investments on its own.

Various estimates suggest that EU funds have contributed at least 0.5 percentage points to Poland's GDP annual growth since 2004 (Ministry of Regional Development 2013). Campos, Coricelli and Moretti (2014) estimate that without the EU, GDP per capita in CEE countries would have been 12 percent lower than otherwise. But these estimates do not account for many additional positive spillover effects from the EU funds on the economy and society: without a proper highway network, strong institutions and billions of euros invested into research infrastructure, higher education and training, economic growth would have slowed a long time ago. Without the billions invested into urban rejuvenation and beautification, Polish cities would continue to underwhelm. And without the billions invested into the social and well-being infrastructure, Poles' happiness would be much lower.

Overall, without the allure of European values, the strength of imported Western institutions, the benefits of open borders and the high returns on invested EU funds, Poland's economic miracle would never have happened. If it had been left outside the EU, Poland could have ended up like Belarus, at best, or as poor as Ukraine, at worst.[15]

5.4.3 Comparison with Peers Outside the EU

Looking outside the EU, Poland's performance could be compared to its global peers such as South Korea, Mexico, Malaysia and South Africa,

---

[15] Poland and Ukraine had a similar GDP per capita in 1990. In 2018, Poland's GDP PPP was almost four time higher than in Ukraine. From: https://data.worldbank.org/indicator/NY.GDP.PCAP.PP.KD?locations=PL-UA

which in 1990 had a similar starting point in income and which share some characteristics such as size, economic structure and dependence on key trading partners.[16]

Among the five countries, South Korea did better than Poland in terms of GDP growth, although most of the difference is due to Poland's underperformance during the first years of transition (Fig. 5.5). Malaysia did similarly well to Poland: in 2018, it had only a marginally lower income per capita. However, Mexico—despite a much higher income in 1990, proximity to the US market and a similar cultural background—did much worse than Poland, ending up in 2018 with less than two-thirds of Poland's income. South Africa did even worse, increasing its income since 1990 by only one fourth.

Poland's GDP growth has also been much less volatile, with a lower standard deviation of growth than its peers and all emerging markets (World Bank 2017). This stability of economic performance can be largely attributed to the benefits of the EU's institutional framework, which limits

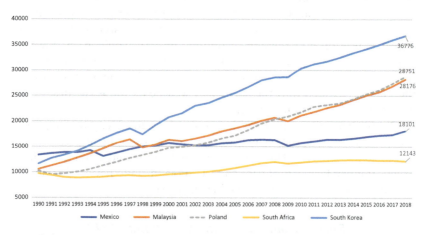

Fig. 5.5 Changes in GDP per capita for Poland, Mexico, Malaysia, South Korea and South Africa, 1990–2018, PPP, in constant 2011 international $. (Source: author's own based on the World Bank World Development Indicators database)

---

[16] Mexico's economy much depends on the USA, Malaysia on China and Poland on Germany. World Bank (2017) selected Mexico and Malaysia as Poland's peers in their comparative analysis of Poland's performance.

the scope for economic populism.[17] There is also evidence that because of the EU, global financial investors are ready to accept a lower yield on Poland's debt than what would be suggested by its economic fundamentals alone. This "EU halo effect" lowered the cost of capital, increased investment and spurred Poland's growth (Luengnaruemitchai and Schadler 2007).

Looking beyond GDP, Poland has also succeeded in eliminating extreme poverty (calculated at the highest poverty threshold of $5.50 a day, rather than the usual $1.90 threshold). Only South Korea and Malaysia achieved the same success. The poverty rate in Mexico has come down since 1992, but in 2016 still exceeded 10 percent of society. In South Africa, almost one-third of the country's citizens lived in poverty (Fig. 5.6).

What sets Poland apart from its peers is also a relatively low level of income inequality, as reflected by the Gini coefficient: Poland's inequality is similar to South Korea's, but significantly lower than in Malaysia and Mexico and drastically lower than in South Africa, one of the most unequal countries in the world (Fig. 5.7).

Thanks to the much lower level of inequality, the fruit of Poland's economic growth have been shared much more equally than among its peers. This is reflected in the median household income level, for instance, which is higher in Poland than a simple comparison with the GDP per capita of its peers would suggest. In 2016, in Mexico and South Africa, the annual median equivalized disposable household income amounted to less than US$ 5000.[18] At the same time, Poland's median household income exceeded US$15,000, more than triple Mexico's and South Africa's level (OECD 2019).

Finally, Poland could be compared to its peers on the level of overall well-being, using the OECD's Better Life Index. Poland outranks both Mexico and South Africa: it ranks 26th, behind Slovakia and ahead of Portugal, while Mexico and South Africa occupy the last two places in the

---

[17] Despite much criticism of the current Law and Justice party's government, including its attempts to undermine the rule of law, the economic policy has been far from populist: over the last four years, 2015–19, the government has presided over an almost 20 percent increase in GDP per capita, one of the highest growth ratios in the EU, a decline in inequality and poverty and a falling public debt.

[18] Annual median equivalized disposable household income measures median income for families adjusted for taxes, social security contributions and social benefits. It is also adjusted for purchasing power parity (OECD 2019, p. 76).

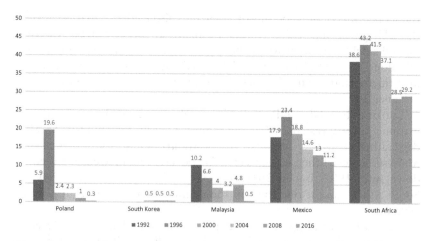

Fig. 5.6 Changes in poverty headcount for Poland, Mexico, Malaysia, South Africa and South Korea, 1992–2016, poverty gap at $5.50 a day (2011 PPP) (%). (Note: Poland and South Africa: 1992 = 1993; Malaysia: 1996 = 1997; Malaysia: 2000 assumed to equal 4; South Africa: 2004 = 2005, Malaysia: 2016 = 2015 and South Africa: 2016 = 2014, South Korea: 2006 = 2004, 2016 = 2012. Sorted by the lowest poverty rate in 2016. Source: author's own based on the World Bank World Development Indicators database)

ranking.[19] In Boston Consulting Group's Sustainable Economic Development Assessment (SEDA), an alternative index of well-being, Poland is ranked in 31st place, behind South Korea (in 22nd place), put ahead of Malaysia in 45th place, Mexico in 71st place and South Africa in a distant 107th place.[20]

The bottom line is that largely thanks to the EU and the European social model, Poland has grown faster than its global peers and it has also been able to translate this growth into much higher well-being for society as a whole.

5.4.4 The European Union as a Convergence Machine

Poland has not been the only beneficiary of the EU: all new member states in Central and Eastern Europe have benefited too. As a result, they now

---

[19] From: http://www.oecdbetterlifeindex.org/#/11111111111
[20] https://www.bcg.com/publications/interactives/seda-2019-guide.aspx

5 HOW THE EUROPEAN UNION MADE POLAND EUROPEAN AGAIN 165

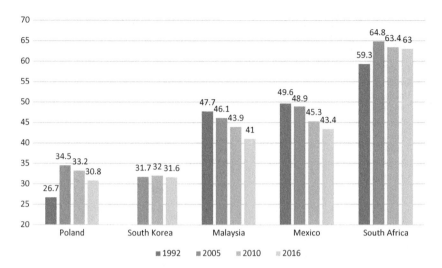

Fig. 5.7 Changes in Gini coefficient for Poland, Mexico, Malaysia, South Korea and South Africa, 1992–2016. (Note: Poland and South Africa: 1992 = 1993; Malaysia: 2005:2004; 2010 = 2011, 2016 = 2015; South Africa: 2016 = 2014, South Korea, 2005 = 2006, 2016 = 2012. Sorted by the lowest Gini coefficient. Source: author's own based on the World Bank World Development Indicators database)

all live in their new Golden Ages, defined as the shortest distance to the Western European level of income. But the EU's positive impact goes way beyond the new EU member states: it has been a "convergence machine" that has been taking poor countries in and making them rich for much longer (Gill and Raiser 2012). The EU has been responsible for two-thirds of 27 high-achieving countries that made it to the group of high-income countries since 1960 (Table 5.1).

5.5 Growth Projections

Given its strong growth fundamentals—high quality of human capital, low labor costs, flexible factor markets, relatively strong institutions, improving infrastructure, macroeconomic stability, entrepreneurial spirit and open borders—Poland's economy is not likely to stop growing any time soon. Poland's human capital is constantly improving, with university

Table 5.1 Countries that have become high-income since 1960

Non-European Union	European Union
1. Chile	1. Bulgaria*
2. Israel	2. Croatia
3. Puerto Rico	3. Cyprus
4. Panama	4. Czech Republic
5. South Korea	5. Estonia
6. Singapore	6. Greece
7. Taiwan	7. Hungary
8. Trinidad and Tobago	8. Ireland
9. Uruguay	9. Latvia
	10. Lithuania
	11. Malta
	12. Poland
	13. Portugal
	14. Romania*
	15. Slovakia
	16. Slovenia
	17. Spain

Note: excludes rich OECD countries, small island states and oil-rich countries. *Romania and Bulgaria are projected to become high income in the near future. World Bank's definition of high income: https://datahelpdesk.worldbank.org/knowledgebase/articles/906519-world-bank-country-and-lending-groups
Source: author's own based on Piatkowski (2018)

enrollment rates exceeding 66 percent in 2017 (Fig. 5.8), much above its global peers except South Korea (the global leader).

Infrastructure has also improved: the length of highways, largely thanks to the EU funding, has increased from less than 500 km in 2000 to almost 4000 km in 2019. The high-speed road network will reach 5000 km within the next few years (Fig. 5.9).

Poland's labor costs continue to be one of the lowest among high-income countries, amounting to only 20 percent and 22 percent, respectively, of the German and the US level of wages in manufacturing in 2016 (Fig. 5.10). Relatively flexible factor markets have so far helped ensure that real wage growth has not outstripped real productivity growth,[21] which helped sustain cost competitiveness.[22]

[21] In Poland, real labor productivity per person increased by 23.8 percent during 2010–2018, the second fastest rate of increase in the EU, after Romania. In Germany, it increased by only 5.5 percent. Source: https://appsso.eurostat.ec.europa.eu/nui/show.do?dataset=nama_10_lp_ulc&lang=en

[22] Although rapidly growing labor market shortages over the last few years, only partially filled by a significant increase in labor immigration, especially from Ukraine, have spurred a

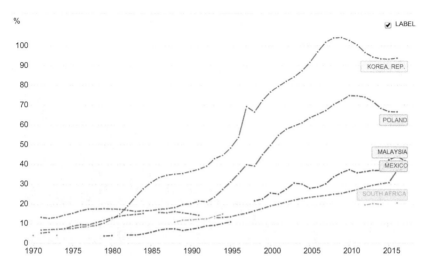

Fig. 5.8 Tertiary school enrollment in Poland and selected global peers, % gross, 1970–2017. (Source: World Bank's World Development Database)

Finally, Poland's economy has become much more open than its global peers and more open than even Germany: in 2018, Poland's total exports amounted to 55 percent of GDP versus 47 percent in Germany and 44 percent in South Korea (Fig. 5.11). High openness will help keep the economy productive by increasing competitive pressures, contributing to higher economies of scale and keeping costs in line with fundamentals.

Given these strong growth fundamentals, the European Commission and the IMF project an average GDP growth of above 3 percent in the next few years (although Poland is likely to outperform these projections again: in 2019, it is likely to grow at more than 4.5 percent, more than the IMF's projection of 3.6 percent GDP growth). This should allow Poland to become richer than Portugal in 2019 (on a PPP per capita basis) and exceed 70 percent of the Western European level of income by 2022. If these trends continue, by 2030, Poland's income would reach 80 percent of Western European's income, the highest level ever (Piatkowski 2018).

That said, Poland's speed of convergence will slowly decline during the next decade, as the country's growth potential becomes stymied by

much faster increase in wages. That said, growth in unit labor costs continues to be subdued (IMF 2019).

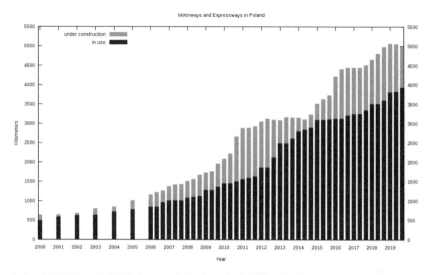

Fig. 5.9 Length of highways and expressways in Poland, 2000–2019. (Source: https://en.wikipedia.org/wiki/Highways_in_Poland#/media/File:PL-Motorways-en.svg)

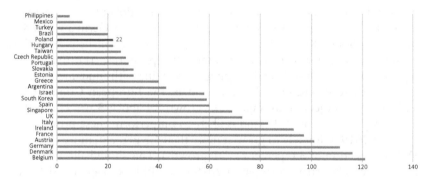

Fig. 5.10 Hourly compensation costs in manufacturing, as a percent of costs in the United States (US = 100), 2016. (Source: author's own based on The Conference Board)

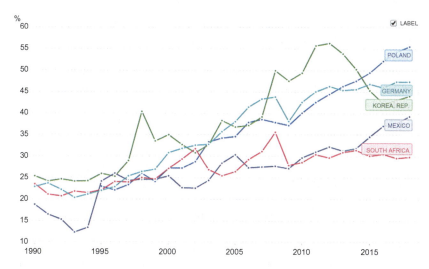

Fig. 5.11 Exports of goods and services as % of GDP in Poland, Germany and selected global peers, 1990–2018. (Source: World Bank's World Development Database)

growing labor shortages due to population ageing, a relatively low level of innovation and a low level of domestic savings. The worsening quality of institutions, especially of the rule of law, may also undermine growth.[23] Policies will need to be adjusted accordingly, ideally in line with a new growth model that I propose—The Warsaw Consensus—that would help mitigate growth challenges and maximize developmental potentials (Piatkowski 2014, 2018).

5.6 Conclusions

Poland has just lived through its best 30 years ever. Poles have never been more prosperous, safe, or happy. The country is living through its Golden Age. The European Union has been the key driver of this unprecedented success.

But past success is not a guarantee of future success. Poland is not immune to policy reversals and may struggle to deal with its growing

---

[23] See the World Bank's Worldwide Governance Indicators for the current reading of Poland's institutional quality: https://info.worldbank.org/governance/wgi/#reports

challenges. The Polish "soaring eagle" could crash to the ground, as it has many times before, in Poland and in many other seemingly "invincible" countries.

The future of Poland will fundamentally depend on three key factors: the success of moving from imitation to innovation, the strength of its inclusive society and the robustness of the European Union.

First, Poland will never catch up with Western Europe, especially the core countries of Europe that have been at the forefront of European and global civilization for centuries, unless it becomes a source of ideas, products and services that inspire others, in Europe and worldwide. This has hardly ever happened before and it will be hard to do in the future. But Poland should not stop trying to fully leverage its intellectual potential: it is there, but it needs stronger institutions, a more open culture, and more investment to truly flourish.

Second, Poland needs to sustain an inclusive society, where every citizen has a chance to develop regardless of their hometown, personal connections or the wealth of his or her parents. This requires that Poland shares the fruits of growth with all members of society, especially the poor. The key guiding principle should be to ensure that the incomes of the bottom half of the society grow faster than the rest, that high-quality public services are available to everyone and that markets are open to every ambitious entrepreneur.

Finally, without a strong, open, integrated and competitive EU, Poland's miracle will quickly end, and the country will revert back to the dark economic periphery of the continent, where it has languished before. It is in Poland's strategic interest to ensure that the EU—probably the most successful institutional invention in mankind's history—continues to grow in strength. While building the United States of Europe will take some time, there is no need to wait.

REFERENCES

Acemoglu, D., & Robinson, J. (2012). *Why Nations Fail: The Origins of Power, Prosperity, and Poverty*. New York: The Crown Publishing Group. Kindle Edition.

Acemoglu, D., Johnson, S., & Robinson, J. (2005). Institutions as the Fundamental Cause of Long-Run Growth. In P. Aghion & S. Durlau (Eds.), *Handbook of Economic Growth* (Vol. 1A, pp. 385–472). Amsterdam/San Diego: Elsevier/North-Holland.

Bąk, M. (2009). Uwarunkowania transformacji gospodarczej w krajach Europy Środkowej i Wschodniej. In G. W. Kolodko & J. Tomkiewicz (Eds.), *20 lat transformacji. Osiągnięcia, problemy, perspektywy*. Warsaw: WAIP.
Blanchet, T., Chancel, L., & Gethin, A. (2019). *How Unequal Is Europe? Evidence from Distributional National Accounts, 1980–2017*. WID, World Working Paper No. 2019/06.
Bolt, J., Inklaar, R., de Jong, H., & van Zanden, J. L. (2018). *Rebasing 'Maddison': New Income Comparisons and the Shape of Long-Run Economic Development*. Maddison Project Working Paper 10.
Bukowski, M., Koryś, P., Leszczyńska, C., Tymiński, M., & Wolf, N. (2018). Wzrost gospodarczy ziem polskich w okresie I globalizacji (1870–1910). *Ekonomista, 2018/2,* 127.
Campos, N., Coricelli, F., & Moretti, L. (2014). *Economic Growth and Political Integration: Estimating the Benefits of Membership in the European Union Using the Synthetic Counterfactuals Method*. IZA Discussion Paper No. 8162.
Czapiński, J. (2015). Główne wyniki i wnioski. Diagnoza Społeczna 2015, Warunki i Jakość Życia Polaków—Raport. *Contemporary Economics, 9*(4), 16–24.
EBRD. (2016). *Transition Report 2016–17. Transition for All: Equal Opportunities in an Unequal World*. London: European Bank for Reconstruction and Development.
Gill, I., & Raiser, M. (2012). *Golden Growth. Restoring the Lustre of the European Economic Model*. Washington, DC: The World Bank.
Gomułka, S. (2018). Poland's Economic Performance in Global and Long-Term Perspective: Surprises So Far and Risks in the Years Ahead. *Central European Economic Journal, 5,* 109–117.
IMF. (2019). Republic of Poland: 2018 Article IV Consultation.
Kolodko, G. W. (2000). *From Shock to Therapy: The Political Economy of Postsocialist Transformation*. Oxford/New York: Oxford University Press.
Kolodko, G. W. (2009). *A Two-Thirds Rate of Success*. UNU/WIDER Research Paper No. 2009/14.
Kolodko, G. W. (2011). *Truth and Lies: Economics and Politics in a Volatile World*. New York: Columbia University Press.
Kolodko, G. W., & Tomkiewicz, J. (Eds.). (2019). *Strategia dla Polski. Ćwierć wieku później*. Warsaw: PWN.
Koryś, P. (2018). *Poland from Partitions to EU Accession. A Modern Economic History, 1772–2004* (pp. 1–390). Cham: Palgrave Macmillan.
Luengnaruemitchai, P., & Schadler, S. (2007). *Do Economists' and Financial Markets' Perspectives on the New Members of the EU Differ?* IMF Working Paper No. WP/07/65, International Monetary Fund, Washington, DC.

Malinowski, M. (2016). Little Divergence Revisited: Polish Weighted Real Wages in a European Perspective, 1500–1800. *European Review of Economic History*, *20*(3), 345–367.

Ministry of Regional Development. (2013). Wpływ polityki spójności na rozwój społeczno-gospodarczy Polski w latach 2004–2015 w świetle wyników badań makroekonomicznych.

OECD. (2019). Household disposable income database. Organisation for Economic Co-operation and Development.

Piatkowski, M. (2009). *The Coming Golden Age of New Europe*. Center for European Policy Analysis Report Nr. 26.

Piatkowski, M. (2013). *Poland's New Golden Age: Shifting from Europe's Periphery to Its Center*. World Bank Policy Research Working Paper, Working Paper Series Nr. 6639.

Piatkowski, M. (2014). The Warsaw Consensus: The New European Growth Model. In W. Grzegorz & W. Kołodko (Red.), *Management and Economic Policy for Development*. Hauppauge, NY: Nova Science Publishers.

Piatkowski, M. (2018). *Europe's Growth Champion. Insights from the Economic Rise of Poland* (pp. 1–400). Oxford: Oxford University Press.

Roaf, J., Atoyan, R., Joshi, B., Krogulski, K., & an IMF Staff Team. (2014). *25 Years of Transition, Post-Communist Europe and the IMF*. Regional Economic Issues Special Report, The IMF, Washington, DC.

Roland, G. (2014). Transition in Historical Perspective. In A. Aslund & S. Djankov (Eds.), *The Great Rebirth: Lessons from the Victory of Capitalism Over Communism*. Washington DC: Peterson Institute for International Economics.

Székely, I. P., & Ward-Warmedinger, M. (2018). *Reform Reversal in Former Transition Economies (FTEs) of the European Union: Areas, Circumstances and Motivations*. IZA Policy Paper No. 142.

Vonyo, T. (2017). War and Socialism: Why Eastern Europe Fell Behind Between 1950 and 1989. *Economic History Review*, *70*(1), 248–274.

World Bank. (2017). *Lessons from Poland, Insights for Poland: A Rapid and Inclusive Transition to High-Income Status*. Warsaw: World Bank.

CHAPTER 6

Transformation of the Trade and Financing Model of the Hungarian Economy After EU Accession

Anna Boldizsár, Zsuzsa Nagy-Kékesi, and Erzsébet-Judit Rariga

6.1 INTRODUCTION

Enlargement of the European Union in 2004 provided a significant development opportunity for the new member states involved. They were afforded the opportunity for rapid economic growth through easier access to European export markets, the expansion of external funding channels and the improvement in investor perception solely resulting from the fact of the country's accession to the EU. It is no coincidence that in almost all

---

The authors would like to thank to Bálint Dancsik, Balázs Kóczián, Péter Koroknai, Zsolt Szőrfi and Barnabás Virág for their help in preparing this paper.

A. Boldizsár (✉) • Z. Nagy-Kékesi • E.-J. Rariga
Magyar Nemzeti Bank, Budapest, Hungary
e-mail: boldizsara@mnb.hu; kekesizs@mnb.hu; rarigaj@mnb.hu

© The Author(s), under exclusive license to Springer Nature Switzerland AG 2021
M. Landesmann, I. P. Székely (eds.), *Does EU Membership Facilitate Convergence? The Experience of the EU's Eastern Enlargement - Volume I*, Studies in Economic Transition,
https://doi.org/10.1007/978-3-030-57686-8_6

of the new member states the accession period was characterised by very positive economic expectations for the second time since the change of regime in 1989. The one-and-a-half decades that have passed since then provide an opportunity to compare former expectations in 2004 and the actual macroeconomic changes.

Accession countries used the opportunities associated with EU membership differently, resulting in significant differences in their actual economic performance. The growth path, and in particular the growth performance achieved during the 2008/2009 crisis, was determined by the opportunities offered by EU membership as well as the (until then) lesser-known dangers of accession and the economic policies applied in each country. While some countries achieved sustained higher growth rates with well sequenced and executed reforms, the opening up of European export and financial markets enabled other countries (unfortunately including Hungary until 2010) to temporarily counterbalance the negative impacts of their unsustainable economic policy. In the latter case, of course, the painful recognition was triggered by the global financial crisis.

In our study, we present the impact of EU accession on the integration of foreign trade and macrofinancial processes of the economy based on data for Hungary. The study is structured as follows: Sect. 6.2 provides an overview of Hungary's trade structure, highlighting the years following EU accession. Section 6.3 outlines the processes that influenced the financing structure at the time of EU accession – in the period of external indebtedness up until the outbreak of the crisis. In Section 6.4, we discuss the behaviour of Hungarian economic actors after the outbreak of the crisis and describe the changes in the external balance of the economy. We conclude with presenting the main pillars of the new financing model of the Hungarian economy and the period of self-financing.

6.2 Developments in Trade After EU Accession

6.2.1 An Open Economy

Hungary is one of the most open economies in the European Union, where developments in international trade play a significant role in the growth performance of the economy. EU accession brought about a sharp rise in Hungarian trade openness compared to the average openness of the EU-15 countries or that of new EU member states (Fig. 6.1).

After 2005, the share of exports and imports to GDP increased and – except for the year marking the onset of the Great Recession, when

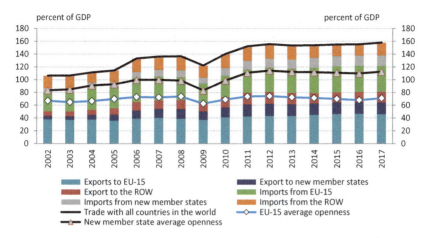

Fig. 6.1 Developments in trade openness in Hungary. (Source: Eurostat 2019, UN Comtrade, Fred. Note: Exports and imports as a share of GDP. New member states are countries joining in 2004 or later)

international trade collapsed – exports and imports relative to GDP continued to increase at a moderate rate. In the pre-EU accession period, trade openness was around 110 per cent of GDP; by 2007, it was close to 140 per cent, reaching almost 160 per cent of GDP by 2017. Exports to and imports from old EU member states (EU-15) account for the largest share of trade and both show a small, but steady increase relative to GDP throughout the period under review. New EU member states also play an important role in trade developments in Hungary: exports to new member states grew from 5 per cent to 18 per cent of GDP by 2017, whereas imports from new EU member states grew from 5 per cent to 16 per cent of GDP.

The rise in trade with old and new EU member states reflect the nature of Hungarian trade integration in the past decade. The increase in Hungarian trade intensity with other EU member states is mostly explained by two factors: easier access of foreign (multinational) companies to the Hungarian market and increased global value chain (GVC) participation. After EU accession, the entry barriers faced by foreign companies were reduced. More broadly, the pre-crisis years coincide with a period of rapid global value chain (GVC) expansion. Disentangling the effects of these two factors on the developments of the openness of the economy is difficult, but it is likely that GVC participation and the effects of globalisation were enhanced by EU accession.

Hungary's exports are highly concentrated at a few EU-15 member states, but after 2012 new EU member states also become significant export partners (Fig. 6.2). Germany is the main export partner of Hungary, with a share in total exports decreasing from 35 per cent in 2002 to 27 per cent in 2017. The other top export partners of Hungary are Austria, Italy, France and the United Kingdom in the pre-2012 period. The share of Hungarian exports towards new member states increased by 2012, and a few years after the eastern enlargement, the neighbouring countries of

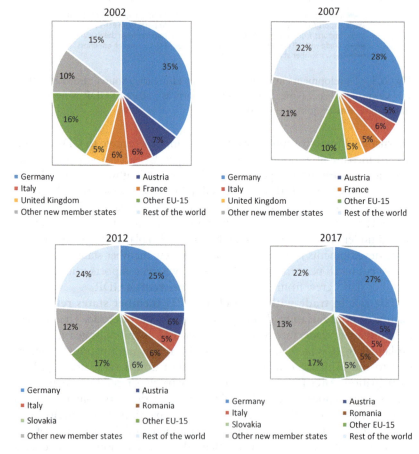

Fig. 6.2 Top export partners of Hungary. (Source: UN Comtrade)

Romania and Slovakia became top five export partners of Hungary, with a 6-per cent share in total Hungarian exports for both countries.

Developments in imports by partner country show a clear pattern of opening up to imports from EU-28 member states (Fig. 6.3). Germany is the main source of Hungarian imports, with its share rising from 24 per cent in 2002 to 27 per cent in 2017. The import share of new EU member states increased to 14 per cent by 2007, with Poland and Slovakia gradually becoming one of the main import partners of Hungary

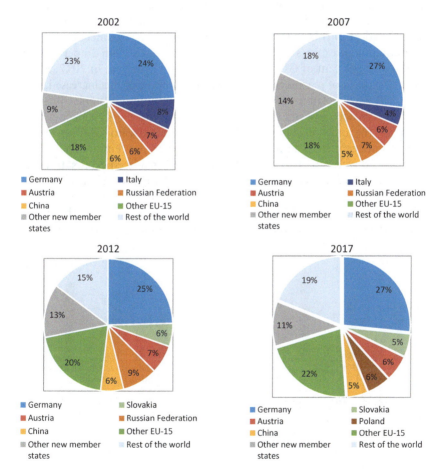

Fig. 6.3 Top import partners of Hungary. (Source: UN Comtrade)

by 2017. The share of imports sourced from outside the EU-28 countries (considering China, Russian Federation and the rest of the world) decreased from 35 per cent at the beginning of the period to 30 per cent in 2007 and 24 per cent in 2017.

6.2.2 Age of Specialisation

Concerning the products traded, machinery and transport equipment account for the highest share of both exports and imports as a share of GDP, both within and outside the EU-28 (Fig. 6.4). **After EU accession, specialisation in this type of product rose further.** Machinery and transport equipment exports to EU-28 countries increased from 26 per cent of GDP to 33 per cent of GDP in 2007, reaching 37 per cent in 2017. Extra EU-28 exports of machinery and transport equipment also increased, but remained small relative to GDP. Import patterns offer a similar picture: imports of machinery and transport equipment from the EU-28 countries comprise the bulk of imports and their share relative to GDP increased from 18 per cent in to 24 per cent in 2007 and 28 per cent in 2017.

These developments point to increased trade specialisation in machinery and transport equipment for Hungary. As this product group represents medium to high technology according to classifications, trading in machinery and transport equipment is associated with knowledge transfer, productivity gains and transition towards higher value added

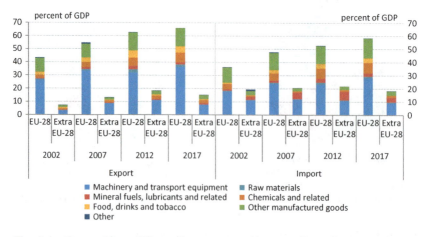

Fig. 6.4 Composition of Hungarian exports and imports. (Source: Eurostat 2019)

trade. However, the high concentration of exports and imports in this product group makes the country more vulnerable to global shocks affecting this specific sector.

6.3 From EU Accession to the 2008–2009 Crisis: The Curse of Easy Access to External Debt Financing

6.3.1 Dependence on External Funding

From the political transition in 1989 until the onset of the crisis, the gross saving ratio of domestic participants fell short of the investment ratio, resulting in persistently high current account deficits. Investments – which mostly related to corporate sector – typically exceeded 25 per cent of GDP, whereas domestic savings amounted to 20 per cent of GDP. Domestic participants made up for the difference by taking recourse to external funds; consequently, in the 2000s the current account[1] showed a continuously high deficit of 6–8 per cent of GDP (Pellényi et al. 2016). However, the high level of corporate investment was essential for maintaining economic growth, i.e. for the convergence of the economy (Fig. 6.5).

The relatively low level of internal savings can be partly attributed to a decline in household savings, which reflected stronger convergence expectations in the wake of EU accession. The willingness of Hungarian households to borrow started to increase only in the late 1990s. On the one hand, income expectations improved owing to the further convergence expected from EU accession in an environment of favourable domestic and global economic activity. In addition, the positive income expectations were also boosted by fiscal policies that had become undisciplined and accumulated substantial deficits starting from 2002. On the other hand, the impatience motive may also have raised households' credit demand: the recession following the political changeover required significant adjustments and subdued consumption on the part of households. The improvement in growth prospects, however, encouraged households to "make up for" the deferred consumption. Thus, the net savings of the Hungarian population decreased gradually until EU

---

[1] Saving-investment balance or I-S balance is a balance of national savings and national investment, which is equal to current account.

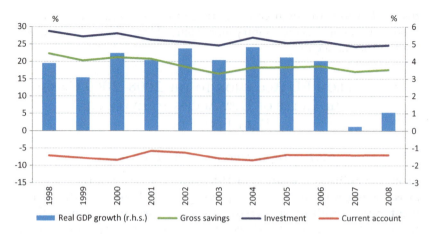

Fig. 6.5 Hungary's investment-to-GDP ratio, financing and real growth (as a percentage of GDP). (Source: Pellényi et al. 2016)

accession, mainly due to significantly lower inflation[2] than before and bank credit growth. Although the government attempted to stabilise the situation with unsuccessful fiscal austerity measures in 2006, amid continued positive income expectations and ostensibly favourable borrowing options, households opted for smoothing consumption; in other words, they reduced their saving even further. On balance, households' low propensity to save gave rise to problems because the household sector became even less capable of financing other sectors. Consequently, these sectors were forced to take recourse to external resources, mainly denominated in foreign currency (Fig. 6.6).

6.3.2 *The Spread of Debt Liabilities*

While for most of the 1990s, the current account deficit had mainly been financed from FDI inflows, after the beginning of the 2000s external debt provided the resources required for growth. When the sum of investment and consumption exceeds the available resources of an economy, the country must resort to borrowing, which may take the form of external debt or foreign direct investment inflows. In the case of

---

[2] Lower inflation reduces savings, as households need smaller savings to maintain the real value of their wealth.

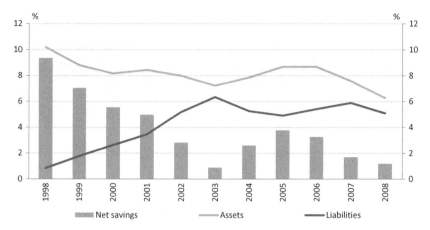

Fig. 6.6 Changes in households' net savings (as a percentage of GDP). (Source: MNB, own compilation)

Hungary, FDI inflows were dominant up until the early 2000s: external liabilities reached Hungary through the purchases of shares and in the form of greenfield investment. The FDI inflows financing the projects not only ensured fast-paced economic growth but also significantly improved the economy's future growth potential. Due to the nature of the external inflows and the high investment ratio, foreign investors deemed Hungary's high net borrowing (amounting to 6–8 per cent of GDP) sustainable. The total financing need of the economy did not change considerably after the early 2000s, but the structure of external financing changed: instead of FDI funds, debt financing gained increasing prominence (Fig. 6.7).

Rising foreign indebtedness continued after EU accession: stronger confidence stemming from the abundance of global liquidity and EU accession resulted in a decline in lending rates, thus further encouraging debt financing. Hungary's risk spreads already saw a significant decline before the country's accession to the EU. The deepening of economic relations and the integration of financial systems prompted by accession provided even better access to external borrowing. The increase in debt financing was also supported by the decline in yields on Hungarian securities up until the 2008–2009 crisis, partly as a result of the yield-reducing effect of the expectations linked to EU accession. On the whole, not only Hungary, but all other recently joined member states shifted

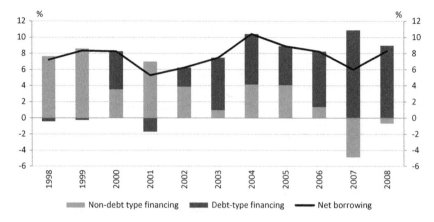

Fig. 6.7 Main financing factors of external net borrowing (as a percentage of GDP). (Source: MNB, own compilation)

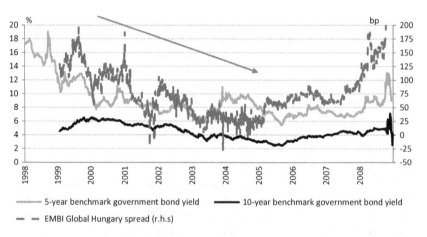

Fig. 6.8 Changes in the yields on Hungarian government securities. (Source: Bloomberg, own compilation)

towards debt financing, but there were significant differences in the extent. A particularly strong surge in external debt ratios was observed only in Hungary among the new EU member states as a result of the rise in the borrowing of both the government and households (Fig. 6.8).

Box: Changes in Investor Sentiment in Response to EU Accession
The positive effect of the 2004 EU enlargement on the economic perception of new entrants also pointed to indebtedness. At the beginning of the 2000s, the countries which joined the EU in 2004 had a credit rating of "BBB+" on average, six grades below the "AA+" average credit rating of the older member states. After the Irish referendum of 2002 and the 2004 accession as well, credit rating agencies formed increasingly positive expectations about the economic outlook of the Accession States. Consequently, the average credit rating of new entrants was only four notches below that of the older member states immediately prior to the start of the 2009 financial crisis. In the post-crisis recovery period, investor perception in the older and newly joined member states continued to converge (Fig. 6.9).

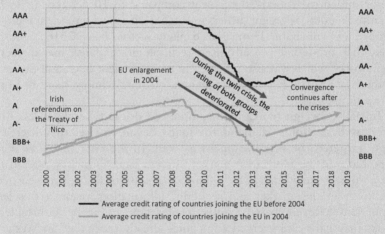

Fig. 6.9 Changes in the average credit rating of countries acceding to the EU prior 2004. (Note: The respective credit rating of the countries is calculated as the average of the ratings provided by Fitch, Moody's and S&P. The credit rating shown for the two groups is calculated as the average credit rating of the countries belonging to the given group. Source: tradingeconomics.com, own calculations)

6.3.3 The Unsustainable Financing Model of the Banking System

The process leading to EU accession entailed numerous changes that later significantly affected the operation of the Hungarian banking sector. The liberalisation of external capital flows had special relevance for the Hungarian financial system, as it led to the rapid appearance of foreign ownership in the domestic banking sector in the 1990s and early 2000s. The share of foreign ownership began to rise in 1994 when the government decided to privatise state-owned banks, which were often on the verge of bankruptcy. Foreign banks were attracted by the regional banking market: in view of the relatively low bank coverage, the expected economic convergence, the legal harmonisation process and the saturated Western banking sectors, regional markets promised higher profitability. As a result of the privatisation and subsequent bank acquisitions, by 2004 the share of banks in foreign ownership in the total assets of the banking sector surged to around 70 per cent compared to 10 per cent in 1990 (Zsámboki 2006). Foreign owners injected fresh capital into the underdeveloped and vulnerable Hungarian banking sector (Banai 2016a); moreover, they brought more advanced technologies and risk management frameworks, which was also reflected in more efficient operation (at least in the case of greenfield investment) and in the declining share of non-performing loans.

Initially, foreign banks mainly financed domestic companies. But later, as households' demand for loans began to rise, they increasingly targeted the retail segment as well. In the first years after their appearance in the Hungarian market, foreign banks primarily catered to the corporate credit market for a number of reasons: firstly, entry barriers are lower in this market and secondly, information asymmetry is less prominent here compared to the retail segment. Finally, nonresident banks may have often served companies already recognised in Western European markets or their Hungarian subsidiaries (Banai 2016b). Owing to their international activity, these companies often needed FX financing, which could be more easily satisfied by foreign-owned banks with easier access to the global capital markets. However, as the corporate credit market became saturated and competition picked up, the margins available in this segment narrowed, which also eroded the profitability of foreign banks. Consequently, foreign participants increasingly turned their attention to the household credit market, which had been previously dominated by domestic banks.

In addition to improving income prospects after EU accession, households' indebtedness was also facilitated by the introduction of new banking products. Households' demand for credit started to pick up in the early 2000s, at the time of the state's generous interest rate subsidisation. The upswing in retail lending was encouraged by easier access to credit. On the other hand, households' exceptionally positive expectations about future real wages also contributed to an increase in household borrowing. Given these expectations, and ignoring risks, a fairly high level of indebtedness appeared to be rational on the part of households (Erhart et al. 2015). The loans taken out were primarily allocated to consumption. Households' demand for cheap loans persisted even after the subsidy of HUF-denominated[3] housing loans had been curbed. Therefore, taking advantage of their easier access to FX funds, foreign-owned banks came up with a new product: the FX (foreign currency)-denominated loan. Foreign-owned banks sharply raised the volume of FX-loan contracts with households first through the financial enterprises owned by them and subsequently through direct disbursements, while the domestic banks caught up with the trend with some lag (Banai et al. 2016b). Banks with an Austrian background were vanguards in this process, as they launched in the Hungarian market the CHF-based lending which was popular in Austria at the time.

Expectations about the adoption of the euro in Hungary may also have contributed to the rapid increase of FX lending to households. EU accession, and in particular the processes leading up to it (primarily the increase in financial openness, the stronger inflow of FX funds and the rising share of foreign bank ownership), coupled with loose fiscal policies, contributed to the introduction and spread of FX lending in Hungary and in certain countries of the CEE region (Neanidis 2010; Rosenberg and Tirpak 2008).[4] Although Hungary's expansive fiscal policy did not point in this direction at all, from time to time government communication during the EU accession period set the goal for Hungary to join the euro area by the second half of the first decade of the 2000s. Upon joining the euro area, the Hungarians would have earned their incomes in euro, which

---

[3] HUF refers to forint which is the domestic currency in Hungary.

[4] Neanidis (2010) found that EU accession significantly facilitated the spread of foreign currency lending, whereas Rosenberg and Tirpak (2008) found no evidence for the significance of accession in itself but demonstrated that a number of processes related to accession (easier access to foreign funds, growing hedging options, adjusted expectations) did indeed point to an increase in the share of foreign currency lending.

would have eliminated the exchange rate risk. Another motive for taking out FX loans was the fact that due to high inflation compared to the region, HUF interest rates significantly exceeded euro rates. In addition, households expected the long-term persistence of FX loans' relative cost advantage, in view of the stable HUF exchange rate and the low international interest rate environment. Moreover, households increasingly shifted their focus to FX loans due to the tightening conditions of subsidised housing loans in domestic currency. As a combined result of these processes, the increase in retail HUF lending came to a halt in 2005 with a parallel, continued expansion of FX loans, which surpassed the stock of outstanding HUF loans by 2007.

On the whole, banks' financing model changed: the sector borrowed an increasing amount of funds from abroad. In addition to raising funds in Hungary, banks borrowed a substantial amount of funds from abroad to cover their domestic FX lending activity, as the domestic sources of funding proved insufficient, due to the low level of households' savings. Moreover, the rise in FX lending also led to the opening of the banking sector's currency position,[5] which was hedged by off-balance sheet swap contracts. In parallel with the spread of FX loans, banks took more and more risk to maintain their competitiveness where long-term stability considerations were regularly overridden by short-term market share acquisition plans. In addition, the Financial Supervisory Authority was also unable to set limits on the spread of FX lending (Matolcsy 2015). Consequently, the vulnerability of the Hungarian banking sector increased significantly in this period: the high loan-to-deposit ratio, the rising share of external liabilities and reliance on the swap market pointed to liquidity and financing risks, while the increased credit risk associated with FX debtors implied potential losses for banks (Fig. 6.10).

6.3.4 Rising Foreign Debt of the Public Sector

Due to the global abundance of liquidity, fiscal policy remained financeable although its unsustainability became more and more evident. At the same time this resulted in an increase of both the share of external borrowing in total government borrowing and the share of FX debt in GDP. Fiscal policy was significantly eased after 2002, leading to a persistently high budget deficit. At the same time, the global

---

[5] An open position represents market – in this case FX – exposure for the investor.

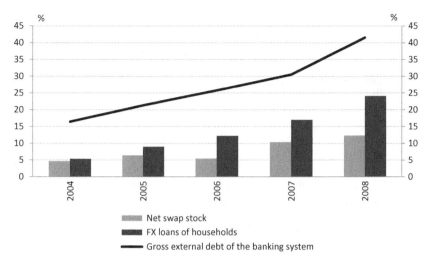

Fig. 6.10 External debt, swap holdings and retail FX loan portfolio of the banking sector (as a percentage of GDP. (Source: MNB, own compilation)

abundance of liquidity and the general underpricing of risks allowed for the short-term financing of the high deficit and public debt. As a result of years of high government deficits, public debt surged, which in turn gradually undermined Hungary's risk perception. In the context of high-yield HUF-denominated instruments, lower interest rates on FX loans became more attractive, and this also fuelled the public sector's rising FX indebtedness. The FX debt ratio of Hungarian public sector rose to 30 per cent, while the share of external funding amounted to almost 50 per cent by the end of 2007. HUF-denominated government securities were mainly purchased by non-resident investors, leading to an increase not only in the FX debt ratio but also in the share of external funding (Fig. 6.11).

The pre-crisis financing model of the Hungarian economy became unsustainable, as – in the absence of sufficient internal savings – it relied increasingly on external financing. In addition, the rising debt only led to a temporary increase in consumption and was not followed by investments, thus the growth potential remained unchanged. The government borrowed funds from non-residents directly, while households took out foreign loans through the banking sector. Although the high level of external financing temporarily allowed for a faster growth rate in Hungary in the period following EU accession, the growth

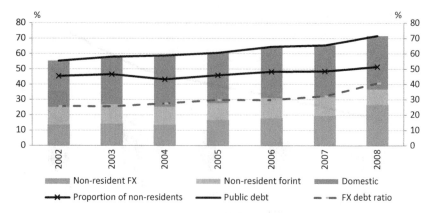

Fig. 6.11 Structure of public debt (as a percentage of GDP). (Source: ÁKK, MNB, own compilation)

potential of the economy did not improve. External sources increasingly financed consumption rather than investment. In addition, the income balance – and hence, the external position of the Hungarian economy – was undermined by the interest paid on the rising external debts.

6.4 Adjustment Prompted by the Crisis: Failed Corrective Measures, International Safety Net

6.4.1 Waning Market Financing: EU/IMF Bailout

When the crisis erupted, the previous sources of funding were no longer available and Hungary was among the first ones to apply for an international rescue package (Matolcsy and Palotai 2018). The outbreak of the crisis in 2008 hit Hungary in an extremely vulnerable position: the economy was confronted with structural growth weaknesses and the unsustainability of the financing model at the same time. Combined with investors' risk aversion, Hungary's high external debt and public debt (with a large share of FX debt) prompted a large-scale sell-off of government securities in the autumn of 2008. In addition to dumping their Hungarian instruments, non-residents' participation in Hungarian government securities auctions dwindled, ultimately leading to the suspension of government bond issuance for a period of six months. In the context of persistently weak demand and the market's liquidity shortage, Hungary necessarily had to resort to loans provided by international institutions in order to continue to finance its public debt (Hoffmann et al. 2013). In subsequent quarters, the country's temporary financing difficulties were resolved thanks to the drawdown of the FX loans extended by the IMF/EU, but these loans further increased non-residents' role in the financing of Hungarian debt; in addition, the share of FX debt jumped to 50 per cent of total debt.

> **Box: Loans from the EU and the IMF**
> **Hungary's unsustainable financing model in the first decade of the 2000s necessitated the conclusion of a credit agreement with the IMF/EU after the outbreak of the crisis.** Recourse to the credit facility was justified mainly by the tensions in the government securities market, but the loans also represented funds for distressed banks. Beyond the need to ensure the financeability of the public sector, the FX loans borrowed by the state were also warranted by reserve adequacy considerations, as the loans boosted the FX reserves of the central bank. Funds received by the budget and by the central bank under the credit facility amounted to EUR 14.5 billion, of which a total of EUR 9 billion was extended by the IMF in 2008 and 2009, and an additional EUR 5.5 billion was provided by the EU.
> **The international organisations attached conditions and a number of economic policy criteria to the package.** The loan extended by the EU was disbursed in four instalments. The disbursement of the first, EUR 2 billion instalment was conditional upon reducing the budget deficit target for 2009 and the implementation of supporting fiscal measures. The EU made the disbursement of individual instalments conditional upon the attainment of increasingly stringent budget deficit targets; moreover, it made recommendations for the regulation and supervision of the financial sector and the implementation of specific policy steps in relation to structural reforms. The EU verified compliance with the conditions before the disbursement of the next instalment and during ex-post supervision. Moreover, a monitoring and reporting system was also introduced, including the requirement of regular reporting on the foreign exchange reserve, the budget, public debt, financial stability and inflation. The strict ex-post supervision, which was part of the loan conditionality, ended in January 2015, and the country repaid the loan in full by 2016 (Kicsák 2016).

6.4.2 Changed Savings Behaviour of the Private Sector

Against the backdrop of declining incomes and tightening credit conditions, households became increasingly cautious which decreased consumption and investment, and turned the current account deficit into a surplus. The drying-up of external funds took its toll on private sector lending as well: credit supply slumped and liquidity constraints worsened. In addition to credit supply, credit demand also fell. Corporations were reluctant to take out loans in view of the downturn in external and internal demand, while households refrained from borrowing because of growing unemployment, decreasing incomes, increasing uncertainty and the rise in monthly instalments on their FX loans due to the depreciation of the HUF. On the whole, the intensification of precautionary motives triggered a quick adjustment in the private sector, leading to a sharp decline in borrowing. Thus, in addition to the reduced net borrowing of the public sector compared to early 2000s, the private sector increasingly became a net saver: on the one hand, corporations' previously substantial net borrowing first declined and then the sector turned into a net saver; on the other hand, households' financial savings also increased. The high level of private sector savings now enabled national savings to satisfy investment, which subsided after the crisis. All of this resulted in a sustained current account surplus after years of sizeable deficits (Hoffmann et al. 2013; Fig. 6.12).

A transformation of the country's financing model started: in the aftermath of the crisis the private sector began to repay its foreign debt. As a result of the credit crunch, the level of indebtedness came to a halt in 2009; in fact, debt repayment gradually intensified, and Hungary's external debt embarked on a slow decline (Hoffmann et al. 2013). A key contributor to this process was the fact that the private sector's increased loan payments and rising deposit holdings enabled banks to shed their external debts. However, the growth in outstanding debt stemming from the depreciation of the HUF exchange rate decelerated the decline in external vulnerability. As a result of the depreciation of the HUF exchange rate after the outbreak of the crisis, debt expressed in HUF surged, along with the debt servicing burden (Koroknai and Lénárt-Odorán 2012). Accordingly, although the country's external financing decreased according to transaction data, due to the revaluation, the reduction of outstanding debt relative to GDP only started later, from 2011. The stabilisation of the HUF exchange rate and the policy measures presented in the next section were indispensable for the reduction of the external debt ratio (Fig. 6.13).

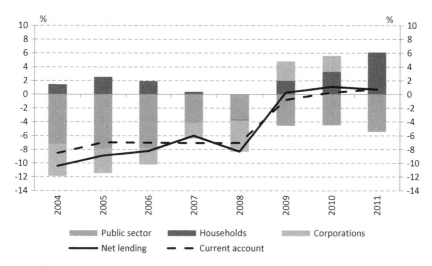

Fig. 6.12 Net lending of the sectors (as a percentage of GDP). (Source: MNB, own compilation)

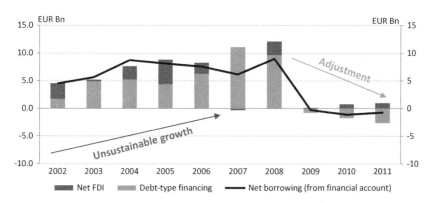

Fig. 6.13 Financing of external net borrowing (in EUR billions). (Source: Pellényi et al. 2016)

In addition, the large share of foreign banks in the Hungarian banking sector mitigated the effects of the crisis on the financial flows of the economy. Since after the crisis a significant share of – previously well performing – loans to the private sector started to turn into non-performing loans, the banking sector faced significant losses, which meant that additional funding was needed to maintain operations. The foreign banks – by way of their owners with more access to funding – could finance those, meaning that the crisis' effect on credit supply was somewhat mitigated by the presence of foreign banks. These efforts were formalised in 2009 within the boundaries of the Vienna Initiative, by which foreign investors undertook that they would maintain their investments in the region, resulting in a more stable macro environment and reducing the stress on the governments as well.

6.4.3 EU Transfers Also Alleviated the Financing Gap

The rise in EU transfers during this period helped reduce foreign debt and increase the level of the foreign exchange reserves, which is a key factor in a country's external perception. The accumulation of the substantial net lending in the aftermath of the crisis was also supported by the Hungarian economy's growing absorption of EU funds from 2009. A dominant part of the resources came from the Structural Funds and the Cohesion Fund, the primary objective of which is to foster convergence, increase regional competitiveness and expand employment. Therefore, the funds received from the EU not only offered an alternative financing for corporate and public investment projects, but also provided the means for the refinancing of foreign and domestic loans. By increasing the surplus on the transfer balance, EU transfers supported the improvement in the Hungarian economy's external balance position. The EU funds also boosted the level of the foreign exchange reserves, as the government converted the transfers received in euro to HUF at the central bank. The EU transfers mitigated the economy's reliance on external funding and facilitated a decline in the external indebtedness of the economy (Boldizsár et al. 2016).

6.5 New Financing Model: Strengthening Self-Financing

In the decade following the crisis, a new financing model relying upon domestic sources instead of external indebtedness was established in Hungary. This was allowed by the high net savings of the economy and was also generally supported by the changes in economic policy. Together with significant inflows of EU funds, these developments contributed to the financing of domestic investment in a sound structure, facilitating economic growth over the long run as well. As a result of the decline in external vulnerability, the external assessment of the country improved considerably, as was also reflected in the assessments of credit rating agencies and international organisations. The choice of sources available for financing corporate investment has widened significantly, and domestic sources have become prevalent in funding the state as a result of high household savings. The following section presents an overview of the factors that facilitated the development of a healthier financing structure which supports the convergence of the Hungarian economy, along with the fundamental pillars of the new financing model.

6.5.1 Rising Household Savings and Shift in Economic Policy

The state used numerous targeted measures to reduce the external vulnerability of the Hungarian economy and develop a sounder financing structure. The measures resulted in a decline in the high debt indicators, broadened companies' opportunities to raise funds and contributed to the development of a healthier financing model, which relies more strongly on domestic funding. Public institutions (the government, Government Debt Management Agency, central bank) took coordinated steps, which supported economic policy and strengthened and/or complemented one another's effects, exerted their impact by expanding the domestic sources (which had proven to be insufficient during the crisis) and facilitated the reduction of external funding (Fig. 6.14).

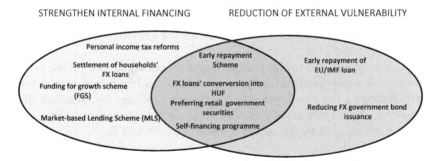

Fig. 6.14 Measures affecting the change in the financing structure. (Source: own compilation)

Net household savings increased considerably in the years after the crisis, and their sustained high level represents an important source of funding for other sectors of the economy. As seen during the crisis, an inadequate level of domestic savings leads to serious vulnerability risks for the country. In the past decade, households' savings rose from the low pre-crisis level to a steadily elevated level (5–6 per cent of GDP on average), with contributions from the accumulation of financial assets as well as the repayment of loans.

This change, which was favourable in terms of external vulnerability, was supported by the underlying trends in savings as well as economic-psychological factors and various government measures. The growth in financial assets was facilitated by a considerable expansion in employment and a dynamic rise in wages, resulting in a significant increase in real income in a low inflation environment. In addition, fiscal measures such as the personal income tax cut, the family tax allowance and the utility cost reduction also contributed to the substantial improvement in households' income situation. As a result of the crisis, households' attitude about savings also changed: borrowing tapered off and precautionary considerations came to the fore. The change in economic policy priorities (e.g. efforts to make retail government securities more popular, wider product choice and higher interest rates) and targeted measures (e.g. the possibility of early repayment of FX loans at a fixed exchange rate, later the settlement due to the unilateral interest rate hikes and the conversion of FX loans as well as the rules limiting the possibility of the development of excessive lending) also contributed to the rise in households' financial savings and to the change in the composition of the financial asset portfolio. In the past years, as a result of favourable income developments, the sector's financial savings rate remained high, even while households' consumption and investment expenditures were expanding, i.e. supporting economic growth (Fig. 6.15).

The targeted economic policy measures managed the problem of households indebted in foreign currency, in addition to limiting the possibility of the development of excessive lending. As a result of the conversion into HUF at the end of 2014, households' exposure to foreign-exchange rates practically ceased to exist, which was a favourable change in terms of external vulnerability and banks' loan portfolio quality. As the foreign currency necessary for the conversion into HUF was provided by the central bank's FX reserves for the banking sector, the measure contributed to the reduction of credit institutions' external debt and the decline in Hungary's gross external debt.

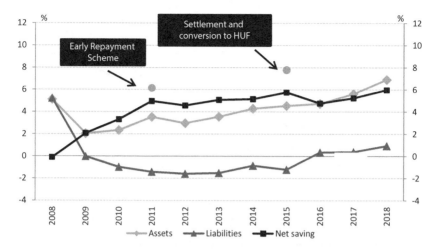

Fig. 6.15 Net savings of the household sector (as a percentage of GDP). (Source: MNB, own compilation. Note: * The values reflect underlying trends and are adjusted for the effect of pension savings, the early repayment scheme, real yield payments, the indemnification of the depositors of liquidated savings cooperatives and the HUF conversion and settlement. Two points show the original data without the corrections)

6.5.2 New Public Debt Strategy

The most spectacular change concerning the composition of households' savings and at the same time the most important one in terms of the financing structure of the economy took place in the retail government securities market. Households' government securities purchases started to rise quickly from 2012, and the holdings have been steadily expanding since then. All of this was due to the fact that as a result of the government's new strategy, the accumulation of government securities has become a new form of investment that provides competitive saving opportunities. This occurred because the economic policy priority shifted from the previous external sources of financing to domestic savings, and a number of measures were taken to encourage domestic actors to buy government securities. As a result of interest rate increases, government securities offer a major yield advantage compared to other forms of investment in the low yield environment as well. In addition, the government securities market demand was supported by a marketing campaign to raise

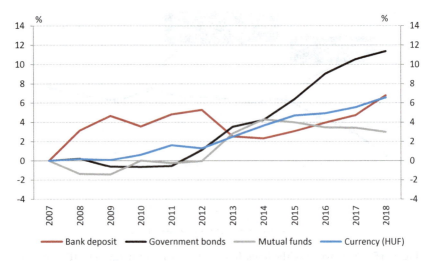

Fig. 6.16 Cumulative change in households' main financial assets. (Source: MNB, own compilation)

investor awareness as well as the better availability of government securities, which was the result of infrastructure development and steps aimed at strengthening the participation of market service providers (Kékesi et al. 2015). **Households' strong demand for government securities increased the ratio of domestic financing of the state, which played a key role in the reduction of Hungary's external vulnerability** (Fig. 6.16).

After 2010, savings from domestic income holders gradually took over the main role from external sources in the financing of the government debt. From 2012, external debt indicators declined considerably, i.e. a turnaround occurred in external debt, which had surged as a result of the loan from the IMF and the EU at the outbreak of the crisis and increased further due to the need for external borrowing. These developments were attributable to the fact that initially the repayment of the loans from international organisations had been covered by international FX bond issues, but in 2012, as a result of the change in the debt management strategy of the Government Debt Management Agency (ÁKK), increasing amounts of domestic funds were used to finance government debt.

Central bank measures also helped to strengthen domestic savings, thanks to the concept of self-financing. The shift towards self-financing was realised as a sequence of successive government measures and decisions, aimed at increasing the government security holdings of domestic agents (households, banking sector), and facilitated safer public financing and the reduction of external indebtedness (Matolcsy and Palotai 2016). As a result of the increase in government securities purchases by households, which was related to the factors presented above, and the growth in banks' demand for government securities, HUF-denominated securities played an increasingly dominant role in the net issuance of the public sector (Fig. 6.17).

The MNB's self-financing programme may have also contributed to the rise in banks' demand for government securities. The programme, which was announced in 2014 contributed to the banks' acquisition of government securities by the restructuring of central bank instruments. The central bank policy instrument changed into deposits instead of bonds in August 2014. Another instrument was the introduction of a floating rate-payer new interest rate swap (IRS) tool, in order to support banks in increasing and stabilising their holdings of long-term government securities. These measures helped reduce external vulnerability and strengthen financial stability. As a result of the conversion into deposits, due to the less favourable liquidity properties, some of the funds

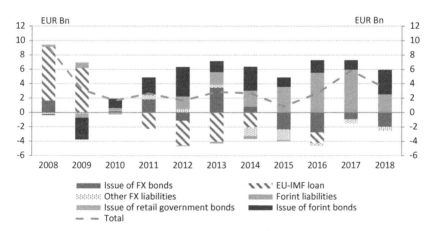

Fig. 6.17 Breakdown of the net issuance of the public sector. (Sources: ÁKK, MNB, own compilation)

of banks flowed out from the central bank's policy instrument and likely appeared on the government securities market due to the IRS tool (MNB 2015).

The increase in the share of domestic financing was reflected in a change in the ownership structure of government securities as well, which was a favourable development for the national economy as a whole. The declining dependency on external sources is well illustrated by the fact that the ownership share of non-residents gradually decreased from the level of above 55 per cent in 2011–2012 to 32 per cent in 2018. In parallel with that, the weight of households in government debt financing rose by roughly 15 percentage points to 20 per cent in 2018. All in all, public debt owned by residents already accounts for nearly two thirds of the total debt, and the share of FX debt within the total public debt fell to 23 per cent by 2018. The strengthening of domestic financing is a favourable change for the national economy in various respects. Firstly, domestic sources represent more stable financing for the state than foreign funds, as was demonstrated by the withdrawal of funds due to the erosion of investor confidence during the 2008 crisis. In addition, the increase in financing by households may result in a decline in market yields as the state has to undertake fewer market issuances. Overall, it has a positive impact on the country's external balance indicators and, through that, on the external assessment of the economy as well (Fig. 6.18).

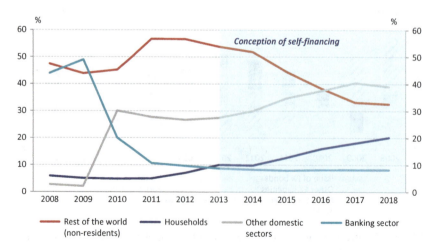

Fig. 6.18 Ownership share of debt securities issued by the central government. (Source: MNB, securities statistics)

6.5.3 Turnaround in Lending: Support for Domestic Lending to Corporations

Sources of loanable funds available to companies have expanded since the crisis, mostly because of the MNB's Funding for Growth Scheme. The MNB launched the Funding for Growth Scheme (FGS) in June 2013 with the aim of restarting SME lending and reviving the corporate credit market. Within the framework of the FGS, the central bank supported small and medium-sized enterprises' access to loans through the banking sector, by way of targeted lending. In the scheme, the central bank provided loans at a 0 per cent interest rate to the banking sector, allowing banks to extend loans with a fixed interest margin (of up to 2.5 per cent per annum) from these funds to domestic micro, small and medium-sized enterprises for specific loan purposes. In the 3 phases of the scheme, nearly 40,000 enterprises had access to financing in a value of more than HUF 2800 billion (EUR 9,2 billion) over 4 years. The individual phases of the scheme were characterised by different features:

- **Phase 1 restarted SME lending, directed attention to the SME sector**, and stimulated competition among banks. Serving loan refinancing, a considerable portion of the lending contributed to the decline in companies' interest burdens, and through the refinancing of FX loans it reduced the sector's exchange rate exposure.
- **In Phase 2, investment loans became prevalent,** allowing the implementation of longer-term investment projects, and the share of business credit was also significant.
- **Phase 3 of the scheme facilitated the financing of investment only,** allowed more targeted funding, also provided FX financing for companies that had natural hedge.

The FGS had a positive impact on both loan demand and supply, contributing to economic growth through the financing of SME investments and improving the income situation of the sector. The loans granted within the FGS had a positive impact on investment activity directly and through their spill-over effects as well. More than 60 per cent of the total lending of more than HUF 2800 billion (EUR 9,2 billion) provided in the three phases of the FGS financed new investment. The investment projects implemented from these funds had direct positive impacts on growth and employment as the value of some of these would

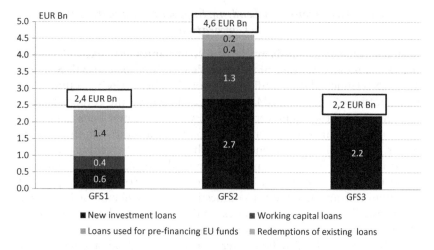

Fig. 6.19 Distribution of loan purposes in the individual phases of the FGS. (Source: MNB 2017)

have been lower without the introduction of the FGS. As a result of the improving liquidity situation of companies, business credit contributed to the improvement in the competitiveness of the sector, thus directly supporting growth in investment, while loan refinancing persistently improved enterprises' income situation and creditworthiness due to the lower interest costs. The funds for refinancing FX loans helped reduce companies' external debt, and thus facilitated the decline in external vulnerability and in FX exposure as well (Fig. 6.19).

Following the end of the third phase of the FGS, the central bank launched new, targeted programmes to increase the outstanding loans of SMEs and to achieve a favourable change in their composition. Banks' smooth return to market-based lending was facilitated by the Market-based Lending Scheme launched by the central bank in 2016, providing – without central bank refinancing – interest rate swaps to support banks' interest rate risk management and deposit placement possibilities, facilitating their liquidity management. The scheme contributed to the expansion in loans outstanding but was unable to exert a favourable effect on the structure of the portfolio. Starting from early 2019, the FGS Fix programme is intended to facilitate a favourable change in the structure of SME loans outstanding by supporting the granting of long-term loans with fixed and favourable interest rates (MNB 2018).

6.5.4 Shift in the Absorption of EU Transfers

EU funds have increasingly become sources of investment for both the private sector and the public sector after the crisis, supporting economic recovery. For domestic companies, due to lack of a developed capital market, in addition to funds from the banking sector, cohesion funds – the role of which became more important in the period following the crisis – represent the most important external financing possibility for investment. After the crisis, companies faced narrowing opportunities to obtain funds, and this situation was eased by the financing provided by EU funds. Net EU fund absorption in Hungary between 2008 and 2017 amounted to more than EUR 40 billion, nearly EUR 27 billion of which financed the private sector. EU funds contributed to corporate investment but facilitating the revival of SME lending – as a main channel of monetary transmission – by the MNB was crucial in terms of recovery from the crisis and strengthening financial stability. The absorption of EU funds helped the growth of the Hungarian economy through financing the public sector's investments. Within the funds utilised, the ratio of capital transfers financing investment increased gradually, and by 2015 the transfers used by the private sector exceeded those of the state. In addition, the inflows of EU funds resulted in a rise in FX reserves, improving the reserve adequacy of the country. On the whole, when the possibilities of obtaining funds were scarce and bank lending was weak, EU funds helped avoid a major decline in domestic investment, and via the financing of investment they may have contributed to the recovery from the recession after the crisis.

Although net EU fund inflows dropped with the 2007–2013 programming period coming to an end, the financing model based on internal resources had become self-sustaining by then. Following the end of the 2007–2013 programming period, EU fund absorption reached its peak in 2015. In 2015, EU fund inflows exceeded 6 per cent of GDP, which played an important role in the rise in gross capital formation as a percentage of GDP nearly reaching the level last experienced before the crisis. Following the closing of the 2007–2013 programming period, in 2016, at the beginning of the upswing in funds from the new programming period, the absorption of EU funds dropped. In parallel with that, gross capital formation as a percentage of GDP also declined, but this decline proved to be temporary and more moderate than the one resulting from the fall in EU funds. All of this was the result of the fact that

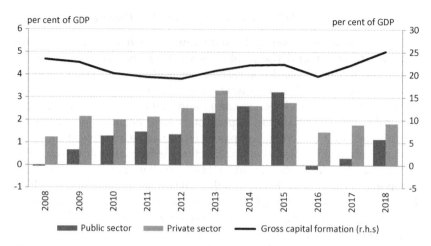

Fig. 6.20 Absorption of EU funds and the investment rate. (Source: MNB)

companies were able to offset the financing need arising due to the decline in EU funds by using funds originating from the growing bank lending. This is corroborated by the fact that in parallel with a still subdued absorption of EU transfers, strong growth in investment was already observed in 2017 (Fig. 6.20).

In the 2014–2020 programming period, the more targeted and efficient use of EU funds will help improve competitiveness and increase productivity. Examining the funds for economic development of the 2007–2013 programming period, the impact assessment by Banai et al. (2017), which relies upon a micro database and concerns Hungarian companies, found that funds with economic development objectives had a significant positive impact on sales revenues, gross value added, the number of employees and, in some cases, on operating income as well. Although in the 2014–2020 programming period the total appropriation provided by the cohesion policy is lower in nominal terms than in the previous programming period, the structure of funding is more favourable in terms of economic growth. According to the Partnership Agreement, during the cycle Hungary may use EUR 22 billion of the funds of the cohesion policy, of which the areas that are crucial in terms of the competitiveness of the Hungarian economy (e.g. support for the SME sector, research and development) may receive higher proportions of funding. The Economic Development and Innovation Operational Programme

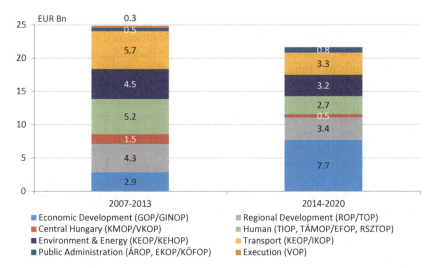

Fig. 6.21 Breakdown of funds of EU programme periods by development objective. (Source: Boldizsár et al. 2016)

(EDIOP) accounts for most of the funds intended to be spent on economic development, including funds aiming at production capacity expansions of small and medium-sized enterprises, increasing funds for research and development and the improvement of competitiveness as well as facilitating higher and more efficient employment (Boldizsár et al. 2016; Fig. 6.21).

6.5.5 Impact of the Changing Financing Model on Developments in External Liabilities

As a result of the above developments, Hungary's external debt has decreased, while FDI inflows continue to constitute a stable source of financing for the economy. As presented in the previous sections, FDI funds have played an important role in financing the growth of the Hungarian economy since the political transformation. As opposed to debt liabilities, these funds proved to be stable during the crisis as well, although their inflows slowed down in the years after the crisis. From 2008, the decline in both gross FDI inflows and outflows (capital exports) contributed to this deceleration. Starting from 2012 net FDI inflows started to increase again, despite the expansion in the gross components (in- and outflows), which was related to significant capital in transit transactions, in which reinvested earnings also played a significant role. Most of the FDI funds in Hungary originated from the countries of the EU following the crisis as well, with these funds accounting for three quarters of the total portfolio. Nevertheless, in the past years an important structural change took place in the FDI portfolio: in contrast to the earlier trend, manufacturing became prevalent by 2017, while the weight of services declined. Looking at the various sectors, the share of vehicle manufacturing, pharmaceutical production and electronics expanded.

The new financing model based on self-financing allowed Hungary's debt indicators to fall, which also improved investors' perception of the country. A continuous decline in debt liabilities was observed in the years following the crisis, resulting in a significant reduction in Hungary's external vulnerability. The reduction of the external debt of the banking and corporate sectors as well as that of the public sector also contributed to this. The decrease in net external debt after the crisis was mainly related to the private sector until 2012: the balance sheet adjustment was coupled with a rise in financial claims and the repayment of bank loans. Banks spent the ensuing household and corporate funds on the repayment of their accumulated external debt, which resulted in a fall in banks' external debt. In this period, due to the borrowing from the EU and the IMF and non-residents' government securities purchases, the net external debt of the state was on a rising path, before declining significantly from 2013, which was particularly attributable to household savings and the government measures that supported the strengthening of domestic financing. By end-2017, the net external debt of the private sector reached a level close to 0, while that of the public sector fell to nearly half of the historical high of 20 per cent of GDP observed in 2012 (Fig. 6.22).

Developments in the net international investment position, including net external debt, are also particularly important in that they induce a change in the open currency position of the sectors (as net external debt equals the sum of the open currency positions of individual sectors). The dynamically rising net external debt of pre-crisis years was accompanied by the opening of the FX position (HUF exposure) of domestic market participants resulting from their FX indebtedness. With the profound change in financing conditions and the elimination of FX lending to households, households' open position began to moderate after the outbreak of the crisis. Thanks to favourable developments in external balance in the recent

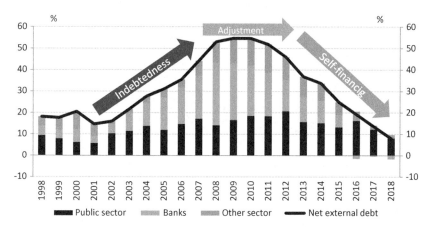

Fig. 6.22 Changes in net external debt by sector (as a percentage of GDP). (Source: MNB, own compilation)

period, exposure to exchange rate risk also subsided significantly in the other two domestic sectors, corporations and the public sector. At present, both the public sector – consolidated with the MNB – and households hold more FX assets than FX liabilities. The turnaround in the open position of households can be attributed to the conversion of FX loans to HUF, the offsetting of which materialised, due to the decline in the FX reserves, in the public sector consolidated with the MNB (that notwithstanding, FX debt decreased owing to self-financing and the inflow of EU funds). By contrast, corporations hold more FX liabilities than FX assets. This, however, does not necessarily imply a vulnerability risk for Hungary thanks to the natural hedge available to numerous firms: their export sales provide sufficient foreign currency to pay off their FX loans. Amid persisting net lending, the downward shift in net external debt may continue and thus the open position of the sectors can moderate further in the coming years.

Generally speaking, the net international investment position of the more developed EU countries is higher than those of the lower income economies (Fig. 6.23). The improving NIIP can be attributed to several factors (Lane and Milesi-Ferretti 2002). In parallel with economic development, domestic marginal product of capital will decrease so investment abroad – which is more profitable – may gain ground. For this reason in developed countries the volume of outward direct investments typically

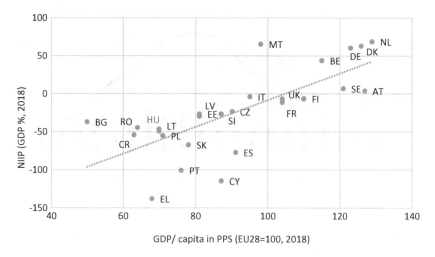

Fig. 6.23 Correlation between economic development and NIIP position (2018). (Source: Eurostat (2019), own compilation)

exceeds the FDI in the respective country. The stock of net foreign assets also increases due to the households' favourable income position in higher income economies. The rise of income and the decline in the marginal utility of consumption leads to a rise in savings and the accumulation of assets takes place partly in foreign assets – or domestic assets can finance other sectors, thus they need less foreign liabilities. Based on international experiences, the country's convergence to higher income Western European economies may result in improving of the NIIP position over the longer term (Balogh et al. 2018).

6.6 Summary

The Central and Eastern European countries joining the European Union in 2004 made the most important step in European integration with the hopes of accelerating economic convergence. The expansion of export markets and rapidly deepening financial integration opened up new growth opportunities.

In the first decade of EU membership, the Hungarian economy was unable to take advantage of the economic potential of accession. The country's export exposure, which was already high at the time of accession, increased further with the deepening of foreign trade integration. While remaining concentrated, exports to the newly joined EU member states also started to grow. However, the improved access to external financing conserved the unsustainable financing model which Hungary had when it joined the EU. This model used foreign loans to finance excessive consumption instead of financing new investments. As this model led to increasing foreign indebtedness while failed to improve the growth potential of the economy, it left the country vulnerable to external shocks. Thus, when the global financial crisis hit Hungary in 2008–09, it caused a deep economic, financial and social crisis. A further deepening of this crisis was prevented by the loan agreement and financial assistance programme concluded with the EU and the IMF. In this period, the EU transfers played an important role as they helped to prevent a protracted economic recession (Fig. 6.24).

Following the crisis, transformation of the country's financing model started in 2010. As a result of a significant increase in domestic savings, the repayment of external loans began.

During the past years, a new financing model took shape in Hungary, which reflected the new economic policy strategy. As before, European

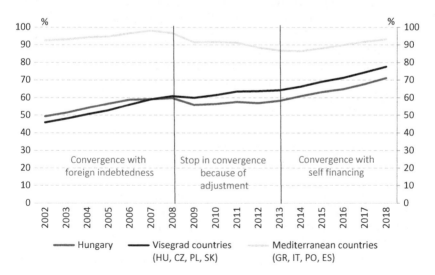

Fig. 6.24 Real GDP per capita calculated from the PPP-based indicator in 2017, EU28 = 100. (Source: Eurostat 2019, own calculation)

Table 6.1 Transformation of Hungary's financing model

	Indebtedness (2002-2008)	Adjustment (2009-2011)	Self-financing (2012-)
Net borrowing	↑	↓	↓
Internal savings	↓	↑	↑↑
FDI	↑	↑	↑
External debt	↑↑	↔	↓↓
EU fund	↔	↑↑	↑↑

Source: own compilation

Union funds supported the development of the Hungarian economy, but now they worked in tandem with the domestic development strategy, the two forces pulled in the same direction. As a result, the external vulnerability of the economy has declined and a turnaround in lending has taken place. The range of funds available to finance corporate investments is steadily expanding as a result of the MNB's Funding for Growth Scheme, and domestic funds have become prevalent in financing the public sector due to high household savings (Table 6.1).

In terms of external vulnerability indicators, Hungary not only worked off its shortfall compared to the Visegrád region but caught up with the average of the region in a number of indicators, sometimes even became one of the leaders. The Hungarian current account balance was persistently above the levels seen in the Visegrád countries, and as a result, Hungary's gross and net external debt declined by more than 35 per cent of GDP in the past 10 years. As these indicators typically increased or only declined slightly in the other countries in the region, by now Hungary's gross and net external debt correspond to the levels observed in the countries of the region. This was an important step forward which helped to improve the country's external assessment and to reduce risk premium on the country's external debt. These improvements were also reflected in the evaluations by credit rating agencies, confirming the stronger resilience of the economy.

REFERENCES

Balogh, E., Boldizsár, A., Gerlaki, B., & Kóczián, B. (2018). Developments in the GDP-GNI Gap in Hungary and the CEE Region. *Financial and Economic Review, 17*(3), 57–84.

Banai, Á. (2016a). *Banki viselkedés a válság előtt és a válságban (Bank Behaviour Before and During the Crisis)*. PhD Thesis, Corvinus University of Budapest.

Banai, Á. (2016b). Drivers of Bank Lending in Hungary – The Roles of Bank-Specific and Macro Factors. *Economic Review, LXIII*, 137–161.

Banai, Á., Lang, P., Nagy, G., & Stancsics, M. (2017). The Effects of EU Economic-Development Subsidies on Micro, Small and Medium-Sized Firms in Hungary. *Economic Review, LXIV*, 997–1029.

Boldizsár, A., Kékesi, Z., Koroknai, P., & Sisak, B. (2016). Review of Hungarian EU Transfers – At the Border of Two Fiscal Periods. *Financial and Economic Review, 15*(2), 59–87.

Erhart, S., Kékesi, Z., Koroknai, P., Kóczián, B., Matolcsy, G., Palotai, D., & Sisak, B. (2015). The Macroeconomic Effects of Foreign Currency Lending and the Economic Policy Responses. In *A devizahitelezés nagy kézikönyve (Big Handbook of FX Lending)*. Nemzeti Közszolgálati és Tankönyvkiadó, Budapest, 121–158.

Eurostat (2019). Eurostat database – European statistics. *European Commission.* https://ec.europa.eu/eurostat/data/database

Fred: Fred Economic Data. *Federal Reserve Bank of St. Louis.* https://research.stlouisfed.org/

Hoffmann, M., Kóczián, B., & Koroknai, P. (2013). Developments in the External Balance of the Hungarian Economy: Indebtedness and Adjustment. *MNB Bulletin, 8*(Special issue), 69–80.

Kékesi, Z., Kóczián, B., & Sisak, B. (2015). The Role of Household Portfolio Restructuring in Financing of the General Government. *Financial and Economic Review, 14*(1), 79–110.

Kicsák, G. (2016). The Repayment of the Last Instalment of the EU Loan Reduced Both Hungary's Vulnerability and the Costs of Debt Financing. *MNB Professional Article.* https://www.mnb.hu/letoltes/kicsak-az-eu-hitel-utolso-reszletenekvisszafizetesemnbhonlapra.pd

Koroknai, P., & Lénárt-Odorán, R. (2012). Developments in External Borrowing by Individual Sectors. *MNB Bulletin, 7*(3), 46–56.

Lane, P. R., & Milesi-Ferretti, G. M. (2002). Long-Term Capital Movements, NBER Chapters. In *NBER Macroeconomics Annual 2001* (Vol. 16, pp. 73–136). National Bureau of Economic Research. https://doi.org/10.1086/654435.

Matolcsy, G. (2015). Economic Balance and Growth. *Magyar Nemzeti Bank Könyvsorozata.* Kairosz Kiadó, Budapest.

Matolcsy, G., & Palotai, D. (2016). The Interaction Between Fiscal and Monetary Policy in Hungary Over the Past Decade and a Half. *Financial and Economic Review., 15*(2), 5–32.

Matolcsy, G., & Palotai, D. (2018). The Hungarian Model: Hungarian Crisis Management in View of the Mediterranean Way. *Financial and Economic Review., 17*(2), 5–42.

MNB. (2015). *The Magyar Nemzeti Bank's Self-Financing Programme*, April 2014–March 2015. https://www.mnb.hu/letoltes/the-magyar-nemzeti-bank-s-self-financing-programme-april-2014march-2015.pdf

MNB. (2017). *The Results of the Funding for Growth Scheme.* https://www.mnb.hu/letoltes/anovekedesi-hitelprogram-eredmenyei-honlapra-20170613.pdf

MNB. (2018, September). *The Central Bank's Considerations with Regard to the Launching of the Funding for Growth Scheme Fix (FGS Fix) and Main Features of the Scheme.* https://www.mnb.hu/letoltes/nhp-fix-hun-vegleges.pdf

MNB: Statistical Time Series. *MNB.* https://www.mnb.hu/en/statistics/statistical-data-andinformation/statistical-time-series

Neanidis, K. C. (2010). Financial Dollarization and European Union Membership. *International Finance, 13*(2), 257–282.

Pellényi, G., Kékesi, Z., Rippel, G., & Sisak, B. (2016). Convergence and Equilibrium in Hungary Since the Political Changeover in Competitiveness and Growth the Road to Sustainable Economic Convergence. In *D. Palotai - B. Virág (Ed.): Competitiveness and Growth.* Magyar Nemzeti Bank, Budapest.

Rosenberg, C. B., & Tirpak, M. (2008). *Determinants of Foreign Currency Borrowing in the New Member States of the EU.* IMF Working Paper, No. 08/173.

UN Comtrade: UN Comtrade Database. *United Nations.* https://comtrade.un.org/

Zsámboki, B. (2006). *Az EU-csatlakozás hatása a magyar bankrendszerre – Szabályozáspolitikai megfontolások (The Impact of EU Accession on the Hungarian Banking Sector – Regulatory Policy Considerations).* PhD Thesis, Corvinus University of Budapest, Budapest.

CHAPTER 7

Macroeconomic Trends in the Baltic States Before and After Accession to the EU

Martti Randveer and Karsten Staehr

7.1 INTRODUCTION

The three Baltic states, Estonia, Latvia and Lithuania, joined the European Union on 1 May 2004 in the first round of enlargement to include countries from Central and Eastern Europe. Developments in the Baltic states have however been intricately linked with those in the EU since the

---

The views expressed are those of the authors and not necessarily those of Eesti Pank or other parts of the Eurosystem.

M. Randveer
Eesti Pank, Tallinn, Estonia
e-mail: martti.randveer@eestipank.ee

K. Staehr (✉)
Eesti Pank, Tallinn, Estonia

Tallinn University of Technology, Tallinn, Estonia
e-mail: karsten.staehr@eestipank.ee

© The Author(s), under exclusive license to Springer Nature Switzerland AG 2021
M. Landesmann, I. P. Székely (eds.), *Does EU Membership Facilitate Convergence? The Experience of the EU's Eastern Enlargement - Volume I*, Studies in Economic Transition,
https://doi.org/10.1007/978-3-030-57686-8_7

countries regained their independence in 1991 and this also applies particularly to the macroeconomic trends in the three countries.

This chapter discusses key macroeconomic and structural developments in the Baltic states before and after they joined the EU. The experiences of the Baltic states are particularly interesting because they are the only EU members from the former Soviet Union. The macroeconomic developments are a consequence of the Baltic states having small and open economies, but they also arise from the institutional frameworks and economic policies of the countries. It follows that there are numerous ways in which the EU has directly or indirectly affected macroeconomic developments in the Baltic states.

The Baltic states aspired to join the European Union at an early stage after they regained their independence, since economic and political integration with Western Europe was widely seen as a cornerstone in the nation building process. The countries joined the EU in May 2004, but their admission was merely the culmination of a gradual process of integration that had first started in the early 1990s. This means that it is often difficult to identify the exact or direct effects of the EU on macroeconomic developments in the countries. Moreover, although there are many similarities between the three countries, there are also important differences that are rooted in history, geography and economic structures, including differences that are important for the relationship of the countries with the EU (Poissonnier 2017).

The rest of the chapter is organised as follows. Section 7.2 discusses briefly the EU accession process of the Baltic states. Sections 7.3, 7.4, 7.5 and 7.6 consider key macroeconomic developments from the early 1990s up to 2019, by which time the countries had been members of the EU for 15 years. Section 7.7 considers selected broader long-term developments. Finally, Section 7.8 provides some perspectives on the key macroeconomic challenges facing the Baltic states.

7.2 Joining the EU

The Baltic states regained their independence from the Soviet Union in August 1991 and the newly elected governments articulated shortly afterwards the ambition of their countries to join the European Union.[1]

---

[1] The *European Union* was known as the *European Community* before 1993 and even earlier as the *European Economic Community*. This chapter uses the terms the *European*

Alongside the processes of nation building and post-communist reform, the countries also took measures to prepare for membership by taking part in a number of EU programmes for the post-communist countries in Central and Eastern Europe. As early as December 1991 the Baltic states joined PHARE, a programme that provided aid and technical assistance, and that initially targeted Poland and Hungary (Kerikmäe et al. 2016). Other agreements on trade and economic and commercial cooperation with the EU were signed in 1992 and extended in early 1995.

Many countries from Central and Eastern Europe aspired at the time to join the EU so a common framework for admitting new members was warranted. This was provided by the Copenhagen criteria of June 1993, which set out the broad requirements for membership. They stated that a country wanting to join the EU had to adhere to democratic principles and exhibit a market economy that was deemed able to cope with the competitive pressures it would face within the EU. Moreover, membership required that applicants comply with the *Acquis Communautaire*, the legal set of rules of the EU. These were divided into 21 thematic *chapters*, each of which was to be negotiated and closed individually.

The Baltic states entered into the *Europe Agreements* with the EU in 1995. The agreements spelled out numerous areas of cooperation and meant that the Baltic states became associated countries and therefore possible future members of the EU. Estonia was in the first wave of countries that were invited to start membership negotiations in December 1997, in part in recognition of the momentum of the reforms in the country. Latvia and Lithuania were invited to start the negotiations in December 1999 as part of the second wave. The negotiations that followed were relatively straightforward for the Baltic states and the chapters were closed without any major administrative or political issues; arguably the thorniest issues were found within the energy, environmental and taxation chapters.[2]

A Council meeting of heads of states held in Copenhagen in December 2002 acknowledged the preparations of the Baltic states and the other applicant countries and confirmed the accession of 10 countries to the EU

Union and its abbreviation *EU* as shorthand also when it refers to the earlier forms that existed before the term was adopted in 1993.

[2] Staehr (2011) uses proxies for the "closeness" of the post-communist countries to the EU, one of which is the proportion of the chapters that were closed each year during the negotiations, and finds that closeness to the EU helped strengthen democratisation in the countries, while the economic reforms appear to have become more government-centred and less market liberal.

by 1 May 2004. The final preparatory step was for referendums on membership to be held. In total 91 per cent of the votes cast in the Lithuanian referendum in May 2003 were in favour of membership, while 67 per cent were in favour in the Latvian and Estonian referendums, both held in September 2003 (Kerikmäe et al. 2016). The referendum results cleared the way for the countries to join the EU on 1 May 2004.

The Baltic states have been full members of the EU since May 2004 although they were subject to some temporary rules for labour movements, agricultural support and other areas. Their membership marked a return to Europe for the Baltic states as they became integral parts of the economic and political structures of the European Union.

7.3 Transition and Aspirations

The 1990s was a decade of rapid change in the Baltic states. The transition reforms established the underpinnings of a market economy, but unlike in the transition countries of Central Europe, the process also encompassed nation building, as independent national administrations and institutions had to be established. The three countries were small in size and had only recently become independent, so administrative and institutional capacities were limited. The three countries chose in consequence reforms that led to a liberal-market economic model where the role of government was limited and policies were rules-based or easy to administer (Laar 2002; Staehr 2017).

International trade is of key importance for small open economies, and trade policy and the supporting domestic policies have helped define developments in the Baltic states. The countries chose from an early stage to have open trading regimes and low duties (OECD 2000). The countries entered into a Baltic Free Trade Agreement in 1993 and extended its scope over time. Trade was also liberalised within the grouping of Baltic Rim countries and increasingly with the EU countries, as this was part of the Europe Agreements. Estonia and Latvia joined the World Trade Organisation in 1999 while Lithuania did so in 2001.

Estonia went the furthest and independently introduced a very liberal trading regime with no duties and no quantitative restrictions on international trade for virtually all products, including agricultural products (Feldmann 2003). This meant that agricultural prices in Estonia were close to world market prices and the agricultural industry was exposed to substantial competitive pressures, while Latvia and Lithuania retained protection of the agricultural sector. The Estonian experiment with having no trade protection was gradually rolled back in the late 1990s as the EU negotiations gained pace.

The introduction of national currencies and the choice of exchange rate regime were important milestones in the process of nation building and of regaining economic independence. The small size of the economies and concerns over administrative capacity were important factors in the choices made (Levenko and Staehr 2016; Staehr 2015b). In June 1992 Estonia became the first of the Baltic states to replace the Soviet rouble with its own currency. The currency was from the outset tied to the German mark at a fixed rate through a currency board with full reserve coverage of the monetary base.

Lithuania initially introduced temporary currencies that circulated alongside the rouble, but these were replaced by a national currency in September 1993. The currency floated at first, but after a period of exchange rate instability and inflation pressure, Lithuania introduced a currency board and tied the currency to the US dollar. Latvia also used a temporary currency for a while before introducing a national currency in March 1993. The exchange rate was tied to the Special Drawing Rights of the IMF using a traditional fixed exchange rate regime, but in the end the exchange rate regime became very similar to those of Estonia and Lithuania since the reserve coverage was very large. The countries liberalised their capital accounts at an early stage, although Latvia and Lithuania in particular retained restrictions on foreign direct investment for longer to encourage domestic ownership of businesses (OECD 2000, ch. 7).

The Baltic states had introduced new national currencies within a few years after they regained their independence. The fixed exchange rate systems and the institutions that gave a high degree of credibility meant that inflation came down gradually, while trade and other international transactions were facilitated. The fixed exchange rate regimes also meant that the exchange rate could not operate as a shock absorber if or when the countries were hit with external shocks.

The Baltic states saw large declines in production in the early 1990s although deficient data mean that the magnitudes of the declines are uncertain. The declines resulted in large part from the dismantling of central planning, the disruption of trade links, and the uncertainties that surrounded the transition process. The economic climate improved from the mid-1990s however, as all three Baltic states exhibited fast economic growth and improved employment prospects.

The upswing was short-lived because of the spill-over from the Russian crisis, which erupted in August 1998 when the Russian government defaulted on its debt obligations and allowed the rouble to float. Economic growth declined in 1998 and came to a halt in Estonia and Lithuania in 1999. The downturn was in large part due to a dramatic decline in exports to the Russian market, but losses in the financial sector also played a role. The knock-on effects from the Russian crisis underscored how vulnerable the Baltic states were to economic developments in their neighbourhood given their small economies and limited options for independent economic policy.

One notable consequence of the Russian crisis was a further reorientation of the Baltic economies away from their traditional trading partners in the former Soviet Union and towards Western markets. The crisis also provided an impetus to the on-going negotiations on EU membership. In the end the downturn proved short-lived and it was followed by a boom that lasted until the global financial crisis.

7.4 The Accession Boom

Economic growth had already bounced back by in 2000. Figure 7.1 shows the annual GDP growth rate in the three Baltic states and for comparison also for the EU15, the group of the first 15 EU countries including the UK, all of which were from Western Europe.[3] The rate of growth in the Baltic states exceeded five per cent in every year from 2000 to 2007. Moreover, the growth rate was trending upwards until the outbreak of the global financial crisis, and in the process reached levels that had previously been seen most commonly in the Asian tiger economies. Indeed the Baltic states were occasionally referred to as the Baltic tigers in this period.

Economic growth was broadly based in the beginning of the boom but at later stages it stemmed mainly from rapid expansion in the construction, retail, transport and financial sectors, while the primary and manufacturing sectors were less dynamic (Kuusk et al. 2017).[4] This pattern suggests

---

[3] The data presented typically start in 1995. By this time the countries had established market-economy systems and the immediate effects of the transition reforms had waned. Moreover, reliable data that comply with Eurostat requirements are typically only available from this year.

[4] Results from decomposition analyses reveal that the contribution to overall economic growth from the sectoral reallocation of employment was very small or even negative during the boom (Kuusk et al. 2017). The boom in demand in sectors such as construction and

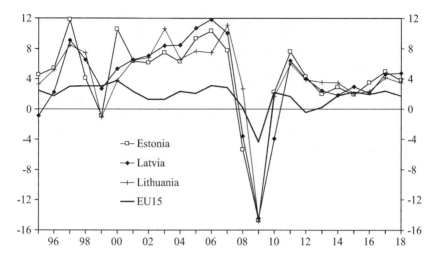

Fig. 7.1 GDP growth, per cent per year, 1995–2018. (Source: Eurostat (code: nama_10_gdp), Ameco (code: OVGD) for 1995)

that the boom was in large part driven by demand, but several factors are likely to have contributed.

The effects of the Russian crisis faded over time and exports from the Baltic states to Russia regained momentum. Economic developments were also benign in Western Europe including in the Nordic countries, and this bolstered exports and financial ties. Moreover, the economic reforms of the 1990s had helped establish dynamic private sectors with substantial growth potential.

The EU negotiations at the beginning of the period and the eventual membership in 2004 may also have played a role. Foreign investors started seeing promising investment opportunities in the Baltic states as regulation was harmonised and growth prospects were seen to improve. Confidence also improved domestically in the Baltic states and this led to increased consumption and greater demand for investment.

A key feature of the boom was the substantial inflows of foreign capital. At the beginning of the 2000s these inflows were mostly of foreign direct investment, driven in some years by Nordic banks buying up domestic

retail meant that in some cases resources were moved from sectors with high productivity to sectors with lower productivity.

banks or establishing new banks. From the mid-2000s however, the capital inflows consisted increasingly of loans and other forms of non-equity credit. The capital inflows were in part mediated by the banking sectors in the three Baltic states, and rapid growth in domestic credit helped finance the consumption and investment booms (Brixiova et al. 2010).

Figure 7.2 shows the current account balance in per cent of GDP. The current account deficits were already substantial in the 1990s but they started growing even wider from 2000 and throughout the boom period. The current account deficits at the height of the boom were exceedingly large, especially that in Latvia. The large and increasing current account deficits were signs at the time that the pre-crisis boom may not be entirely sustainable.[5]

There were other signs of overheating in the Baltic economies towards the end of the boom. The unemployment rates fell markedly and real wage growth was substantial and outstripped productivity growth. The accession to the EU in May 2004 may have contributed to the labour market

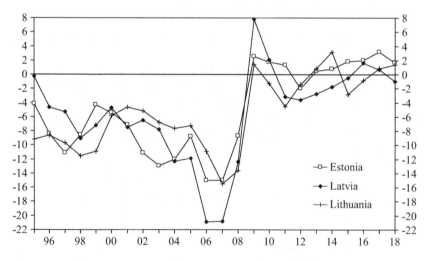

Fig. 7.2 Current account balance, per cent of GDP, 1995–2018. (Source: WEO (label: Current account balance))

[5] It is notable that the developments of GDP growth shown in Fig. 7.1 are broadly mirrored in the current account developments in Fig. 7.2. Economic growth goes hand-in-hand with current account deficits, and this pattern appears to apply to most Central and Eastern European countries (Staehr 2018).

pressure. The free movement of labour is one of the four freedoms of the internal market, although temporary restrictions on labour movements were permitted after the enlargement of 2004. In May 2004 Ireland, Sweden and the United Kingdom opened their labour markets fully, while some other countries operated with quotas or other restrictions. As wage levels in the Western European EU countries were so much higher, the opening of the labour markets was followed by substantial labour outflows from the Baltic states. This was especially the case for Lithuania where net emigration reached 1.5 per cent of the population in 2005. The net emigration from the Baltic states at the height of the boom may have contributed to labour shortages and higher wage growth.

The boom and the increasing overheating in the years before the global financial crisis reflect the susceptibility of the Baltic states as small open economies to changes in fundamentals and sentiments. The accession negotiations and the eventual membership of the EU changed the prospects and perceptions of the Baltic states and may thus have been one of the factors behind the unprecedented growth.

7.5 The Crisis Years

Financial markets in the USA and some Western European countries started showing strains in 2007 and this culminated with the bankruptcy of Lehman Brothers in September 2008. The ensuing global financial crisis affected the Baltic states severely as GDP began to shrink in 2008 in Estonia and Latvia, and it fell by around 14 per cent in 2009 in all three countries. These declines in GDP were much larger than those in Western Europe (see Fig. 7.1).

The fallout of the global financial crisis demonstrated once again how vulnerable the Baltic states were to economic shocks. The countries experienced severe *sudden stops* as the current account balances swung from very large deficits to surpluses within only one year (see Fig. 7.2). The sudden stops crippled the financial sector and the provision of domestic credit dried up. Export volumes contracted as the downturn in the trading partners cut foreign demand for goods and services from the Baltic states. Exports of goods and services dropped from 2008 to 2009 by 20.5 per cent in real terms in Estonia, by 12.3 per cent in Latvia, and by 12.8 per cent in Lithuania (Ameco, code: *OXGS*). Finally, the financial crisis also badly damaged confidence as firms and governments encountered financing problems, unemployment shot up, and the outlook worsened.

The crisis had a profound impact on unemployment in the Baltic states. Figure 7.3 shows the quarterly unemployment rate for those aged 15–74. The unemployment rates were falling rapidly during the boom before the crisis, but they started to rise dramatically from the end of 2008, peaking at 18–20 per cent in 2010 before starting to come back down. The unemployment rate stayed above 10 per cent until the third quarter of 2012 in Estonia and until the first quarter of 2015 in Latvia and Lithuania.

Another consequence of the crisis in the Baltic states was that emigration ticked upwards. The economic hardship and the unemployment caused by the crisis coincided with several EU countries opening up fully for labour migration and with others relaxing their requirements. Figure 7.4 shows the net emigration from the three countries in per cent of the population at the beginning of the year.

While net emigration reached striking levels in 2009–2010 in Latvia and Lithuania, it changed only modestly in Estonia. The difference may have arisen partly because unemployment was typically lower in Estonia than in the other two countries, and partly because wages in Estonia were somewhat higher than those in Latvia and Lithuania (Eurostat, code: *nama_10_gdp*). Moreover, geographical proximity meant that Estonians

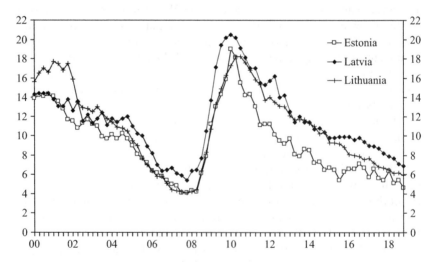

Fig. 7.3 Unemployment rate, 15–74 years, per cent of labour force, quarterly data 2000:1–2018:4. (Note: The quarterly unemployment rate is from labour force surveys. Source: Eurostat (code: *une_rt_q*))

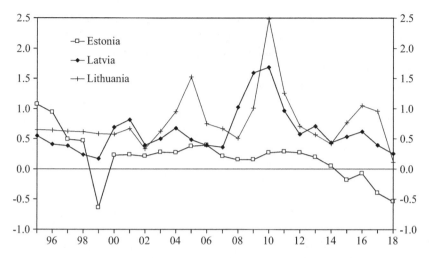

Fig. 7.4 Net emigration, per cent of population, 1995–2018. (Source: Eurostat (code: *demo_gind*))

were able to work in Finland while still living in their own country. Outward migration may have led to overheating during the boom, but it is likely that it helped reduce unemployment and hardship during the crisis, though at the cost of substantial declines in population in Latvia and Lithuania.

The net emigration relative to the population size has generally been larger from the Baltic states, particularly from Latvia and Lithuania, than from most other EU countries in Central and Eastern Europe. The economic crisis was very deep in the Baltic states and this may have strengthened the emigration incentives. Surveys of the motives of emigrants from the Baltic states suggest that outward migration was a strategy for coping with low incomes, high unemployment and limited welfare payments, and also with a perceived lack of prospects for the future (Hazans 2016). Moreover, the countries are small and culturally open, and so the younger generations in the Baltic states may have felt comfortable moving to another country. Finally, the Soviet occupation of the Baltic states meant that there were communities of migrants from the three countries in many Western European countries, and this might have facilitated emigration to those countries.

The crisis affected all three countries severely but Latvia the most. The government faced acute financing problems in the autumn of 2008. Parex bank, the second largest bank in the country, encountered severe liquidity problems after the outbreak of the global financial crisis, and the Latvian government decided to inject capital into the bank and take it over. Meanwhile the fiscal stance deteriorated as the steep downturn hurt tax revenues. Given the disruptions in international capital markets at the time, the Latvian government could not borrow the budgetary shortfall on commercial terms and therefore had to request financial assistance from international public lenders.

In December 2008 the Latvian government signed an assistance programme led by the IMF and the European Union with the participation of the World Bank and a number of north European countries, including Estonia. The agreement contained a total loan commitment of 7.5 billion euros and stipulated a number of *conditionalities*, including requirements for structural reforms and limits on future budget deficits. Latvia's membership of the EU played a key role in Latvia receiving the international assistance, as witnessed by the European Union being a lead organiser of the programme and contributing more than 40 per cent of the total loan commitment. The active role that the EU took reflected solidarity with a new member but was also meant to reduce the risk of contagion from the crisis to other EU countries.

Latvia became a strong proponent of austerity policies in the wake of the global financial crisis (Aslund and Dombrovski 2011). The authorities moved assertively to contain the budget deficit and make structural reforms while at the same time retaining the fixed exchange rate. After a total loss of around 21 per cent of GDP over the years 2008–2010, with soaring unemployment and large budget deficits, Latvia eventually turned the corner in 2011 as economic growth picked up, unemployment continued its decline from 2010 and the budget deficit returned to manageable levels. A total of 4.5 billion euros of the total loan commitment were paid out to Latvia by the lenders. The programme expired in January 2012 and Latvia had repaid the IMF loan by the end of that year, and the loans from the other lenders in the following years.

The economic policies in Estonia and Lithuania were in many respects similar to those in Latvia, and the Baltic states became the standard bearers of austerity policies in the years following the crisis (Staehr 2013). The countries retained their fixed exchange rate systems, pursued tight fiscal policies, and implemented structural reforms that typically sought to improve efficiency and reduce employment.

The policy response to the crisis in the Baltic states was the subject of debate at the time (Aslund and Dombrovski 2011; Hansson and Randveer 2013). The deep recessions in the countries made some observers argue for expansionary measures to soften the impact on unemployment and living standards. Such anti-austerity policies would typically have meant devaluing the currencies or abandoning the fixed exchange rate regimes in order to improve external competitiveness, and using expansionary fiscal policies to stimulate growth in the short term.

The debates on the policy stance in the Baltic states mirrored broader debates on the appropriate policy mix during the downturn caused by the global financial crisis. Expansionary fiscal and monetary policies have increasingly been seen to support economic growth and prevent deepening of the crisis (Blanchard and Summers 2019). Expansionary policies may however be counterproductive if they lead to financial instability or increased uncertainty as might have been the case in some European periphery countries. Countries that pursued austerity policies in the wake of the crisis seem in many cases to have performed better than those that did not (Hansson and Randveer 2013).

In practice the policy options in the Baltic states were somewhat circumscribed. In spite of their austerity measures, the governments of Latvia and Lithuania were still running very substantial budget deficits in the years following the crisis, and although the Lithuanian government managed to borrow at commercial terms, the Latvian government was not able to do so. Altering the fixed exchange rate regimes would have risked negative repercussions since a very large part of private borrowing was denominated in euros or other foreign currencies, and so a rapid depreciation could have led to widespread debt servicing problems and new rounds of financial instability. This meant that expansionary policies could well have been counterproductive for the Baltic states after the crisis.

A factor that is often overlooked in debates on austerity in the Baltic states is that the countries had started receiving substantial funds from the EU after 2004. The bulk of the funding came from the Common Agricultural Policy and the structural and cohesion funds that were in place at the time. The European Commission exhibited substantial flexibility in the crisis years and expedited the distribution of the structural and cohesion funds to the Baltic states and other EU countries. The aim was to help fund projects that stimulated economic growth without exerting additional pressure on the public finances of the member countries.

The total *net* transfer from the EU in 2009 and 2010 was around 4.2 and 4.9 per cent of gross national income (GNI) for Estonia, 2.5 and 3.7 per cent of GNI for Latvia (excluding the assistance programme), and 5.5 and 5.0 per cent of GNI for Lithuania (Danish Parliament 2019). These amounts are sizeable and potentially large enough to have macroeconomic impacts although they are relative small in comparison to the current account deficits which the countries had been running during the pre-crisis boom. Overall the transfers from the EU helped support the economy while relieving the pressure on the public finances in the Baltic states during the difficult crisis years.

7.6 The Recovery

The crisis did not last. Estonia and Lithuania exhibited positive growth rates from 2010 and Latvia did so from 2011. Indeed 2011 saw an upswing in all three countries, as annual economic growth reached 6–8 per cent. This might have raised expectations of a return to the growth trajectory seen before the crisis, but this did not happen; growth rates dipped and hovered for the next five years in the range of 2–4 per cent, which was only slightly above the growth rates in the EU15.

The catching-up process was losing momentum at a point where the Baltic states had only just come out of very deep economic recessions and had income levels that were still substantially below those of most Western European EU countries. Many emerging-market economies in Latin America and Asia have at different times narrowed the income gap to the most developed countries, only to see their income stagnate and the gap start to widen again, leaving the countries trapped at middle-income levels.

The timid nature of the recovery in the Baltic states raised the question of whether the Baltic states risked being caught in a middle-income trap where structural, institutional or governance problems held back productivity growth and competitiveness so that the income gap to Western Europe narrowed only slowly or not at all (Staehr 2015a).

The rates of economic growth in the years after the crisis pale in comparison with the growth rates during the boom, but it must be remembered that the boom was in large part demand driven and unsustainable, with excessive credit growth and large capital inflows. During the recovery from 2010 onwards the current account was broadly in balance and credit growth was moderate. As such the recovery, although timid, had stronger foundations than the boom before the crisis did. The concerns about growth lessened eventually after all three countries exhibited economic growth of around four per cent in 2017 and 2018. The recovery from the global financial crisis has brought a new degree of stability to the economies of the Baltic states with moderate changes in growth rates and few obvious signs of financial or economic imbalances.

A key event during the recovery was that the Baltic states successively joined the common currency area and adopted the euro. When the countries became members of the EU, they took on the obligation to join the euro once they had satisfied the requirements for doing so. The governments in the three Baltic states confirmed at an early stage their intention to join the euro area as soon as possible and thus participate fully in the European Economic and Monetary Union.

The economic rationale for the Baltic states to join the common currency seemed straightforward (Lättemäe and Randveer 2004). The countries have small, open economies and a large share of their trade is with countries in the euro area. They had operated fixed exchange rate regimes for a long time, with currency boards in Estonia and Lithuania and a tightly fixed exchange rate regime in Latvia. Adopting the euro would thus be a minor step that would eliminate any remaining exchange rate risk and reduce or eliminate some transaction costs.

The Maastricht Treaty sets a number of requirements or criteria that must be satisfied when a country is assessed for whether it can join the euro area. The budget deficit must be smaller than three per cent of GDP, the government debt must be smaller than 60 per cent of GDP, the exchange rate must have been relatively stable for a certain time, and the interest rate on government bonds and the inflation rate must be below reference values that are computed using data from all the EU countries. The Maastricht criteria have not changed over time but there is evidently some discretion in how they are applied.

The boom in the Baltic economies prior to the crisis meant that the countries did not at that time comply with the Maastricht criteria, particularly the inflation criterion. The boom was accompanied by relatively high inflation, and the assessments by the European Commission and the ECB in 2006 and 2008 concluded that none of the countries satisfied the inflation criterion. The ability of the authorities to steer the inflation rate was limited, so the political ambition of joining the euro area was put on hold. The crisis changed the outlook.

When the extent of the crisis became evident towards the end of 2008, the Estonian government reckoned that the crisis opened an opportunity for Estonia to satisfy all five Maastricht criteria at the forthcoming assessment in 2010, since the economic downturn and rising unemployment would exert downward pressure on inflation. However, the downturn would also reduce the tax intake and cause public spending to rise, so the main challenge would be to keep the budget deficit below 3 per cent of GDP.

The Estonian government set in motion a comprehensive package of fiscal consolidation measures with rises in the unemployment insurance contribution, value added tax, and excise duties, and wage cuts in the public sector and numerous other cuts to public spending. The fiscal consolidation in Estonia was successful in that the deficit for 2009 ended up at two per cent of GDP. Figure 7.5 shows the fiscal balance in per cent of GDP. The outcome of the Estonian consolidation is particularly striking when it is compared to developments in Latvia and Lithuania.

The convergence assessments by the ECB and the European Commission in 2010 concluded that Estonia had complied fully with all the Maastricht criteria, and the country was invited to join the euro area as the 17th member from 1 January 2011. The roll-out of the euro went

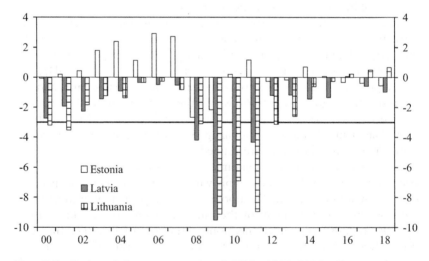

Fig. 7.5 Budget balance, per cent of GDP, 2000–2018. (Source: Ameco (code: *UBLG*))

smoothly and the fear that prices would rise does not seem to have been borne out by the data, although there may have been some minor price rises in the months before the euro was introduced (Meriküll and Rõõm 2015).

The strategy of Latvia and Lithuania for joining the common currency essentially followed that of Estonia. The crisis and the high rates of unemployment meant that inflation was kept in check and so the main challenge was to get the budget deficit below three per cent of GDP. Latvia became a member of the euro area in 2014 and Lithuania did so in 2015. The memberships were at the time seen as a sign that the Baltic states, even as they faced numerous economic challenges, had continued their work towards closer economic and political integration with the EU.[6]

7.7 Longer-Term Trends

The discussion so far has largely focused on cyclical dynamics and some key factors that help explain these dynamics, including the role of EU membership. This section considers some longer-term trends in the Baltic states from the mid-1990s.

Figure 7.6 shows GDP per capita in purchasing power terms (PPP) in per cent of the average level in the EU15. The most striking feature is the rapid convergence towards the EU15 average. The income level or GDP per capita PPP has grown from 25–30 per cent of the EU15 level in 1995 to 65–75 per cent in 2018. For comparison, the income levels in Greece and Portugal in 2018 were 63.6 and 72.3 per cent of the EU15 level (Ameco, code: *HVGDPR*). However, Nordic countries such as Denmark and Sweden, which are often seen as peers for the Baltic states, have income levels that are 10–15 per cent above the EU15 average. The gap to the Nordic countries was still substantial in 2019, 28 years after the Baltic states regained independence and 15 years after they joined the EU.

The speed of convergence has varied markedly over time. The convergence process was halted briefly after the Russian crisis and went into reverse during the global financial crisis, but it resumed afterwards. This

---

[6] The euro has remained popular. According to the Eurobarometer for autumn 2018 the euro is backed by large majorities of the populations in the Baltic states. The statement "A European economic and monetary union with one single currency, the euro" gained support by 85 per cent of those interviewed in Estonia, 81 per cent in Latvia and 67 per cent in Lithuania (Eurobarometer 2018, p. 32).

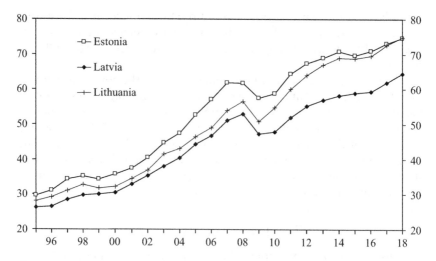

Fig. 7.6 GDP per capita PPP, per cent of EU15, 1995–2018. (Source: Ameco (code: *HVGDPR*))

pattern reflects the notable cyclical volatility in the Baltic states both before and after the countries joined the EU. It is notable however that the cycles have been quite subdued and the convergence relatively steady following the recovery from the global financial crisis.

The income levels in the three Baltic states are somewhat different. The GDP per capita PPP in Latvia has consistently been below those of the two other Baltic states, and the gap does not appear to have narrowed over time. Meanwhile, GDP per capita PPP in Lithuania has caught up with the level in Estonia since the global financial crisis, which is partly because the crisis affected Lithuania less than the other two Baltic states.

The longer-term trends in income reflect factors such as the structure of industry, the knowledge base and the business environment. Although there are areas with high value added in ICT, financial services and manufacturing in all three countries, there are also areas with relatively low value added that is based on exploitation of natural resources, simple mass production and manual services. The convergence process has seen resources shift from less productive to more productive sectors, but productivity growth within the sectors has been of greater importance (Kuusk et al. 2017).

The 2018 issue of the *Global Competitiveness Report* says the Baltic states stand out for their skilled labour force, flexible labour markets and high levels of ICT adoption (World Economic Forum 2018). Moreover, the results from the OECD's Programme for International Student Assessment, PISA, indicate that the primary and secondary education system is of good quality (OECD 2016). There is also a relatively favourable business environment as witnessed by the generally good scores of the Baltic states in the *Doing Business Report* of the World Bank (World Bank 2019).

Economic growth may however have been held back by the limited innovation capabilities in the Baltic states. The level of R&D expenditures, especially those of the private sector, the state of cluster development and the quality of research institutions lag behind those of Western European EU countries (World Economic Forum 2018). According to the *European Innovation Scoreboard* the performance of the innovation systems in the Baltic countries has improved but is still below the EU average (European Commission 2019). Moreover, the financial systems in the Baltic countries are less developed than those in many other EU countries, potentially impairing the financing of small and medium-sized firms.

Another key feature with potentially important macroeconomic effects is the decline in population in the Baltic states. Figure 7.7 shows the population at the beginning of the year over several years. From 1995 to 2018 the population declined by more than 100,000 in Estonia, almost 600,000 in Latvia and more than 800,000 in Lithuania. These downward trends are partly the result of fertility rates that dropped sharply after the countries regained independence while the death rates declined only modestly, but net emigration has over time played a much larger role.

The depopulation in the Baltic states has been more severe in Latvia and Lithuania than in Estonia, but the issue and its longer-term economic consequences are on the policy-making agenda in all three countries. Population forecasts from Eurostat suggest that the decline will continue but the precise rate of decline will depend on demographic developments including trends in emigration and immigration. As discussed in Sect. 7.5, net emigration has been negative in Estonia since 2015 and declining in Latvia and Lithuania since 2017. These developments have been driven by increased return migration and the relatively benign economic climate.

The population declines in the Baltic states have been associated with increasing old-age dependency ratios. Figure 7.8 shows the old-age dependency ratio computed as the population aged 65 or older relative to the population aged 15–64. The ratio increased by around 12 percentage points from 1995 to 2018 in all three countries and this increase is forecast to continue given current trends.

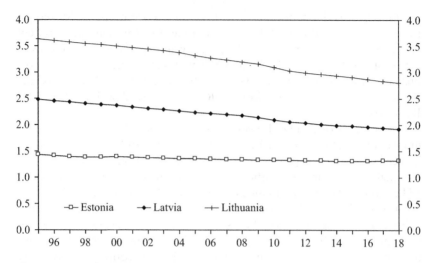

Fig. 7.7 Population at the beginning of the year, millions, 1995–2018. (Source: Ameco (code: *NPTN*))

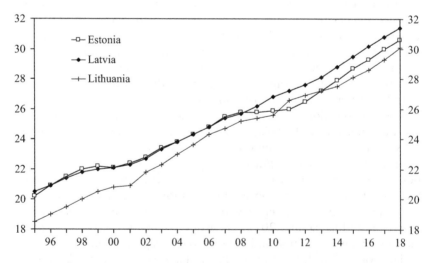

Fig. 7.8 Old-age dependency ratio, per cent, 1995–2018. (Note: The old-age dependency ratio is computed as the population aged 65 or older in per cent of the population aged 15–64 at the beginning of the year. Source: Eurostat (code: *demo_pjanind*))

The upshot is that the demographic structures in the Baltic states increasingly resemble those in Western European countries even though Baltic income levels are substantially below those in most of Western Europe. The increasing old-age dependency ratio and perhaps also the reduction in the populations will affect macroeconomic performance as the labour force declines and public finances come under strain, potentially jeopardising long-term growth in per capita income. The demographic changes in the Baltic states are profound and will affect societal developments and macroeconomic performance. The ageing of society will be a challenge for pension, health, education, employment and tax policies in the future.

7.8 Some Perspectives

This chapter has discussed macroeconomic developments in the Baltic states before and after the countries joined the European Union. The countries regained their independence in August 1991, became members of the EU less than 13 years later, and celebrated 15 years of membership in May 2019. The Baltic states have become fully integrated in the EU, including the euro area, and they participate on equal terms in the policy-making processes (*The Economist* 2018). The membership of the EU is supported by large majorities in the three countries and the public generally trust the EU and its institutions.[7]

The Baltic states spent the 1990s establishing national institutions and setting up the foundations for a market economy. As they went through the transition process the countries were cooperating ever more closely with the EU, and this cooperation intensified after the Baltic states started negotiations on membership in the late 1990s. The gradual adoption of EU rules and increasing economic cooperation meant that joining the EU in May 2004 did not affect the economic trends in the countries abruptly, as any effects have been gradual and spread out over time.

The Baltic states have modernised their economies, and their income levels have converged quite rapidly towards levels in Western Europe. GDP per capita adjusted for purchasing power parity was around 65–75 per cent of the EU15 level in 2018. It remains however a key policy challenge for the countries to sustain the convergence process and reach the

---

[7] The populations in the Baltic states express greater trust in the EU than the average across the EU countries (Eurobarometer 2018, p. 6).

income levels of the Western European EU countries and eventually those of the peer group of Nordic countries. Higher income levels in the Baltic states will affect economic well-being directly, but they could also help stem emigration and entice migrants from earlier waves of emigration to return to their home countries.

The convergence process in the Baltic states will likely become more challenging over time. As the income gap narrows, the returns from capital deepening and technological adaptation will diminish. Moreover, the rapid ageing of the societies implies that an increasing share of the population will be outside the labour force while public spending on pensions and health care will increase. This makes it important to prepare for the ageing of society in ways that do not jeopardise economic development and macroeconomic stability.

The Baltic states must increasingly produce goods and services with high value added. This will require a switch towards a knowledge-based economy where innovation and agglomeration effects contribute significantly to income growth. Parts of this process are likely to emerge over time as businesses adapt to an environment of higher incomes, increased competition and rising demand for advanced products and services. As discussed in Sect. 7.7, the Baltic states have various competitive strengths and are generally conducive to business development. However, there is scope for more emphasis on research and development in the private and public sectors. Governments may also play a greater role in deepening innovation systems and in ensuring that the Baltic states are equal partners in international research and development cooperation (Alnafrah and Mouselli 2020).

An important factor in developing a knowledge-based economy is a workforce with appropriate skills and competences. Continued upgrading of education and training systems is therefore essential. It is in this context encouraging that the Baltic states are seen to have very good primary and secondary education systems (Schleicher 2019). There may however be potential for strengthening the tertiary education systems, including in IT and other technical fields. Vocational education is not always well funded in the three countries and is often seen as an unattractive career choice (Bünning 2016). These concerns are compounded by companies in the Baltic states being among the least inclined in Europe to provide training to their employees (OECD 2019). The quality of education and training at universities and other institutions of higher learning is arguably still to reach the levels in the Nordic peer countries (Staehr 2015a). This is a process that requires reforms of management and financing and perhaps also changes in attitudes in society. Finally, the development of knowledge-based economies may also be aided by the return of people who had emigrated from the Baltic states and who have acquired appropriate skills abroad. The three countries have programmes in place to facilitate this and the resulting return migration may play an important role in future economic and societal development.

The EU plays important roles in the quest for economic growth and steady convergence in the Baltic states. Economic theory and empirical studies generally find that trade openness is conducive to economic growth. Some parts of the EU support programmes also aspire to strengthen economic growth by supporting infrastructure, innovation and education. Closer integration of financial markets within the EU may ease financing constraints in small and medium-sized enterprises and contribute to improving corporate governance in the Baltic states. Several empirical studies have found that EU membership has had substantial positive effects on economic growth (Badinger 2005; Campos et al. 2019).

The direct economic support that the EU gives the Baltic states through the Common Agricultural Policy and the structural and cohesion programmes has been substantial, and may thus have supported economic development and to an extent alleviated pressures on public finances. There is in this context some uncertainty about the amount of structural and cohesion funding the Baltic states will receive after the 2014–2020 funding round has been completed. The negotiations over the details of the 2021–2027 funding round were still on-going at the time of writing (the end of 2019), but Estonia and Lithuania may stand to lose part of their funding given their income levels. EU funding targets regional development in large part, and so funding cuts may over time have an effect on regional inequality.

Another key challenge for economic policy-making in the Baltic states is to ensure macroeconomic stability. The pronounced cyclical volatility has over time led to an uneven convergence process and, more importantly, it has caused economic and social problems, especially during downturns when lower incomes, higher unemployment and heightened uncertainty have brought hardship. Moreover, a more stable macroeconomic environment might also be conducive to long-term economic growth (Dabušinskas et al. 2012).

The Baltic states have generally exhibited relatively stable economic growth and no major macroeconomic imbalances during the recovery after the global financial crisis. Experience shows however that small open economies are highly dependent on external developments and are susceptible to sentiment shifts, so vigilance is in order even in benign economic environments.

Measures that enhance financial stability and dampen excessive credit cycles are of key importance. Surveillance and supervision are vital in this context along with countercyclical reserve requirements. Their earlier experiences suggest that the Baltic states should also pay close attention to developments in their current account balances. The countries should aim to avoid a pro-cyclical fiscal policy and to ensure they have sufficient fiscal space for use in times of distress. This is particularly important given the outlook of reduced funding from the EU structural and cohesion programmes in the future. Labour market policies could also be used actively, for instance by ensuring that spells of unemployment are used for training and for acquiring the skills that will be needed during the next upturn.

The EU has taken numerous measures in the wake of the global financial crisis to reduce the risks of crises occurring in the future. The measures targeting the financial sector include three new European supervisory authorities and rules for the division of supervision between national and EU authorities. Other measures include a strengthened framework for fiscal policy formulation and a system for aiding countries with fiscal problems. The Macroeconomic Imbalance Procedure seeks to identify macroeconomic imbalances at an early stage. How effective these measures are depends in large part on how they are implemented and, equally importantly, how they are incorporated into domestic policymaking. The measures are, however, beneficial for the Baltic states in that they help create a more stable external economic and financial environment, and they may also provide useful frameworks for the policy measures of the Baltic authorities as they seek to reduce the risks of financial crises and deep downturns.

The Baltic states face the challenge of maintaining macroeconomic stability and steady convergence with the levels of income in Western Europe. Membership of the EU has led to increased openness and new opportunities for trade, capital movements and movement of labour. Support from the EU has aided the modernisation processes and has strengthened cohesion and thus the prospects for growth in the region. EU membership has also brought challenges by increasing the exposure of the three countries to external economic developments and by facilitating substantial emigration.

Entering membership of the EU in 2004 was a defining moment for the Baltic states, marking their return to Europe. The following 15 years were eventful, not least in terms of macroeconomic developments. The countries have seen strong economic growth but also episodes of economic and financial instability. It is to be hoped that the next 15 years will exhibit a calmer macroeconomic environment, allowing the Baltic states to narrow or close the income gap with Western Europe. The future is never certain, and it is bound to bring opportunities as well as challenges. However, after 15 years of EU membership the Baltic states are better prepared than ever to address the challenges facing them and to contribute to solving the challenges that face the entire European Union.

REFERENCES

Alnafrah, I., & Mouselli, S. (2020). The Role of National Innovation Systems in Entrepreneurship Activities at Baltic State Countries. *Journal of the Knowledge Economy, 11*(3), 84–102

Ameco: "Annual Macroeconomic database". Ameco Online, European Commission. http://ec.europa.eu/economy_finance/ameco/user/serie/SelectSerie.cfm. Accessed on 11 July 2019.

Aslund, A., & Dombrovski, V. (2011). *How Latvia Came Through the Financial Crisis*. Washington, DC: Peterson Institute for International Economics.

Badinger, H. (2005). Growth Effects of Economic Integration: Evidence from the EU Member States. *Review of World Economics, 141*(1), 50–78.

Blanchard, O., & Summers, L. H. (Eds.). (2019). *Evolution or Revolution? Rethinking Macroeconomic Policy After the Great Recession*. Cambridge, MA: MIT Press.

Brixiova, Z., Vartia, L., & Wörgötter, A. (2010). Capital Flows and the Boom-Bust Cycle: The Case of Estonia. *Economic Systems, 34*(1), 55–72.

Bünning, F. (Ed.). (2016). *The Transformation of Vocational Education and Training (VET) in the Baltic States – Survey of Reforms and Developments*. Dordrecht: Springer.

Campos, N., Coricelli, F., & Moretti, L. (2019). Institutional Integration and Economic Growth in Europe. *Journal of Monetary Economics, 103*, 88–104.

Dabušinskas, A., Kulikov, D., & Randveer, M. (2012). *The Impact of Volatility on Economic Growth*. Working Papers of Eesti Pank, No. 7/2012.

Danish Parliament. (2019). *Which Countries Are Net Contributors to the EU Budget?* Danish Parliament EU Information Centre. https://web.archive.org/web/20190608210211/https:/english.eu.dk/en/faq/net-contribution

Eurobarometer. (2018). *Public Opinion in the European Union*. Standard Eurobarometer, No. 90, European Commission.

European Commission. (2019). *European Innovation Scoreboard 2019*. https://ec.europa.eu/docsroom/documents/36281

Eurostat: "Electronic Database". https://ec.europa.eu/eurostat/data/database. Accessed on 11 July 2019.

Feldmann, M. (2003). Free Trade in the 1990s: Understanding Estonian Exceptionalism. *Journal of Post-Soviet Democratization, 11*(4), 517–533.

Hansson, A., & Randveer, M. (2013). Economic Adjustment in the Baltic Countries. In E. Nowotny, P. Mooslecher, & D. Ritzberger-Grünwald (Eds.), *A New Model for Balanced Growth and Convergence* (pp. 190–206). Cheltenham: Edward Elgar Publishing.

Hazans, M. (2016). Migration Experience of the Baltic Countries in the Context of Economic Crisis. In M. Kahanec & K. Zimmermann (Eds.), *Labor Migration, EU Enlargement, and the Great Recession* (pp. 297–344). Berlin/Heidelberg: Springer.

Kerikmäe, T., Chochia, A., & Atallah, M. (2016). The Baltic States in the European Union. In *Oxford Research Encyclopedia of Politics* (pp. 1–27). Oxford: Oxford University Press.

Kuusk, A., Staehr, K., & Varblane, U. (2017). Sectoral Change and Productivity Growth During Boom, Bust and Recovery in Central and Eastern Europe. *Economic Change and Restructuring, 50*(1), 21–43.

Laar, M. (2002). *Little Country That Could*. London: Centre for Research into Post-Communist Economies.

Lättemäe, R., & Randveer, M. (2004). Monetary Policy and EMU Enlargement: Issues Regarding ERM II and Adoption of the Euro in Estonia. *Atlantic Economic Journal, 32*(4), 293–301.

Levenko, N., & Staehr, K. (2016). To Be or Not to Be in the Rouble Zone. Lessons from the Baltic States. *CESifo Forum, 17*(4), 34–42.

Meriküll, J., & Rõõm, T. (2015). Euro Changeover-Related Inflation in Estonia. *Journal of Common Market Studies, 53*(4), 822–839.

OECD. (2000). *Baltic States. A Regional Economic Assessment*. Paris: Organisation for Economic Co-operation and Development.

OECD. (2016). *PISA 2015 Results (Volume I): Excellence and Equity in Education*. Paris: OECD Publishing.

OECD. (2019). *Economic Surveys: Estonia*. Paris: OECD Publishing.

Poissonnier, A. (2017). *The Baltics: Three Countries, One Economy?*. European Economy Economic Briefs, No. 24, European Commission.

Schleicher, A. (2019). *PISA 2018. Insights and Interpretations*. Paris: OECD Publishing.

Staehr, K. (2011). Democratic and Market-Economic Reforms in the Post-Communist Countries. The Impact of Enlargement of the European Union. *Eastern European Economics, 49*(5), 3–28.

Staehr, K. (2013). Austerity in the Baltic States Since the Global Financial Crisis. *Intereconomics, 48*(5), 293–302.
Staehr, K. (2015a). Economic Growth and Convergence in the Baltic States: Caught in a Middle Income Trap? *Intereconomics, 50*(5), 274–280.
Staehr, K. (2015b). Exchange Rate Policy in the Baltic States: From Extreme Inflation to Euro Membership. *CESifo Forum, 16*(4), 9–18.
Staehr, K. (2017). The Choice of Reforms and Economic System in the Baltic States. *Comparative Economic Studies, 59*(4), 498–519.
Staehr, K. (2018). Capital Flows and Growth Dynamics in Central and Eastern Europe. *Post-Communist Economies, 30*(1), 1–18.
The Economist. (2018, December 8). Gang of Eight. *The Economist*, p. 8.
WEO: "World Economic Outlook data". Electronic Database, April 2019.
World Bank. (2019). *Doing Business 2019: Training for Reform*. Washington, D.C.: World Bank.
World Economic Forum. (2018). *The Global Competitiveness Report 2018*. Geneva: World Economic Forum.

CHAPTER 8

Bulgaria and Romania: The Latecomers to the Eastern Enlargement

Rumen Dobrinsky

8.1 INTRODUCTION: WHY WAS EU ACCESSION DELAYED?

Bulgaria and Romania, two poor countries on Europe's periphery, managed to catch one of the last trains of the big EU Eastern Enlargement at a time that was still dominated by post-communist euphoria and a somewhat idyllic vision of a united Europe. The rationale of their admission to the Club – even with a delay compared to the other New Member States (NMS) – is sometimes still being questioned as some of the old EU member states were (and still are) of the opinion that the two Balkan countries were not sufficiently prepared for accession in 2007. But the late 1990s and the first half of the 2000s was a period of growing prosperity in Europe as well as in most parts of the world. In such an environment it was not uncommon for the incumbent EU members to assign higher priority to

R. Dobrinsky (✉)
Vienna Institute for International Economic Studies (WIIW), Vienna, Austria
e-mail: dobrinsky@wiiw.ac.at

© The Author(s), under exclusive license to Springer Nature Switzerland AG 2021
M. Landesmann, I. P. Székely (eds.), *Does EU Membership Facilitate Convergence? The Experience of the EU's Eastern Enlargement - Volume I*, Studies in Economic Transition,
https://doi.org/10.1007/978-3-030-57686-8_8

benign political arguments over conservative economic logic and dry economic facts in the enlargement decisions.

Bulgaria had experienced a grave transition crisis in the mid-1990s combining a crash of public finances, run on the banks and a collapse of the currency (Dobrinsky 2000). Economic turmoil culminated in a hyperinflationary hike in early 1997, while the real economy nose-dived that same year. In these circumstances the government was forced to seek external assistance to address the grave problems it was facing. In the first place this was the IMF, which offered financial support, but under the conditions of a clear role in the macroeconomic management of the country (Dobrinsky 2013). The key component and instrument of the new policy approach was a currency board arrangement which started operations in July 1997. The IMF support programme envisaged also radical structural reforms, something that the Bulgarian authorities had avoided until that time.

In the second half of the 1990s, Romania also faced serious economic problems and was forced to introduce harsh macroeconomic stabilisation measures. Consequently, the economy fell into a second transformational recession, which continued for three years from 1997 to 1999. GDP, industrial output and investment plummeted while the chronic balance-of-payments problems led to skyrocketing of foreign debt and depletion of foreign reserves. Soft bank lending to loss-making state-owned firms led to a general weakening of the banking system. The crisis reflected deep structural problems in the economy which required radical but painful economic reforms that, similarly to the case of Bulgaria, the authorities had been postponing (Smith 2001). To cope with the crisis Romania also had to request IMF assistance.

While Bulgaria and Romania were preoccupied with macroeconomic turmoil, crisis management and lack of clarity about the reform course, the majority of the other Central and Eastern European countries (CEECs) had already started accession negotiations with the EU and were advancing towards membership. The two Balkan countries opened accession negotiations only in 1999; furthermore, the negotiations did not advance promptly due to the delays in market reforms compared to the other CEECs.

Nevertheless, the process of accession negotiations played an essential role for the transformational reforms in Bulgaria and Romania, especially in their institutional aspect. The realistic prospect of EU membership was for the two Balkan economies – as for the other CEECs – the single most important driver and catalyst of reforms, providing a powerful impetus for the economic and political transformation in these countries. Thus the transition phase leading to EU accession in 2007 was for Bulgaria and Romania both a period of difficult transition and change but also a time of great expectations of a new era of prosperity that was about to materialise with EU membership.

The objective of this chapter is to present an analytical assessment of some of the important changes that took place in the period after formal accession to the EU. Obviously, the scope and ambition of such an assessment is limited by the nature of the chapter so I try to focus only on some key aspects of the ongoing economic transformation. The narrative also seeks to identify the channels through which EU membership exerted its effect on the evolution of economic structures and institutions in the two countries and the way these effects translated into economic change.

Despite the numerous similarities between Bulgaria and Romania, including those that led to their "packing" into a duo in their relations with the EU, the two economies also feature important differences in terms of the policies followed by the authorities and, consequently, the process of economic restructuring, macroeconomic adjustment and institutional change. The main analytical approach in the chapter is that of comparative analysis juxtaposing the two countries with each other and also with what has been happening in the other participants in the Eastern Enlargement. One of the objectives of such a comparative perspective is to identify the factors that can bring about different outcomes in different countries despite the fact that EU membership implies a common general framework of economic policy and institutional development.

Following the broad objective of the whole volume, another objective of this chapter is to analyse to what extent EU membership has helped Bulgaria and Romania to converge to the EU frontier(s). Convergence has many different facets such as real convergence (or convergence in per capita incomes); technological convergence; structural convergence; institutional convergence; convergence in value systems, etc. A comprehensive assessment of all aspects of convergence is obviously beyond the scope of the chapter.

Furthermore, there are ambiguities related to the definition of the "frontier" as regards many of these facets. One of the questions that calls for an answer is: Convergence to what frontier? Or, how can we define the "best practice" with respect to performance that is not quantifiable? Moreover, the EU (even the old EU-15) is by no means uniform as regards the achievements of individual countries vis-à-vis the above facets. In fact, heterogeneity prevails and within-EU dispersion in performance is usually quite high. Is it legitimate to claim that the frontier is the best performing EU member state by each of these facets? Can we expect that all countries should seek to converge to such frontiers and is this indeed the desirable future state?

In view of these methodological uncertainties, the chapter often refrains from taking a definite position as to the degree of convergence to a frontier but rather reduces its analytical focus with a rough assessment as to how the economies of Bulgaria and Romania fare in comparison with other EU members.

8.2 Deepening of Integration with the EU and Economic Restructuring

The process of trade reorientation and economic restructuring in all CEECs started immediately after the demise of central planning and its accompanying international structures such as COMECON. During the first years of transition this was a forced restructuring due to the loss of the previously guaranteed international markets. Geographic proximity played a central role in the reorientation of the CEECs' trade towards the leading economies of Western Europe. This process was facilitated by the liberalisation of trade with the EU and among the CEECs. Thanks to the Association Agreements and a set of complementary free trade agreements, the CEECs opened their markets and were granted privileged access to the EU market with immediate or gradual elimination of existing barriers in trade with industrial goods. These policy measures were vital both for the revival of the CEECs after the transformational recession and for the rejuvenation of their economies.

Bulgaria and Romania did follow the general pattern of economic opening and gradual integration with the EU. By the end of the 1990s, the EU was already their main trading partner; however the degree of trade integration in Bulgaria and Romania was lower than that of the Central European and Baltic states (hereafter denoted as NMS-8). Thus in 2000 the EU-15 accounted for 56.3% of Bulgaria's total merchandise exports and 72.4% of Romania's total exports whereas the corresponding average figure for the NMS-8 was 84.1% (source: Eurostat). After EU accession in 2007, there were ups and down in the dynamics of trade flows but on average the share of the EU as the main trading partner of Bulgaria and Romania increased: in 2018 it accounted for 68.7% and 77.1% of Bulgaria's and Romania's total merchandise exports, respectively. It is interesting to note that in the same period this share declined for the NMS-8 (to 80.5% on average in 2018) but this was due to their increased potential to export to other global markets.

Trade integration with the EU was an important factor for the economic restructuring in the tradable sectors of all CEECs. Their reintegration into the large EU market and, especially, the realistic prospects of future EU membership as well as the gradual liberalisation of capital flows were also the most important factors for the attraction of FDI which became the main driver of growth and economic restructuring. In most CEECs, multinationals entering the new markets sought to incorporate the manufacturing industries of these economies into global value chains and this played a crucial role in shaping the new economic structure. Indeed, the last two decades witnessed a process of major relocation of European multinationals into this part of Europe coupled with the integration of the FDI firms in the CEECs into global production cycles. The emergence of new, FDI-driven production facilities contributed to the expansion of the production base and the raising of the value added content of exports (Grela et al. 2017).

Bulgaria and Romania were no exception to this pattern: already in the late 1990s, when the prospects for EU accession became firmly grounded, FDI started flowing into the two countries. The FDI inflow accelerated in the 2000s and became the main engines of growth in Bulgaria and Romania and this continued until the global financial crisis struck in 2008–2009 (Fig. 8.1).

In relative terms, as a proportion to GDP, Bulgaria was among the CEECs that attracted the largest quantities of FDI in the past two decades. The stock of FDI accumulated in this period in Bulgaria was considerably higher than the average in the NMS-8 and about twice as high as that in Romania (Fig. 8.2). This was partly due to the sectoral composition of inward FDI (discussed below) as Bulgaria attracted significant inflows in real estate activities and these were the most abundant international FDI flows during the "bubble years". Notably, FDI originating in EU member states accounted for the largest shares of the FDI inflows to Bulgaria and Romania underscoring the leading role of the EU in the economic restructuring of the two economies.

However, there was one significant difference in the initial FDI penetration into Bulgaria as compared to other CEECs and that was the

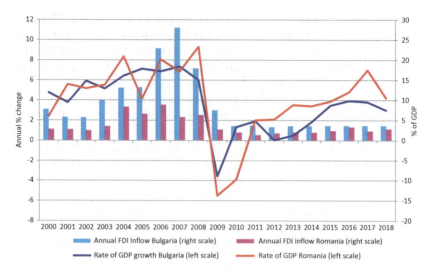

Fig. 8.1 FDI inflows and GDP growth in Bulgaria and Romania, 2000–2018. (Source: wiiw macroeconomic database)

relatively low FDI participation in the privatisation process, especially in the first phases of transition. Privatisation in Bulgaria was delayed by almost a decade as compared to other CEECs and by the time the country opened its market to such type of investment, many of the inherited industrial giants oriented towards the Soviet market were just closed down and liquidated. The big crisis of 1996–1997 was another deterrent to foreign investors in this period. The absence of Bulgaria in the radar screen of foreign investors in the important first phase of economic transformation laid its mark on the nature of the subsequent FDI inflows: up until the present days no large manufacturing multinational is present in Bulgaria with a big production facility.

By contrast, a first wave of privatisation was accomplished in Romania already in the 1990s and it was followed by a second wave conducted between 2001 and 2013 (Popescu and Ciora 2015). Thus already during the first wave, Romania sold its existing automotive facilities to foreign investors: in 1994, 51% of the shares of Automobile Craiova were sold to Daewoo and, more importantly, Renault purchased in 1999 Romania's automotive giant Dacia. Later on, Romania managed to attract also a number of flagship greenfield FDI projects such as Nokia which moved its

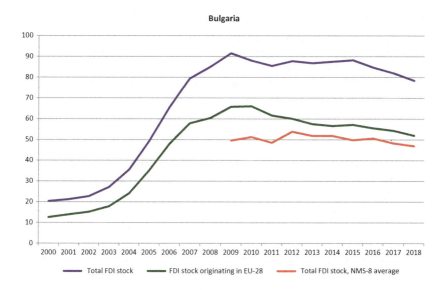

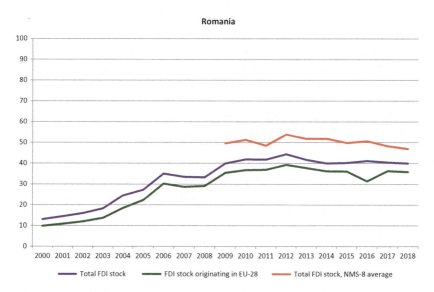

Fig. 8.2 Stock of inward FDI in Bulgaria and Romania, % of GDP. (Source: wiiw macroeconomic database)

Bochum plant to the Romanian city of Cluj in 2008. Despite the fact that not all of these projects turned out to be successful, the fact that big multinationals settled in Romania served as a positive signal that attracted further large investments.

These differences are partly reflected in the structure of the FDI stock in the two countries (Fig. 8.3).

The manufacturing industry in Romania has been by far the main recipient of FDI inflows which, in particular, reflects the presence of large multinationals. FDI has been the main driver of modernisation of Romania's manufacturing since the mod-1990s: already by 2000, when the stock of FDI invested in Romanian manufacturing amounted to just USD 2 billion, foreign affiliates accounted for 38.6% of the total manufacturing turnover, employed a quarter of the manufacturing labour force and were responsible for 44% of the direct manufacturing exports (Hunya 2002).

These effects were further amplified in the years after EU accession contributing to a complete overhaul of the Romanian economy. While traditionally Romania was largely specialised in agriculture, food processing and light industry, FDI supported the expansion of high-value added manufacturing sectors such as electrical engineering, electronics, manufacture of motor vehicles.

Probably the most notable success story has been the development and transformation of the Romanian automotive sector (Pavlínek 2017), especially after the decision of Renault to turn Dacia into its global low-cost brand. Thanks to that a number of Renault's key suppliers also invested in Romania and developed their own local production facilities. Daewoo's investment into Automobile Craiova was not so successful but this was mostly due to the global financial problems of the Korean multinational during the Asian financial crisis. Its local facility went bankrupt in 1998 and remained closed until 2006 when it was repurchased by the Romanian government. However, the next steps were much more productive after Ford purchased the Craiova facility in 2007. Subsequently Ford made a large investment into its development and encouraged dozens of its suppliers to set up local operations. In 2018 Romania entered the Top 10 of Europe's largest producers of motor vehicles and developed its own local automotive cluster which is well integrated into the global production and value chains of this important industry.

Most of Romania's manufacturing is now well integrated into European corporate networks and is mostly export-oriented. Of course, not all developments have been smooth and trouble-free both due to the effect

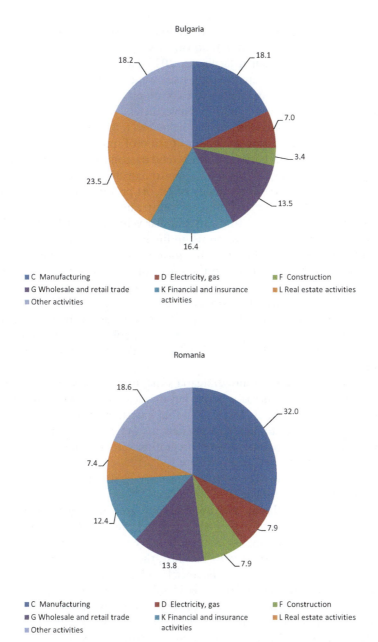

Fig. 8.3 Breakdown of the inward FDI stock in Bulgaria and Romania by NACE sectors, 2017, %. (Source: wiiw macroeconomic database)

of the global financial crisis in 2008–2009 and to specific business trouble in some multinationals. Thus following its forced global restructuring, Nokia closed its Romanian facility in 2011 laying off more than 2000 employees. Faced with rapidly rising local wages, both Renault and Ford have been repeatedly threatening to relocate production elsewhere unless workers agree on wage moderation. Nevertheless, on balance the presence of big multinationals in Romania has helped to fully transform Romania's manufacturing within a relatively short period of time.

Economic research based on firm-level data confirms that FDI inflows have facilitated the export upgrading by Romanian firms revealing a positive relationship between the quality of export products and the presence of multinationals enterprises both in the upstream and downstream industries (Bajgar and Javorcik 2019). In a similar vein, Jude (2019) finds that in the long term FDI tends to crowd in further investment, thanks to the integration of foreign affiliates in the local market and the emergence of trade linkages. Mostly thanks to the effect of FDI, Romania's economy underwent a radical transition away from agriculture and light industry to more sophisticated manufacturing and services (Hunya 2017). The integration of Romania's manufacturing into global value chains also contributed to a significant diversification of the geographic structure of foreign trade. The country's full EU membership has served as the cornerstone of this transformation.

Although FDI flowed into Bulgaria's manufacturing sector to a relatively smaller extent it has also been a key driver of restructuring and modernisation. While Bulgaria lost most of its inherited Soviet type industry that did not manage to adjust to the new market environment, a process of gradual re-industrialisation and integration into EU and global value chains was set in motion already before EU accession, driven by FDI. The ICT industry also saw a revival and the country became an attractive destination for the outsourcing of such services.

By now many FDI manufacturing projects are running successfully in Bulgaria; however, these are mostly small and medium sized production facilities. Symptomatically, so far no FDI-driven car assembly facility has been launched in the country. By contrast, the presence of foreign capital is more visible in the sector "Financial and insurance services" which reflects the fact that virtually the whole banking sector in Bulgaria at present is owned by foreign banks. Real estate activities also attracted relatively large FDI inflows mostly through the acquisition by foreigners of hotels and housing at the Black Sea and mountain resorts. This is also the sector that attracted most of all non-EU FDI, especially from Russia and other post-Soviet countries.

Empirical analysis suggests that FDI inflows to CEECs that were targeted at the real estate sector have had the most sizeable direct impact on GDP growth, outweighing the impact on growth of inflows destined to non-real estate related activities where indirect effects prevail (Mitra 2011). The comparison of the dynamics of FDI inflows and GDP growth in Bulgaria and Romania both during the years preceding the global financial crisis and after it (Fig. 8.1) is consistent with such a finding.

The ongoing process of economic restructuring in the two countries is reflected in the changing structure of their exports (Fig. 8.4)

Notably, a comparison of the changes in composition of exports structures between 2002 and 2018 indicates, even at a rather aggregated level, major structural shifts. In Romania, the key structural changes took place in the leading manufacturing sector, away from fuels and light industry and towards the exports of machinery, electrical and electronic devices, as well as transport vehicles. By contrast, food industry and fuels retained their importance in Bulgaria but there was a similar reduction in the relative importance of the exports of the light industry and a growing importance of the exports of machinery and transport equipment. Overall, while there was a stark contrast between the structure of exports of Bulgaria and Romania with that of the EU-15 in 2002, the dissimilarities were reduced considerably 16 years later.

A closer look into the dynamics and structure of the exports of machinery and transport equipment (Fig. 8.5) provides further evidence about the different evolution of the manufacturing sectors in Bulgaria and Romania.

In the first place, as also evidenced in Fig. 8.4, machinery and transport equipment account for a much larger share of Romania's total merchandise exports compared to Bulgaria. And more importantly, the share of commodity group "road vehicles" is almost by one order of magnitude larger than in the case of Bulgaria, which is probably one of the most important differences in the export structures of the two countries. Actually, Romania as well as the NMS-8 taken as a whole are by now more specialised in the exports of machinery and transport equipment than the EU-15 as a whole.

As noted, the FDI-led transformation of Romania's manufacturing industry was underpinned by a further sophistication of exports, increase in its technological content as well as a general upgrading of its quality.

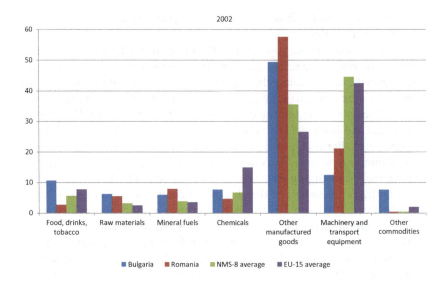

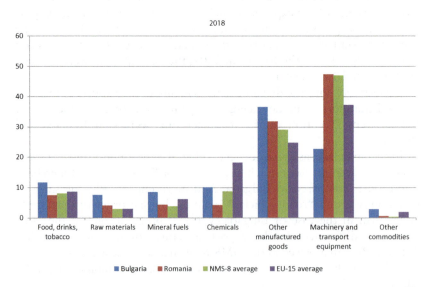

Fig. 8.4 Breakdown of exports from Bulgaria and Romania by SITC categories, 2002 and 2018, % of total. (Source: Eurostat)

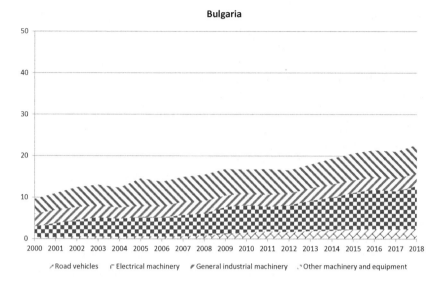
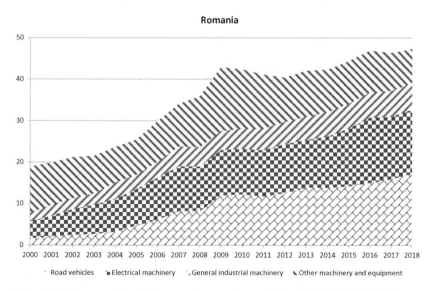

Fig. 8.5 Exports of machinery and transport equipment (SITC 6) from Bulgaria and Romania, 2000–2018, % of total exports. (Source: Eurostat)

The sophistication of Romania exports as measured by the so called "EXPY index" which reflects the productivity and income level associated with a country's specialisation pattern (Hausmann, Hwang and Rodrik 2007) increased by almost 20% between 1996 and 2016 (World Bank 2018). This has been the largest increase among all NMS in this period: for a comparison, Poland's EXPY increased by 12% in the same period; that of the Czech Republic and Slovakia – by 8 and 7%, respectively, while Bulgaria's index actually dropped by 0.5% between 1996 and 2016. The fast growth of the automotive sector played the key role for rise in the average sophistication of Romania's exports.

Overall, the economic restructuring that took place in Bulgaria and Romania during the past two decades mostly thanks to their accession to the EU has been bringing the two economies closer to the economic structures prevailing in the more developed EU members with Romania being more advanced in this process so far. One lesson from the comparative assessment of their experience is that if a country fails to avail of an opening window of opportunity (as did Bulgaria during the whole first decade of transition), some of these opportunities as the attraction of large multinationals that were relocating in this period may be foregone forever.

8.3 Coping with Shocks as EU Members

Both the theoretical and empirical literature are ambiguous as to the effect of closer integration on the vulnerability of an economy to adverse external shocks. Empirical research prior to the Eastern Enlargement did not come to definitive conclusions as regards the effect of closer trade and financial links with the EU on the susceptibility of the NMS to external shocks and the nature of the implied effects (Babetskii 2005; Fidrmuc and Korhonen 2003). However, the global financial crisis of 2008–2009 was a painful real life experiment to this effect and, with the benefit of hindsight, we now know more about the degrees of vulnerability of the NMS to external shocks and whether and to what extent EU membership helped mitigate the adverse effects. The experience of Bulgaria and Romania during and after the crisis provides some interesting evidence about the readiness of the two countries to cope with major external shocks and the role of national policies in mitigating the adverse consequences within an economic union such as the EU.

The global crisis had the effect of a multidimensional adverse shock on the NMS, including Bulgaria and Romania and had wide-ranging repercussions. Given the fact that the whole of the EU was hit by the global crisis one cannot speak of shock asymmetry; what we observed was rather uneven shocks in different countries (across their numerous dimensions) as well as asymmetric responses to the shocks, depending on the different context and policy agenda in different EU countries. The most profound negative aspects of the crisis in the case of Bulgaria and Romania were the sudden drop in external demand as well as the drying out of capital inflows; indeed, their reversal after 2009.

Prior to the crisis both Bulgaria and Romania experienced a boom in domestic and import demand which was associated with real exchange rate appreciation and a significant widening of their current account deficits related to massive capital inflows (Fig. 8.6).

Apart from the large inflows of FDI, this period was also marked by significant inflows of financial capital as local banks were massively borrowing abroad to be able to respond to the growing demand by credit-hungry investors and consumers. However, the accumulating domestic and external imbalances were unsustainable and increased the vulnerability to external shocks. Plus, the growing trade integration with the EU meant a closer synchronisation of the business cycle with the EU and greater susceptibility to cyclical effects coming from the EU core.

The pattern of economic performance prior to the crisis was broadly similar in both countries but differed in two important features. In the case of Bulgaria, it was the private sector that was exclusively responsible for the hike in external borrowing and the widening current account deficit. The latter spiked to above 20% of GDP in 2006 and 2008 and was associated with the build-up of large foreign debt which rose above 100% of GDP in 2008 and 2009 (Fig. 8.7).

By contrast, while the Romanian government kept dis-saving even during the benign period of high growth and thus added to the current account deficit, it was only borrowing in the domestic market. As a result domestic public debt increased considerably both before and after the global crisis; at the same time, while the external debt rose after the crisis, its level did not pose threats to macroeconomic stability (Fig. 8.7).

The crisis brought a sudden stop of the massive FDI inflows seen in the past and a reversal in financial flows. The process of macroeconomic adjustment and unwinding of the accumulated imbalances in the two countries featured some similarities but also some important differences. Exports plummeted both in Bulgaria and Romania in 2009 due to the global drop in import demand and the two economies fell into a recession.

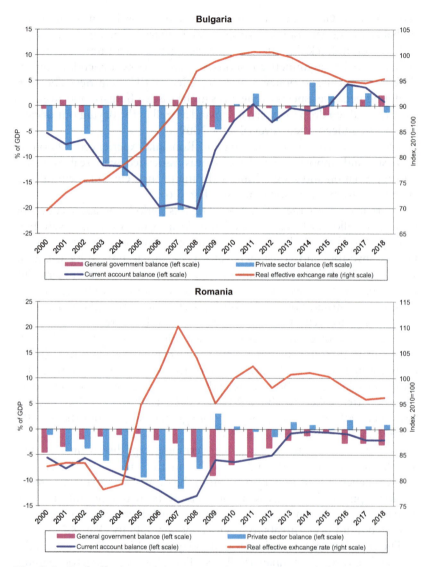

Fig. 8.6 Real effective exchange rate and current account balance by sectors in Bulgaria and Romania, 2000–2018. (Source: Eurostat, wiiw macroeconomic database, author's calculations)

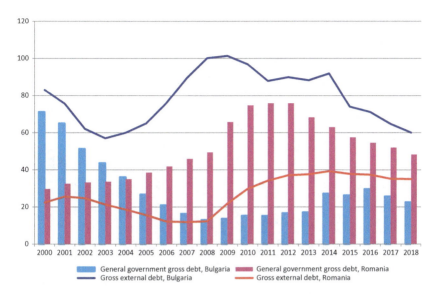

Fig. 8.7 Public and gross external debt in Bulgaria and Romania, 2000–2018, % of GDP. (Source: wiiw macroeconomic database)

The crisis-related recession in Romania was deeper and continued for two years but afterwards the economy regained its pace whereas Bulgaria's economy fell into a prolonged slump which lasted for several years (Fig. 8.1).

The main characteristic that distinguished the adjustment process in the two countries was the markedly different behaviour of the labour market. The labour markets in Bulgaria and Romania featured different dynamics already during the 1990s. While both countries experienced emigration of a massive scale mostly to Western Europe which lead to an unprecedented population decline, the transition-related drop in employment in Romania during the 1990s was relatively gradual thanks to the more gradualist approach to market reforms and enterprise restructuring. In the same period, Bulgaria experienced an abrupt decline in employment accompanied by skyrocketing unemployment rates (Fig. 8.8).

The differences were even more pronounced during the global crisis of 2008–2009 especially as regards the responses of employment and wages. Thus the crisis triggered massive layoffs and sharply rising unemployment rates in Bulgaria with lasting consequences: the labour market started to

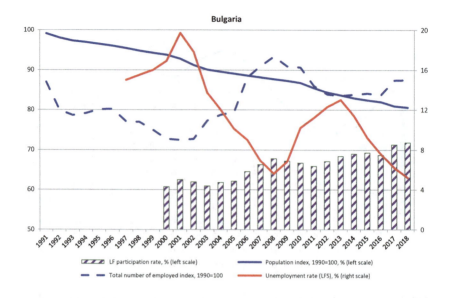

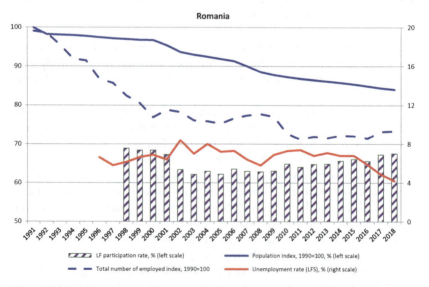

Fig. 8.8 Population, employment, activity rate and unemployment rate in Bulgaria and Romania, 1991–2018. (Source: wiiw macroeconomic database)

recover only around 2014. At the same time, the shock on the level of employment and unemployment in Romania was relatively moderate (Fig. 8.8). The wage responses of the two economies differed in the opposite direction: real wages actually declined in Romania in the period 2010–2012 while those in Bulgaria only moderated their pace of growth (Fig. 8.9).

The differences in the pattern of macroeconomic adjustment in Bulgaria and Romania reflect the fact that while both countries were EU members in this period they adhered to different monetary regimes and applied quite dissimilar macroeconomic policies. The currency board in Bulgaria reduced considerably the degrees of policy freedom: under this arrangement monetary policy is absent altogether whereas the conduct of fiscal policy is heavily restrained by sustainability considerations. Under these conditions, the economy becomes a hostage of the tidal movements of capital flows: periods of continuous inflows are generally benign for the economy; however, when capital inflows stop or change direction, policy makers have virtually no policy instruments to offset the adverse effects.

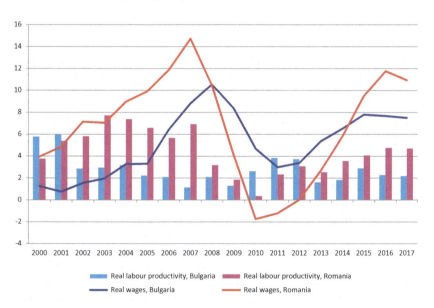

Fig. 8.9 Labour productivity and real wage dynamics in Bulgaria and Romania, 2000–2017, annual % change, 3-year moving averages. (Source: wiiw macroeconomic database)

Under these circumstances, if the labour market is flexible enough, it can act as an adjustment mechanism absorbing some of the effects of negative real external shocks. As suggested by Bulgaria's experience, its labour market de facto did demonstrate such flexibility with respect to labour input but not so much as regards wages. This type of adjustment proved to be sufficient for the continued rise of labour productivity also during the period of recession of near stagnation (Fig. 8.9). While the nominal exchange rate remained unchanged under the currency board arrangement, the moderation in the pace of growth of real wages helped arrest the growth of the real effective exchange rate and contributed to its subsequent gradual decline (Fig. 8.6).

The Romanian authorities had more degrees of policy freedom and they did use them in their attempts to mitigate the negative effects of the crisis but the country's monetary regime of inflation targeting implying a flexible exchange rate exposed to economy to additional risks. Thus the sudden capital outflow that started in 2008 led to a sharp depreciation of the leu and a surge in inflation. In consequence, the National Bank of Romania tightened considerably its monetary policy by raising its key policy rate. At the same time the government reverted to policies of wage restraint: starting from 2009 wages in the public sector were subject to a series of cuts, including a 25% reduction in 2010. The latter was announced as temporary but its residual effects lasted for several years. Wage restraint proliferated also the business sector and taken together this wage dynamics produced the drop in real wages in 2010–2012 (Fig. 8.9). These developments and the accompanying policy measures also contributed to a sharp drop in the real effective exchange rate and its subsequent relative stabilisation (Fig. 8.6).

The fiscal stance of the two countries also played an important role in shaping their adjustment process. In the case of Bulgaria, the mandatory fiscal reserve (established as part of the currency board arrangement) was combined with a persistently conservative fiscal policy stance which produced surpluses in the consolidated general government balances during the boom period preceding the crisis. These surpluses were mostly used to beef up the fiscal reserve, which at its peak in 2007–2008 reached levels above 12% of GDP. Once the crisis hit, there was a reversal in Bulgaria's fiscal balance as well (Fig. 8.6). This change mirrored a process of rebalancing between the public and private sectors: while the government was a net saver during most of the previous decade, it switched to dis-saving during the crisis to offset the process of deleveraging by the private sector that was triggered by the crisis.

Romania's fiscal stance was much more lax, especially before the crisis. As noted, the general government balance was in chronic deficit even during the boom period, suggesting a persistent structural deficit which added to the current account deficit (Fig. 8.6). Public finances were badly hit during the crisis and further destabilised by populist policies. The magnitude of the structural deficit surfaced in 2009 when the general government balance hit -9.1% of GDP in 2009 and prompted a sizeable and painful emergency correction in the fiscal policy course, including the above noted cuts in public sector wages.

The asymmetric policy responses of the two countries to similar external shocks reflected both the different degrees of policy freedom at the disposal of the authorities but also embodied different policy objectives pursued by policy makers. The macroeconomic outcomes are indicative of both the strengths and weaknesses of the policy approaches followed in each country.

As noted, the policy course of the Romanian authorities made it possible to cushion to a large extent the labour market from a shock impact on labour input: the effect of the crisis on unemployment was rather marginal. On the other hand, part of the shock was absorbed by cuts in real wages. And, more importantly, the macroeconomic destabilisation in Romania in 2009 was of such a magnitude that the authorities were forced to seek assistance from the IMF. The rescue programme offered to Romania was actually jointly agreed by the EC-IMF-WB troika. This was also a way for local politicians to pass – and anchor – some of the responsibility for undertaking harsh and unpopular policy measures to an external authority.

The 24-month Stand-By Arrangement approved by the Executive Board of the IMF in 2009 was earmarked to support an economic programme to cushion the effects of the sharp drop in capital inflows while addressing the country's external and fiscal imbalances and strengthening the financial sector (IMF 2009). The programme envisaged consolidation of public finances through reductions in government expenditure in the short run and the introduction of longer-term fiscal reforms as well as a range of associated policy measures. This arrangement was followed by two similar IMF stand-by arrangements jointly endorsed by the troika (in 2001 and 2013); however, the Romanian authorities did not draw funds under these subsequent arrangements.

Ultimately, after absorbing the shocks and helped by the foreign assistance (both financial but also in the form of external policy anchoring), Romania's economy emerged from the crisis in a strong position and embarked on a path of robust export-led growth. The strong and lasting upturn that followed the crisis was made possible thanks to the rejuvenated production base of the manufacturing industry invigorated by FDI.

By contrast, Bulgaria avoided macroeconomic destabilisation both during and after the global crisis. The presence of a fiscal reserve on top of the persistently conservative fiscal policy stance provided the authorities with a macroeconomic buffer that they could use at their discretion to cushion the negative effects of external shocks. As an example, the government was able to finance some of the deficit resulting from the global financial crisis by drawing from the fiscal reserve rather than through new borrowing at unfavourable conditions. The existence of such a cushion enabled the Bulgarian authorities to avoid the need to revert to an external "lenders of last resort" such as the IMF in this period of global turmoil.

While Romania was also forced to introduce corrections in its policy course in order to comply with IMF conditionality, the fiscal reserve in Bulgaria also served as a "cushion" for the authorities against external interference in local policy making. On the one hand the available evidence can be interpreted in the sense that the Bulgarian authorities self-imposed on themselves such excessive fiscal austerity that they did not need an external anchor as the IMF for maintaining macroeconomic stability. But in the absence of needed policy reforms targeting sustained long-term growth, stringent policies may become self-serving: maintaining balanced public finances just for the sake of the balance. Bulgaria's experience during the past 10–15 years bears some features of such a policy model. One could possibly argue that its excessively tight fiscal policy stance over a prolonged period of time came at the expense of some growth sacrifice during this period. On the other hand, policy sovereignty may also be regarded as a mixed blessing for a still immature emerging economy as Bulgaria: it likely averted the re-introduction of some degrees of external anchoring of the policy course which might have supported the initiation of needed policy reforms, including those targeting long-term growth.

In conclusion, Romania's fairly loose fiscal policies in the past decade (sometimes in violation of EU's Stability and Growth Pact) resembled more the policy attitude of a sovereign economy which is not bound under jointly agreed macroeconomic policy norms and rules such as those in the EU. By contrast, in the absence of independent monetary policy and given its specific policy approach, Bulgaria probably resembled a eurozone economy (but without access to ECB funding) excessively preoccupied with its fiscal sustainability at the expense of growth considerations.

8.4 COHABITATION AND SOLIDARITY IN THE CLUB: THE CARROTS AND THE STICKS

The broader definition of convergence is the tendency of group members to become more alike over time and if we consider the EU as a club this definition is probably a good match to the requirement that countries that join the club or aspire to do so have to abide by the rules and norms that define the club as such. Such a requirement is formally embodied in the EU's acquis communautaire and all candidate countries need to pass a rather severe test during the accession process in order to prove that they have adopted the common rules and norms and that these function efficiently. The acquis communautaire – which actually refer to the requirement for institutional convergence – were established under the combined effect of two main driving forces: on the one hand, a shared vision of the future embodied in common objectives and, on the other hand, shared values embodied in the design of the common mechanisms and instruments to achieve these objectives.

However, the design and implementation of norms defining a degree of institutional convergence is the making of humans and hence is prone to human error or error of judgment. The human factor is present also in the evaluation of the degree of fulfilment of certain criteria when sometimes political considerations may outweigh expert judgment. On the other hand, the geographic widening of the EU was associated with a growing heterogeneity of its membership which, in turn, narrowed the scope of integration issues and common policies the members could easily agree upon. Moreover, the rapidly changing external environment often calls for the updating, adjustment and modification of some EU common rules and norms that have been instituted under different circumstances and the process of required change resembles attempts to intercept moving targets. In this context decision-making in the EU becomes even trickier.

These processes affected the adjustment of all NMSs and, especially of the two latecomers, to the complex multilateral decision-making environment in the EU. The cohabitation with some of the old EU members has been somewhat awkward and uneasy as some of the old members preserved – and still preserve – the reservations they had had towards the accession of Bulgaria and Romania to the Union.

Actually back in 2006, the EU was not unanimous whether the two countries were ready to join the club in 2007. The areas that raised most numerous concerns were related to the institutional capacity of the two countries to fight against corruption and organised crime as well as the overall unsatisfactory situation in their judicial systems. Concerns were also raised as regards the administrative capacity of the two economies to absorb EU transfers in an efficient way. However, as noted earlier, political considerations prevailed when the subsequent enlargement decision was taken. To mitigate the existing reservations, the EU decided to impose regular monitoring on Bulgaria and Romania in order to assess progress under the Cooperation and Verification Mechanism (CVM) in areas related to the rule of law.

Another sign of persistent scepticism has been the stubborn reluctance by some members of the Schengen Area to admit Bulgaria and Romania into the Area although, even according to the rigorous assessment by the European Commission, the two countries have already met the technical criteria for membership. The latter situation, however, is also a typical demonstration of the difficulties in hitting a moving target in a situation when the EU is contemplating changes (and even an overhaul) in the Schengen system itself.

The post-accession experience of institutional convergence in the two countries has been mixed and did not bring satisfactory progress in some of the areas that had been problematic prior to accession. As regards Bulgaria, in the first place this concerns the judiciary system which, despite the numerous legislative, regulatory and administrative changes introduced during the past decade (to a large extent in response to criticisms in the CVM reports), remains highly inefficient and is perceived as corrupt. Up to a point, it was considered that Romania made more radical and effective steps in this direction, mostly thanks to the activity of the National Anticorruption Directorate which has been investigating and prosecuting corruption-related offences such as bribery and embezzlement (Hunya 2017). However, subsequent domestic political pressure largely watered down these efforts and the overall effect of the fight against corruption in Romania remains limited.

These unsatisfactory outcomes also demonstrate a low efficiency of some of the "sticks" that the EU has at its disposal to deal with non-compliance with its rules and norms. Recent research (Dimitrov et al. 2016) found that despite the fact that the CVM has been exerting continuous pressure for reforms, it did not produce a sustained progress in bringing Bulgaria and Romania up to the required EU standards in the monitored areas. What has been observed was rather a fluctuation around a status quo of a blocked judicial reform, produced by an institutional vicious circle of state capture and corruption at a high political level. Such a vicious circle embedded in vested interests is difficult to be broken from within while the CVM proved to be an inefficient external stick to break it from the outside. Basically, resolving such problems requires a major bottom-up political overhaul driven by a democratic process, something that has not happened so far in either of the two countries.

On the other hand, the pre-accession concerns about the absorptive capacity of the two economies turned out to be unsubstantiated, especially as regards Bulgaria. In retrospective, the main European focus of the efforts by Bulgaria's political elite during the past decade has been on the management of fund allocations from the EU budget. Actually, the buzz word on European policy as delivered by local politicians to the Bulgarian public has been "European funds". These specific efforts were generally fruitful, although success varied over time: after 2012 Bulgaria surpassed the average of the NMS-8 and in 2015 and 2016 it actually reported the largest net financial balance with the EU among all EU member states. Romania was slower to embark on the utilisation of EU transfers but thanks to learning-by doing and continuous EU pressure it also surpassed the NMS-8 average after 2014 (Fig. 8.10).

The bulk of EU budget allocations to both countries was apportioned to infrastructure development. Thus Romania managed to undertake several large public infrastructure projects such as the expansion of water and sewage infrastructure and the modernisation of public heating systems, while the efficiency of the funds allocated to motorway construction was only partial (Hunya 2017). The one genuine success story in Bulgaria was the rapid extension of the metro network in Sofia which was funded under different EU programmes. Highway construction as well as the upgrading of the railway network were also among the successful infrastructure projects.

At the same time, the successful absorption of EU funds in infrastructure development was both a blessing and a curse for Bulgaria. In particular, over time, the preoccupation with "EU funds" led to serious undesirable shifts, indeed distortions, in Bulgaria's public investment policy and practice. In the first place, while total public capital expenditure as percentage of GDP generally increased after EU accession thanks to the allocations from EU budget, the share of public capital expenditure financed from the general government budget declined rapidly (Fig. 8.11). Apart from that, the domestic public funding was allocated with priority as co-financing of the EU-funded projects while public investment programmes which were outside the reach of EU funding enjoyed lower priority. And thirdly, the relative abundance of EU funding gave rise to

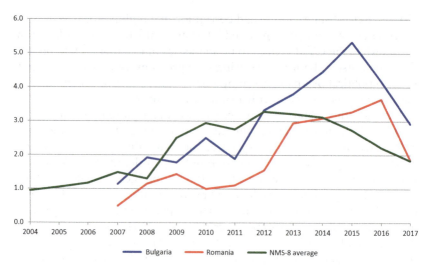

Fig. 8.10 Net financial position of the new EU member states, 2004–2017, % of GNI. (Source: Eurostat)

expectations similar to an aid addiction syndrome. Similar developments were taking place in Romania as well, but to a significantly lesser extent. Plus, on average the Romanian government has been allocating relatively more local public funds for public investment (Fig. 8.11).

Summarising, in the absence of adequate public investment policy EU funding de facto may be crowding out, rather than crowing in, local public investment funding. Thus Bulgaria's public investment programmes became skewed towards infrastructure development at the expense of other areas of needed public investment such as the upgrading of dilapidated urban and municipal infrastructure (including schools and hospitals, public spaces, sewage and water supply infrastructure) and the rehabilitation of the secondary and tertiary roads; the abundance of EU funding also gave rise to policy complacency.

These problems came to the surface in 2016 when, on the one hand, the carryovers from projects under the EU 2007–2013 Multi-annual Financial Framework (MFF) were exhausted whereas both Bulgaria and Romania incurred serious delays in the launching of new projects under the 2014–2020 MFF and the finalisation of previously launched projects. As a result, total public investment dropped in proportion to GDP (in the case of Bulgaria significantly) after 2016.

8 BULGARIA AND ROMANIA: THE LATECOMERS TO THE EASTERN… 265

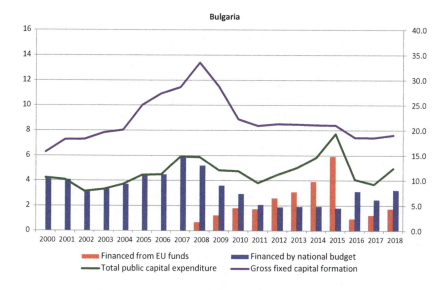

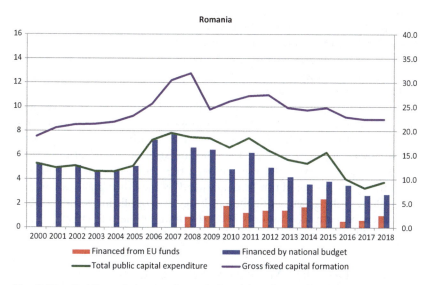

Fig. 8.11 Public capital expenditure (left scale) and gross fixed capital formation (right scale) in Bulgaria and Romania, 2000–2018, % of GDP. (Source: wiiw macroeconomic database, author's calculations)

One of the lessons of these experiences is that the EU "sticks" (as embodied in the CVM) were not very efficient as instruments for enforcing institutional and policy change in the accession countries with an unfinished reform agenda regarding some aspects of institutional convergence with the EU. Actually the role of the EU as an external anchor for reforms virtually faded away after Bulgaria and Romania became full EU members in 2007. In the lead-up to EU membership, local politicians regarded accession as a possible reward to their own personal efforts and sought to appropriate as much as possible of this reward. Therefore they were ready to endure considerable sacrifices in return for the expected reward. However, once accession was a fact, the reform zeal of local politicians waned and the critical remarks contained in the CVM reports were not considered as forceful threats to their political standing and to the existing status quo. In the absence of alternative bottom-up pressure, further reform progress may be next to nil as evidenced in Bulgaria and partly in Romania. The only way to re-invigorate the reform efforts would be the engineering of continuous and strong local bottom-up public pressure based on a democratic process. However, for this to happen the public needs to be well informed (thus transparency is essential) and must be well organised so that to be able to exert its demands through a democratic political process. This was not happening in Bulgaria where the political system is still dominated by descendants of the old elites; such pressure did emerge in Romania but so far it has not been able to trigger genuine systemic change.

On the other hand, the efficiency of EU's "carrots" as embodied in the EU transfers, a key symbol of EU-wide solidarity, seems to have been higher than that of its "stocks". The mobilisation and utilisation of large amounts of EU funds has been considered as another form of a tangible reward by local politicians and they did invest effort and zeal in making this happen. However, the efficiency of the actual investments funded from these sources could not be guaranteed by the existing EU norms and rules. Plus, in the absence of coherent long-term public investment policy, the obsession with EU transfers may have undesirable side effects, as also evidenced by the experience of Bulgaria and Romania.

8.5 Does EU Membership Bring About Prosperity on the Eastern Periphery?

In the whole of Central and Eastern Europe, EU membership has been associated with the expectation of growing prosperity, matching or approaching the wealth enjoyed by the old EU members that served as role models for the future. However, as the EU was born and initially evolved as a club of equals real convergence, the reduction of differences in per capita incomes within the club, was not a major common policy issue prior to the Eastern Enlargement: most of the newly acceding countries in that period used to enjoy relatively high per capita income levels at the time they joined the Union. Thus membership was not formally coupled with a condition or expectation of achieving certain levels of per capita income by the candidate countries prior to accession. Income disparities did exist in the EU but mostly at the regional level and the structural and cohesion funds served as the policy instruments intended to mitigate and reduce such disparities.

The Eastern Enlargement brought about a radical change in this situation with the accession of a numerous group of relatively poor countries. However, the EU which was undergoing a difficult internal constitutional reform process that ended with the adoption of the Lisbon Treaty did not have and was not willing to put in place new EU-wide policies and instruments and mechanisms facilitating real convergence across countries. Thus the task of supporting a catch up process was basically left as a responsibility of policy makers in each of the new member states.

Obviously, as already discussed and as substantiated by abundant academic research, the process of integration with the EU itself served as a powerful impetus invigorating economic growth and catching up by the NMS. EU integration affected positively economic growth in the accession countries both directly and indirectly through numerous channels such as, among others, the acceleration of systemic and structural reforms, the access to a large market, the massive FDI inflows, the integration with EU financial markets, the effect of growing competitive pressure on productive efficiency and, not least, the positive effect of EU cohesion policies and the access to EU cohesion and structural funds. However, the degree to which each acceding country could avail of the potential positive effect offered by the opening of these new opportunities depended to a large degree on the local context, the existence of a conducive business environment and investment climate and the creativity and initiative of local policy makers. Naturally, factors such as geography, historic links and cultural tradition also mattered.

Indeed, all CEECs benefited from these opportunities and experienced a period of high economic growth, at least until the global financial crisis. Growth was uneven, however, reflecting the degree to which each country could avail of the newly opening opportunities (Table 8.1). Bulgaria and

Table 8.1 GDP growth in the NMS-10, national accounts data

	Annual average rate of GDP growth, %			GDP index, 2000=100	Annual average rate of GDP per capita growth, %			GDP pc index, 2000=100
	2001–2010	2011–2018	2001–2018	2018	2001–2010	2011–2018	2001–2018	2018
Bulgaria	4.6	2.3	3.6	188	5.6	3.0	4.5	219
Czech Republic	3.2	2.3	2.8	164	3.0	2.1	2.6	158
Estonia	3.3	3.8	3.5	187	3.6	4.0	3.7	194
Hungary	2.0	2.6	2.3	150	2.2	3.0	2.6	157
Latvia	3.8	3.6	3.7	193	5.1	4.7	4.9	237
Lithuania	4.3	3.6	4.0	203	5.6	4.9	5.3	254
Poland	3.9	3.5	3.7	194	4.0	3.4	3.7	194
Romania	4.2	3.8	4.1	205	5.3	4.3	4.9	236
Slovakia	4.9	2.9	4.0	203	4.9	2.8	3.9	201
Slovenia	2.7	1.8	2.3	150	2.4	1.7	2.0	144

Source: wiiw macroeconomic database

Romania were actually among the NMS that reported the highest rates of growth of GDP and GDP per capita in the period 2001–2018.

High growth in per capita income, as approximated by the increase of GDP per capita is the foundation of catching up by poorer countries and of real convergence among a group of countries. Ironically, in the period 2001–2018, GDP per capita in most NMSs was growing faster than GDP per se. This reflects one of the gloomy aspects of the recent socio-economic developments in these countries: population decline. While this was partly due to the general problem of population ageing in Europe, emigration accounted for the largest share of the population decline. This was the other side of the coin of EU integration as most of the people emigrating from the NMSs moved to the more prosperous parts of the EU. The EU eastern periphery (Romania, Bulgaria and the Baltic states) suffered the most from the exodus.

Faster economic growth underpinned a process of sustained catching up by the NMSs and in the period from 2000 to 2018 all of them reduced the differences in per capita GDP levels relative to the more prosperous old EU members (Fig. 8.12). Numerous research on this issue also provides abundant evidence that real convergence has been taking place

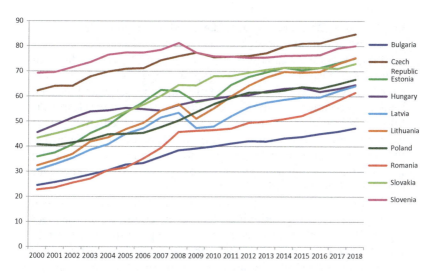

Fig. 8.12 Real GDP per capita at PPS in the NMS-10 relative to the EU-15, 2000–2018, %. (Source: Eurostat)

through various channels (see, among others, Dobrinsky and Havlik 2014; Grela et al. 2017, Rapacki and Próchniak 2009).

Figure 8.12 illustrates the process of catching up within the EU in dynamics as reported by Eurostat and measured by real GDP per capita at the purchasing power standards (PPS) of the latest available year, 2018. While the graph confirms that a catch-up process was underway in all NMS, it also reveals some puzzling discrepancies with the rates of GDP growth reported by the countries' statistical offices. Thus while Table 8.1 indicates only a marginal difference between the rates of growth of GDP per capita in Bulgaria and Romania in the period 2001–2018, Fig. 8.12 suggests that the catch up process in Romania was much faster during the same period: in 2000 real GDP per capita at PPS in Bulgaria was 24.3% of the EU-15 average and that in Romania stood at 22.8%; in 2018 the respective figures were 47.3% and 61.6%. The implied highly differentiated speed of catching up in the two countries is not consistent with the rates of growth of GDP per capita as reported using national accounts (Table 8.1). This inconsistency may be due to the imperfection of the measurement system based on real GDP per capita at PPS and the mixing up of real convergence and structural effects (Box 1).

Box 1 Do We Measure Correctly the Speed of Catching Up?
The most commonly approach to measure real convergence and catching up is the comparison of per capita GDP levels in different countries as measured at purchasing power parities (PPP). Eurostat coordinates these assessments among EU member states and selected non-EU economies using a common methodology (Eurostat-OECD 2012). The results are presented at the accepted common measurement unit, the purchasing power standard (PPS), which is the technical term used by Eurostat for the common currency in which national accounts aggregates are expressed when adjusted for price level differences using PPPs.

Notably, Eurostat's PPS assessment are static measures which present the relative positioning of different countries by their per capita GDP levels as measured at the average price structures within the EU member states. Eurostat's methodological manual contains a disclaimer as regards the possible use of such measures for the assessment of catchup dynamics to the effect that computed year-to-

(*continued*)

Box 1 (continued)

year changes in real per capita GDP levels at PPS may be due to changes in the numerous relative price and volume levels that form the aggregate assessment (Eurostat-OECD 2012). Hence, the rates of relative growth derived from the indices are not consistent with those obtained from national accounts data.

Nevertheless, Eurostat does publish retrospective estimates of "real GDP per capita at PPS" (measured at the most recent EU PPS) and in reality these are widely used to illustrate the catchup dynamic, as also presented in Fig. 8.13. However, these measures present a different picture of the historical economic growth as compared to national accounts data. This is illustrated in Table 8.2 which presents the implied retrospective growth of GDP and GDP per capita in the NMS-10 as computed from the most recent Eurostat estimates of real GDP per capita at the PPS of the EU-28 in 2018.

A comparison with the respective rates of economic growth computed from national accounts data (Table 8.1) reveals considerable discrepancies between the two sets – and a very different picture of the underlying catchup process in the NMS-10.

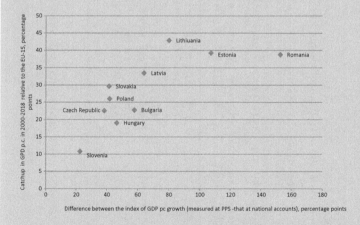

Fig. 8.13 Speed of catching up and structural effects. (Source: author's calculations based on Eurostat and wiiw macroeconomic database)

(*continued*)

Table 8.2 Implied rates of GDP growth in the NMS-10 (GDP at PPS of 2018, Eurostat)

	Implied annual average rate of GDP growth, %			GDP index, 2000=100	Implied annual average rate of GDP per capita growth, %			GDP pc index, 2000=100
	2001–2010	2011–2018	2001–2018	2018	2001–2010	2011–2018	2001–2018	2018
Bulgaria	6.4	3.2	4.9	263	7.2	4.2	5.8	277
Czech Republic	4.3	3.7	4.0	216	4.0	3.5	3.8	196
Estonia	6.7	5.0	5.9	321	7.2	5.2	6.3	301
Hungary	4.5	2.9	3.8	213	4.7	3.2	4.0	204
Latvia	5.4	4.7	5.1	263	6.7	5.8	6.3	301
Lithuania	6.3	4.8	5.6	288	7.6	6.1	6.9	334
Poland	5.5	4.1	4.9	249	5.5	4.1	4.9	236
Romania	8.6	5.5	7.2	364	9.6	5.7	7.8	389
Slovakia	6.7	3.0	5.1	259	6.7	3.0	5.0	242
Slovenia	3.3	2.8	3.1	184	3.0	2.7	2.9	166

Source: author's calculations based on Eurostat and wiiw macroeconomic database

(*continued*)

Box 1 (continued)

To highlight some of the implications of these discrepancies, I juxtapose, on the one hand, the difference between the index of growth of GDP per capita 2001–2018 as computed from PPS data (the last column of Table 8.2) and that from national accounts data (the last column of Table 8.1) and, on the other hand, the degree of catchup by the different countries vis-à-vis the EU-15 as measured by the change in their relative positioning during the same period (the starting and ending points in Fig. 8.12, i.e. the years 2000 and 2018, respectively). This juxtaposition is illustrated in Fig. 8.13 which suggests a positive correlation between the degree of catchup measured at current PPS in the individual countries and the difference between the two indexes of growth of GDP per capita.

A possible explanation of these discrepancies is the bias caused by ongoing structural change. One of the underlying assumptions of the PPP-based assessment is that price and volume structures do not change over time. As Eurostat makes this assessment on the expenditure side of GDP, this refers to volume and price structure of final demand. However, in reality these structures do change and over long periods this may produce a biased picture of the relative economic developments of the countries (Eurostat-OECD 2012). Hence one of the likely causes of the discrepancies is a differential dynamics of the structural change in the different countries.

Coming back to the comparison of the two measures of economic growth (Tables 8.1 and 8.2) one can note that the growth of GDP per capita measured at PPS in all NMS is higher than the respective growth based on national accounts. This can be interpreted in the sense of structural effects (structural convergence or divergence of volume and price structures) vis-à-vis the EU average (for a discussion on the issue of structural convergence and its measurement see Alexoaei and Robu 2018; Coevering 2003). When relative prices and relative volumes change vis-à-vis the reference structures, their weights in the computation of the aggregate also change and this results in a "bias" of the estimation of the aggregate. In our case, all NMSs display a positive difference which intuitively is likely to reflect structural convergence. Furthermore, when such structural convergence in one catching up country is faster than that in another coun-

(*continued*)

> **Box 1 (continued)**
> try, then the corresponding "bias" may be even larger and vice versa. This can explain the variation in the differences between the two indexes of growth of GDP per capita among the NMS (presented on the horizontal axis in Fig. 8.13). Moreover, if the reference structures also change, such effects will depend on the comparative dynamic structural effects. The size of the difference between the index of growth of GDP per capita 2001–2018 as computed from PPS data reflects the size of the structural effects captured in the dynamics of real GDP per capita at PPS.
>
> On the other hand, such an interpretation suggests that not all of the dynamic catchup effect as measured at current PPS (the vertical axis of Fig. 8.13) may be due to higher economic growth but also to more pronounced structural effects. To put it figuratively, the degree of catchup measured in this way depends not only on the speed with which you run but also on whether you run in the right direction.

Despite the ambiguities regarding the degree and speed of convergence, it is obvious that both Bulgaria and Romania have been catching up successfully to the more affluent old EU members. Apart from the statistical indicators, everyday life provides numerous visible signs of the rising prosperity and welfare of the population in the two countries and these are obvious also for visitors who have seen the decay prevailing in the 1990s.

However, another facet of this process is the nature of growth in these countries and to what extent it has been inclusive in the sense of creating opportunity for all segments of the population and distributing the dividends of increased prosperity fairly across society (OECD 2014). Internal solidarity and the inclusiveness of growth have always featured in the spirit of EU's social policies and are also embodied in the EU Strategy 2020 (European Commission 2010). However, the actual implementation of these policies is a prerogative and responsibility of national governments; the EU and its bodies have no say either on the design of national policies in this area or on their outcomes.

A key distinguishing feature of the notion of inclusive growth is its dual emphasis on outcomes as well as opportunities. Inclusive growth refers simultaneously to the process itself and to its upshots, i.e., people should both contribute to and benefit in a broad sense from economic growth. From this point of view and judging from some of the observable outcomes of the recent pattern of growth in Bulgaria and Romania, one could conclude that internal solidarity has been to a large extent a neglected issue by local policy makers.

Moreover, in the case of Bulgaria, the degree of income inequality as characterised by the Gini coefficient, has been persistently increasing both prior to the global crisis and after it (Fig. 8.14). In 2018, Bulgaria featured by far the highest Gini coefficient of equivalised disposable income in the EU and within the Union it has been the only country with such dynamics of income inequality in the past two decades.

Income inequality in Romania is also relatively high: it increased substantially in the lead up to the global crisis but in the period thereafter this tendency was reversed. For a comparison, the CEECs are among the EU countries with the lowest degree of income inequality within the EU.

The differential dynamics of income inequality across countries is entirely an outcome of national policies and framework conditions in the different countries. Among other things, the systems of taxation undoubtedly play a role for the distribution of the benefits of economic growth.

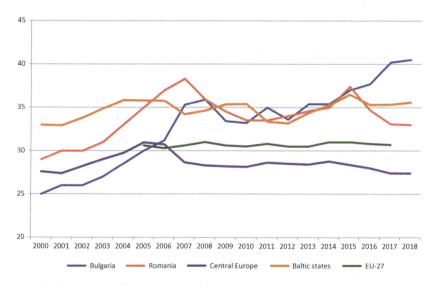

Fig. 8.14 Gini coefficient of equivalised disposable income in selected EU member states, 2000–2017, %. (Source: Eurostat)

Immediately prior to EU accession both Bulgaria and Romania introduced tax reforms based on a flat tax streamlining the system of taxation but also seeking to make the business environment even more attractive to foreign investors. In Romania, initially both employment income and corporate profit was taxed at 16%; later on the tax rate on personal income was reduced to 10%. In Bulgaria the flat tax rate of 10% applied to all types of income (both personal income and corporate profit).

The tax competition effect of these reforms was questionable due to their ill-fated timing as the global crisis triggered massive outflows of capital from emerging markets including Bulgaria and Romania. At the same time, these changes in taxation did exert a distortive effect on income and wealth distribution, especially in Bulgaria, where the flat rate applies to all personal income (except pensions), without a non-taxable minimum income. Such taxation of income directly contributes to the deepening of income inequalities as it favours high-income groups, eliminating the solidarity tax component contained in the progressive scale. Of course, taxation of income is only one element of the policies contributing to the disproportionate distribution of the benefits of economic growth and the widening of social stratification. However, the fact is that growing income inequality has not been recognised by local policy makers as an issue of concern and no policy efforts have been undertaken to address this issue.

Besides, income inequality itself is just one of the unfavourable outcomes of the pattern of growth prevailing in Bulgaria and Romania. The massive emigration which continues up to this moment reflects the disappointment of parts of the population with the current economic situation and prospects. The labour markets in the two economies also feature some serious distortions. Thus while the labour force participation rate in the two economies has been increasing in recent years, especially in Bulgaria (Fig. 8.8), in both countries there is a stable segment of the population that has never been integrated into the formal labour market. Thus the proportion of young people neither in employment nor in education and training in Bulgaria and Romania is the highest among all EU member states, albeit decreasing in recent years (Fig. 8.15).

Furthermore, one needs to take into account the fact that a large chunk of the idle young people come from within the sizable Roma minorities in the two countries, reflecting the persistent failure to integrate these minorities into the education system and the labour market. The fact is that within these minorities one can now observe several subsequent generations living under one roof none of whom has ever attended formal education or has been formally employed.

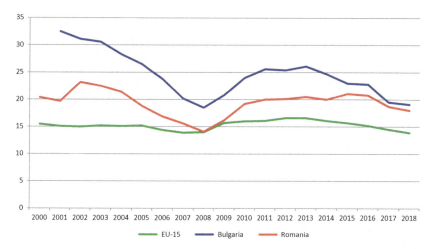

Fig. 8.15 Young people neither in employment nor in education and training in Bulgaria and Romania, 2000–2018, %. (Source: Eurostat)

These regrettable outcomes indicate that the pattern of growth in Romania and, especially, in Bulgaria produced some results that are not consistent with the philosophy of inclusive growth. Instead of supporting a broader sharing of the benefits of the growing overall prosperity, this pattern contributed to further social stratification and a lasting marginalisation of some segments of the population. Thus according to Eurostat data, in 2017 Bulgaria and Romania were the two EU countries featuring the highest share of people at risk of poverty and social exclusion: 38.9% and 35.7%, respectively. For comparison, the EU-28 average in that year was 22.4%. According to the UN Global Sustainable Development Goals Indicators Database (https://unstats.un.org/sdgs/indicators/database/), the proportion of population living below the national poverty line in Bulgaria even increased in recent years: from 14% in 2000 to 22.9% in 2016. The proportion of people below the national poverty line in Romania on average has been even higher but a full time series is not available.

Apart from the growing social stratification as measured at the country level, regional disparities have also been increasing in the past couple of decades. Thus according to data of the National Statistical Institute based on SILC statistics, in 2012 the incidence of poverty in Bulgaria's poorest

NUTS2 region (the Northwest region) was more than 2.5 times higher than that in the wealthiest region (the Southwest region which includes the capital Sofia): 29.9% and 11.6%, respectively. At the NUTS3 level the gap was even higher: 38.7% in the poorest region (Sliven) vis-à-vis 6.6% in the wealthiest one (Sofia). These disparities have been setting in motion a vicious circle of interrelated undesirable changes: internal migration of economically active population from poorer to the wealthier regions and cities, accelerated degradation of physical infrastructure in poor regions and, especially, remote areas; worsening of the quality of health care, education and public transport in these areas. All this has been associated with further widening of the income gaps.

On the whole one could say that the process of overall catching up in per capita income levels that has been underway in Bulgaria and Romania and which has been largely associated with the integration within the EU, has not been equitably distributed and did not bring about prosperity to all segments of the population in the two countries. These outcomes are not at all due to EU accession but are entirely the result of domestic policies pursued in the two countries. Even more, such outcomes are not consistent with the spirit of external and internal solidarity and cohesion embodied in the European project.

8.6 Concluding Remarks

This chapter seeks to analyse and assess to what extent the process of integration of Bulgaria and Romania into the EU played a role in some of the important socio-economic changes that took place in the two countries during the past two decades and the extent to which they have been part of a process of convergence to EU frontier(s).

The most visible positive effect of EU integration has been the reconstruction and modernisation of the two economies driven by FDI which, in turn, was directly associated with EU accession. In both countries and, especially in Romania, one can clearly observe the dynamic sprouts of a modern new economy, closely integrated with global value chains and competitive in the international markets. Also, Bulgaria and Romania joined successfully many EU programmes and benefited from considerable funding from the EU budget. The ongoing reconstruction of public infrastructure has been greatly supported by the transfers of EU funds. However, the mobilisation of large allocations from the EU budget did not always result in overall efficiency of public investment in the two countries.

Real convergence or the catching up in per capita income levels is probably the best recognised facet of convergence. In lower income economies like Bulgaria and Romania, the widespread expectations of rising prosperity associated with prospective EU membership has been a key and broadly shared inspiration for joining the EU. The irony in the case of the two countries is in the pure coincidence of the timing of accession to the EU with the global financial crisis which caused a reversal in capital flows and put a break on the pace of solid economic growth that had prevailed in the years ahead. In consequence, the first years of EU membership turned out to be a period of recession or near stagnation and lack of visible catching up. During and after the crisis these immature economies also had to cope with the destabilising macroeconomic effects of external shocks. Bulgaria was more successful in this; however, at the expense of a growth sacrifice.

Despite certain setbacks on the way, over the period from 2001 to 2018 Bulgaria and even more so Romania managed to reduce substantially the gap in average per capita income levels compared to the more developed EU members. However, the degree to which the population of these countries senses and acknowledges growing prosperity depends to a great degree on the perception of an equitable distribution of the rising total wealth. This is an area where both Bulgaria and Romania were actually falling behind vis-à-vis the European frontiers of solidarity and cohesion. Moreover, the failure of society and its political establishment to deliver broadly benefits of EU membership to all layers of the population signifies a mismatch between ex ante expectations and ex post outcomes which can be a source of disappointment with the way the EU functions.

Both Bulgaria and Romania are still learning to fully adhere to the norms and rule of the European club. The visible effects of the unfinished institutional reforms in the two countries such as corruption and dysfunctional judiciary have been a source of tension between them and the old EU members. However, the EU's Cooperation and Verification Mechanism applied in a monitoring process has proved to be inefficient as an external anchor in that its critical conclusions have not been sufficient to instigate relevant response actions on the ground. Genuine change of policies and attitudes towards EU best practice still remain a task for the future.

In a broader sense many aspects of the visible gaps vis-à-vis the EU frontier(s) can be qualified as gaps in the overall convergence of Bulgaria and Romania towards "Europeanness" (defined by the Oxford Dictionary as "the quality or fact of being European, or having or sharing a European heritage"). In this sense one could question whether we observe a process of convergence of the people's mindset in this part of the EU's eastern periphery towards a European common identity and shared values? Is Europeanness part of the self-perception of Bulgarian and Romanian citizens and their political elites and to what degree? The answers are not clear-cut. It has been suggested that there is a conflict between the traditional political establishment (which is engaged in clientelism and corruption) and a new generation of people, movements and institutions representing democratic ("European") values (Hunya 2017). Thus the convergence to Europeanness may also necessitate a generational change and a challenging learning process. But a radical change may also be triggered by a democratic bottom-up political process.

Such a change is a necessary remaining step towards Bulgaria's and Romania's full-fledged membership in the EU. Only when the European identity proliferates widely in the mindset of the population at the European Eastern periphery and when the domestic political process is genuinely driven by European values, Bulgaria and Romania will have a weighty voice in EU-wide debates and the two countries will be able to fully benefit from EU membership.

REFERENCES

Alexoaei, A. P., & Robu, R. G. (2018). A Theoretical Review on the Structural Convergence Issue and the Relation to Economic Development in Integration Areas. *Proceedings of the International Conference on Business Excellence, 12*(1), 34–44.

Babetskii, I. (2005). Trade Integration and Synchronization of Shocks. Implications for EU Enlargement. *Economics of Transition, 13*(1), 105–138.

Bajgar, M., & Javorcik, B. (2019). *Climbing the Rungs of the Quality Ladder: FDI and Domestic Exporters in Romania.* mimeo. http://users.ox.ac.uk/~econ0247/Romania.pdf.

Coevering, van de C. (2003). *Structural Convergence and Monetary Integration in Europe.* Netherlands Central Bank, Monetary and Economic Policy Department, MEB Series 2003-20. https://www.dnb.nl/en/binaries/serie2003-20_tcm47-147349.pdf

Dimitrov, G., Haralampiev, K., & Stoychev, S. (2016). *The Adventures of the CVM in Bulgaria and Romania.* Freie Universität Berlin, MAXCAP Working Paper No. 29.

Dobrinsky, R. (2000). The Transition Crisis in Bulgaria. *Cambridge Journal of Economics, 24*(5), 581–602.

Dobrinsky, R. (2013). Bulgaria and Political Economy of Transition. In P. Hare & G. Turley (Eds.), *Handbook of the Economics and Political Economy of Transition* (pp. 217–227). London/New York: Routledge.
Dobrinsky, R., & Havlik, P. (2014). *Economic Convergence and Structural Change: The Role of Transition and EU Accession.* wiiw Research Report 395.
European Commission. (2010). *Europe 2020. A European Strategy for Smart, Sustainable and Inclusive Growth.*
Eurostat-OECD. (2012). *Methodological Manual on Purchasing Power Parities (2012 Ed.).* Luxembourg: Publications Office of the European Union.
Fidrmuc, J., & Korhonen, I. (2003). Similarity of Supply and Demand Shocks Between the Euro Area and the CEECs. *Economic Systems, 27*(3), 313–334.
Grela, M., Majchrowska, A., Michałek, T., Mućk, J., Stążka-Gawrysiak, A., Tchorek, G., & Wagner, M. (2017). *Is Central and Eastern Europe Converging Towards the EU-15?* NBP Working Paper No. 264.
Hausmann, R., Hwang, J., & Rodrik, D. (2007). What You Export Matters. *Journal of Economic Growth, 12*(1), 1–25.
Hunya, G. (2002). Restructuring Through FDI in Romanian Manufacturing. *Economic Systems, 26*(4), 387–394.
Hunya, G. (2017). Romania: Ten Years of EU Membership. *Romanian Journal of European Affairs, 17*(1), 5–15.
IMF. (2009). *Romania: Request for Stand-By Arrangement.* IMF Country Report No. 09/183.
Jude, C. (2019). Does FDI Crowd Out Domestic Investment in Transition Countries? *Economics of Transition and Institutional Change, 27*(1), 163–200.
Mitra, P. (2011). *Capital Flows to EU New Member States: Does Sector Destination Matter?* IMF Working Paper 11/67.
OECD. (2014). *All on Board. Making Inclusive Growth Happen.* Paris: OECD.
Pavlínek, P. (2017). Foreign Direct Investment and the Development of the Automotive Industry in Eastern and Southern Europe. *SSRN Electronic Journal.* https://doi.org/10.2139/ssrn.3015163.
Popescu, D. D., & Ciora, C. (2015). The Second Wave of Restructuring in Romania. A Change of Paradigm. *Procedia Economics and Finance, 32*, 1289–1304.
Rapacki, R., & Próchniak, M. (2009). *The EU Enlargement and Economic Growth in the CEE New Member Countries.* European Commission DG ECFIN, Economic Papers 367.
Smith, A. (2001). The Transition to a Market Economy in Romania and the Competitiveness of Exports. In D. Light & D. Phinnemore (Eds.), *Post-Communist Romania.* London: Palgrave Macmillan.
World Bank. (2018). *Romania Systematic Country Diagnostic. Background Note Trade.* Washington, DC: The World Bank.

PART III

Convergence to Frontier as a Future Member of the European Union

CHAPTER 9

Convergence of Non-EU Countries in the CESEE Region

Richard Grieveson and Mario Holzner

9.1 INTRODUCTION

Almost every country in Central, East and Southeast Europe (CESEE) has converged with Germany over the past three decades. However, the pace of convergence has been far from even. This chapter sets out to do three main things. First, to trace the patterns of convergence of non-EU CESEE countries over the past three decades. Second, to identify the key factors that have determined relative convergence success or failure.

R. Grieveson (✉)
Vienna Institute for International Economic Studies (WIIW), Vienna, Austria

Diplomatic Academy of Vienna, Vienna, Austria
e-mail: grieveson@wiiw.ac.at

M. Holzner
Vienna Institute for International Economic Studies (WIIW), Vienna, Austria

University of Vienna, Vienna, Austria
e-mail: holzner@wiiw.ac.at

© The Author(s), under exclusive license to Springer Nature Switzerland AG 2021
M. Landesmann, I. P. Székely (eds.), *Does EU Membership Facilitate Convergence? The Experience of the EU's Eastern Enlargement - Volume I*, Studies in Economic Transition,
https://doi.org/10.1007/978-3-030-57686-8_9

And third, to analyse how central the role of the EU accession process, and eventual EU membership, has been in determining convergence progress among CESEE countries.

When analysing convergence in CESEE, it is clear that many factors must be taken into account. To attempt to demonstrate a precise causality in quantitative terms is very difficult. The issues are far too complex, and the differences between countries and time periods too great. It is clear that many factors played a role. Moreover, it is not clear which are causes and which are consequences of convergence. There is also a broader debate as in all social sciences about structure versus agency: it is likely that the role of individuals or groups of people at certain points may also have been very important in setting countries on convergence paths (or not). This cannot be satisfactorily captured in an economic model (although we will use regression analysis at one point in the analysis to get more insight).

External conditions have also certainly played a role. The period of CESEE transition and convergence was concomitant with a rather momentous change in the global economy, the era of what Dani Rodrik calls "hyper-globalisation". Since the 1980s, many countries around the world have seen significant increases in trade/GDP ratios. China has entered (and come increasingly to dictate fluctuations in) the global economy. In addition, the scale of global capital flows has increased dramatically, with a role for both "hot money" and FDI. Global value chains have been significantly expanded, with the dominant role and long reach of multinational corporations calling into question the whole concept of macroeconomic accounting on a national basis.[1] Most of CESEE has participated rather significantly in this process. Here, many EU-CEE countries have enjoyed a significant advantage, both in the sense of proximity to Germany, and the large amount of EU funds that have been available for infrastructure upgrading (the importance of these factors will be investigated below).

In this chapter, we focus on the 12 non-EU CESEE countries covered by the Vienna Institute for International Economic Studies (wiiw). This includes six countries in the non-EU Western Balkans (North Macedonia, Montenegro, Serbia, Kosovo, Albania, and Bosnia and Herzegovina), four in the CIS (Russia, Kazakhstan, Belarus, and Moldova), Ukraine and Turkey.[2] Where relevant, we compared these non-EU CESEE countries

---

[1] https://www.bis.org/speeches/sp190410.htm
[2] In this chapter we use the following country groups: EU-CEE 2004 (the eight CEE countries that joined the EU in 2004); EU-CEE 2007–13 (Bulgaria, Romania and Croatia);

with Germany or other Western European countries as a benchmark, as well as the countries in CESEE that joined the EU between 2004 and 2013. Within this latter group, we split the countries into the 2004 joiners and the post-2004 joiners, as there are important differences between them. These latter points are particularly crucial in attempting to understand the role that the EU accession process played in convergence, and how important it was for countries that played only a partial or no role this this.[3] Our hypothesis at the outset is that the role of the EU accession process was quite large and positive.[4]

9.2 Starting Points

All countries discussed here except Turkey started the transition from Communism to market capitalism and something like democratic politics around 30 years ago.[5] All had the typical inefficiencies in resource allocation that stemmed from this system. However, even under Communism there were important differences (Blanchard 1997). Four seem to have been particularly important.

First, the basic economic models under Communism were not always the same, or even similar. The differences between the Yugoslav and the Council for Mutual Economic Assistance (COMECON) models, for example, were significant, with the former Yugoslavia applying a more liberal system. Albania also had a different model, leaning towards a fairly extreme version of autarchy.

The influences of these different models can be seen in economic structures in the early 1990s. One way to look at this is rural population, which as a share of the total was very different in 1990 in the various countries, indicating variance in stages of development. The share ranged from only

WB6 (Albania, Bosnia and Herzegovina, Kosovo Montenegro, North Macedonia, Serbia); and CIS+UA (Russia, Belarus, Ukraine and Kazakhstan).

[3] We do, however, acknowledge that the 2004 joiners acceded to the EU earlier in part because they were already doing better than Romania and Bulgaria (Croatia is a different case, due to its involvement in the wars of the 1990s), rather than doing better because of having joined the EU.

[4] We try to provide as broad a picture as possible, by assessing a large number of relevant indicators. As much as possible, we assess trends back to 1989. However, for a lot of the issues we look at, data back to 1989 are not available, so we can only look at more recent levels.

[5] Here we acknowledge the particular case of Belarus, which has remained an outlier both politically and economically. This is addressed where relevant throughout the chapter.

around one quarter in Russia to two thirds in Albania and Bosnia (according to World Bank data for 1990). In general the countries of the former Yugoslavia, as well as other Balkan countries, were less urbanised, while some in central Europe and the former Soviet Union had similar urbanisation rates to Japan, the US and Germany.

Agriculture's share in GDP provides a further illustration of these differences. In 1995 (the first year for which generally comprehensive data are available), the agriculture/GDP ratio ranged from 6.7% in Russia to 56.6% in Albania. In general, among non-EU CESEE countries, the Former Soviet Union was more industrialised (and wealthier) in 1990, while the former Yugoslav (non-EU) countries were more agriculture-based and less developed. There are different ways to think about the importance of this, but one is that a lot of the easier "catch up" gains to productivity from moving workers from agriculture to industry and services is still to be made in South-East Europe.

The second key difference among CESEE countries was the level of integration into the regional and global economy. For example, outward migration from the former Yugoslavia was much easier than for the rest of the Communist bloc. As a result, the former Yugoslavia exported a lot more workers, and also received a lot more remittances, than other countries of the region. Yugoslavia also experimented with more reforms before the end of Communism than the others.

A fairly comprehensive picture of economic openness can be obtained from around 1995. CESEE economies stand out as generally very open by regional and global standards (Fig. 9.1). Countries of the former Soviet Union in particular show a much greater export/GDP ratio than the global average, non-European developing countries, or developed states (this ratio is actually higher for the non-commodity exporters, indicating that resource endowment was not necessarily the determining factor in trade openness at this stage[6]). In the Western Balkans, the picture is more mixed, although these data were influenced by the wars of the period. Across all of CESEE, it should also be kept in mind that the export/GDP ratios could be artificially boosted by the collapse in domestic demand in

---

[6] Indeed, this is also the case today. Russia is, along with Turkey and Kosovo, the least "open" economy (in terms of exports/GDP) in the whole CESEE region. These are the only three CESEE economies where the exports of goods and services/GDP ratio is below the global average (29%) according to World Bank data.

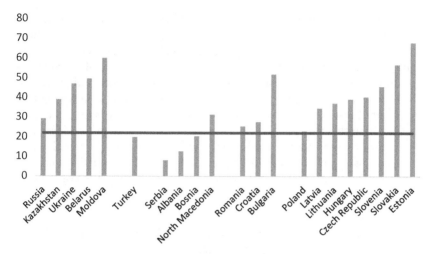

Fig. 9.1 Exports of goods and services, % of GDP, 1995. (Note: Horizontal line indicates the global average. Source: World Bank)

many places in the early 1990s (discussed in more detail later in the chapter).

The third key difference between the non-EU CESEE countries is the legacy of Empire. This has proven to be a very tricky subject for economists and economic historians to study and to establish objective facts, but it seems likely that the hangover from the various Empires in the region is highly important in explaining developments right up to the present day. Several studies appear to show that legacies of the former Empires in the region (German, Habsburg, Ottoman) left a legacy which survived Communism. In a previous paper, we found lasting negative effects from being part of the Eastern block's Council for Mutual Economic Assistance and years under Ottoman rule (Holzner et al. 2016). In particular, we found that this left a legacy of poor institutions, misallocation of resources, and a substantial technology gap. Countries that were formally part of the Habsburg Empire (in the case of non-EU CESEE this means only parts of a few countries, such as certain parts of Ukraine and Serbia), generally enjoy a more positive institutional and infrastructural legacy.

The final key difference in terms of starting points among the countries covered is the variance in experience of state formation, state collapse and war in the years immediately following the end of Communist rule. One can juxtapose the differing fortunes of neighbours from the same multi-ethnic state (e.g. Slovenia and Croatia) or the different ways in which states broke apart (e.g. Yugoslavia and Czechoslovakia). For countries caught on the "right" side of this, such as the Czech Republic, Slovakia and Slovenia (i.e. where disintegration was relatively quick and peaceful), the implications were very positive, and it provided these countries with a significant boost in the convergence race relative to many neighbours. For those where this was not the case (for example Croatia or Serbia, which experienced years of war), the implications were significant, negative and long-lasting. Even a country like Croatia, however, fared relatively favourably compared with those where frozen conflicts emerged and continue to this day (several places in the Western Balkans and Former Soviet Union).

9.3 Growth Performance and Convergence Over the Past 30 Years

9.3.1 Overview of Growth Performance

The pace of real GDP growth over the last three decades in CESEE has been highly uneven (Fig. 9.2). Between 1990 and 1994, per capita GDP in most countries in CESEE for which data are available fell, reflecting largely the "shock therapy" of the early 1990s, plus the war in the case of some former Yugoslav countries. Among countries not yet members of the EU, a decline of over 10 percentage points during these years was recorded in Moldova, Montenegro, Serbia and Ukraine. Among non-EU countries in CESEE, only one country recorded growth: Turkey (not a transition story).

This "shock therapy" meant a liberalisation of trade and prices, including early opening of the capital and financial accounts. Broadly, there were two key components of early transition: reallocation of resources and restructuring of state firms (Blanchard 1997). This contributed to very high inflation and in many cases deep recessions. Some societies are arguably still recovering from this shock.[7] According to the EBRD's 2016–17 Transition Report, "the social, economic and physical costs of these

---

[7] The legacy in Russia is clear, where the memory of the 1990s still exerts a powerful role on contemporary politics. There was also a well-documented negative impact on birth rates (https://www.ncbi.nlm.nih.gov/pmc/articles/PMC2842562/), which has been a contributing factor to the demographic challenges that the region currently faces.

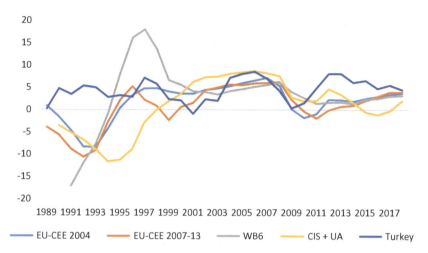

Fig. 9.2 Real GDP, % per year, 3-year moving average. (Note: simple averages for each region. Data for the early years are missing for some countries. Source: wiiw)

reforms were so substantial that men and women born at the start of the transition process are on average 1 cm shorter than those born just before or after that period" (EBRD 2017).

In the second half of the 1990s (1995–1999), the performance of the region was more positive. All countries except Moldova and Ukraine recorded positive real per capita GDP growth. The painful reforms of the early 1990s started to produce some results. However, this period also included the Russian financial crisis in 1998 (following on from the Asia crisis of 1997 and the Mexico crisis of 1994), which had wider implications for the region.

Growth rates picked up even further in 2000–2007. This reflected in part higher global growth, and CESEE's increasingly significant participation in global trade and financial markets. FDI and "hot money" inflows increased, as did export ratios. Every economy in CESEE posted positive growth in this period. However, foreign capital inflows also contributed to the build-up of dangerous imbalances in some countries. Capital inflows financed to a large extent consumption rather than investment in non-EU CESEE countries, which in turn led to wider trade deficits, especially in the Western Balkans. External debt also increased, although in general this was more visible in EU-CEE countries rather than non-EU CESEE, reflecting the latter's more restricted access to international capital markets.

Some parts of CESEE were hit particularly hard by the global financial crisis. Those countries most reliant on short-term foreign capital inflows were often the most badly affected, but Russia also experienced a deep recession as the oil price collapsed. In non-EU CESEE;, the biggest 2009 contractions in growth were recorded by Ukraine (-15.1%), Russia (-7.8%), Moldova (-6%) and Turkey (-4.7%). However, some EU-CEE countries were hit at least as hard, if not harder. The three Baltic economies registered contractions of over 14% in 2009, while the economies of Slovenia and Croatia shrunk by over 7% in the same year. Especially in the case of the Baltic states, this also reflected the vulnerability of large external deficits financed by "hot money". The extent of CESEE countries' external deficits and reliance on short-term capital flows therefore appears to have been more important than EU membership in determining the severity of their post-2008 recessions.

The post-crisis period has seen generally less impressive growth in most parts of CESEE, including the non-EU members. For the post-crisis period as a whole (2008–2018), compound real per capita growth rates ranged from -1.6% in Ukraine to 6.4% in Turkey. The simple average for the CESEE region was 2.9% (2.7% for the non-EU member states in the region). This growth was achieved with significantly smaller external imbalances than during the pre-crisis years in most countries. It should be noted that the still relatively large current account deficits in many Western Balkan countries in the post-crisis period reflects the role of foreign aid and loans on highly favourable terms (low interest rates, long maturities), which provides structural support and makes the external deficits far less potentially destabilising than could be assumed from the headline data.

An additional important factor suppressing growth in the CIS and Ukraine during the post crisis-period has been political conflict and international sanctions. Especially since the annexation of Crimea by Russia in 2014, conflict in Eastern Ukraine has significantly weighed on economic activity there.[8] Meanwhile a series of Western sanctions have affected the Russian economy, combining with lower oil prices and structural problems to suppress growth both there and in many neighbouring countries that rely on Russia for remittances or export demand.

[8] https://wiiw.ac.at/economic-consequences-of-the-ukraine-conflict-n-60.html. This news article summarises a longer research report only available in German.

9.3.2 Growth Drivers

Taking a broad sweep of the past 30 years, it is possible to identify econometrically three key drivers of convergence within CESEE[9]:

1. Over the whole period poorer countries tended to grow more quickly than richer ones (per capita GDP in 1990 is negatively correlated with growth performance), allowing for some convergence within CESEE.
2. A higher investment share in GDP was positively correlated with overall GDP growth.
3. EU accession appears to have played a very important role. All else being equal, non-EU countries from CESEE grew by 1.5 percentage points less than EU member states in the region. The Western Balkan countries plus Turkey underperformed EU-CEE by 1.2 percentage points (holding all other factors constant), while for the CIS and Ukraine the negative gap was a notably larger 1.9 percentage points. These differences are considerable and hint at the large costs that are involved by not acceding the EU.

9.3.3 Convergence with Germany

Germany is often used as the comparison country when measuring convergence within Europe. Going back to 1990, where data are available, per capita GDP starting points versus Germany were very low (subregional averages are shown in Fig. 9.3). In that year, among non-EU CESEE countries per capita GDP at PPS ranged from 9.6% of the German level in Albania to 36.7% in Kazakhstan. For CESEE as a whole, the highest level reached was 47.3% in the Czech Republic. Interestingly, the starting points for at least some non-EU CESEE countries compare quite well with many of the EU member states. Kazakhstan, Russia and Ukraine were all significantly wealthier than Poland at this point, for example.

By 2000, after a very tough first transitions decade for reasons outlined above, most non-EU CESEE countries had fallen back relative to Germany. At this point, Turkey (not affected by the post-Communist shock therapy) had reached the highest level of convergence, at 34.4%. Among the former

---

[9] This section reports the conclusions of an econometric analysis, the results of which are included in the Annex.

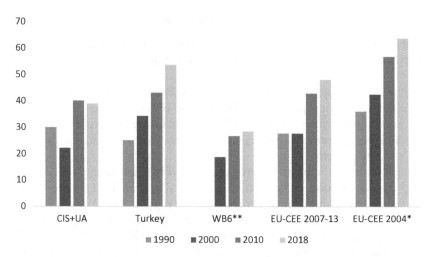

Fig. 9.3 GDP per capita, PPS, Germany = 100, simple averages for each subregion. (Note: *Does not include Estonia for 1990; **Insufficient data available for 1990. Source: wiiw)

Communist countries, Kazakhstan was still the highest, but at 28.6% of the German level had fallen back considerably since 1990. Albania had converged somewhat, but at 14.1% was still the second-lowest level of convergence in the region, just ahead of Ukraine (13.7%).

By 2018, after a generally positive almost two decades—albeit interrupted by the global financial crisis—all countries had achieved some level of convergence with Germany compared with 2000. The highest level in the non-EU CESEE region was Turkey (53.7%), followed by Kazakhstan (52.1%) and Russia (50%). By some distance, the lowest was Ukraine (16.8%).

9.3.4 Convergence with Spain, Greece and Portugal

It is also reasonable to compare CESEE countries with Southern European EU member states. In many ways, CESEE has more in common with these countries, such as a more recent history of non-democratic rule, weaker institutions, and that it mostly missed out on the first phases of the industrial revolution in the nineteenth century. With the exception of Italy, Southern EU countries also joined the EU much later. Spain,

Portugal and Greece (SE3) in particular are interesting countries to compare with CESEE: they only had around a 10–15 year head-start in terms of transition to democracy and market capitalism.

Versus the SE3 average, the extent of catch-up is quite strong. Among EU members, four countries by 2018 had passed the SE3 average level: Czech Republic, Slovenia, Estonia and Lithuania. Among the non-EU CESEE countries, the three frontrunners (Turkey, Kazakhstan and Russia) had all reached around 80% of the SE3 average. At the other end of the scale, however, Ukraine had only reached a convergence level of 26%.

9.4 Economic Structures

The economic structures of CESEE economies have generally converged with those of Western Europe since the end of Communism. As detailed above, many economies were still quite rural and reliant on agriculture in 1990, and this has gradually been replaced by services and industry. However, the pace of this convergence of economic structures has not been equal everywhere, and many non-EU countries in CESEE have not converged to anything like the extent of most EU-CEE members.

9.4.1 Production Structures

The Visegrád countries, Slovenia and Romania in particular have much higher manufacturing gross value added (GVA) as a share of GDP than anywhere in non-EU countries except Turkey and Belarus (both outliers for different reasons). These EU-CEE countries have integrated strongly into regional value chains, and are fully part of the German manufacturing core (Landesmann and Stöllinger 2018). Many EU-CEE countries have been able to benefit both from proximity to Germany, as well as substantial upgrading of their infrastructure (largely financed by EU funds), both of which are of major importance to foreign investors in the manufacturing sector. Proximity to the home market, as well as the quality of infrastructure, play a particularly important role in "just-in-time" manufacturing chains, for example.

However, the situation is changing somewhat, at least in the Western Balkans. Serbia and North Macedonia have both had some success in following the Visegrád model of attracting FDI into the manufacturing sector in recent years, reflected in a substantial increase in the share of exports in GDP. However, so far in North Macedonia this has been generally at the low value-added level (Gligorov 2017). We believe that the prospect of future EU accession has played a role in this process for both countries, by making them more attractive to foreign investors. The resolution of Greece's name dispute with North Macedonia could provide a further boost to FDI inflows for the latter, as it makes both EU and NATO accession more likely.

Albania, Ukraine and North Macedonia in particular stand out for still having very big agricultural sectors. However, it is interesting (and positive) that non-EU CESEE countries do not seem to be behind EU members of the region in ICT and financial and insurance activities, indicating less of a competitive disadvantage than in manufacturing. We put this down to decent education systems (in part a reasonable legacy of technical education standards from Communism), less of a lock-in to old technology and infrastructure than in other industries (because ICT is quite new for everyone), and the fact that the bad infrastructure doesn't matter as much in these industries as in, say, manufacturing. Many parts of CESEE, including non-EU countries, have established themselves as outsourcing locations for ICT firms in Western Europe and North America.

9.4.2 Trade Integration with Western Europe and Competitiveness

A further way to assess convergence of economic structures is in terms of international trade integration with Western Europe. This has been a key part of the convergence of the most successful EU-CEE countries. Using the share of exports to the EU15 as a percentage of the total (Fig. 9.4), in general EU-CEE countries are much more integrated with the West of the continent than non-EU overall (with some exceptions, specifically Albania and North Macedonia). Some of this is obviously just a gravity effect (all else being equal, countries trade more with their neighbours), but if that was the only factor, Romania's share would not be so high. In the case of CIS countries, the share going to the EU15 has been falling in recent years, reflecting political factors.

A key factor affecting external trade, and the ability to export a large share to rich countries in Western Europe, is countries' external competitiveness. Right from the start of transition, there were huge differences in trade balances within the region. Deficits were particularly pronounced in the Western Balkans and Moldova. Some future EU members also had deficits at that time, albeit smaller (the Baltics and the post-2004 accession

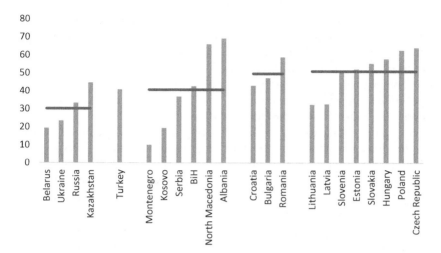

Fig. 9.4 Share of merchandise exports going to EU15, %, 2018 or latest data. (Note: Horizontal lines represent simple averages for each sub-region. Source: wiiw)

countries). Over time, these trade shortfalls in EU-CEE countries have either shrunk or disappeared completely, reflecting the building up of large, competitive export sectors. This has not really happened in the non-EU member states (the oil exporters are an exception, for obvious reasons).

It is likely that EU accession explains a major part of the difference, by acting as a strong advantage for CESEE countries looking to attract foreign investment into the tradeable sector. As already noted, EU accession brought major funds for public infrastructure upgrading (in many parts of EU-CEE, EU funds finance basically all public infrastructure), which is very important for manufacturing firms that want to move large quantities of goods quickly and reliably. EU accession also had an important impact on the quality of institutions (discussed below), another important factor for foreign investors.

However, another big part of the trade deficits in non-EU CESEE, both in the 1990s and now, is likely to be the particularly large share of emigrants leaving these countries, and the big income gap between the host (normally, but not always, Western) and source countries. This means remittances make up a very big share of GDP, and finance a lot of imports. Fundamentally, this model hasn't really changed, indicating rather limited convergence of economic structures in this regard.

Since 2017, the EBRD has also been providing composite indicators to measure how "competitive" and "integrated" economies of the region are.[10] These give a further indication about convergence levels of CESEE in terms of economic structure.

The *competitive* indicator measures both market structure and ability to generate value added. No country in non-EU CESEE ranks at the level of even the weakest EU-CEE country (Croatia), with the best performer being North Macedonia at 5.73, indicating a quite considerable distance to the frontier. Most countries rank at or close to 5, while Kosovo and Moldova are somewhat below that level.

The *integrated* indicator assesses both internal and international integration, taking into account factors such as openness to trade and investment, transport infrastructure quality, and ICT performance. Again, no non-EU country reaches the levels of EU members in the region. However, the performance relative to the frontier is somewhat better than for "competitive", with three countries in the Western Balkans scoring higher than 6 (Serbia, Montenegro and North Macedonia). In the case of Serbia and North Macedonia, this likely reflects at least partly the building up of larger export sectors over the past decade. However, in combination with the "competitive" score, it also points to manufacturing being skewed towards lower-value added activities. Kosovo and Ukraine are the weakest performers, both scoring less than 5.

9.4.3 Inward FDI Stock and Structure

Foreign direct investment (FDI) is an important part of the convergence of economic structures between CESEE and Western Europe. Many of the non-EU CESEE countries have been quite successful at attracting FDI, often from Western Europe, indicating quite a high degree of convergence in this sense. As of 2017, the countries in CESEE with the highest FDI stock in GDP were Montenegro, Serbia and Kazakhstan, all ahead of the frontrunners among EU member states in the region (Bulgaria and Estonia). However, round-tripping plays an important role and therefore significantly distorts the figures. Moreover, a wiiw report in 2017 found that Central European Free Trade Agreement (CEFTA) countries were not attracting very good quality FDI compared with the Visegrád countries (Hunya et al. 2017), with a relatively low share going into

---

[10] https://2018.tr-ebrd.com/reform/

high-value-added export. Countries in the Western Balkans are not as integrated into regional value chains as EU-CEE.

The discrepancy between sometimes higher levels of FDI in non-EU CESEE countries, but generally lower level of integration into regional value chains, can also be partly explained by an examination of where the FDI comes from. The non-EU member states generally receive a much lower share of total FDI from the EU15 than EU member states in the region. As an extreme example: 87% of Poland's inward FDI stock comes from the EU15, compared with 10% for neighbouring Belarus. Among current EU member states in CESEE, the average level is 71%, whereas for non-EU members states in the region it is 44%. There are many reasons for this, including proximity. However, it is likely that other factors probably play a role, including infrastructure quality, business environment, perceptions of corruption, and the anchor of EU membership.

The split of inward FDI by industry also reveals some interesting differences in convergence patterns (Fig. 9.5). By the standards of most EU-CEE countries, non-EU CESEE economies have generally received substantially less FDI into manufacturing as a share of the total (Turkey is an exception). This reflects many of the factors listed above (e.g. infrastructure, investment climate and distance from Western Europe), but also

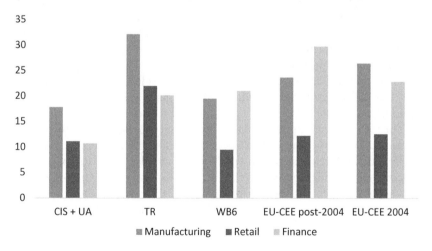

Fig. 9.5 Inward FDI stock, % of total in CESEE countries, selected industries, 2017 or latest data. (Source: wiiw FDI database. Simple averages for each country group)

for some CIS countries the dominance of the energy industry. The non-EU countries have also received substantially less FDI into their financial sectors as a share of the total, relative to EU member states. Patterns for FDI into the retail sector are more similar between EU and non-EU countries in the region. The generally lower levels of FDI into industry have likely affected the convergence performance of non-EU CESEE countries. Plenty of studies bear out that industrialisation is important for economic growth (Peneder 2003; Rodrik 2009; Szirmai and Verspagen 2011). Manufacturing is a source of technological progress and a high productivity growth sector (Stöllinger et al. 2013).

9.4.4 Longer-Term EBRD Transition Indicators

The EBRD transition indicators, which stopped in 2014, also gave an indication of convergence in terms of economic structures and particularly the development of conditions for the private sector in each country. Here, six areas were assessed: large-scale privatisation, small-scale privatisation, governance and enterprise restructuring, price liberalisation, trade and forex system, and competition policy.[11] Broadly, two conclusions can be drawn about long-term developments in CESEE.

First, reform progress in non-EU CESEE countries between 1989 and 2014 was on average significantly worse than in the countries of the region that joined the EU between 2004 and 2013 (Fig. 9.6). Within non-EU CESEE, the performance of the Western Balkan countries in particular has been disappointing, with the exception of Albania. Particularly in the case of small-scale privatisation, but also across all indicators, the other four Western Balkan countries included have not made very good progress by regional standards.

The CIS + Ukraine's performance was on average better over the whole period, particularly for small-scale privatisation, price liberalisation and trade and the forex system. However, there are also some disappointing aspects here as well, especially in the case of Belarus. For the CIS + Ukraine region as a whole, large-scale privatisation, governance and enterprise restructuring, and competition policy have been quite disappointing.

---

[11] Data for the early years of transition are not available for Turkey and Kosovo, while for the Czech Republic the series stops in 2007. We therefore excluded these countries from parts or all of the analysis.

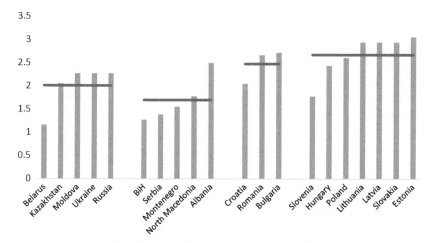

Fig. 9.6 Average EBRD transition indicators score, change 1989–2014. (Note: Simple average of change in six scores: large-scale privatisation, small-scale privatisation, governance and enterprise restructuring, price liberalisation, trade and forex system, competition policy. Orange line = sub-regional simple average. Source: EBRD)

The second key take-away from the EBRD data is that on four of the six categories—large-scale privatisation, small-scale privatisation, governance and competition policy—the hierarchy within CESEE was clear and roughly what would be expected. In all cases, the EU member states ranked significantly higher than non-EU countries. In most cases, the EU joiners of 2004 ranked notably higher than the 2007 and 2013 joiners. Within non-EU CESEE, the Western Balkan states tended to score somewhat higher than the CIS and Ukraine. Perhaps the stand-out indicator is governance and enterprise restructuring: the large gap between non-EU CESEE countries and the 2004 EU joiners points strongly towards one key barrier to further development of the former.

9.5 Social Aspects of Convergence

The social aspects (and consequences) of convergence are often neglected, but are a key component of how the past three decades have been experienced and perceived in the region. Although the EBRD reported that the "happiness gap" between CESEE and Western Europe finally closed in

2016, this reflected more a decline in life satisfaction in the latter (Guriev and Melnikov 2017). For most of the past 30 years, citizens in CESEE have generally reported a low level of life satisfaction than those in Western Europe. This reflects, among other things, the impact of the volatility of the 1990s, a perceived increase in inequality, a decline in the quality and availability of public goods, environmental issues, and concerns about their children's life chances.

9.5.1 Inequality

Within CESEE, income inequality is highest in parts of the Western Balkans (especially Albania and Bosnia and Herzegovina) and Turkey. For the rest of the non-EU CESEE countries inequality is no higher than in most of the current EU member states of the region, albeit often higher than France and Germany (but not Italy). In some parts of the CIS + Ukraine, inequality is actually very low in comparison with EU member states in both Western Europe and CESEE. This is particularly the case in Belarus, Kazakhstan and Ukraine.

These levels, however, disguise some important changes in the level of inequality in the CIS, Ukraine and Turkey over the past three decades. Both Russia and Ukraine started out with fairly low levels of inequality, but this changed sharply in the early years of transition, roughly until 1995. In both countries, inequality rose significantly in this period, before levelling off. Since then, inequality has declined in both countries, but much more significantly in Ukraine than in Russia. Ukraine's disposable income Gini coefficient was 26 as of 2016, compared with 23 in 1988. For Russia, the Gini in 2016 was 33, up from 25 in 1988. The past three decades therefore appear to have had a more long-lasting negative impact on equality of income in Russia than in Ukraine.

By contrast, Belarus clearly has had very little change in inequality over the whole period, reflecting its quite specific development model. It remains one of the most equal countries in Europe. Both Belarus and Ukraine have similar levels of inequality to the Czech Republic and Germany, i.e. fairly low. Moldova underwent a similar process to Russia and Ukraine, albeit less dramatic, but starting from a higher level. Its inequality level now is very similar to Russia. Turkey has had a much higher level of inequality over the whole period than any other country for which full data are available.

Comparable data for the Western Balkans do not go back as far, reflecting the break-up of Yugoslavia and wars in the region. For the whole period inequality in the region has been above Czech and German levels. However, the difference has become smaller in relation to Germany as inequality has increased there. This is especially true of Kosovo and Montenegro. The highest inequality in the region by far is in Bosnia and Herzegovina and Albania, and this has remained consistently the case over many years. Serbia and North Macedonia are somewhere in between, but in both cases inequality has increased since the mid-1990s.

9.5.2 Inclusivity

EBRD transition quality indicators assess how "green" and how "inclusive" economies of the region are. Nowhere in CESEE has it reached more than 80% of the frontier level, with the levels for even the best-performing non-EU members of the region even lower.

The *inclusive* indicator measures convergence in terms of gender, youth and regional inclusivity. Factors taken into account include the share of women in government and on company boards, education quality, difference in unemployment rates between age groups, and how broadly access to various services are spread among the population. Among the on-EU members, the highest levels were reached in Russia and Belarus, with the lowest in Kosovo. In two cases, non-EU CESEE countries represented the "frontier": Moldova for share of women in total employment, and Russia for share of establishments with savings accounts. In general, the CIS + Ukraine score more highly than the Western Balkans and Turkey (and in many cases the post-2004 EU joiners).

9.5.3 Environment

The EBRD's *green* indicator measures climate change mitigation and adaptation. Here, non-EU CESEE countries are generally even further away from the frontier than for the "inclusive" indicator. This may reflect the generally lower profile of green politics in much of CESEE relative to Western Europe.

The simple average for non-EU CESEE countries is 5.13, barely more than half the frontier level, and well below 6.64 for the region's EU member states. Kosovo is again the weakest performer (3.42), and Belarus the best (6.26). After Belarus, the highest scores were achieved by Turkey, Serbia and Ukraine.

9.5.4 Education

A further indicator of convergence in the social sphere is provided by education standards. An international comparison is provided by the PISA rankings (Fig. 9.7), which include most of the countries studied here (Ukraine, Belarus, Serbia and Bosnia are unfortunately missing). 2015 data (latest available) show a mixed picture for non-EU CESEE countries. Russia in particular scores very highly, above many EU-CEE countries, and roughly comparable with Western countries such as Austria, France and the US. However, the other parts of non-EU CESEE do not show this level of convergence in education standards. Kazakhstan is the next best performer, but does not come close to the OECD average. The weakest performers are Kosovo and North Macedonia. The rest of non-EU CESEE scores roughly equal to or slightly below Romania and Bulgaria, which are comfortably the weakest performers among EU countries.

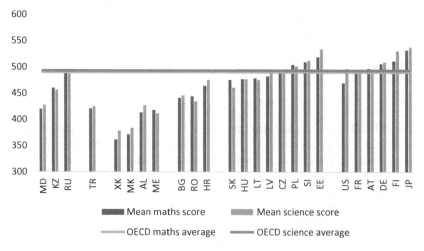

Fig. 9.7 PISA scores, 2015. (Source: OECD)

9.6 Institutions

The restructuring of institutions and governance practices was a key element of reform of formerly Communist countries in the 1990s. However, it is still incomplete, especially in the non-EU countries.

9.6.1 Governance

Most non-EU member states started out in 1996 (first year available) at a weaker level than countries that would go on to join the EU on the following World Bank Worldwide Governance indicators: control of corruption, government effectiveness, rule of law, regulatory quality and voice and accountability (Fig. 9.8). This could have been influenced by the early years of transition, but it is quite likely that it was more deep-seated, linked both to different communist experiences and maybe some pre-Communist institutional characteristics.

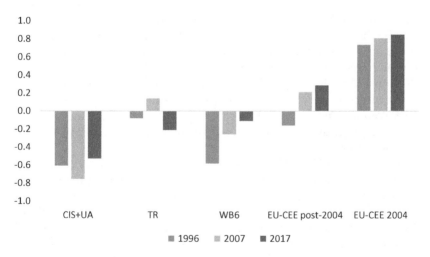

Fig. 9.8 Average World Bank Worldwide Governance Indicators scores, simple averages for each country group in selected years, 2.5 = best, -2.5 = worst. (Note: Scores represent simple averages of change in five categories: control of corruption, government effectiveness, rule of law, regulatory quality, voice and accountability. Source: World Bank Worldwide Governance Indicators. Some 1996 data unavailable for Kosovo and Montenegro)

In 1996, the countries that would go on to join the EU in 2004 were already clearly ahead, with the exception of Latvia and Slovakia on the corruption and rule of law indicators. The countries that joined the EU in 2007–13 were some way behind, including being behind the non-EU members on some indicators. Countries that have not yet joined the EU scored on average quite badly, indicating a weak starting point. Turkey was somewhere in between, generally ahead of the non-EU members, but behind the future EU members.

By 2007, on the eve of the global financial crisis, the picture was actually not especially different, at least in terms of levels. The basic hierarchy observed in 1996 was largely in place: the 2004 EU member states clearly ahead, followed by the 2007–13 member states and Turkey, with the non-EU member states ex-Turkey at a lower level. For the non-EU member states, voice and accountability and regulatory quality were relative strengths, with the rule of law, government effectiveness and control of corruption relative weaknesses.

As for 2017, the latest year of full data, the situation in relative terms remained largely unchanged, with one difference: Turkey has now fallen behind the 2007–13 EU joiners on most or all indicators. Parts of EU-CEE may be slipping back, especially Hungary, but remain generally far ahead of the non-EU member states. However, apart from Turkey, across indicators and countries, there were far more improvements than declines for the non-EU CEE countries in 2007–2017 (this was not the case for the EU members in the region). Improvements in absolute terms for non-EU CEE countries are particularly apparent in government effectiveness, rule of law and regulatory quality. This is visible in both the CIS and Western Balkan countries.

Taking the 1996–2017 period as a whole, and averaging across the five scores, non-EU CEE countries are well represented among the top convergence performers (Fig. 9.9). The most significant improvements relative to Germany were recorded in Albania, Kazakhstan, Serbia and North Macedonia (along with Croatia, Estonia and Latvia among current EU members). However, considering the low starting point, even for the top performers in non-EU CESEE, this has been insufficient to even significantly catch up with the EU member states in the region, never mind Germany. In addition, it is notable that, even in the context of a low starting level, four non-EU CESEE countries have gone backwards versus Germany over the period (using average scores): Russia, Turkey, Belarus

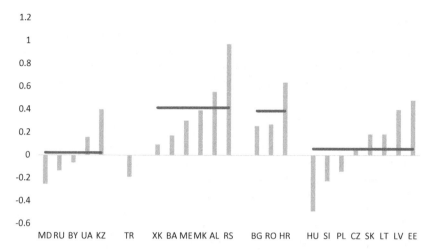

Fig. 9.9 Average World Bank Worldwide Governance Indicators scores; Change versus Germany, 1996–2017. (Note: Scores represent simple averages of change in five categories: control of corruption, government effectiveness, rule of law, regulatory quality, voice and accountability. Source: World Bank Worldwide Governance Indicators. Some 1996 data unavailable for Kosovo and Montenegro)

and Moldova (it should be noted though that several EU member states have also gone backwards, especially Hungary).

9.6.2 Corruption

Many improvements have been made, but overall CESEE still has a problem with corruption. The Transparency International Corruption Perceptions Index for 2018 shows that most countries are far from the German level (Estonia is an exception). In general, even the best performers in non-EU CESEE (Belarus, Montenegro and Turkey) only manage to reach the level of the worst performers among the EU countries (Bulgaria, Hungary, Croatia and Romania). Cross-country comparisons can be problematic with data based on perceptions, but this seems to be an area where convergence has not gone especially far. It is also notable that, according to Transparency International, many countries are going backwards. Since 2012, the index has registered declines in Turkey, North Macedonia, Bosnia and Moldova among non-EU member states (several EU member states have also gone backwards over the same period). In addition, in a recent report, Transparency International highlighted particular concerns regarding recent developments in Russia, Kazakhstan, Serbia, Kosovo and Montenegro.[12] Taken together, this suggests that most countries in non-EU CESEE are either already seeing backsliding on anti-corruption efforts, or are at serious risk of going in this direction.

9.6.3 Electoral Democracy and State Capture

A further insight into the process of institutional convergence can be provided by measures assessing how well democracy has been established in the region since the end of communism. The Varieties of Democracy (V-Dem) Electoral Democracy Index indicates an initially sharp improvement in the transition economies in the late 1980s and early 1990s (Fig. 9.10). Most countries at this point made the transition to democracy and competitive elections. The clearest improvement was visible in the future EU-CEE countries. An initially much bigger improvement was

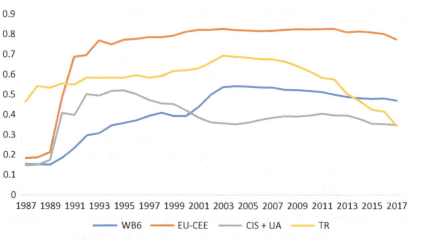

Fig. 9.10 V-Dem Democracy Index for CESEE countries, 1 = best, 0 =worst. (Note: Simple averages for each country group. Source: V-Dem)

[12] https://www.transparency.org/news/feature/weak_checks_and_balances_threaten_anti_corruption_efforts_across_eastern_eu

registered in the CIS and Ukraine rather than the Western Balkans (although in absolute terms both improved). However, whereas the CIS and Ukraine index peaked in the mid-1990s, and has trended down almost consistently ever since, the Western Balkan scores continued to rise, at least until the mid-2000s, including a notable pick up from around 2001 as the war in Kosovo ended. Turkey remained above both the Western Balkans and CIS + Ukraine, but fell below the former in around 2013 and the latter in 2017.

9.7 Infrastructure

A key part of the convergence process is related to infrastructure. Extensive, well-maintained and properly planned infrastructure is a crucial component of industrial and regional development, and countries' ability to integrate into regional value chains. This in turn is a major part of per capita GDP convergence, as demonstrated by the regression discussed above.

The EU member states in the region have benefitted from massive inflows of EU structural and cohesions funds, which have contributed substantially to infrastructure upgrading. Over recent years, these inflows have been equal to 2–5% of GDP per year for most EU-CEE countries. The superior infrastructure of countries such as the Czech Republic are a major part of why they are able to attract lots of FDI into high-value manufacturing, even recently in the context of labour shortages and rapid wage increases.

This money has not been available from external sources on anything like the same scale for non-EU CESEE countries. As a result, non-EU countries of the region tend to have substantially worse infrastructure as measured by the World Bank's Logistics Performance Index (LPI, Fig. 9.11). The exception is Turkey, which for both infrastructure and the overall LPI scores higher than many EU member states. Otherwise, non-EU CESEE still has some way to go, especially in the cases of Moldova and Ukraine (data for Kosovo are not available, but would probably also be very low).

These findings are backed up by recent EBRD estimates of current investment needs. Unsurprisingly, the estimates suggest that the annual infrastructure needs for the period 2018–2022 are particularly high in the CIS, Ukraine and the Western Balkans, with Moldova leading in the CESEE comparator group (Fig. 9.12). There, as well as in several other

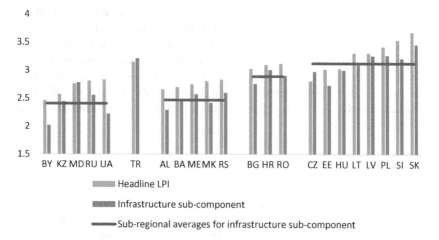

Fig. 9.11 World Bank's Logistics Performance Index (LPI), 2018. (Source: World Bank)

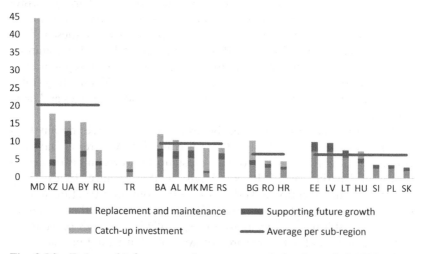

Fig. 9.12 Estimated infrastructure investment needs for the period 2018–2022, in % of GDP, by investment type. (Note: Catch-up infrastructure investment needs refer to the cost of catching up with the levels expected on the basis of the experiences of more advanced comparator economies. Supporting future growth infrastructure investment needs refer to the cost of improving infrastructure to support future growth in GDP and population. Source: EBRD Transition Report 2017–18)

non-EU CESEE economies, catch-up investment to infrastructure levels found in the more advanced comparator countries is quite substantial. However, replacement and maintenance investment is also important. For non-EU CESEE countries, the annual investment needs in infrastructure are estimated to be in the range of 4% (Turkey) to 45% (Moldova) of GDP, with a mean of 14% and a median of 11%.

The EBRD found that throughout CESEE, investment needs are greatest in the transport and electricity sectors. ICT and water and sanitation account for a generally much smaller share of the total. In non-EU CESEE countries, electricity infrastructure is generally higher (as a share of the total) than in EU-CEE economies. This is particularly the case in Turkey.

9.8 Financialisation

The financial system worked very differently during Communism compared with today. It had a largely passive role supporting state enterprises and fulfilling political priorities (Roaf et al. 2014).[13] At the end of communism, therefore, a financial sector had to be built basically from scratch. This included areas such as regulation, supervision, competition, and the role of the central bank. There was lots of involvement of IFIs and other external stakeholders.

The speed of financial deregulation or liberalisation after the fall of the iron curtain was very different in the CESEE region. Capital account liberalisation was an important first step towards the financialisation of the former communist economies and actively supported by the International Monetary Fund and the World Bank. It was hoped that deregulation would improve the efficiency of local financial markets and thereby the allocation of resources, and hence generate economic growth. Potential risks of increased financial openness to macroeconomic stability were widely ignored.

The degree of success of this approach was mixed, and depended a lot on the quality of domestic legislation. Many of the old state banks soon hit asset quality problems, which was not surprising given that (a) they were suddenly exposed to competition, and (b) the depth of downturn in almost every transition economy. In addition, lots of smaller non-bank providers of financial services sprang up. This new landscape was difficult

---

[13] Turkey is the an exception to this among the countries covered here.

for populations with little financial literacy to navigate, and plenty of people ran into financial difficulties as a result. These various factors combined to cause banking crises in most countries of the region in the 1990s. In Albania the collapse of Ponzi schemes even contributed to the start of a civil war. Meanwhile The Asian financial crisis and a decline in the oil price triggered the 1998 Russian financial crisis.

In the second half of the 1990s, another wave of reforms to the financial sector was initiated. At this point, a division started to open up within non-EU CESEE, between the CIS on one hand and the Western Balkans on the other. In the CIS, state oversight of the financial sector was increased, and the CIS economies from then on did very little to further open their capital accounts. By contrast, most of the rest of CESEE (EU and non-EU) sought increased privatisation of the banking sector. From the mid-1990s, financial deregulation was strongest in the EU-CEE countries that joined in 2004 (Fig. 9.13). Foreign banks arrived in the region in big numbers, either taking over existing lenders or investing in greenfield operations. For many countries in EU-CEE and the Western Balkans,

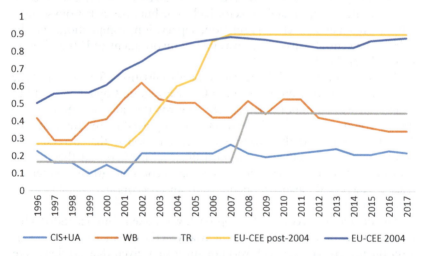

Fig. 9.13 Chinn-Ito Financial Openness Index. (Note: The index is normalised with the highest degree of financial openness captured by the value of one and the lowest by the value of zero. The CIS+UA average is constructed from data for BY, MD, KZ, RU, UA; the WB average from data for AL, BA, MK. Source: Chinn and Ito (2006), 2016 update, own calculations)

by around the year 2000, banking and financial services were the sectors with the highest foreign participation.

The financial sector played a fairly important role in convergence during much of the period.

Foreign firms brought technology transfer and knowhow, but also greater exposure to external shocks. This would become very important in 2008, when the banking sector was an important channel of contagion from the global financial crisis in many countries in the region.[14] In the CIS, generally lower foreign participation means less integration into global markets, although banks here were also certainly not spared. Similar to other institutions, differences in the quality of the banking sector mattered a lot, as well.

Following the crisis, the banking sectors of the region generally underwent retrenchment, as pre-crisis leverage was gradually reduced. Loans/deposits ratios fell, and many foreign currency loans were forcibly converted to local currency, with banks (often foreign-owned ones) taking most of the pain. However, most foreign parent banks remained, with the Vienna Initiative a crucial part of restoring stability and preventing a bigger crisis.

Asset quality became a problem almost everywhere in these years, with the NPL ratio rising quite rapidly, especially in the Western Balkan countries. Although they mostly stayed, foreign banks were reluctant to put in more money, and as a result credit growth had to be financed largely from local deposits. This, combined with weaker credit demand after the shock of the crisis, kept credit growth quite subdued in most places by pre-crisis standards. Nevertheless, the share of credit in GDP in the Western Balkans is not fundamentally lower than for the EU member states (and in many cases it is higher). For the CIS and Ukraine, especially when Russia is excluded, the share is mostly lower.

In general, the stability of the banking sector in CESEE is much improved from the immediate post-crisis years (EU and non-EU members). However, the situation in at least some non-EU CESEE countries appears more problematic than for the EU member states of the region. Many Western Balkan countries still have clear (albeit reduced) asset quality problems. Perhaps the most challenging situation though is faced by

---

[14] Although this is true in general, there are important exceptions. For example, the fact that Slovenia's banking sector was mostly domestically owned did not prevent it suffering a banking crisis.

lenders and policymakers in the CIS and Ukraine. Here, asset quality is also a problem (at least in Ukraine), state support has recently been required for banks (Russia, Ukraine and Kazakhstan), and credit growth in some segments looks uncomfortably and unsustainably high. This all suggests that structural issues remain in many non-EU countries of the region.

9.9 The New Geopolitics

Economics cannot be separated from geopolitics, maybe especially in the CESEE region. Currently, the world in general and Europe in particular stand at what appears to be a fairly significant geopolitical juncture. Two aspects of this are particularly important for the economic fortunes of CESEE: the rise of China to become a serious threat to US hegemony, and the hardening of the conflict between Russia and the West over the past decade. Although the implications are not automatically negative in all respects, there is a serious risk that parts of non-EU CESEE will be stuck on the fault lines of these two geopolitical conflicts, and that this will represent a barrier to economic development and convergence (as it clearly already has in some cases, most obviously Ukraine).

9.9.1 *The Arrival of China in CESEE*

The emergence of China as a military, political, financial and economic rival to the United States in particular and the West in general is the most important geopolitical development for at least three decades. In reality, the financial and economic aspects of China's power make it an even more formidable rival than the Soviet Union.

The implications for non-EU CESEE of China's rise are very important. China's 16+1 plan and Belt and Road Initiative (BRI) include large amounts of planned investment in CESEE, particularly for infrastructure upgrading. In that sense, especially in the Western Balkans, China is filling a gap (see above). Smaller countries involved in the BRI, such as Serbia and Montenegro, are those that are likely to benefit the most (Barisitz and Radzyner 2017). Moreover, at least in certain respects, it is possible to see complementarity between the Chinese and EU roles in non-EU CESEE. For example, in theory Chinese infrastructure investments in the

Western Balkans could be strategically combined with the EU's own spending in the region.

However, the challenges to Chinese-EU (and Chinese-US) cooperation in the Western Balkans are significant. China's growing role in the region creates risks around political influence (unwelcome from a Western perspective at least), potentially unsustainable debt loads[15] (the money is in the form of loans) and corruption,[16] and questions around whether positive spill-over effects will materialise for countries in CESEE. China has very different ideas about public procurement and environmental standards compared with the EU. It is far from clear that a rules-based organisation like the EU will be able to cooperate with a country like China in the Western Balkans (Bieber and Tzifakis 2019).

9.9.2 A harder Divide Between Russia and the West

The second key geopolitical shift, the hardening of the conflict between Russia and the West, has deep roots, but became more concrete following the Russian invasion of Georgia in 2008, and the annexation of Crimea in 2014. These two invasions demonstrated in very concrete terms that Russia saw a limit to the eastward expansion of euro-Atlantic institutions (most obviously NATO), and was both willing and able to enforce this in its "sphere of influence".

In the case of Russia, there are also implications for the Western Balkans. Russia plays an important role in Serbia and the Republika Srpska of Bosnia and Herzegovina. However, in economic terms, it cannot commit anything like the resources of China.

Where Russia plays a much more important role is in the former Soviet Union. For those countries in the Russian orbit, the difficulties are significant. Some have tried to play a balancing act and maintain good relations with both sides, including in economic terms. This may be possible for smaller countries like Moldova (or, further east, Armenia), but much more difficult for a country as large and strategically significant as Ukraine. Ukraine appears condemned to be divided for the long term between Russia and the West, which will make it even harder to achieve sustainable

---

[15] https://www.imf.org/en/News/Articles/2018/04/11/sp041218-belt-and-road-initiative-strategies-to-deliver-in-the-next-phase

[16] https://foreignpolicy.com/2019/01/15/the-belt-and-road-initiative-is-a-corruption-bonanza/

economic reform and kick-start what has been probably the whole region's most disappointing convergence story since 1989.

This does not mean that the CIS and Ukraine are or will be completely cut off from economic integration with the EU. Association Agreements, and Deep and Comprehensive Free Trade Agreements (DCFTAs), represent an important way for these countries to increase their economic engagement with the EU. The EU recently signed DCFTAs with Ukraine, Georgia and Moldova. Over the long term, the DCFTAs will help improve institutions, the predictability and transparency of the legal system and the investment climate (Adarov and Havlik 2016). However, one should not expect too much from these agreements on their own, especially if the current hard divide between Russia and the West continues. Moreover, the agreements create significant upfront costs for the beneficiary countries, while the real benefits are only likely to arrive over a longer time horizon.

9.9.3 Staying on the EU Path

For non-EU members, a realistic accession perspective has been an important reform anchor (itself a key factor in the decisions of foreign investors about where to put their money). Countries without an accession perspective have found sustainable and positive reforms much more difficult to achieve. For this reason, they tend to have a much bigger problem with issues like state capture and rent seeking. Consequently, the quality of life for the majority of their population is worse than in EU member states in the region.

In this context, while the situation of the CIS and Ukraine may be different, it seems clear that the only feasible future for the six Western Balkan countries discussed here is the EU. Forced to choose between the interests of competing great powers, it is hard to make a case that they have any realistic alternative to the EU, even if the bloc is not always extremely popular among their populations according to some opinion surveys. Even in the case of Serbia, which has a strong historical link to Russia, the pros of EU accession significantly outweigh anything concrete that Russia can offer.

However, faced with massive financing gaps and few options with which to fill them, the lure of Chinese investment will remain strong. Whether and how this is compatible with the EU accession process for Western

Balkan countries is likely to be a key question for policymakers in Europe in the coming years.

9.10 Conclusions

Countries that did not join the EU, and especially those that did not join in 2004, have faced an uphill task in converging with Western European, or even Southern European, per capita GDP income levels. Separating out EU accession from other factors of convergence is impossible, and it is clear that there were many other significant influences. One issue, as noted above, is that those countries joining the EU, especially the 2004 joiners, were anyway more advanced. Therefore, it is not always clear that EU membership itself was the decisive factor in driving the generally better performance of these countries. However, the evidence presented here implies that the 2004 joiners in particular, but also to an extent those that acceded later, have had a significant helping hand in the convergence process relative to their regional peers.

The EU has been able to offer many things to its future and current members. However, three perhaps stand out above all else. First, transfers, which represent a serious component of aggregate demand in EU-CEE countries, as well as underpinning a large share of total public investment, which in turn has meant having much better infrastructure than non-EU members of the region. Second, the reform anchor, perhaps particularly during the accession process, when the EU's power to demand change is stronger. Third, EU accession has been part of a broader integration into Euro-Atlantic institutions, which have had a host of positive spill-over effects. The "protection" that this affords may have been particularly important for the Baltic states, but more generally has been supportive of foreign investor sentiment.

Aside from the fact that EU-CEE countries have achieved a generally much higher level of convergence with Western Europe than non-EU CESEE countries, two other indicators suggest strongly to us the importance of EU accession. First, available measures of transition progress (such as those proposed by the EBRD) highlight much more progress in the EU member states of the region. Second, the convergence of economic structures and trade and investment integration with Western Europe appears to have been much stronger among EU-CEE countries, even those that are geographically further away from Western Europe (such as Romania).

Nevertheless, it would not be credible to attribute all convergence developments in CESEE since 1989 to the EU. The legacies of empires in the region, and of the different types of communism experienced within CESEE, were both clearly very important. Different 1989 starting points, in terms of for example economic structure, infrastructure quality, or trade openness, also played a role. Geography was also often key: the location of the Czech Republic, for example, is clearly much more advantageous than that of Bosnia and Herzegovina in a host of ways. Resources also played a role. Finally, the way that Communism ended was crucial: some countries experienced very little disruption, while others were plunged into multi-year civil wars.

Within non-EU CESEE, the three countries that achieved the highest level of convergence with Western Europe are Russia, Kazakhstan and Turkey. All face uncertain futures. For Russia and Kazakhstan, developments in the energy industry will be crucial (unless they manage to diversify significantly their economies). Meanwhile for Turkey, a growth model built on foreign credit and large current account deficits appears to have reached its limit, and there is little sign of what will come next. Especially for Russia and Turkey, trend growth rates are likely to be much lower in the next ten years than for much of the past two decades. For non-EU CESEE as a whole, this chapter has demonstrated several areas where they remain far behind EU-CEE countries. Among these are inequality, education, corruption and institutions. All require improvements in order to achieve a higher level of convergence.

In this sense, within non-EU CESEE, the future of the Western Balkan countries may in fact be brighter. Serbia and Montenegro, for example, have already reached a level of per capita GDP convergence with Germany roughly equal to that of Romania and Bulgaria when they joined the EU in 2007 (Grieveson et al. 2018). The anchor of EU membership makes significant, positive reforms much more likely in the Western Balkans than in the CIS and Ukraine. This is not to say that the Western Balkan countries do not also have problems with state capture, but that their chances of successfully tackling these challenges are higher under the umbrella of an EU accession process.[17] The EU reform process could also have a positive impact on the ability of at least some Western Balkan countries to attract better quality FDI into export-oriented industries, and to increase their integration into regional and global value chains. Finally, unlike in some parts of EU-CEE, many non-EU CESEE countries have continued to show positive progress on governance and institutional reforms over the past decade.

Convergence is likely to continue in the future. However, as the non-EU CESEE countries continue to get richer, they will increasingly encounter the challenge faced by the wealthier parts of EU-CEE: how to move from imitation to innovation (Aghion and Bircan 2017; Berglof et al. 2019). So far, the signs across CESEE regarding innovation are not too promising (for both EU and non-EU members). Moreover, in terms of automation and digitalisation, almost all CESEE countries are well behind the frontrunners in Western Europe (Grieveson et al. 2019). Combined with the scale of the demographic decline that the region is set to experience in the coming decades (Leitner and Stehrer 2019), policymakers in CESEE have a lot to think about.

Annex

We constructed a cross-sectional regression model explaining compound annual growth rates of GDP per capita at PPS in percent between 1990 and 2018, consisting of the following explanatory variables:

(i) the log of the initial 1990 GDP per capita in euro at PPS in order to capture the conditional convergence;
(ii) the average 1990–2010 investment share in GDP as a proxy for physical capital investment;
(iii) the compound average growth rate of population between 1990 and 2018 as a proxy for the development of the labour force;

---

[17] It should be noted that, at the time of writing, the whole process of EU integration for the Western Balkans is in question, owing primarily (albeit not only) to reservations in France, and a desire to integrate the existing EU before admitting new members.

(iv) an average human capital index for the period 1990–1999 as an additional factor relevant in Cobb-Douglas-style growth regressions;
(v) a non-EU dummy variable (and alternatively a Balkan and a CIS dummy variable) in order to test whether non-EU countries in CESEE had lower than average growth even after controlling for all the other growth-related factors.

Cross sectional regression results explaining the compound annual growth rates of CESEE economies (1990–2018)

	1	2	3	4	5	6
GDP per capita 1990	-1.32	-2.57	-2.57	-2.40	-2.83	-2.71
	(-1.81)*	(-3.67)***	(-3.62)***	(-3.03)***	(-6.21)***	(-5.08)***
Investment share 1990–2010		0.26	0.26	0.28	0.17	0.16
		(2.36)**	(2.40)**	(1.92)*	(2.13)**	(2.18)**
Population growth 1990–2018			0.05			
			(0.10)			
Human capital index 1990–1999				-0.80		
				(-0.95)		
Non-EU dummy					-1.53	
					(-3.08)***	
Balkan dummy						-1.17
						(-2.20)**
CIS dummy						-1.87
						(-2.27)**
Constant	15.37	21.12	21.14	21.62	25.76	24.86
	(2.39)***	(4.18)***	(3.98)***	(3.83)***	(6.90)***	(5.54)***
N	21	21	21	18	21	21
R^2	0.099	0.369	0.369	0.365	0.572	0.598

Note: Figures in brackets are t-values; * significant at 10% level, ** significant at 5% level, *** significant at the 1% level

Source: wiiw Annual Database, Penn World Table 9.0, own calculations

REFERENCES

Adarov, A., & Havlik, P. (2016). *Benefits and Costs of DCFTA: Evaluation of the Impact on Georgia, Moldova and Ukraine (with Peter Havlik)*. Joint Working Paper, No. 2016-12, Vienna.

Aghion, P., & Bircan, C. (2017). *The Middle-Income Trap from a Schumpeterian Perspective*. EBRD Working Paper No. 205.

Barisitz, S., & Radzyner, A. (2017). *The New Silk Road, Part II: Implications for Europe*. Focus on European Economic Integration Q4/17, OeNB.

Berglof, E., Guriev, S., & Plekhanov, A. (2019). The Convergence Miracle in Eastern Europe: Will It Continue? In I. P. Székely (Ed.), *Faces of Convergence* (pp. 19–27). Vienna: The Vienna Institute for International Economic Studies.

Bieber, F., & Tzifakis, N. (2019). *The Western Balkans as a Geopolitical Chessboard? Myths, Realities and Policy Options*. BiEPAG Policy Brief.

Blanchard, O. (1997). *The Economics of Post-Communist Transition*. Oxford: Clarendon Press.

Chinn, M. D., & Ito, H. (2006). What Matters for Financial Development? Capital Controls, Institutions, and Interactions. *Journal of Development Economics, 81*(1), 163–192.

EBRD. (2017). *Transition Report 2016–17—Transition for All: Equal Opportunities in an Unequal World*.

Gligorov, V. (2017). *Macedonian Exports*. wiiw Research Report No. 420.

Grieveson, R., Grübler, J., & Holzner, M. (2018). *Western Balkans EU Accession: Is the 2025 Target Date Realistic?* wiiw Policy Note/Policy Report No. 22.

Grieveson, R., Bykova, A., Hunya, G., Holzner, M., Pindyuk, O., & Richter, S. (2019). *Forecast Report: CESEE Moving into the Slow Lane*. wiiw Forecast Report No. Spring 2019.

Guriev, S. M., & Melnikov, N. (2017). *Happiness Convergence in Transition Countries*. EBRD Working Paper No. 204. Available at SSRN https://ssrn.com/abstract=3044935 or https://doi.org/10.2139/ssrn.3044935.

Holzner, M., Adarov, A., & Sikic, L. (2016). *Backwardness, Industrialisation and Economic Development in Europe: The Development Delay in Southeast Europe and the Impact of the European Integration Process Since 1952*. wiiw Balkan Observatory Working Papers No. 123.

Hunya, G., Ghodsi, M., Gligorov, V., Grieveson, R., Hanzl-Weiss, D., Holzner, M., & Stöllinger, R. (2017). *CEFTA Investment Report 2017*. CEFTA Secretariat, Brussels.

Landesmann, M., & Stöllinger, R. (2018). *Structural Change, Trade and Global Production Networks*. wiiw Policy Note/Policy Report, No. 21, Vienna.

Leitner, S., & Stehrer, R. (2019). *Demographic Challenges for Labour Supply and Growth*. wiiw Research Report No. 439.

Peneder, M. (2003). Industrial Structure and Aggregate Growth. *Structural Change and Economic Dynamics, 14*(4), 427–448.

Roaf, J., Atoyan, R., Joshi, B., Krogulski, K., & an IMF Staff Team. (2014). *25 Years of Transition: Post-Communist Europe and the IMF*. Regional Economic Issues Special Report, IMF, Washington, DC.

Rodrik, D. (2009). *Growth After the Crisis*. CEPR Discussion Paper, No. DP7480.

Stöllinger, R., et al. (2013). *A Manufacturing Imperative in the EU—Europe's Position in Global Manufacturing and the Role of Industrial Policy*. wiiw Research Reports, No. 391.

Szirmai, A., & Verspagen, B. (2011). *Manufacturing and Economic Growth in Developing Countries, 1950–2005*, UNU-MERIT Working Paper, No. 2011-069.

Index[1]

A
Absorptive capacity, 263
Accession boom, 216–219
Accession negotiations, 240
Acquis Communautaire, 213, 261
Agglomeration, 124, 125, 128, 133–136, 140, 142–145, 144n17
Aging, 97, 107
Albania, 34n4, 35, 37, 42n13, 86, 286–288, 287n2, 293, 294, 296, 300, 302, 303, 306, 312
Algeria, 35, 37, 86
Argentina, 35, 37, 86
Association Agreement, 242
Austerity, 222, 223
Austria, 34, 37, 44, 60, 76, 86

B
Balcerowicz, L., 155, 157n10, 158
Balkan countries, 239, 240
Baltic states, 211–235
Banking Union (BU), 50, 58, 59, 59n24, 59n25, 81
Belarus, 286, 287n2, 287n5, 295, 299, 300, 302–304, 306, 307
Belka, M., 157n10
Beveridge curve, 106
Bosnia, 286, 287n2, 288, 302–304, 307, 315, 318
Brain drain, 98, 108, 111, 120
Budget balance, 226
Bulgaria, 13–15, 22, 37, 39, 42, 64, 66, 77n33, 86, 157, 166, 239–280

C
Capital Market Union (CMU), 50, 59, 81
Catching up, 267, 269–271, 273, 274, 278, 279

---

[1] Note: Page numbers followed by 'n' refer to notes.

© The Author(s), under exclusive license to Springer Nature Switzerland AG 2021
M. Landesmann, I. P. Székely (eds.), *Does EU Membership Facilitate Convergence? The Experience of the EU's Eastern Enlargement - Volume I*, Studies in Economic Transition,
https://doi.org/10.1007/978-3-030-57686-8

323

324 INDEX

Central and Eastern Europe, 151, 164
Central and Eastern European countries (CEECs), 240, 242–244, 249, 267, 275
Champion of inclusive growth, 152
Chile, 35, 37, 86
CIS, 286, 292, 293, 296, 300–302, 306, 309, 312–314, 316, 318, 320
Cohesion funding, 223, 233
Cohesion policy, 223, 233, 234
Competitiveness, 223, 224
Conditionality, 222
Control of corruption, 68, 71n32, 74, 75, 79n35
Convergence (beta β, sigma σ), 92–95, 93n2, 98, 99n10, 100, 103, 117, 120, 126, 126n5, 226–228, 231–234, 285–320
Cooperation and Verification Mechanism (CVM), 262, 263, 266
Corruption risk, 74
Costa Rica, 35, 37, 86
Croatia, 6, 6n2, 20, 37, 61, 62n28, 86
Cross-border banking, 112, 112n20, 117
Cross-border capital flows, 51, 59, 117, 120
Cross-border migration, 10, 12
Currency board, 215, 225, 240, 257, 258
Current account, 218, 218n5, 224
Current account balance, 218, 219, 234
Czech Republic/Czechia, 13–15, 37–39, 42, 56–57, 60, 64–66, 85, 86

D
Dangers of convergence, 75–81
Demographic change, 231
Denmark, 34, 37, 44, 76, 86
Digitalisation, 100, 101

E
Eastern enlargement of the European Union, 43, 51, 59, 60, 79
Economic convergence, 2–8, 11–13, 15, 17–19, 22, 28–31, 33, 35n7, 36–40, 38n10, 47, 54, 56, 70–75, 77, 81–84
Economic growth, 215, 216, 222–225, 229, 233, 235, 267, 269, 271, 273–276, 279
Economic model, 2, 4
Economic restructuring, 241–243, 249, 252
Economic transformation, 241, 244
Education, 229, 231–233
Effect of EU membership on economic and social convergence, 82
Emerging economy, 260
Emigration, 95, 97, 105, 105n14, 107, 109, 219–221, 229, 232
Estonia, 37–39, 42, 86, 211, 213–216, 219, 220, 222, 224–229, 233
EU accession, 173–208
EU candidate countries, 32, 34n4, 42, 43, 45, 46, 52, 67, 70
EU11, 1–22, 1n1, 9n3, 27–87
Euro, 225–227
Euro adoption, 225
Euro area, 225–227, 231
Europe Agreement, 213, 214
European Union (EU), 1–22, 1n1, 9n4, 27–87, 123, 124, 127, 132, 139, 140n15, 142, 143, 151–170
EU transfers, 262, 263, 266
Export openness, 45, 46
Export structure, 249
External anchor, 260, 266, 279
External funds, 179, 190
External imbalance, 253
External shock, 252, 253, 258–260, 279

F

Finance channel, 5, 10, 30, 47, 50, 51, 82, 83, 83n39
Financial integration, 31–33, 81, 83n39
Fiscal policy, 73, 76, 82
Fiscal reserve, 258, 260
Fiscal stance, 258, 259
Fixed exchange rate, 215, 222, 223, 225
Flat tax, 276
Foreign direct investment (FDI), 8–13, 15, 21, 30–32, 46–49, 51, 56–58, 64, 66, 75, 77–80, 77n33, 82, 84, 92, 94–97, 97n7, 99, 111, 112, 119, 120, 243, 244, 246, 248, 249, 253, 260, 267, 278, 286, 291, 295, 296, 298–300, 309, 319
Former Yugoslavia, 6n2
France, 152, 154n3
Frontier of economic development, 2, 3, 6, 9
Frontier of social development, 2, 3

G

GDP, 286, 288–291, 288n6, 293–295, 297, 298, 309–311, 313, 317–319
Germany, 152, 162n16, 166n21, 167, 169
Gini coefficient, 36, 41–43, 41n12, 42n13, 275
Global financial crisis, 7, 216, 219, 222, 223, 225, 227, 228, 234, 243, 248, 249, 252, 260, 267, 279
Global frontier of economic development, 28, 30, 34, 69, 85, 86
Global frontier of institutional development, 28, 30, 34

Global frontier of social development, 28, 30, 34, 69, 85, 86
Global value chains, 243, 248, 278
Governance Indicators, 68, 71
Government effectiveness, 68
Greece, 7, 35, 40, 44, 55, 60n26, 86
Growth champion, 152, 155

H

Happiness, 152, 154, 161
Herzegovina, 286, 287n2, 302, 303, 315, 318
Historical Human Development Index (HIHD), 44
Human Development Index (HDI), 36, 38, 43, 84–86
Hungary, 20, 22, 37, 39, 44, 46n16, 54, 58, 64, 77n33, 79, 80, 86, 152, 174–178, 180–182, 185–190, 185n3, 192, 194, 196, 201–205, 207, 208

I

Imbalances, 12–13, 70, 74–84
IMF, 31, 50, 52n19, 67, 240, 259, 260
Inclusive growth, 274, 277
Income inequality, 275, 276
Indonesia, 35, 37, 86
Inequality, 154, 154n3, 154n7, 163, 163n17
Inequality-Adjusted HDI (IA-HDI), 36, 42, 43
Innovation, 92, 93, 97–105, 99n10, 110, 119, 120
Institution building, 155, 157–159
Institutional channel, 5, 11, 13, 15, 18, 29, 31, 32, 38, 49, 50, 59, 67, 70, 72, 73, 80–82, 84, 85

Institutional convergence, 3–5, 7–9, 11, 30, 35n7, 72, 241, 261, 262, 266
Institutional model, 2, 4
Institutional quality, 32, 50, 70, 70n30, 71, 71n31, 74, 75, 78, 80n37, 83, 85
Institutions of macroeconomic policymaking, 72
Investment channel, 5, 9, 11, 30, 32, 46, 47, 49, 70, 77, 78, 82, 84
Inward FDI, 9, 12, 32, 46n16, 48, 49, 75, 76, 78, 83
Ireland, 7
Italy, 6, 7, 35, 40, 44, 85, 86

J
Jordan, 35, 37, 86

K
Kazakhstan, 286, 287n2, 293–295, 298, 302, 304, 306, 308, 314, 318
Knowledge-based economy, 232, 233
Kolodko, G.W., 155, 156, 157n10
Korea, 35, 37, 85, 86
Kosovo, 286, 287n2, 288n6, 298, 300n11, 303–305, 307–309

L
Latam, 35, 37, 43, 86
Latvia, 37, 39, 49, 86, 211, 213–215, 218–227, 227n6
Lisbon Treaty, 267
Lithuania, 37–39, 63, 86, 211, 213–216, 219–229, 227n6, 233
Loan-to-deposit ratio (LTDs), 94, 114, 115
Locational Gini coefficient, 135

M
Maastricht criteria, 225, 226
Maastricht Treaty, 225
Macroeconomic adjustment, 241, 253, 257
Macroeconomic stabilisation, 240
Macroeconomic stability, 232–234
Malaysia, 35, 37, 86, 161–165, 162n16
Manufacturing, 243, 244, 246, 248, 249, 260
Mexico, 161–165, 162n16
Middle-income trap, 97, 98n8
Migration, 134
Migration channel, 10–12, 80
Minorities, 276
Moldova, 286, 290–292, 296, 298, 302, 303, 307, 309, 311, 315, 316
Montenegro, 34n4, 35, 37, 42, 86, 286, 287n2, 290, 298, 303, 305, 307, 308, 314, 318
Moran scatterplot, 139
Moran's I, 139–141
Morocco, 35, 37, 86
Multi-annual Financial Framework (MFF), 264

N
Nation building, 212–215
Netherlands, 34, 37, 44, 76, 86
New financing model, 174, 192–206
New growth model, 98, 99, 108, 110, 120
New Member States (NMS), 239, 252, 261, 267, 269, 270, 273, 274
New public debt strategy, 195–199
Non-performing loans (NPLs), 115–117
North Africa, 35, 37, 86

INDEX 327

North Macedonia, 34n4, 37, 86, 286, 295, 296, 298, 303, 304, 306, 307
NUTS (level 2, level 3), 126, 126n2, 127, 128n6, 142

O
Outward FDI, 12, 48, 49, 58, 75, 76, 83
Outward migration, 60–62, 64, 75, 79, 83

P
Pension system, 65, 74, 83
PHARE, 213
Philippines, 35, 37, 86
Poland, 22, 37, 38n9, 42, 44, 58, 64, 77n33, 79, 80, 86, 151–170
Poland's new Golden Age, 154
Policy reform, 260
Policy reversals, 75–81
Political Stability, 68
Population dynamics, 219–221, 229–232
Portugal, 7, 35, 40, 44, 55, 60n26, 86, 163, 167
Post-socialist transformation, 156
Potential growth, 95, 97, 117
Potential output, 76, 77
Private investment, 94, 96, 98
Privatisation, 244
Productivity, 92–94, 97–99, 103, 105, 118–120
Prosperity, 239, 241, 266–279
Public debt, 73
Public investment, 96, 263, 264, 266, 278
Public procurement, 71n32, 74, 75, 79n35
Purchasing power parities (PPP), 270

R
R&D, 106n17
Real convergence, 241, 267, 269, 270, 279
Recovery, 224–228, 233
Referendum, 214
Reform reversals asymmetries, 13
Regional differences, 78
Regional disparities, 277
Regional inequalities, 12
Regulatory quality, 68
Research and development (R&D), 102–104, 120, 232
Rise in trade openness, 174
Romania, 13, 22, 37, 39, 42, 60, 63, 64, 66, 77n33, 86, 239–280
Rostowski, J., 157n10
Rule of Law, 33, 68
Russia, 157, 286, 287n2, 288, 288n6, 290n7, 292–295, 302–304, 306, 308, 313–316, 318
Russian crisis, 216, 217, 227

S
Self-financing, 174, 192–206
Serbia, 34n4, 35, 37, 42, 86, 286, 289, 290, 295, 298, 303, 304, 306, 308, 314–316, 318
Shift in economic policy, 193–194
Shock reforms, 158
Single market for trade, 9
Skills, 93, 97, 97n7, 103, 105–112, 106n17
Slovakia, 13, 37, 38, 38n9, 42, 49, 65, 86, 163
Slovenia, 6n2, 13, 20, 37–39, 42, 49, 54–57, 64, 66, 77n33, 85, 86
Social coherence, 13–17
Social consensus, 157

Social convergence, 2–5, 7, 11, 15, 17, 28, 30, 31, 33, 35n7, 37–40, 38n10, 70, 72–74, 81, 84
Social model, 2, 4
South Africa, 161–165
South Korea, 154, 161–167
South-East Asia (SEA), 35, 37, 85, 86
Soviet Union, 212, 216
Soviet-type central planning system, 5
Spain, 7, 35, 40, 44, 53, 60n26, 85, 86
Spatial clusters, 141
Spatial dependency, 125, 126, 139–142, 140n15
Structural change, 249, 273
Sudden stop, 219
Sweden, 34, 37, 44, 76, 86

T
Theil index, 127, 129, 136
Total factor productivity (TFP), 94, 95, 97
Trade, 286, 288, 290, 291, 296–298, 300, 301, 317, 318
Trade channel, 5, 9, 11, 47
Training, 99, 109
Transformational recession, 240, 242
Transition, 214–216, 216n3, 231
Tunisia, 35, 37, 45, 86
Turkey, 286, 287, 288n6, 290, 292–295, 299, 300n11, 302–304, 306, 307, 309, 311, 311n13, 318
Turnaround in lending, 208

U
Ukraine, 157, 161, 161n15, 166n22, 286, 287n2, 289–296, 298, 300–302, 304, 309, 313–316, 318
Unemployment, 218–223, 226, 227, 233, 234
Urbanisation (level of), 128, 129, 131, 134
Uruguay, 35, 37, 86

V
Venture capital, 93, 117–119, 121
Voice and Accountability, 68

W
Welfare, 10
Welfare gains, 79, 84
Well-being, 152, 154, 161, 163, 164
Well-being champion, 152
Western Balkans, 286, 288, 290, 291, 295, 296, 298, 299, 302, 303, 309, 312–315, 318, 319n17
World Bank, 31, 42, 42n13, 43, 50, 67
Worldwide Governance Indicators, 31, 67

Printed in the United States
By Bookmasters